Lajos Kossuth

Memories of my Exile

Lajos Kossuth
Memories of my Exile
ISBN/EAN: 9783743345935
Manufactured in Europe, USA, Canada, Australia, Japa
Cover: Foto ©ninafisch / pixelio.de

Manufactured and distributed by brebook publishing software (www.brebook.com)

Lajos Kossuth

Memories of my Exile

MEMORIES OF MY EXILE.

BY
LOUIS KOSSUTH.

TRANSLATED FROM THE ORIGINAL HUNGARIAN,
By FERENCZ JAUSZ.

PREFACE.

An indescribable rush of feeling overwhelmed me, when the surrender at Világos rendered me homeless.

No words can adequately express my feelings.

Before I stepped across the frontier I lay down on the soil of my native land; I pressed upon it a sobbing kiss of filial love:—I took a handful of earth; one step, and I was like the hull of a wrecked ship, thrown up by the storm on a desert shore.* A Turkish staff officer greeted me courteously in the name of "Allah." He led me to a place which he had kindly caused to be prepared for me to rest for the night under God's free heaven, and—asked for my sword with downcast eyes, as if ashamed that a Turk should disarm a Hungarian.

I unbuckled it and gave it to him without uttering a word; my eyes filled with tears, and he, wishing me sound rest, left me alone with my sorrow.

Rest to the homeless!

Could Adam rest when the gates of the Garden of

---

* Shortly afterwards a farewell address to the Hungarian nation in my name went the round of the European press. It was a fabrication. I wrote neither that nor any other.

Eden were closed behind him—behind him, who was driven out because he had eaten of the fruit of the tree of knowledge of good and evil?

I too had eaten of that fruit, and I too knew good and evil: I had raised my hand for the defence of the good against the evil. Evil was victorious and I was driven from my home, my Eden.

There I stood in silent meditation on the bank—but no longer the Hungarian bank—of the Danube, the waves of which were mingled with the tears of the Hungarian nation—and which not far from me grumbled and roared through the rocky pass of the Iron Gates, as if protesting against an undeserved fate.

I listened to this roaring, in rude harmony with the storm in my heart; and as I contemplated the annihilation of patriotic hopes so undeservedly extinguished, tears of indescribable grief unconsciously showered down my cheeks.

Those tears contained every grief that can afflict the patriotic heart, every grief but one! Hopelessness there was none; no despair for the future of my country.

It appeared to me—in the first feverish attack of pain—as if a ray of hope were coming from the glimmering light of the stars, penetrating through the veil of my tears—hope that though my nation would suffer terribly, *it would not perish*.

It was only one of those whispers which, in the heat of emotion, rush through the heart without passing through the reflecting brain, like the balm poured into the souls of sufferers by the God of mercy lest they should become insane through grief.

Later on, the Turks magnanimously defended my life,

and the lives of my homeless compatriots. They defended them, not without danger to themselves. The two neighbouring Powers, flushed with victory, threatened them with war if they refused to give us up. And when the situation assumed such a threatening aspect that the counsellors of the Sultan thought they could no longer avoid our extradition unless the fugitives embraced the Turkish faith, and thus became Turkish subjects, the Sultan, Abdul Medjid, rose from his seat in the Divan, and, raising his hands to heaven, used these words solemnly—"Allah is powerful. I trust in his protection. But, if I must perish, may I perish with honour. I will not bring upon my name the disgrace of violating the rights of hospitality, by surrendering to the vengeance of their enemies the unfortunates who have sought my protection. It is my determination that, having sought it, they shall also obtain it. Come what may, I will not surrender them. This is my determination, and thus shall it be. Consider the means of defence."

He did not surrender us, and no war resulted, but we were detained as prisoners in distant Asia, in obedience to the dictates of European diplomacy.

And there, in the distant solitude, we pondered the past, present, and future of our country, and I examined in my mind's eye the origin, character, and course of our struggle for liberty, and the causes which rendered a collapse possible. The more I considered the situation, and the more I examined the historical and psychological elements of our nation's vitality, the more was I confirmed in my conviction that the faith and hope which flooded my soul in the first rush of grief at my homelessness, while I stood on the banks of the Danube, were but strengthened by mature consideration.

My nation cannot sink under the suffering which has been dealt out to it. The Hungarian question has a historical, legal, geographical, national, political, and arithmetical basis; it is closely connected with the interests of European freedom and the equilibrium of power. Such questions appeal to the logic of universal history. The cry may be silenced for a time, but cannot be effaced from the record of facts upon which it has been inscribed by history. This question will demand a place amongst the open questions of Europe until it is solved according to right and justice, or until the nation renounces it.

This was my own view, and that of all the other emigrants. Whatever dissensions embittered our homeless existence—so bitter in itself; however far we were scattered over the world like a second Israel; and however heavily the burden of patriotic sorrow, or the cross of the uncertainty of winning an honest livelihood, rested on the shoulders of most of us as we trod the varied path of misery, strangers amongst strangers, all of us, everywhere, and at all times, were agreed that the holy duty of active and steadfast patriotism was expected of the Hungarian emigrants in their exile, whether they were united as friends or sundered in loneliness.

They must remain a living protest before God and man against the suppression of Hungary's existence as a state.

They must raise their voices in the name and for the defence of the nation itself, now condemned to silence;

they must act for the nation fettered with the chains of the oppressor.

They must hold aloft the banner which was surrounded with the nimbus of immortal glory through the heroic and patriotic deeds of our " nameless demi-gods," and the fall of which created a sorrowful consternation amongst the races of the earth.

They must preserve the Hungarian question amongst those questions which demand solution from the logic of history, according to the unchanging truth of the eternal laws that govern the moral universe.

They must represent this article of faith of the Hungarian nation's political religion—that, though the three hills in the coat of arms of our country became in 1849 a Golgotha, soaked with the gore of heroes, as they had been several times before, the cross which stood on that Golgotha was not the wooden monument over a grave, but the symbol of resurrection.

They must proclaim their belief in the future independence of their country, in order that the world might believe in it, and, in consequence of this belief, render due consideration to the Hungarian nation.

And while, by their untiring activity, they sent a stimulating magnetic current home to their country, so that the nation should not languish under her sufferings, they must personify the just and natural aspirations of the Hungarian nation, and form a connecting-link between these aspirations and the events of the world.

I cannot say that the "domestic life" of the family of refugees was quite free from those petty dissensions which we meet with in the history of exiles everywhere and at all times. We are men, and man is a frail creature. The constrained laxity of that statuteless society, which was called the "nation of refugees," was but little adapted to keep human frailty within bounds.

Yet the trivial miseries of exile are but evanescent bubbles; they do not permanently stain the page of history.

On the other hand, history owes to the Hungarian refugees the acknowledgment that they have faithfully responded to, and honourably performed, the duty demanded of them by their country.

I can even affirm that the activity of the Hungarian refugees was not without influence on that turn of events which at home they call a new era of constitutional life.

As far as I am personally concerned—in consequence of the events of the past, there rested upon me, to a great extent, the responsibility of exerting myself to the utmost to *smooth the way* for my nation to the reclamation of her rights of existence as an independent state, which the history of a thousand years, the sacred legacy of her ancestors, has handed down to posterity as an inalienable inheritance.

The words "smooth the way" mark out the limits of the activity which we could display abroad. We did not over-estimate our abilities. We never flattered ourselves with the fanciful idea that we could reclaim for our nation that place at the round table of independent nations to which it has an incontestable right, by virtue of its history of a thousand years, and by virtue of the diplomatic agreements which form an integral part of European international law. Only the nation herself can do this.

Our duty was to see that, if she should wish to do it, she may find such support in her foreign relations as to make success—as far as human calculation can make sure of anything — solely dependent upon her own determination.

Starting from this point of view, I deemed it my duty faithfully to strive in three directions.

One direction was indicated by the knowledge that the frustration of the Hungarian nation's gigantic exertions in 1849 could be traced to the decrease of self-confidence.

The second I took from the knowledge of the state of European affairs, which, in the case of a general European commotion, or of some European question now pending being raised, might lead to the possibility of such combinations as, on the basis of the identity of interests, might facilitate the work of our nation's liberation.

The third direction was defined by the consciousness of the fact that, even if favourable circumstances arose, there could only be a prospect of success if on the one hand a solidarity in aim and intention were to spring up between the nation and the refugees, and if on the other hand the favourable opportunities did not take the nation by surprise.

With regard to the first point, namely, that fatal misfortune, which I call the decrease of self-confidence, I was, and am still convinced, that however many feeders may have swelled that subterranean current which undermined the banks of the stream of the national self-confidence, all of them together could not have swept the public spirit of the nation on to despair, had she not felt herself so utterly forsaken by the whole world.

But the cause of the Hungarian nation was much less hopelessly forsaken than we in our unfortunate isolation had imagined.

The governing classes of Europe became more and more convinced of the truth that events in Hungary did not belong to that class of revolutionary commotions, such as had for their object the acquisition of rights not possessed before by the people, which had at that time shaken the whole of Europe. The conviction gained ground that, in our case, it was not the people that had made revolution against the governing power, but that the governing power had so acted as to upset by force of arms a legal *status* based on diplomatic agreements, and forming an integral part of the international law of Europe and an essential factor of the European equilibrium.

The fact gradually came to be more appreciated, that it was not the nation who first tore up the compact between the Hungarian nation and her sovereign, but he who attacked the country which he was bound to defend, and who proclaimed it to be deprived of its existence as a state, and debased to the level of an Imperial province.

The Russian intervention had created indignation all over the world. In the French National Assembly a resolution was passed declaring it to be "dangerous to the future of liberty." In the English Parliament the Foreign Secretary, though not at all a friend of our cause, officially expressed the opinion of the Government that what was going on in Hungary was "*an important European transaction*," and this acknowledgment has its own necessary corollary in international politics. The powerful Republic of North America, indeed, had just sent a diplomatic agent to Hungary—a preparatory step towards the acknowledgment of our independence, and—for us—towards the utilisation of all those political and material advantages assured in such cases by international law.

Above all, the public opinion of civilised states commenced to express itself strongly in favour of our righteous cause. I can affirm without hesitation, that there is scarcely an instance in the history of the world where a struggle for independence has called forth greater sympathy than ours.

But we were excluded from the world. The sympathy did not penetrate to the heart of our nation engaged in a struggle for dear life; and I set out on my wanderings as an exile with the oppressive feeling that it was the thought of being forsaken that had opened the gate to those intrigues for undermining the self-confidence of the people which became the cause of our overthrow.

I considered it my duty as a patriot to see that the interest in the cause of Hungary's independence should take root to such a degree in the public opinion of the free and independent nations, that we might not be afraid, if the Hungarian nation did again raise the banner of independence on the soil of their country, soaked with the gore of her heroes, that the feeling of being forsaken would paralyse her consciousness of strength.

Comparatively speaking my task has been an easy one, for I found ready sympathy, bordering on enthusiasm, such as our "nameless demi-gods" had aroused everywhere; and I found ready response in the condolence which such an undeserved defeat, and the martyrdom following the fall, evoked in the human heart.

And this sympathetic interest was not of a transient nature. More than two years had elapsed since the dark night of oppression had settled over Hungary, when fate transported me from Asia to the hospitable shores of free Albion, and thence shortly to free America, and notwithstanding these two intervening years the sympathy was so warm that it manifested itself in demonstrations such as the world had never seen before.

I can say this, I am permitted to say it, because my person was but the occasion, and not the object of these demonstrations and sympathy; I can say that the down-trodden Hungarian nation held a triumphal procession in two continents such as is not recorded in the history of any victorious Imperator.

Finding so much spontaneous sympathy, I considered it my duty to render it permanent by directing attention to the legal side of the Hungarian question, to its righteousness, and to the importance of its bearings far beyond the limits of our country.

And I believe this sympathy has become permanent. The change in the state of affairs may have moderated the fervour of sympathetic interest in the Hungarian name which had become familiar all over the world at the domestic hearths of the people, who pray to the *one only* Divinity of liberty. It is possible that it has done so. It is difficult to recognise in the Hungarian of to-day, who moves in the whirlpool of the policy of the so-called Austrian power, the Hungarian of thirty years ago, who at the point of the sword demanded from the same power his inalienable ancient right. But if it is written in that book which religion calls the book of Providence, that the whirling wheel of events turns in the future the past into the present, the Hungarian phœnix which rises from its ashes will perceive that the smouldering flames of the world's sympathy will again blaze up, and the Hungarian will have no reason to feel forsaken.

With regard to the second direction in which I turned my activity from knowledge of European affairs:—

After the ebullition of 1849 that particular state supervened all over Europe which one perceives on the battle-field after the struggle is over—that peculiarly awe-inspiring stillness which makes us shudder. The dead lie about; the wounded groan, and their groaning is so dreadful! but for this sound, dead silence would prevail. Only the birds of prey shriek in the polluted atmosphere; only the "hyænas of the battle-field" move about, plundering the dead and killing those who are still alive.

Such was the state of Europe at the end of 1849 and after 1849. The man who died, died; he who was hanged, was hanged; he who was thrown in prison, languished there; he who was in hiding, was hunted; he whose property was confiscated—well! his family learnt to starve; the sons of the people were taken from

their homes and enrolled as soldiers—well! they went;
heavy taxes, "*de plenitudine potestatis*," were imposed on
the people, who paid them with the sweat of their brow.
Orphans and widows wept—in silence, in some hidden
corner of their homes, behind well-closed doors and
windows. But for this sound there was stillness, and the
silence of the grave prevailed. And potentates called it
the state of "order and peace." They have a dictionary
of their own. They called it "Europa ordini et tranquillitati asserta" in 1849, "libertati asserta" in 1815.

But the reaction of 1849 did not create anywhere a
state which it could expect would be permanent. To
strike the sword out of the hand does not mean to
appease the heart. The continent of Europe was a
volcano; it did not smoke, but it rumbled perceptibly.
It was only necessary to stoop to the ground to hear
how it was roaring in the depths. The roaring even
reached my ear in the barracks of Kutahia; and when
I arrived at Marseilles it roared round my ship in the
powerful strains of the "Marseillaise." The very air
was full of conspiracy. On the right or on the left,
all were conspiring—even those conspired who thought
that they did not do so. Even such men conspired
as are nowadays astonished and horror-stricken at the
very idea of ever having been conspirators.

We Hungarian refugees did not conspire. There
was no need for it. A nation of exiles is in a certain
sense a free nation;—theirs is a mournful liberty, but
still it *is* liberty. The political exile has written on his
forehead to which party he belongs. He need not conceal
the symbols of his faith and religion in his cartridge-box.
He could not hide them even if he wished. As long as

he does not violate the laws of the country which has given him an asylum, he may freely sacrifice at the altar of his political religion.

But, even if we did not conspire, still, even now, in the desert of frustrated hopes, it appears to me that, as one of the custodians of the Hungarian banner of 1849, it was my duty, under the circumstances then prevailing, to keep before my eyes the phases of the agitated European volcano, lest its eruption should take me by surprise, and, in consequence of this surprise, should pass away without being turned into what it might perhaps be—an *opportunity* for my unfortunate country.

The connections arising from this position belong to the history of my life in exile. I cannot say that I could have used these connections for the practical good of my country. The events of the world have taken a different turn. The volcano, which had shown all the prognostics of a powerful eruption extending over the whole world, was in one place appeased; in a second place it found a safety-valve; in a third place it was set at rest by a partial outbreak; in a fourth place (just where our interests were most identical) the force of the volcano was led into a proper channel of strength by a power wisely identifying itself with the national aspirations.

Amongst my experiences appertaining to this circle of ideas is one trait, which is not of a private character, nor is it confined to the domestic life of the band of Hungarian refugees. It belongs to the history of the Hungarian nation.

When at Boston, twenty-seven years ago, I stepped on the grand staircase which leads up to the superb building of the Capitol, in the open portico of which stood, bareheaded, the Senators and Deputies of the State of Massachusetts, with their Presidents and the Governors of the State at their head, in order to pay the tribute of esteem and brotherly sympathy—in my person—to the Hungarian nation, which had succumbed under the weight of the violated law of nations. I perceived the triumphal arch erected in front of the building, bearing the coat of arms of the State of Massachusetts, with this inscription : " Ense petit placidam sub libertate quietem,"* and underneath it these words quoted from one of my speeches:

" *There is a community in the destinies of humanity.*"

And the Governor of that free, cultivated, happy, model state (in which there is not a single person who cannot write, not a single pauper, not a single tumble-down house) took me by the hand and, pointing to those words in the face of God's free heaven, asked me to tell my nation to trust in that sacred truth, and to be assured that the powerful Republic of the United States would act towards her in accordance with that sacred truth.

And this assurance was re-echoed by the acclamations, which reverberated through the heavens, of hundreds of thousands of people who had gathered together for the occasion.

It refreshed me, the homeless wanderer, to witness this solemn acknowledgment of the solidarity between nations by a state, the legislature of which, after having

---

* The coat of arms shows a hand clasping a sword, the motto being that of Algernon Sidney. In extenso it reads as follows : " Manus haec inimica tyrannis, ense petit placidam sub libertate quietem."

well sifted the Hungarian cause, declared that our struggle for independence was legitimate and just, that the Russian intervention was a rude violation of international law which ought to have been strongly reprimanded by the nations interested in preserving constitutional liberty, and that it was the duty and the interest of all constitutionally governed nations to enter into the closest relations with each other, in order to be able to unite their strength the more effectually for the repulsion of the attacks of despotism.

Of course I found the feeling of this solidarity, which was proclaimed with such solemnity beyond the ocean, in all the nations of Europe, but, what very characteristically illustrates the European influence of the independence of the Hungarian nation is the immense importance which, in connection with the interests of European liberty, acknowledged to be solidarity, everybody has attributed to our nation, even those who in consequence of their geographical position stood beyond the immediate sphere of the influence of events in Hungary. They were all impressed with the knowledge that the Hungarian struggle for independence, from its very beginning, but especially since the Russian intervention, was an event, the importance of which, reaching far beyond the boundary of our country, was of European interest; that in our struggle —as I myself said at Szeged—the struggle of European liberty was fought out. This knowledge and the circumstance that the Austrian Emperor was obliged to have recourse to foreign help against us,—that not only the total military strength of two great powers, but also the ignoble services of treason and intrigue, undermining the very bases of souls in the dark, were needed to force the arms of justice from our hands, and obscure the nimbus of glory which surrounded the name of "Honvéd;" and finally the fact that, when every other nation in Europe had already succumbed, we were still able to stand upright, and with Venice, still brave, but in its isolation insignificant, held out last on the battle-field of independence; all these facts lent such importance to the Hungarian nation, that I may say the authority of an elder member was given to her in the family of European liberty, upon which everybody looked with confidence and hope.

This is a coin treasured up in the past, which, though at present it may have gone out of circulation, may become valuable in the future.

To another category of the activity entered upon from a knowledge of European affairs belong those connections into which we endeavoured to enter with the belligerent powers in the Crimean war, and into which the Hungarian refugees practically entered during the wars of 1859 and 1866.

The issue of the last Russo-Turkish war—which will have a terrible influence on the future of Europe—clearly demonstrated how right I was when, at the time of the Crimean war, I endeavoured to gain practical acceptance for the political axiom, that only by taking up simultaneously the causes of Hungary and Poland could the Eastern question be saved from the catastrophe—which has, unfortunately, since set in—leading to the ominous extension of Russia's sphere of power. The Turkish Porte has seen this, and wished nothing more than that the reasonable political combination should be carried out. But her Western allies, out of consideration for Austria, stopped her hand, and the hopes of my country attached to the providential opportunity vanished.

The Italian war of 1859 temporarily brought the Hungarian refugees, as allies, into closer connection with the then powerful Emperor of the French; more permanently with the Italian Government until 1867; and during the war of 1866 with Prussia also.

It appears that on both occasions, just as the angel of God's compassion was handing the cup of liberation to the much-suffering Hungarian nation, it became a bitter cup of vanished hopes. On the first occasion, the sanguinary but speedy victory over the Austrians, and the victorious Emperor's fear of that conflict which occurred twelve years later, and which he could have forestalled in 1859, dashed the cup from our lips. On the occasion of the war of 1866 the cup was dashed from our lips by the speedy victory of the Prussians, and still more—by the nation herself. The germs of the Austro-Hungarian dualism were then already in the air.

But these two incidents in the corporate life of the Hungarian refugees are not without interest; their record is a page not without importance in the history of Hungary; and they also have a connection with the history of the world.

In my letter addressed in 1867 to Francis Deák, I wrote as follows: — " The gigantic revelations of the vitality of the Hungarian nation in 1848 and 1849—when, save a little more pertinacity, nothing was wanted to attain success — have at least brought about this much, that in the policy of the Powers, as well as in the feelings of the people, our nation, even in her fall, has been counted among those vital factors that have an aim of their own, that may—nay, must—be considered in the historical evolution of Europe."

This was so, while a Hungarian question existed. The historian will find the fact that it was so illustrated in an interesting manner by those incidents in the life of the Hungarian refugees.

To me and those who shared my endeavours, the only thing which throws a faint ray over the night of disappointed hopes is the recollection that we have disinterestedly saved our nation amidst the enticements of the Powers, and that we could so far control the impatience of fervent longings as to prevent the Hungarian nation from being used as mere means to alien objects.

Thus I have indicated the nature of my activity —demanded of me by duty—in the first two directions; for the indication of the third direction, which refers to our connection with our country, only little is needed; and it will therefore be sufficient if I restrict myself to a few words.

We refugees possessed no independent weight, we could gain weight only by becoming the representatives of the national aspirations, and by being known as such. Therefore, in the interest of our nation, it was our duty to maintain solidarity with her, and also to see that the nation maintained the solidarity with us. This reciprocal influence formed the leading idea that always directed our actions throughout our connection with our country. I must only add that I have always recommended, always enjoined upon my political friends at home to take steps that the opportunity—when it presented itself—should find the country awake, and not unprepared; but I always cautioned and reminded them also, that Hungary's independence was not a matter which could be fought out behind street barricades. If it had to be striven for with arms, it presupposed war — not a mere internal insurrection, but a war carried on on a large scale like a great foreign war. It was neither advisable nor permissible to have recourse to "émeutes;" for the lives of Hungarian patriots were precious; it would be a crime to jeopardise them uselessly. I have never lost sight of this peculiar feature in the cause of Hungarian independence, neither among the various vicissitudes of my connections at home nor among those abroad.

Thus the nature of the question gave to the Hungarian refugees that privileged character which induced the Emperor Napoleon III., when, after the war of 1859, he was reproached by the German press with having allied himself to revolutionary elements, to reply, in the journal edited by Granier de Cassagnac (not " Paul" but " Granier " de Cassagnac): " *The Hungarians are not revolutionists, but patriots.*" *

This was the sphere of the patriotic exertions of the Hungarian refugees.

To-day all this belongs to the past.

The nation has decided differently.

* " Ces messieurs ne sont pas des révolutionnaires, ce sont des patriotes illustres."

It has broken the shaft of that standard which we carried so high on the rugged roads of exile.

I wrote to Francis Deák that the power the Hungarian question possessed, as a factor in political calculations, "*was a great acquisition, and to surrender it would be a crime.*"

It was surrendered.

A Hungarian question may exist, I believe it does exist hidden deep in hearts, but not before the world.

There are no longer Hungarian refugees.

I, with my sons and a few faithful friends, stand alone,—forsaken, solitary wanderers in the desert.

To me, the old wanderer who has arrived at the verge of his grave, who has no hope in the future, and in whose past there is no consolation, the conviction of my heart says, that as I was right once in the controversy with the enemies of my country, so am I now in the diversity of opinion with my own nation; I *am* right.

The " Judge of the World" will decide.

***

But all that I have described in these pages belongs to the history of the past.

And because it belongs to the past I have entered into a contract with the *Athenæum** publishing firm, for the publication of the " Memories of my Exile" of which these pages form the preface.

I do not give a complete collection of my " Memories "—partly on account of the necessity of discretion ; but chiefly because it is one of my shortcomings that I

* In Budapest. (Translator's Note).

have scarcely ever thought of preserving in writing what I have done. I have only preserved records in my exile of what others have done—as the reader will see. I have recorded my own doings but scantily.

Yet I think that what I have written during my exile will form material not unimportant for the historian of our time.

And with this I hand the "Memories of My Exile" to the public—" sine me liber ibit in urbem."

LOUIS KOSSUTH.

*Collegno (al Baraccone), Italy,
Nov. 5th, 1879.*

POSTSCRIPT TO THE PREFACE.

LETTER TO MR. IGNATZ HELFY, Member of the Hungarian Parliament.

"*Collegno, al Barracone, November* 19, 1879.
"DEAR FRIEND,

"You were kind enough to undertake the task of arranging my writings for the press. Since then, however, my position has undergone a material change, to which it may be your duty to call the reader's attention.

"In my Preface and in the 'Memories' about to be published I appear as a member of the Hungarian nation.

"Foreign Governments and nations even believed to see in me the personified idea of the Hungarian national existence.

"This qualification of being a Hungarian, however, has in the last few days been turned into an anachronism by the law passed by the representatives of the Hungarian nation.

"That Hungarian people in' whose elevation to the rank of citizens I had a small share, has chosen representatives who have decided that he who, though a born Hungarian, resides without authorisation ten years abroad, loses his qualification as a Hungarian citizen unless he goes home to become a member of a community, or unless he presents himself at an Austro-Hungarian consulate.*

"What damage, harm, or difficulty would have reached Hungary if this 'dis-Hungarianising' law had not been voted, I do not understand.

* This law, by which Mr. Kossuth lost his birthright of Hungarian citizenship, was voted by the Hungarian Parliament after the above Preface had been forwarded for publication.—(Translator's Note.)

"What may be its use, or how it answers the exigencies of modern civilisation to pass such laws—I understand still less.

"Why the free Englishman should necessarily grope about in the darkness of the Middle Ages because he considers it his birthright, which nobody in this world can take away from him, that he is an Englishman—and, being an Englishman, is necessarily an English citizen*—this I understand least of all; but I know that if anybody said such a thing to an Englishman he would receive the answer : 'Put on sackcloth, throw dust and ashes on your head, and do penance, for you have outraged God, humanity, nature, and civilisation.'

" But the law has been passed.

" I have now been thirty years abroad, and certainly not with the sanction of the Austro-Hungarian Government.

" I do not acknowledge the present state of Hungary to be *legitimate*, because it clashes with the inalienable right of existence of the Hungarian nation.

"I cannot, therefore, become the member of a community, because I should thereby incur obligations as a subject which are opposed to my national feeling of justice.

"Of course I cannot present myself to an Austrian consul, because I do not acknowledge his authority over me.

" I will not become an apostate.

" Therefore I, as well as my children, will belong to the *outcasts*.

" Along with some Hungarians, we are the only men all over the world who are not members of any nation. We are the Pariahs of the world.

"' *Consummatum est.*'

" We shall take notice of it.

---

* In the course of the debate it was stated in the Hungarian House of Representatives that free England and free Switzerland knew nothing about the loss of citizenship by an absence abroad. Whereupon one of the deputies who supported the Bill made the extraordinary statement that in this respect England and Switzerland were still "groping about in the darkness of the Middle Ages."—(Translator's Note.)

"My sons, who have yet a life before them, after having, from love of their country, wasted the better part of it on a footing with galley-slaves—*i.e.*, without being possessed of the *rights of citizens*—will, nay they must, look out for themselves not to remain Pariahs of the world.

"I shall remain one.

"Please remind my readers, therefore (if readers there should be any !) that where in these writings they meet with me as a Hungarian they put the word 'late' or the word 'outcast' before it.

"Besides, as regards the object of my life and the feelings of my heart, I am to-day what I was yesterday, and I shall remain through the morrow meted out to me what I am to-day.

"Driven from the bosom of my mother, I shall retaliate by bearing unchangeable, faithful, filial love until my death.

"With kind compliments,
"Your friend,
"LOUIS KOSSUTH."

A FEW WORDS FROM THE TRANSLATOR.

In undertaking the translation of the present work I had serious misgivings as to my ability to acquit myself satisfactorily of the task. Only the admiration which I share with other Hungarians for the name of our illustrious patriot induced me to take it in hand. The task has proved most arduous, and I am painfully sensible that, in spite of my earnest endeavours, I have not been able to do justice everywhere to the genius of the author, and must therefore appeal to his indulgence and to that of the English public. Considering the exceptional difficulties of Mr. Kossuth's style, I trust that he himself will be ready to make allowances for any shortcomings on my part.

The natural anxiety of the Publishers to bring out the English translation simultaneously with the Hungarian original also made it necessary that the work should be accomplished in a short time, and I had not, therefore, as much leisure as I might have desired.

I have much pleasure in expressing here my gratitude to my beloved wife, and to my friend Mr. Lajos L. Kropf, for the valuable assistance they have each rendered me.

F. J.

5, *Cheverton Road, Hornsey Lane,*
May 10*th*, 1880.

CONTENTS.

CHAPTER I.—(SECTION I.)
ORIGIN OF THE ITALIAN WAR OF 1859.

Historical Retrospect—Struggle for Unity—Hatred of the Foreigner—Hotbeds of Conspiracies—Congress of Vienna—Metternich's Opinion—Charles Albert and the Revolution of 1848 1

(SECTION II.)

Victor Emmanuel—Cavour—Readiness of the Piedmontese to Make Sacrifices—Conference of Dresden, 1851—Attempt of the Court of Vienna to enter with all its Territory and Provinces into the German Confederation—The Memorandum of the Hungarian Refugees—Napoleon Bonaparte . . 11

(SECTION III.)

Endeavour of Austria to Consolidate its Power in Italy—Project of the League of Baldasseroni—Ravings of the Duke of Modena—Mazzini and the Cabinet of Turin 22

(SECTION IV.)

The Crimean War—Endeavour of the Western Powers to draw Austria into their Alliance—Austria's Conduct—Piedmont's Offers and Conditions—Cavour's Audacious Step—Journey of Victor Emmanuel and Cavour to Paris—Congress of Paris 29

(SECTION V.)

Attempt of Orsini—Opinion of Senator Pietri—The Emperor Napoleon and Cavour—The Meeting at Plombières—Diplomatic Campaign—Cavour's Deep Insight and Wonderful Ability—The Archduke Albert in Berlin—The Ultimatum of Baron Kellersberg—Cavour's Answer—*Alea jacta erat*. 49

CHAPTER II.

Preliminary Conference of the Belligerent Powers and the Hungarian Exiles—Incidents of the Complication—Endeavours of the English Government to Prevent War—Kossuth's Position—His Invitation to Paris . . . 88

CHAPTER III.

My Journey to Paris May 3rd-8th, 1859—Preliminary Conference with Prince Napoleon on May 5th 155

CHAPTER IV.

The Question of Neutrality in England—Speeches at Public Meetings— Change of Government 188

CHAPTER V.

EVENTS THAT HAPPENED IN THE INTERIM.

The Hungarians at Genoa—Organisation of an Army—Agreement with Prince Couza, and Explanation of this Relation—Conference with Prince Michael Obrenovics—Mission to Belgrade 277

CHAPTER VI.

Journey to Italy 349

CHAPTER VII.

The Catastrophe of the Armistice—End to our Hopes 409

MEMORIES OF MY EXILE.

ORIGIN OF THE ITALIAN WAR OF 1859.

CHAPTER I.

I.

Historical Retrospect—Struggle for Unity—Hatred of the Foreigner—Hotbeds of Conspiracies—Congress of Vienna—Metternich's Opinion—Charles Albert and the Revolution of 1848.

"ITALY is only a geographical expression," said Metternich. It was nothing else; and the Congress of Vienna decided that it should still be nothing else. We Hungarians were the only nation which called it "the Italian *country*" (Olasz-Ország). The name was one which foretold its future, but Italy was not then a united country. Yet the Almighty, whose work is continually progressing, converted this geographical expression into the garden of Europe, giving it cohesion, and bounding it with the Alps—the symbol of the Everlasting—and the sea, which, like the arm of a mother, embraces it on three sides. And this united garden was the home of races to whom the proud traditions of the past, and the universal genius which belongs to them, said, "You are destined to become a *Nation*. Be a *Nation*."

The apprehension of this destiny, sometimes conscious, sometimes instinctive, and the spirit thereby disseminated everywhere, run like endless threads through the past of these peoples.

Races mixed very differently in different parts of Italy. The northern, the western, the eastern countries, and even Africa, contributed elements to their formation. Here Norman, there Goth, elsewhere Gallic, Ostrogoth, Heriul, Longobard, Greek, Saracen blood flows in their veins; but the element which unites all these constituents is everywhere the same,—that which remained when Rome fell to pieces—the Latin element. And this element, which conquered the conquerors, has imprinted the type of unity upon them all.

They did not speak one language, did not even understand each other; but the characteristic of their languages is the same Latin stem; and as soon as the mighty genius of a poet spoke to these people, in the language in which that common characteristic comes out most prominently, they all felt that, besides the language of their different tribes, they had a common *national* language, which destined them to be one nation in the home marked out by God.

As there is a difference among the individual members of a family, so there was, and is still amongst these races, a difference caused by the region they inhabit. The traces of the history of centuries are not easily effaced. But these differences did not prevent national feeling from knitting them together.

Powerful foreign potentates came, and, striving with each other for the beautiful possession, divided it between them, as the soldiers around the Cross divided the garments of Christ; but they could not succeed in annihilating, even when sundered, the vital power which strove for unity. There were some who sought for the symbol of unity in the Pope. Others looked to those who called themselves Emperors of the "Holy Roman Empire."* Both ideas were wrong. But the source of both was the idea of unity.

There was a time of internal dissension, too. Brother vied with brother. Every one tried to exert his individual strength to the utmost in order to hold his place against his rivals. This strength was displayed most in municipal liberties—the remnants of the broken Roman Empire—and in republican customs. It was a disorganised liberty, but it was liberty; and liberty always breeds strength, even when disorganised. Therefore individual strength has developed in these disjointed members to an astonishing degree. The small town of Asti withstood the might of the whole army of the German Emperor, though its only fortification was a fence. Pisa defeated the Saracens on the shores of Spain, and also in Africa, and conquered Athens, Corinth, Sardinia, Negropont, Corsica, and the Balearic Islands. Genoa alone equipped a fleet with 35,000 combatants, and Venice planted the standard of St. Mark above Constantinople.

This growth of the spirit of individualism did not appear to have a favourable tendency in the direction of unity, but it favoured the spirit of independence, which leads to unity. The Italian wanted to be master in his own house. Hatred of the foreign yoke united the disjointed members, and the small Republics of Lombardy crushed the power of the mighty Barbarossa.

* "Das heilige römische Reich—weder heilig, noch römisch, noch Reich," said Boerne

This inextinguishable hatred of the foreign yoke also took hold of the Popes now and again. Pope Julius II. had this inscription put on his banners: "*Italia ab exteris liberanda*" (Italy must be liberated from the foreigner); and on his deathbed called out, "*Drive the foreigner out of Italy.*"

The small Republics could save Italy from foreign dominion, but could not defend themselves against tyrants at home. The despot lives only for himself, and therefore likes the people to be weak, and makes them weak. This weakness, caused by internal despotism, again allowed foreign dominion to enter Italy. The Spaniards and French vied with each other as to who should rule over the Italians; and the former were victorious. At the beginning of the last century their place was, to a great extent, taken by the Austrians, who were hated most of all. This hatred actively vented itself first amongst the Piedmontese, who dispersed the Austrian armies at Guastalla; then amongst the Neapolitans, who defeated them at Velletri; and last, but not least, amongst the Genoese, who, in an improvisate insurrection, drove the Austrians out,—and the world was shown how deep and how universal was the hatred of the foreign yoke in Italy.

It would be difficult to say whether this hatred would have yielded to the reconciling sentiment of national unity if Napoleon I. had united Italy into one body when, except in the case of Sicily and Sardinia, the fate of the Italians was placed in his victorious hands; but certain it is that the hatred of foreign government was only intensified in the bosom of the Italians when, out of the Italy that yearned so for unity, the conqueror erected three separate kingdoms for the benefit of his own family.*

Such was the state in which, after the overthrow of Napoleon, the Congress of Vienna found Italy.

And that Congress which boasted of having placed Europe on a stable foundation, did not think, in its self-sufficiency, either of the interests or of the feelings of the people, but considered only the dynasties and the division of power between them.

Thus Italy became a geographical expression, over which Austria ruled, and dictated where she did not rule. Not only was Lombardy restored to her, but in addition thereto she received Venice and Istria; and the fortresses of Piacenza and Ferrara were put into her hands, in order that she might make her influence felt also on the right hand side of the river Po. Besides this, Tuscany and Modena were given back to Austrian archdukes, and Parma fell to an Austrian archduchess, under the protection of an imperial Austrian deputy.

Taken altogether, this meant nothing less than that the Austrians were the masters of a divided Italy.

Thus, the Congress of Vienna, instead of creating a consolidation promising stability, converted Italy into a political volcano that was never at rest.

Hatred of the Austrian rule then became the religion of the Italian people. Italy was the hotbed of chronic conspiracies.

When one or another of the governments occasionally endeavoured to pacify the malcontents, and

* As we shall see further on, this plan of the Three Italies was tried by the heir of the Napoleonic ideas in the negotiations preceding and following the war of 1859.

to calm down agitation by concessions and reforms, it met at every step with such an answer as this: "What good are such things to us whilst Italy is not a country, and not independent? Liberty is but an empty name, without independence! Independence there is none, nor can it exist side by side with foreign rule. *Turn the Austrians out of Italy!*" With this exclamation the Italian rose from his bed; he mingled it with his prayers, gnashing his teeth the while; it beat in his pulse, whatever he did; with it he went to rest; and even in his sleep he dreamt of it.

No words can describe what the people in the Papal States suffered through bad government in the time of Gregory XVI. And yet, when those indescribable miseries were inquired into by the Delegation of Forli, the members of the moderate party—not the revolutionists—said openly in a memorandum to the Pope: "All this is painful, bitterly painful, but what is more painful than anything else is that the Pope has made himself a servant of the foreigner." And they also told him that whenever their Italian kindred thought the moment opportune for taking up arms, they would be there too, whatever the Pope might do.

The "Carbonari" were spread all over Italy. There was scarcely an Italian patriot who was not of their number. Liberty in its widest sense always had a place in their programme, but that on which every member took an oath was the independence of Italy, and that meant hatred of the foreigner—the Austrian.

Then came the time of bloody reprisals and martyrdom. The best sons of Italy died on the scaffold, took refuge in exile, or languished in prisons,—the horrors of which were so touchingly described, with the simplicity of truth, by Silvio Pellico, the renowned prisoner of Spielberg. There was scarcely a prominent family even amongst the aristocracy of Italy which had not furnished one martyr or more as an illustration of the hatred of the foreigner; but the inexorable rigour, the executioner, the prisons, the heavy fetters, the confiscation of property, the proscriptions—these all fell without force on the indestructible shield of Italian independence. There were always some who took up the thread of conspiracy as it dropped from the hands of a martyr on the scaffold. Machiavelli, who studied the Italian character so deeply, detected the want of discipline as a fault of the Italians. "Those who are intelligent," he says, "cannot obey, and every man makes pretensions to intelligence." The hatred of the foreign rule, and what was synonymous with it, the desire for national independence, cured the Italians even of this shortcoming. They acquired discipline.

Thus the electricity in the cloud of the Italian Question was gathering for three-and-thirty years, till at last it burst forth in a tremendous storm at Milan in 1848, with the war-cry, "Long live Italy! Drive out the foreigner!"

This outburst was not a consequence of the French Revolution. The French were not yet even thinking of Revolution. The French Chambers were still talking with great solemnity about the eternal stability of the Citizen-King's charter, when the eruption of the Italian volcano was so far foreshadowed by menacing signs, that the English Government sent advice upon advice to all the Governments in Italy, urging them to forestall the outburst by concessions, reforms, and amnesties.

As if a high-spirited people's aspirations for national existence and independence could be extirpated by concessions! Woe to the nation whose aspirations can be thus quelled! It has no future before it. It is like Esau, who sold his birthright for a dish of lentils.

It is really astonishing that, amongst all the diplomatists of Europe, it was Metternich alone who completely understood the whole significance of the Italian movement. Eight months before the Lombardo-Venetian outbreak he thus made answer to the counsels tendered by England:—"This is not a question of reforms. The Italians desire to become a *Nation*. They do not want Italy to be merely a geographical expression. They wish to unite Italy; and Austria, on the other hand, wishes to retain her Italian possessions. This is the question—a question which cannot be solved by concessions and reforms."

And indeed such a question cannot be so solved: at least, with the Italians it could not. It is only because this was impossible with them that they could become what they are. Obstacles are removed, and even Fate bends before a nation which not only determines to gain what it has a right to, but sticks to its determination with inexorable firmness.

The Lombardian people drove Radeczky out of Milan. Charles Albert, King of Sardinia, hurried to assist in the Revolution, which by this time had assumed a decidedly *national* character. But in his note addressed to the European Powers he stated that he did so only because, if he did not interfere, the Revolution would take a republican direction, which might place his throne in jeopardy, *as in Piedmont, Genoa, Sardinia, the Italian national feeling was very strong.* Before I was better informed in the matter, I myself was inclined to take this note literally;* but later on, when I had a more intimate knowledge of the facts, I arrived at the conclusion that this was only one of those diplomatic tricks in which, according to the custom of diplomatists, words are used, not to express thoughts, but to conceal them.

Charles Albert was not always consistent in his views; occasionally he was to be found ranged under the standard of principles opposed to those which he at other times maintained; but it is certain that there were several moments in his life which show distinctly how he felt that of all the Italian princedoms or powers the house of Savoy alone was destined to put itself at the head of the *Italian national* movement, and that he identified himself with this movement. It is a fact that, at the beginning of the third decade of this century, he took part in the Piedmontese Revolution, which led to the abdication of King Victor Emmanuel I., and which, far from being exclusively Piedmontese, had decidedly an *Italian national* character. That the Revolution was national is clearly proved by the fact that the revolutionist committee, or "Giunta," formed with the knowledge and consent of Charles Albert, led the movement *in the name of Italy.* It is also a fact that Charles Albert, before he laid down the regency which at the command of the abdicated King he had assumed till the arrival of King Charles Felix, used his last

* See Note 1 at end of this chapter.

moments of power to put the direction of the War Ministry into the hands of Count Santa Rosa, who was one of the most conspicuous leaders of the Italian Revolution.

And there is another fact besides which supports this view. The Lombardo-Venetian insurrection, happily inaugurated by the five glorious days at Milan (March 18th to 22nd, 1848), and in Venice by the capitulation of Zichy, was victoriously carried on for four months by Charles Albert, at the head of his own excellent army and of the Lombardians, Venetians, and "crusaders" from central Italy. Even the fortress of Peschiera was captured, but on the 25th of July Radeczky defeated the Italians at Custozza, on the very plain where later, in 1866, they again lost a battle, in spite of the indisputable bravery of the Italian soldiers. On the 6th of August Radeczky was again in Milan, and Charles Albert took refuge in Piedmont when he had concluded an armistice.

Even if, in the opinion of the Italians, that diplomatic note may have thrown doubt on the political character of this campaign, which ended so disastrously, it is a fact beyond dispute that when Charles Albert, in March, 1849, again entered the lists against Austria, this resumption of hostilities without any diplomatic intrigues already possessed a purely *Italian national* character. He was defeated at Novara, and his defeat cost him his throne. He died in exile. But the sword that fell from his hand at Novara became the sword of the independence of Italy.

II.

Victor Emmanuel—Cavour—Readiness of the Piedmontese to make sacrifices—Conference of Dresden, 1851—Attempt of the Court of Vienna to enter with all its territory and provinces into the German Confederation—The Memorial of the Hungarian Refugees—Napoleon Bonaparte.

THE sword which fell from the hands of his father was taken up by King Victor Emmanuel II. with an unflinching resolution. He chose for the task of his life the fighting out the independence of Italy, and to this task, as to a sacred duty, he remained steadily true until his death. Many times I have heard him say, " They call me King, and a King I am; that is my profession (*C'est mon métier*). But of that I am not proud; I have another title which I value more. That title is my being the first soldier of Italy. I will gladly risk my throne and my life in the fulfilment of the duties connected with this title. Come what may: come good or come evil, I will not yield." And he did not yield, and his firmness was rewarded by good fortune, which he so well deserved. He accomplished what he had set before himself as the task of his life.

On the whole, the relation of the House of Savoy to the question of the independence of Italy is put forth with manly frankness in that comprehensive memorandum which, shortly before the Peace Conferences that followed the Crimean War, Cavour sent to Count Walewski, the French Foreign Secretary, on January 21st, 1856. It was in reply to the question of Napoleon III., " What can be done for Italy ? "

" The enemies of Italy," writes Cavour, " talk of the thirst for aggrandisement (*soif d'agrandissement*) of the House of Savoy. Change the expression, and instead of 'thirst for aggrandisement,' say 'national aspiration,' and we are ready to acknowledge the fact of its existence. Never was this aspiration disowned since the day when, in 1003, Humbert, Count of Maurien, took for his wife the Marchioness of Susa, and thereby gained the right of citizenship on the Italian Peninsula. The dukes of the House of Savoy, pursuing this aspiration, have often been deprived of their possessions, their courage and sword being left to them as their only hope; but they never wavered, and never despaired of the noble hereditary aim of their family— the liberation of Italy from the foreign yoke. Let men say that in their steady and consistent advance they were perhaps actuated as much by personal ambition as by unselfish patriotism; this too we will admit. But we add, that this was the happiest, the noblest kind of ambition; the interests of this ambition are blended (*se confondent*) with the interests of Italy."

This was clear speaking, and a correct description of the situation.

The requirements of an age create its men. King Victor Emmanuel II. was surrounded, as well in the council-chamber as in the camp, by men who, however much their opinions may have differed in other respects, were steady and faithful champions of the idea of the independence of Italy as personified in their King.

Amongst these men Cavour (Count Camillo Benso di Cavour) was prominent as a giant in intellect—one of those few statesmen in whom the spirit of the age and the genius of a nation are embodied,—one of those who, combining deep penetration with wonderful tact, untiring activity, and the warmth of patriotism, which is the perennial source of unceasing energy, are destined to realise the aspirations of centuries, and form an epoch in the history of their race.

But it remains the everlasting glory of the Piedmontese people, that it was their public spirit of ready self-sacrifice which gave to their King and his counsellors a solid foundation on which to erect the superb pyramid of Italian independence.

It is one of the frailties of human things that the rays of light are accompanied by shadows. Even the stupendous discoveries of natural science by which the hidden forces of nature have been made subservient to the welfare of the human race have this peculiarity—that the splendid lustre they shed on the history of mankind is accompanied by the dark shadow of selfish materialism, which pushes everything else into the background.

If the Piedmontese (and they are a sober, calculating people, who work,—and save too) had simply consulted their own material interests, they would have felt that, amongst all the communities of Italy, they were the only one which had no reason whatever for desiring a change. Piedmont was not subject to a foreign yoke; it was a small principality, but was master in its own house. It had a constitution under the protection of which it felt itself free; and it could feel free, for its King respected its constitution and its liberty with scrupulous fidelity. It had a government that watched faithfully over their inviolability; though in so doing it had to brave the threatening frowns of the foreign potentates.* Besides this the government was

* See Note 2 at end of this chapter.

also studious to promote the welfare of the commonwealth.

And this care, together with the industrious and economical spirit of the people, had an evident success. The state debt—that great curse of our age— was withal not oppressive, though the unhappy result of the struggle undertaken in 1849 for the realisation of the Italian idea, had cast on Piedmont the penalty of a heavy ransom. The taxes were not intolerable. The tax-gatherers did not take away the bread from the mouths of the indigent; neither did they carry off the pillow from under the head of the sick. The art of government, which in many other countries has degenerated into an ingenious method of imposing new taxes upon the people, did not know in Piedmont the cruel maxim which says to the citizen: Pay! then live if you can; but whether you can live or cannot live, pay! You exist for the benefit of the state; the state does not exist for yours.

Such was the situation of small but happy Piedmont. It could not gain in liberty, its burdens could only be increased if it changed its insignificant but independent position for that of a region of· united Italy. And the Piedmontese knew that their burdens would be increased by the change. But Italian patriotism bade them silence the pennywise and selfish calculation of individualism; and, animated by the lofty passion of soul-elevating patriotism, they were not only ready to sacrifice everything with joy in order to convert Italy—"the geographical expression"—into a free, independent, and united country, but they even urged and impelled the government to make use of their readiness for self-sacrifice.

And as a reward for this they did not everywhere meet even with acknowledgment. When—with the exception of Rome, which was garrisoned by French troops—all Italy was independent and united, I heard with astonishment an Italian statesman in high position make this exclamation, in reply to my praise of the unselfish patriotism of the Piedmontese:—" Don't let us speak of Piedmont; Piedmont is not Italian at all" (*L'Italie est hors de Piémont*).

And what would Italy be to-day without the self-sacrificing spirit shown by Piedmont? But what matters it? Patriotism is the spring of self-sacrifice, for the very reason that it does not reckon on acknowledgment when performing its duty.

Yet though this happy harmony of the people, the King, and his government afforded the constitutive elements for that united effort which is the condition of success, there were great difficulties to overcome or remove before even a master-mind like Cavour's could create an opportunity, and surround it with such favourable circumstances as to be able to commence the realisation of the ideal.

Amongst these difficulties I must first mention one which touched Hungary as directly as it did Italy.

Early in 1851 a Congress of Princes was held at Dresden. At this conference the Court of Vienna came forward with a proposal that all the lands and provinces subject to the rule of the Austrian dynasty, Hungary and the Italian possessions included, should be incorporated in the German Confederation. By this means the Court of Vienna would have been able to make sure that every attack and every conflict that might be directed against it on Hungarian and Italian soil would carry with it the character of an attack on the German Confederation, and the Confederation would in consequence have been obliged in case of such attack to defend the Court of Vienna in Hungary and Italy.

At that time I was still a prisoner of European diplomacy in Asia Minor, and our oppressed nation at home was condemned to silence.

But the refugees who had found a shelter in the west of Europe on this occasion also did their duty faithfully to their country.

A comprehensive memorial loudly protested in the name of the nation against this renewed attack on the independence and constitutional rights of Hungary. This memorial, signed by Teleki (Ladislaus), Szemere, Vukovics, Klapka, and Czecz, was addressed to the French Government. Vukovics, my late lamented friend, who shared my political principles, and who was Minister of Justice in Hungary during my Governorship, was kind enough to send this important document to me, in my confinement in Asia Minor.

In it the legal nature of the relations of Hungary to the Hapsburg-Lotharingian dynasty were soundly explained. It was shown that the ascendency of that dynasty in Hungary was not gained by right of conquest, but was based on a bilateral treaty, in which the complete independence of Hungary was made a condition of this rule. The constitutional guarantees by which this independence of the country was encompassed were enumerated and authenticated. These were the oaths of the kings, the diplomas of coronation, and the fundamental laws of the country, to which kings of the House of Hapsburg were obliged to swear observance, to which, with one single exception, each of them swore. It was mentioned that, during the last three centuries, the Hungarian nation had repeatedly been compelled to take up arms for the defence of their national existence and constitution, and that in each case this ended in a solemn treaty, in the negotiation of which the Hungarian nation and the Austrian dynasty acted as independent combatants. The memorial proceeded to remind the French Government that, during the wars for the assertion of our liberty, the kings of France upon several occasions took up the position of mediators, or allied themselves with us; that our several treaties with the Austrian dynasty were put under the guarantee of France, England, Sweden, and Holland, and that in consequence of this the liberty and the independence of Hungary form an integral part of the European system.

Further, there followed a discussion of the question whether this legal relation of Hungary to Austria may be considered as having been changed *de jure* by the events of 1848 and 1849; and on this point the memorial answers with a decided negative. It shows that our reforms of 1848 were not revolutionary, either by their nature, or by the way in which they were carried out, and that they have changed nothing in the legal relations existing between Hungary and Austria. The fact was established that Hungary did not attack, but only defended itself when attacked. It was proved that on this occasion it was the Court of Vienna which revolted against the law: Hungary was the champion of legality. Stress was laid upon the fact that Hungary, though thus attacked, stretched out her hand for peace, and made every effort to preserve peace, but that all her endeavours were arrogantly repulsed; and that the responsibility of the war rested entirely with the Court of Vienna. The memorial called attention to the absurd plea with which the Court of Vienna endeavoured to palliate the enormity of its unjustifiable attack—the plea that it took up arms, not against the nation, but against a party, while in flagrant contradiction to this absurd plea it confiscated the nation's rights. And after briefly recalling the fact that Hungary, in the war that was forced upon it, was not defeated by the Austrian dynasty, but fell a prey to treason coupled with foreign interference, the memorial establishes that there can no longer be a legal basis for the sovereignty over Hungary of the Court of Vienna, which went so far as to use the military power of a foreign State to upset the treaties on which its rule was based and the laws which it was bound to defend. Vienna's motto was, "Right is on my side, because I am the stronger," but this right, the correlative to which is the right of resistance, raises civil war into a system.

The memorial draws a parallel between the conduct of Austria and that of Russia during the Hungarian war. The comparison is in favour of the latter, but the memorialists call attention to the dangers that threaten Europe through the expansion of the sphere of Russia's power and influence in consequence of her intervention in Hungary. They discuss the question of nationalities from this point of view, and point to the increase of danger which would arise if, in consequence of the incorporation of Hungary, Croatia, Dalmatia, Galicia, and Lombardy into the German Confederation, the Russian power could exercise a preponderating influence on German affairs by means of that very Austria which, in consequence of the intervention of 1849, became, so to speak, a vassal of Russia.

The memorial does not neglect to recall to memory two remarkable circumstances—first, that the Emperor Francis, when he assumed the title of Austrian Emperor in 1804, solemnly declared that he did not intend thereby to make any alteration in the public law of Hungary, and that such law should, in every respect, remain unviolated; secondly, that the Treaties of 1815, which are still the foundation of European public law, clearly establish the principle that the German princes can be considered members of the German Confederation only in regard to those of their possessions which formerly belonged to the defunct German Empire. Hungary, however, and the other countries which it was now intended to embrace, never belonged to that empire.

In consequence of all these reasons, set forth at some length, the memorial expresses the hope that the French Republic will not allow the carrying out of the designs of the congress of Dresden, especially as by the projected union the number of the inhabitants of Germany would be increased by 38,000,000, and in the heart of Europe would be formed a state comprising 70,000,000 people, standing, too, within the influence of Russia. Such a state of things would entirely upset the European equilibrium.

There is only one point in the memorial upon which the authors do not seem to have been sufficiently informed, but this perhaps is not to be wondered at.

I mean the supposition that Russia was likely to approve of the projected union, and might even have originated it. This supposition was not confirmed by facts, as we shall see farther on; and, moreover, if this project had been carried out, the Court of Vienna would have been so secured by the support of all the German Powers against the Hungarian and Italian nations, and would have acquired such an ascendency over the whole German Confederation, that it would scarcely have required any further protection from Russia. Russian diplomacy can calculate much too well not to have seen that this growth in strength would have assisted Austria to emancipate herself from the yoke of Russian protection, which, by her interference in 1849, she had so thoughtlessly assumed.

This memorial of the exiled Hungarian patriots is, nevertheless, a memorable incident in the history of our nation. It is a truly diplomatic document to which I call the attention of the future historians of our times.

I need not show that the only aim of this attempt of the Court of Vienna was to secure, for itself the armed assistance of the German Confederation against any struggle of the Hungarian nation for its independence, and against the realisation of the national aspirations of the Italians. But sincerity does not form part of the moral code of diplomatists. The Viennese statesmen palliated their intentions by saying that as it was purposed to give the same political constitution to the whole monarchy, the Court of Vienna found itself reduced to the alternative of either withdrawing from the German Confederation entirely, or of incorporating with it all its "possessions" (of course nations are only "possessions").

Fortunately, this plea, the very aim of which involved a new violation of the rights of our country which could on no account be tolerated, was not accepted by the European Powers. As may easily be understood, the smaller German States did not show much enthusiasm in support of Austria's ambition, which placed before them the prospect of a servile dependence. The Cabinet of Turin did everything it could in London, Paris, and Berlin to frustrate the execution of this audacious plan, which would necessarily have converted the Italian states into vassals of Austria. England put in a decided veto at Vienna, Berlin, and Dresden; but the greatest opposition was manifested by Napoleon Bonaparte, at that time still President of the French Republic, who declared openly that he would be obliged to consider the entrance of Austria, with all her provinces, into the German Confederation as a *casus belli*. In consequence of this intimation—which was sent to St. Petersburg by a special diplomatic agent—the Emperor Nicholas hinted to the Emperor Francis Joseph, in an autograph letter, that it would be well not to throw difficulties in the way of the President of the French Republic in his international relations. This admonition coming from such a quarter was naturally effectual, and the Court of Vienna gave up the audacious plan in February, 1852, after having pertinaciously clung to it for more than a year.

III.

Endeavour of Austria to consolidate its power in Italy—Project of the League of Baldasseroni—Ravings of the Duke of Modena—Mazzini and the Cabinet of Turin.

THE Court of Vienna endeavoured to obtain compensation for defeat on this field by leaving nothing undone that could consolidate its power in Italy by extending its paramount influence over the Governments of Parma, Modena, Tuscany, Rome, and Naples, so as to be able thereby to dispose indirectly of the whole of Italy; while by occupying several important strategical points on the right of the river Po, it speculated on obtaining a direct command of central Italy, with the exception of Rome. To accomplish the former design it left no field of action neglected, and made every exertion in order to convert the foreign policy, the armed forces, the economical and commercial system, the custom-houses, railways, and post-offices of all the governments of the Italian peninsula (except sorely-tried Piedmont) into instruments of domineering Austrian preponderance.

This consolidation of the Austrian power in the Italian Peninsula was the second obstacle which stood in the way of the plans of the Cabinet of Turin. Austria had secured a position from the Alps to Terracina. It not only possessed Lombardy and Venice with the powerful Quadrilateral, but also occupied the Papal Legations and the Romagna. In Commachio, Ancona, Ferrara, Bologna, Piacenza, Austrian troops were stationed, and the Duchy of Parma was simply an Austrian province under a military administration. An Austrian general commanded at Parma, Austrian judges sat in the courts-martial, and under the pretence of maintaining public security, the lives, liberty, and honour of citizens were placed in the hands of the Austrian police.

The history of this extension of the power of Austria does not come within my province, but I have heard and read so much about the mad fanaticism of the so-called demagogues, that for the sake of contrast I do not think it without interest to bestow a moment upon the madly fanatical turn of mind of a partisan of the doctrine of " divine right."

In order to unite the Italian principalities (Piedmont always excepted) into a political whole, under the leadership of Austria, the formation of a league was brought forward in 1851. The subject was discussed in Rome; and Baldasseroni, the Minister President of Tuscany, was charged to elaborate a plan for the organisation of such a league.

Baldasseroni considered it wise to think not only of the princes, but also in a small degree of the people, and included in his plan some ideas " for the better administration of justice."

This "liberalism" did not at all please Francis V., Duke of Modena, but he liked very much the notion of an Austro-Italian League, which he expected would lead to the realisation of the fond desire of his heart, a war with France. Fearing, therefore, that by opposing the project he might mar this chance, he wrote to Count Forli, his Secretary for Foreign Affairs (under date of Venice, April 27th, 1851) to accept the idea of a league, notwithstanding the liberal phrases which accompanied it. These he would take good care to have interpreted in his own way, trusting above all things to Austria, which as a rule does not trouble herself much with "phrases," and understands how to throw dust into people's eyes, as shown by her promise of the "most liberal constitution" of March 4th. Austria would not be likely to feel fettered by such equivocal expressions.

Having thus consoled himself about those "liberal phrases" by his reliance on the "lofty character" of the Austrian Government, he gave himself the pleasure to put down, with his own princely hand, his wise views on the war which the Austro-Italian League was to undertake against France. Some of his profound reflections, which, to the eternal glory of his name, saw the light of day, read as follows:—

"While an English fleet, equipped with guns, sails up the Seine, it will be necessary that the army of the Austro-Italian League, in correspondence with the army of the German Confederation, shall as soon as possible enter on French soil and advance against Paris, the head of the Hydra, which, besides being the sewer of European roguery (*scelleraggini*), is more than ever the capital of the French. I have neither the pretension nor the ability to point out here the detailed movements of the armies, and I only say that I wish fervently that when Paris is taken, Europe may give the French a memorable lesson. Their capital should be transferred to another place; their fortresses in the interior should all be razed to the ground, those lying near the frontier should be occupied by the allies; and, in all the districts that border on Germany and Italy, military colonies should be established similar to those of Austria along the Turkish frontier. I would even propose that to some extent Croatians and Slavonians should be transferred from the Austrian colonies to those French districts, that the regions thus colonised should be subject to the original masters of the colonists, and that the restless inhabitants who now live in those frontier districts should be driven into the interior of France or transported to America. France should not be allowed to build one fortress, or more than a stipulated number of ships. It should provide for the enemy's army while these things are being arranged. It should pay the costs of the war and the expenses of the new colonisation, and should destroy the fortifications of Paris. Oh! what joy it would give me to see the Austro-Italian flag waving amongst the others on the heights of Montmartre."

Have ever the fields of the wildest demagogism produced a crop of fanaticism that could be compared to the madness of this prince, whose *"courteous. and wise judgment"* (*cortese e sapiente giudizio*) and *deep insight* were emphasised with "such feelings of reverence" by the Duke of Schwarzenberg, the Austrian Minister for Foreign Affairs, in his correspondence addressed to the prince with reference to the Customs Union.

If, by Austria's taking up a powerful position, the work of liberating Italy has been made difficult, it cannot be denied that the work was made easier by the Italians having been condemned by the wrath of God to be ruled by princes of such calibre. For these made it sure that whosoever unfurled the banner of Italian freedom with any hope of success would be followed by all the Italians.

But, if no hope of success was held out, it could scarcely have been expected that the universal discontent would vent itself in a general and earnest national movement, unless a political earthquake, like the one of 1848, were to take place throughout Europe. Therefore if we take into consideration how extended, and, by the occupation of the most important strategical positions, how secure was the dominion of Austria in Italy, we cannot at all wonder that the statesmen of Turin did not join in the watchword "*Italia farà da se*" (Italy will do it herself), but thought that assistance from outside was also necessary.

The efforts made in this direction were rendered very difficult by the repeated attempts of Mazzini and his party, which, though intended to be revolutionary, had only the character of isolated insurrections. I decidedly condemned such attempts whenever I became cognisant of them, and endeavoured to restrain Mazzini, though, to my regret, without success.

My view of the matter was always this, that what is permissible and may even be judicious in the case of a nation rising merely to change the form of its government or to transform its internal organisation, is neither judicious nor permissible when the end in view is national independence and delivery from foreign dominion.

In the former case, revolution does not really mean war. It is but an internal contest in which the people are confronted only by governmental power; and such a revolution has in more than one instance been decided by a few days' fighting in the streets. But in the latter case, revolution is a real war against a foreign enemy, whose centre of power cannot be reached in the country because he has at his disposal armies and resources outside the country. Such a war cannot be decided by fighting from behind barricades. In this case the activity of patriotism must confine itself to keeping alive the aspirations for independence, and to taking care that the nation may be in readiness to seize such an opportunity for the realisation of its aspirations as will make the probability of success, according to human calculation, depend solely upon the will of the people. To do this much is a patriotic duty for him who possesses in a sufficient degree the confidence of his fellow-citizens. But to organize local outbreaks is a political error by which no reasonable purpose can be gained; and from a moral point of view it is to be condemned, for it unnecessarily compromises those who are ready for sacrifice, and the lives of such should not be risked in vain.

These views served to guide me under all circumstances since I became a refugee, and from them I have never swerved. Mazzini's more sanguine temper led him into another path. He always lived in the illusion that everything depended upon the beginning. He did not take circumstances into due account. He always believed that if an audacious *coup de main* in one or two places succeeded, it would have the same influence upon the Italian people all over the country as is exercised upon the soldiers by the sound of the drum. He believed that all Italy would rush to arms, and the end of this illusion was that not only did Italy not rush to arms, but that not even a single *coup de main* succeeded. There were cases when Mazzini, after the failure of such attempts, confessed to me, in correspondence, that I was right and he mistaken; but this confession, after the deed, could not undo what had been done.

These attempts caused great difficulties to the Government of Turin. Its enemies, on all sides, declared that they were the outcome of that sufferance, not to say protection, which the Italian revolutionary spirit met with at Turin. Its friends, on the other hand, charged it with want of foresight and with weakness. Austria's indignation at the liberty of the Piedmontese press, and at the protection accorded to the Italian patriots who had taken refuge in Piedmont, was supported even by the Paris Government. It happened that Baron Hübner, the Austrian ambassador at Paris, said bluntly to the Duke of Guiche, the French envoy at Turin, that there would never be peace in the Italian peninsula until he (Guiche) and Apponyi, the Austrian minister at Turin, should go together to King Victor Emmanuel to tell him *that he must kick over the liberal institutions in Piedmont.* The remark which the king made to his minister, General Dabormida, when informed by him of the intrigues of Austria, is worth reproduction. Said the king, "I do not aspire to any other glory than that history should say of me, He was an honest king (*Re galantuomo*); the very moment it became impossible for me to make my people happy, to redeem my promises, and do my duty, I would descend from my throne."* Under these circumstances, it was necessary that an extraordinary turn in European affairs should take place, to enable the statesmen of Turin to find opportunity for introducing the Italian question into the list of European questions, and thus open the way towards the attainment of help from France or England.

* Letters of Dabormida to Villamarina in Paris, April 26th and 28th, 1853.

IV.

The Crimean War—Endeavour of the Western Powers to draw Austria into their Alliance—Austria's Conduct—Piedmont's Offers and Conditions—Cavour's Audacious Step—Journey of Victor Emmanuel and Cavour to Paris—Congress of Paris.

SUCH an opportunity was offered by the Eastern war of 1854, when France and England united to defend Turkey against the Russians. These two powers, before actually declaring war, directed all their efforts to gaining the alliance of Austria. They would not, or could not, see that this was utterly impossible. In their councils there prevailed the absurd prejudice so detrimental to the hopes of Hungary, that for this war the help of Austria was indispensable; and to this view they clung feverishly throughout the war. Austria threw dust in their eyes, protracting the negotiations by doubtful promises and conditional prospects. The Western Powers suffered all this; they wanted Austria's help at any price. They did not get it, and the result of their obstinately courting the favour of Austria was, that while they could have secured Europe for ever from the ambition of Russia, had they, conformably with the logic of the situation, taken the Polish and Hungarian nations into account, the great objects set forth at the commencement of hostilities came to nothing, from considerations to Austria. The huge mountain gave birth to a miserable little mouse, and a situation was patched up in the East, which necessarily resulted in the last Russo-Turkish war—which led to the fall of the

Turkish Empire, and has so frightfully extended the sphere of Russia's influence, that the unavoidable consequences are fraught with the danger of seeing powers vanish and of the ruin of whole nations. These dangers are, indeed, in their final results incalculable.

"*The Eastern Question in* 1854 *and at the Present Time*" forms the subject of the third volume of my Memories: here I will only mention so much as is necessary to elucidate the origin of the Italian war of 1859.

Austria, when sounded by the Western Powers, without loss of time, and, it must be admitted, skilfully made use of the opportunity to damage Piedmont. "How can you expect me," said she, "to make the Russians my enemies, when behind my back I am threatened with an Italian revolution, instigated and supported by Piedmont? Austria cannot even enter on any discussion with the Western Powers until the Government of Turin is forced to give safe guarantees for the maintenance of order and tranquillity." General Radeczky even went so far as to demand as a guarantee for Austria the temporary occupation of Alessandria, the chief fortress of Piedmont.

Of course, in making this demand Radeczky spoke as a soldier only. He confounded tactics with politics, and diplomacy, disregarding his demand, passed to the order of the day. Yet in a political sense even more was offered to Austria by the Western Powers. They offered to guarantee all her Italian possessions, and defend her against any attack from without, if she joined them in the war against Russia. This offer was not even kept secret. It was made public in the *Moniteur* of February 22nd, and gave rise to an irritated exchange of notes between Turin and Paris.

But Austria did not think for a moment of taking up arms against Russia, which was made a condition of the proffered guarantee; therefore she had recourse to other excuses and pretexts to hide her want of inclination. Thus the matter dragged on for months, till at last it occurred to the statesmen of the Western Powers that the Government of Turin might be persuaded to become the ally of France and England and send an army into the Crimea. This arrangement would surely allay the scruples of Austria; for it was madness to suppose for a moment that the insignificant Piedmont could send an army to the far East and at the same time attack powerful Austria at home.

When sounded upon this subject, a cabinet council, presided over by King Victor Emmanuel in person, decided on December 13th, 1854, that Sardinia was ready to take part in the war against Russia, with an army of fifteen thousand men, under the following conditions (besides a loan of two million pounds from England):—1. That the Western Powers should give assurances that when peace was concluded the services and sacrifices of Sardinia would be taken into due account; 2. That Sardinia having by this alliance become an integral part of the European system, should take part in the congress to be called upon to negotiate peace and re-establish the European political equilibrium; 3. That the Western Powers—by a separate secret treaty—should bind themselves to induce Austria to exonerate the property of Sardinian subjects, situate in Lombardy and Venice, from the confiscation they have been struck with without any judicial proceedings,* and that they should further bind themselves *to take the state of Italy into serious consideration at the conclusion of peace.*

But consideration for Austria stood in the way of the acceptance of these conditions by the Western Powers. Austria had no positive knowledge of these negotiations, but she suspected them, and tried by every means to frustrate them. She continually urged that great importance would be given to Sardinia, were it received into alliance with the Western Powers; that such an alliance, increasing its political credit, would enable it to exercise a dangerous influence on the Italian Peninsula. These representations had their effect: all hope of Victor Emmanuel's conditions being accepted was gone, and the matter had arrived at such a stage, that either all negotiations would have to be dropped, or else the alliance for a participation in the Eastern war would have to be concluded without any conditions and guarantees for the state of Italy.

At this juncture of affairs Cavour decided upon an audacious and hazardous game. I know not whether, had I been in his place, I should have dared to risk it. Scarcely.

He started from the position that if Sardinia were to draw back she would remain outside the pale of the European system, and could have no hope whatever of gaining assistance for the realisation of Italian aspirations. "Let the King therefore join in the

* See Note 3 at the end of the chapter.

Western alliance without any condition or guarantee; it is impossible that such loyalty should not be appreciated. Who knows what turn events may take? Do not let us be debarred from making use of any chance that may offer itself. The growth of Piedmont's political credit, of which Austria is so much afraid, is of great importance. Therefore go on bravely! Let us show the world that the colours of the House of Savoy are worthy to be in the company of those of France and England."

So said Cavour. The King and the Council of Ministers agreed with Cavour's views, with the exception of General Dabormida, the Minister for Foreign Affairs, who strongly opposed them; and as he stood alone, he left the Cabinet. The portfolio of Foreign Affairs was given to Cavour himself.

Events proved Cavour to be right. "*Partem fortuna sibi vindicat,*" says Cicero, speaking of victories in the field. This also applies to diplomatic victories. Success justifies much. But it was an audacious and a hazardous part to play.

The alliance was formally concluded on the 25th January, 1855. Sardinia undertook to provide an army of 15,000 men at its own expense for participation in the war against Russia, and to maintain its strength at that figure until the end of the campaign. There is no condition, no stipulation in favour of Sardinia in the treaty; but the sixth paragraph mentions that England and France guarantee the integrity of Sardinia, and bind themselves to defend it against any attack so long as the war then contemplated should last.

That was all. It was not even stipulated that

Sardinia should have a voice in the peace congress. The Sardinian Parliament was persuaded with difficulty to approve this treaty. But still it was accepted—in the Chamber of Representatives by a majority of 101 against 60, and in the Senate by 63 against 27—after a fierce debate that lasted for three days.

Sardinia faithfully discharged the obligation she had assumed. But she had to suffer much political humiliation. On the 15th March, 1855, a conference was opened at Vienna for the preliminary settlement of the conditions which were to serve as a basis for the negotiation of peace. This is the conference of the famous *four points*, which will be minutely discussed in the third volume of my "Memories." Sardinia was excluded from this conference. Cavour, though grieved, submitted to this, lest he should cut away from under his feet the ground of Italy's hope. To save the dignity of his king, at least, Cavour, referring to the fact that diplomatic intercourse between Sardinia and Austria was interrupted, showed himself ready to acknowledge that it would have been difficult to devise a proper mode for the representatives of the two powers to sit in the same conference. But still Sardinia had a right to have the peace conditions previously communicated to her by her allies; for she was a party to the struggle, and in the treaty of alliance which she had made with England and France it was clearly stipulated that the contracting parties should not enter into any communication with a view to put an end to hostilities, without having first consulted together. This was of no avail. They negotiated without Sardinia being allowed to be represented and heard; and Austria also succeeded in excluding Sardinia from the conferences that were held later on at Constantinople. Cavour was forced to be content with calling attention to the rights of Sardinia, with *hoping* that they would in future be respected, and with sending notes to Paris and London, in which he put forth his opinion on the famous "four points," as an intimation that he too had a voice in the matter.

The only question still open now was that of Sardinia's participation in the congress to be called for negotiating the peace. Walewski, the French Minister of Foreign Affairs, in reply to a communication from Sardinia on this point, answered verbally that Sardinia could not take part in the conferences, because only general principles having reference to the European equilibrium were under discussion there, and these had to be reserved to the Great Powers according to precedent established by the Congress of 1815. But it being beyond doubt that in those deliberations which would touch the interests of Sardinia also she had a right to be represented, she would have to take part in the settlement of the conditions of peace, and as a party to the treaty of peace would have to sign the same.

The Government of Turin did not allow the advantage of this acknowledgment to be wrested from its hands, and wished to fix in written notes the part it was to take in the congress, declaring at the same time that if it were contemplated to make any distinction between the status of the representatives of the Great Powers and that of the representative of Sardinia, this would place the latter in a very painful and equivocal position.*

* Villamarina's Note of June 5th, 1855.

On June 17th Walewski, after much evasion and hesitation, gave it in writing, by direct command of the Emperor Napoleon, that the Sardinian plenipotentiary would take part personally in all deliberations *which were likely to affect the particular interests of Sardinia.* In addition, the English and French plenipotentiaries would take care that their Sardinian colleague should always be kept informed of negotiations of *general interest;* and, finally, that the Sardinian plenipotentiary should affix his signature to the treaty of peace.

In England, Russell first said evasively that to begin with, it would be necessary to decide some minor questions of etiquette, as on the occasion of the Congress of Vienna; whereupon the Sardinian ambassador, Marquis Azeglio, replied that this really was an anachronism. After this, the English Government, on June 19th, gave a written assurance similar to that of France.

Thus the point that Sardinia should not be shut out from the congress was gained. This result cost an expenditure of two millions sterling and not a little blood. But the blood and the treasure were better invested than the 983 killed, 4,200 wounded and missing, and the 412,000,000 of francs which, twenty years later, the Austrian, now euphonically called the Austro-Hungarian monarchy, has sunk in Bosnia by way of a first instalment, not as a protection against future contingencies, but seriously to compromise its future.

True, the position assigned to Sardinia at the coming congress was not a very splendid one. Sardinia was to be admitted, not to all deliberations, but only to those in which its own particular interests were discussed. But the Italian, when he meets with difficulties, says, "*Pazienza!*" Cavour was an Italian, and thought to himself, "Let me get in, and *pazienza.*" Patience in this instance really was rewarded.

The first rays of dawn which thus appeared on the dark horizon of Italy gave rise to the idea that it would be well for King Victor Emmanuel to pay a short visit to Paris and London; and he did this at the end of 1855, accompanied by Cavour.

I was staying at that time in England. The Queen, the Government, and the people showed much sympathy with the young king. But I do not believe that this royal visit had any influence on the future of the Italian question. We witnessed, however, several amusing scenes. It was known in England that the Government of King Victor Emmanuel was engaged in a fierce struggle with the Vatican. The English had also heard that, in consequence of the closing of some hundreds of monasteries, and the subjection of the priests to common law, Turin had been banned with Papal excommunication, which, though much dreaded at one time, has long since ceased to be injurious. Some of the English people, earnest Protestants, thought they saw in Victor Emmanuel, if not a second Luther, at least another Moritz of Saxony. And when the king travelled as far as the Tweed, more than one religious assemblage read to him a handsomely illuminated address, strongly abusive of the Great Babylon; praising the king, to his amazement, as a great reformer, and encouraging him to persevere in the good work. It cost him some trouble to make these people understand that, though a great friend to toleration in religious matters, and to liberty and equality before the law, he was at the same time a good Roman Catholic, and intended to remain one to the end of his days.

It is a real delight to see how thoroughly impracticable are, at times, my dear practical English friends, whom I so much respect and love, and to whom I owe such a debt of gratitude.

In Paris the Royal Visitor met with quite a different train of ideas. The letters of Cavour, addressed to Ratazzi, describe the situation, with regard to Italy, as very promising. One evening the Emperor Napoleon even addressed these words to Cavour: "*What can be done for Italy?*" This question, coming from such a quarter, was of great importance. Cavour politely asked to be allowed to give a well-considered answer in writing. "Well, I will await it," was the Emperor's answer.

Thus came into existence that comprehensive memorial already mentioned by me. This memorial, in speaking of Austria, becomes a powerful accusation, and even questions her right to exist. "What is the *raison d'être* of the Austrian Monarchy? Wherefore does it exist? Is it by that force of cohesion which a feeling of nationality gives?—No. Is it through the inherited prestige of the imperial title, which was so powerful from the time of Charlemagne to that of Joseph II.?—No. Is it through the love which a nation has for a dynasty always worthy of the confidence and mindful of the welfare of its people?—No. Austria, leaning on three races differing from each other in origin, language, and customs, three nations whose interests and aspirations are widely divergent, exists only by virtue of a central power, the authority of which is not even allowed to be brought under discussion, and which, by its powerful pressure, keeps together the distinct fractions of the empire which naturally tend to separate. The principle of this central power is identical with that of the power of Russia. Every government, therefore, whose principle was identical with that of the Government of Austria could always depend upon the assistance of that power. Thus, the west of Europe stands here face to face with a permanent coalition, having an opposite principle of existence. A coalition must be met by a coalition."

It is true that when offering practical suggestions in answer to the question, "What can be done for Italy?" the memorial becomes very reserved in tone, and only speaks of reforms. But a great deal can be read between the lines—for instance, when it says that if, in 1849, the Great Powers had thought of Italy, the power of united Italy, instead of that of Piedmont alone, could now have been placed at their disposal; or when it shows that it is a confusion of thought to designate the efforts for national independence as revolutionary exertions, and that it is an old device of all oppressors to endeavour to cover with contumely those whom they have deprived of their rights.

This memorial, however, was only submitted to the Emperor by Walewski in the following January, just at the time when Austria had succeeded in inducing Russia to accept the famous "four points" as the basis of peace.

The memorial of Cavour bears the mark of the pressure of this unwelcome circumstance. In his letter to Walewski, accompanying the memorial, Cavour says that since by a diplomatic fiction Austria must be regarded as having done a great service to Europe, he must start *unfortunately* from the basis, that *for the present at least (pour le moment du moins)* no sacrifice of territory in Italy will be demanded of Austria. Starting from this melancholy basis, he must of necessity restrict his suggestions to the reforms. To alleviate the iron rule which oppresses Lombardy and Venice, to withdraw the Austrian armies from the Legations of the Pope and from the Romagna; to give a secular government to these provinces, to restrain the King of Naples from continuing to shock civilised Europe; and to force Austria to render justice to Piedmont—to these measures did Cavour in his letter cut down the bolder soaring of his memorial, formerly prepared and submitted, as material for further reflection, and in fact at the congress the little conversation held on Italian matters did not travel beyond these narrow limits.

The peace preliminaries were signed in Vienna by the Great Powers on February 1st, 1856, and the peace congress (or rather conference) was opened on February 25th in Paris. Sardinia was represented by Count Cavour and the Marquis Pes di Villamarina. The conditions of peace were all settled, but Italy had not yet been mentioned.

At last, at the meeting of April 8th, the subject was, by direct command of the Emperor Napoleon, discreetly introduced by the President Walewski, French Minister of Foreign Affairs.

He commenced by saying that it would be wise if, before they separated, the members of the conference were to exchange their ideas on different problems which required solution, and with which it would be well to deal now, in order to prevent fresh complications.

He first referred to the sad condition of Greece,

then passed to Belgium, in the newspapers of which country the most offensive and hostile attacks on the French Government were daily published, and at last proposed that as the Congress of Westphalia had sanctioned liberty of conscience, and the Congress of Vienna the suppression of the slave-trade, and the freedom of river navigation, the Congress of Paris should also make an important step forward in international law, by laying down the foundation for regulating the equality of rights of neutrals on the high seas in time of war.

Then, enlarging on different topics in the course of his exposition, he confined himself to the following remarks about Italy :—" The Papal possessions are in an abnormal state. The necessity that they should not be exposed to anarchy has induced France to occupy Rome, and Austria to occupy the Legations. That a power should require the assistance of foreign armies to maintain itself is a state of things which it would be impossible not to pronounce abnormal; France is ready to withdraw her army as soon as this can be done without prejudice to public order and to the dignity of the Papal Government, and France hopes that Austria will accede to this declaration."

Then he put the question whether it would not be desirable that some of the governments in Italy should of their own accord, by some well-understood concessions, put an end to the existing state of affairs, which, far from doing harm to the enemies of public order, only weakened the rulers and made proselytes for the demagogues. Great service would be rendered to the cause of public order not only in Italy, but also in the Kingdom of the Two Sicilies, if it were explained to them that they are following a wrong course.

Lord Clarendon, the first plenipotentiary of England, entered thoroughly into the question. He began by saying that it was necessary to remove the causes which rendered necessary the occupation by foreign armies of some parts of the Italian Peninsula, for if reliance were placed in armed force, instead of the evils justifying the universal discontent being remedied, there could only result the tendency to establish permanently a system which reflected but little credit on the government, and was simply deplorable in its effects upon the people. For the last seven years Bologna, besides being occupied by the Austrians, had been in a state of siege, and the consequence was that the country round about was infested by brigands. The government in the Papal possessions must be secularised, and a new system of administration in harmony with the spirit of the age introduced. It was possible that a sudden change in Rome itself might create some difficulties, but it would be easily carried out in the Legations, now occupied by the Austrians. With regard to the Neapolitan Government, it was the duty of the Congress to protest against the system it was pursuing, as it was only fomenting revolutionary excitement, intead of calming it down. "We want peace for Europe, *but no peace is possible without justice.*"

Count Buol, the Austrian plenipotentiary, took up the other questions, but did not enter into the Italian question owing to want of instructions. The congress was not convoked to inform independent sovereigns of the wishes of others with respect to their system of government. He agreed with the views of the President, but could not follow Lord Clarendon, and would not give any opinion about the duration of the Austrian occupation of the Roman provinces.

Baron Hübner, the second Austrian plenipotentiary, added that his Government would withdraw the troops when it should find that the time for doing so had arrived.

The Russian plenipotentiary preserved silence on the subject; and with regard to what his Prussian colleague said, the Hungarian proverb "Ötöl-hatol" (You are shuffling) may be appropriately quoted.

Cavour, prefacing his observations by the remark that he did not doubt the right of any member to abstain from the discussion of questions on which he had received no instructions, said that he considered it important that the opinions expressed with regard to the occupation of the Roman provinces should be set down in the protocol. Next he referred to Austria. The Austrian occupation of the Roman provinces, he said, was assuming more and more the character of permanency; it had now lasted for seven years, and the state of the country had not at all improved, as it was clearly shown by the circumstance that it was still considered necessary to keep up the state of siege in Bologna in its full severity, in spite of its having lasted as long as the occupation itself. The presence of Austrian troops in the Legations and in Parma upset the political equilibrium of Italy, and constituted a formidable danger to Sardinia. And therefore he deemed it his duty to call the attention of Europe to this abnormal state. With regard to Naples he shared the opinions of Walewski and Lord Clarendon.

Baron Hübner answered these remarks in rather an angry tone. However, he had already at former times given proofs that he was not one of the most self-possessed of diplomatists, particularly when he had to do with Sardinia, about which he was wont to speak in a haughty way.

He told Cavour it was a pity to speak of the Austrian occupation alone, as there was a French occupation too, upon which subject he was silent. And there was even another one, for Sardinia herself had for the last eight years been occupying Mentone and Roccabruna, which belonged to the principality of Monaco. The difference between the two was that while the Austrians and French were called in by the respective sovereigns, Sardinia had entered the possessions of the Prince of Monaco against his will, and remained there to this moment notwithstanding his protest.

Cavour lost no time in replying that Sardinia was ready to withdraw her army of occupation, *consisting of fifty men, all told*, from Mentone, if the Prince of Monaco thought he could return thither in safety. Certainly he (Cavour) wished to see the French occupation come to an end, as well as the Austrian, but he pointed out that the latter was much more dangerous to the independent states of Italy than the former. A weak army removed so far from France did not threaten anybody, but it was undeniably very disquieting to see that Austria, leaning on the fortresses of Ferrara and Piacenza, and continually increasing the number of her fortifications, extended all along the Adriatic Sea as far south as Ancona.

According to the protocol of the congress the discussion on the affairs of Italy ended here, with the exception of a few concluding words from the president, summing up the opinions which had been expressed. But in reading the minutes it is impossible not to feel that something must have happened that is not mentioned in them. The conclusion of the debate at this point is unnatural, and one feels almost inclined to turn over a few leaves to see whether something pertaining to this debate has not been transposed by the binder.— No, there was no such mistake. However, Cavour's letter to Ratazzi, Nerli's telegram to the Minister President of Tuscany, and that of Antonini to the Minister of Foreign Affairs of Naples, inform us that the protocols do not mention everything that happened.

There was in fact a stormy scene. Cavour was warmly supported by the English plenipotentiaries, especially Lord Clarendon, who said of the Papal Government that it was a disgrace and outrage on Europe, and strongly urged Count Buol-Schauenstein, the first Austrian plenipotentiary, to indicate the intentions of Austria with regard to affairs in Italy. Buol answered, in a cold and peremptory manner, that Austria declined to give an account of her intentions to Lord Clarendon. The noble lord felt offended, and said that if the Cabinet of Vienna refused to give reassuring promises it thereby threw down the gauntlet to liberal-minded Europe; but he bade them beware, and said that the challenge would be accepted, and the Italian question be solved by stronger means than had yet been mentioned at the congress. Count Buol replied to this in such passionate language that Lord Clarendon, at the end of this stormy sitting, sent Lord Cowley, the second English plenipotentiary, to Baron Hübner, to tell him that if the scandalous language of the Austrian plenipotentiary were brought to the knowledge of the English public there would be an outburst of indignation all over England.

However, nothing was made known. The congress, on the motion of its president, agreed that these words, and in general all that might damage the credit of the censured governments, should not be inserted in the protocols. But the consequences show that what was left out of the protocols was of greater influence on the events that followed than what was inserted; not as regards England, for the English Government did not carry out Lord Clarendon's threat, which he repeated again, in the course of the next few days, in the presence of the Emperor Napoleon and Count Cavour—and to which he added more weight by his opening a prospect of armed assistance;* but it was of influence elsewhere. Count Buol felt the ground was beginning to tremble under his feet. He would have liked to gain information about the approaching storm, and, therefore on paying his farewell visit to the Emperor Napoleon, he remarked that Austria would not be disinclined to come to an understanding with France about the means of satisfying the wishes uttered at the congress with regard to Italy. But the Emperor, without letting him finish, answered to this feeler: "Too late! it would have been better to say this at the meeting of April 8th." To Cavour he said: "I have a presentiment that peace will not last." "A presentiment" is of great importance when felt by a man like the Emperor Napoleon, at the climax of his power!

* So writes Nicomede Bianchi in his *Storia Documentata*, vol. vii., page 278, but he does not give his authority.

There are two other circumstances connected with the Congress of Paris which I think are worthy of being recorded.

The one is, that Count Hatzfeld, the second plenipotentiary of Prussia, said to Cavour, in a very significant manner, that the political relation of Prussia to Austria was the same as that of Piedmont; they had both common grounds of complaint against her.

" . . . . den grossen Geschicken schreiten ihre Geister schon voran, und in dem *heute* wandelt schon das *morgen*" (Schiller).

With the "*heute*" of 1856 was already bound up the "*morgen*" of 1866.

The other circumstance refers to the question of "armed intervention," a word of terrible memory in the history of Hungary. It appears to be the fate of the Hungarians, that advances in international law come too late for them. But who knows? though late, perhaps after all not fruitless. "Sors incerta vagatur, Fertque refertque vices," wrote Lucan, and writing thus, he wrote history.

The eighth paragraph of the Treaty of Paris stipulates: Should any dispute arise between the Sublime Porte and one of the contracting parties prejudicial to their political relations, an opportunity for mediation should be given to the other powers before having recourse to arms.

Lord Clarendon availed himself of the occasion to propose, in the sitting of the congress of April 14th, that a more general application should be given to this auspicious innovation in order to prevent armed collisions.

Walewski, on the part of France, accepted the proposal, and hoped to see it inserted in the protocol as an idea corresponding to the spirit of our age, while, moreover, it could not interfere with the freedom of action on the part of any government.

Prussia acceded to this, Russia took it *ad referendum*. Austria, though not taking exception to the proposal as formulated by Walewski, could not accept it as an absolute obligation, on the ground that it might interfere with the independence of her Cabinet.

Cavour wished to know whether the proposal was to be understood as referring also to armed intervention entered upon against "*de facto*" governments (*gouvernements de fait*), as was the case for instance in Austria's interference in Naples in 1821.

Clarendon replied that he wished his proposal to have the widest application, and he recalled the endeavour of Great Britain to prevent the armed intervention against the Spanish "de facto" government in 1823. (Had Hungary been represented at the congress, the noble lord might have been reminded that, in 1849, Great Britain had altogether forgotten her humanitarian principles of 1823. Poor Hungary!)

Count Walewski said that as there was no intention to impose any obligation, but only to give expression to a general wish of Europe, which did not interfere with the liberty of action of any power, he did not see why Lord Clarendon's proposal should not be made to bear the most general and universal application.

Of course, Count Buol turned round on Cavour. The interference of Austria, in Naples, was undertaken in conformity with a decision of the Congress of Laibach. He did not admit that a second-rate power should be allowed to question the intervention, based on the will of the Great Powers. He protested against such a general construction being put upon the proposal as would lead to consequences favourable to "de facto" governments. (There is no denying that a Viennese cabinet remains a Viennese cabinet, even if on a visit to Paris.)

Cavour did not allow himself to be betrayed into passion. He was satisfied, he said, with the explanations of England and France, and agreed to the proposal.

In conformity, therefore, with the wish of Europe, a stipulation was inserted in the protocol that, before having recourse to arms, the hostile parties should avail themselves of the mediation of friendly powers, and a hope was expressed that the powers not represented at the congress would accede to it too. So be it.

V.

Attempt of Orsini—Opinion of Senator Pietri—The Emperor Napoleon and Cavour—The Meeting at Plombières—Diplomatic Campaign—Cavour's Deep Insight and Wonderful Ability—The Archduke Albert in Berlin—The Ultimatum of Baron Kellersberg—Cavour's Answer—*Alea jacta erat.*

It does not come within the province of my records to follow minutely every movement made on the chess-board of diplomacy for the two long years after the Congress of Paris, by which Austria endeavoured, with more or less success, to isolate Piedmont politically. But, before we come to decisive events, I must mention that it appears to me as if the attempt committed by Orsini, and his behaviour while in prison, were not without influence on the turn affairs have taken.

Orsini committed his attempt on January 14th, 1858. It was an awful deed. The moment the carriage which conveyed the Emperor and Empress of the French stopped before the entrance to the Opera in the Rue Lepelletier, Orsini and his companions threw bombs filled with explosive material at the vehicle. A dreadful explosion followed. Among the crowd collected before the Opera House many were killed, and still more wounded, but the Emperor and the Empress escaped unhurt.

At that time Senator Pietri was Chief of the Police in France, the same Pietri who, later on, was commissioned by the Emperor to represent him as his confidential man in all the details of his relations with the Hungarian refugees, conformably to the agreement arranged between us. I am bound to testify that in his dealings with us he was courteous to the last degree, and showed great benevolence towards Hungary. I travelled with him to meet the Emperor at Valeggio. On our way thither he spoke much of Orsini, with whom, in consequence of his official duties, he had often come into contact during the latter's imprisonment. He spoke of him with sympathetic pity. He used all his influence to induce the Emperor to spare his life. As so many human lives fell victims to the attempt, the Emperor did not think he could assume the whole responsibility of a pardon, but intimated that if the Council of State, at which also archbishops were to assist, would pronounce favourably for the prisoner, he would not withhold his sanction, and he also authorised Pietri to endeavour to get his (Pietri's) view accepted by the majority. Pietri canvassed each member of the council personally. He received encouraging assurances and went to the council hoping for success; but when abandoned there, and left in the minority, even by the teachers of charity, he was so much grieved that he resigned his office as Chief of the Police. I was told by Pietri that Orsini was not a ruffian. He was a fanatic, who carried patriotism to the verge of passion for martyrdom. He held the mistaken idea that the Emperor Napoleon stood in the way of the liberty of Italy. There he was quite wrong. The Emperor was always a true friend to it. Pietri explained to Orsini, in his cell, that if the murderous attempt had succeeded he would have killed the one man, amongst all the crowned heads of the world, from whom the Italians could expect support and help.

I heard this from Pietri himself.

This explanation was not without influence on Orsini. On February 21st he wrote a letter to the Emperor from the prison of Mazas. "Do not repulse, sire," he writes, "the words of a patriot, who stands on the verge of the grave. Free Italy and the benediction of twenty-five millions of people will accompany your name to posterity."

The newspapers were permitted to publish this letter. Orsini understood this to mean that the voice he had raised from the verge of his grave had found its way to the Emperor's heart, and on March 11th, this time from the prison of La Roquette, he wrote a second letter, in which he openly condemned political murder, and called upon the youth of Italy "to prepare itself for fighting out the liberty of their country, by practising the virtues of citizens, which alone could free Italy, and make it independent and worthy of its past greatness."

Crime deserves punishment. Would that it found it amongst high and low! Orsini was punished. He died on the scaffold for his crime; but verily this man loved his country fervently and unselfishly. He could only have committed a crime for the benefit of his country.

Fatherland is a sacred word! Alas! that this word, though still spoken, has through the growth of the too materialistic tendency of this age commenced to lose its charm! I trust I may not live to see it cease entirely to stimulate to heroic deeds!

A request was sent from Paris to Turin that these two letters, and the last will of Orsini, might be published in the papers there. Cavour answered—"We shall publish them, but let them bear in mind, in Paris, that this will be a direct attack on Austria, not only by Piedmont, but also by the Emperor." "Have them published," was the reply. And they were published, with an appropriate preface.*

* * * * * *

We are now at the end of March, 1858. In June, M. Conneau, physician in ordinary to the Emperor, went to Turin, to inform Cavour that the Emperor Napoleon would like to meet him at Plombières. It was a custom of the Emperor not to make use of the services of professional diplomatists for confidential missions. To me, too, though I did not know him personally, Conneau was mentioned as an intermediary in case Pietri should be elsewhere occupied. (Pietri often was. It was he who went to Nice, and in his wake "suffrage universel" arose.)

The meeting at Plombières (in July, 1858) was the prologue to the drama enacted in 1859. All the details

* See No. 77 of the *Gazetta Piemontese* of 1858.

are not yet known. The chroniclers of Italian diplomacy still speak of it with reserve. They think, however, that they can go so far as to state that Napoleon made a decided offer to give Piedmont armed assistance, in order to wrest the whole of Italy from the hands of Austria. But the question of fixing the time for commencing the war the Emperor reserved to himself. Meanwhile Piedmont was to prepare, and to foster political agitation in Italy; was to prevent all revolutionary outbreaks; make no advances to Austria, yet refrain from provoking her " too much." But she was to endeavour to make friends with Russia. *A united Italy was not mentioned.* It was settled that the temporal power of the Holy See should be preserved, but within very narrow limits. Both parties spoke with the utmost caution as regarded Tuscany and Naples; *but it was agreed, that for the House of Savoy a kingdom of twelve million inhabitants, in the north of Italy, should be formed.* As compensation for the promised military help, *Savoy was to be ceded to France.* It was decided that the question with regard to Nice should be settled later, when the war was over. Nothing passed in writing. An offensive and defensive treaty was signed after a lapse of six months only.

From what I heard later through Pietri, Cavour, and still higher authorities, I feel justified in asserting that this account is authentic in its essential features.

More than four months after the meeting at Plombières (in November, 1858) Vincenzio Salvagnoli—by whose authority it is not known—handed a memorial to the Emperor at Compiègne, in which the expulsion of Austria from Italy, with the help of France, is assumed as a settled matter, and the question of the distribution of Italy is discussed. A great noise was made at the time about this meeting at Compiègne. I myself do not think it had any great influence on the course of events. It is a fact that the Emperor listened to the proposals without speaking a word, and I only mention it to gain an opportunity of making the remark, that *the inherent nature of the political problems determines the irresistible logic of history. This is a principle which asserts itself in the end, though men may not have dared, at the beginning of the movement, to face all the consequences generated by the nature of the problem.* Thus it always happened—in Hungary in 1848-49, and later again, in Italy. At the beginning of this chapter, I propounded the truth that the Italian question was an historical necessity. The question was—how to become a nation, an independent and united nation. The desire to accomplish this was nourished for centuries, and national union was the result of it. Mazzini and his followers always proclaimed it aloud. How beautiful is his appeal to the youths of Italy, the first line of which runs as follows:—

"You seek the Fatherland ..... and why can you not find it?"

But in the course of all the gigantic activity displayed in originating the war of 1859, *the question of Italian unity was not so much as mentioned by one word.* Not only was it left unmentioned, but plans were concocted which, if carried into effect, would have made the unity of Italy impossible for a long time to come, perhaps for centuries. One of these plans was the one promoted at Compiègne. It proposed, instead of one united Italy, four Italies. One of the four, a Central Italy, under the rule of Prince Jerome Napoleon, would have been equivalent to covering the partition of Italy with the shield of the dynastic interests of imperial France. However, in spite of all this, Italian unity became a reality. The Emperor Napoleon, so far from wishing for a united Italy, steadily opposed its realisation. Italy *was* nevertheless united. Not a single power in Europe wished for it, and still it became an accomplished fact.

This carries with it a lesson for other nations. Let them survey the conditions of their national existence; and if this existence is rooted in history, which alone does create nations, while nature only produces nationalities— and there is a great difference between the two—time will bring the realisation, unless the nation spontaneously abdicates. Abdication alone means death to a nation.

But if the memorial of Compiègne was not of great importance, the incident of January 1st, 1859, was.

When the Diplomatic Corps went to the Tuileries to offer the new year's congratulations, the Emperor Napoleon expressed his regret that *the friendship between Austria and France had become cooler.*

These few words of the taciturn, but at that time powerful man, created a commotion all over Europe, and lest anybody should be in doubt as to their significance, Victor Emmanuel shortly afterwards supplied the explanation of them in his speech from the throne, at the opening of Parliament, in which he expressed the anguish that reigned all over Italy, and declared his firm determination to trust to his rights, *and to await the decree of Destiny.*

This "Destiny" in his case found its personification in Paris, which had inspired him with those courageous words.* This "Destiny" also soon gave its "decree" in writing.

A marriage between Princess Clotilde, daughter of King Victor Emmanuel, and Prince Jerome Napoleon, had been arranged. The Prince went to Turin for his wedding on January 14th, but before the celebration of the nuptials he signed, by authority of the Emperor, the offensive and defensive treaty between France and Piedmont, which was afterwards ratified "with pleasure" by the Emperor.

The conditions of the alliance had already been settled in December. They differed but little from the preliminaries of Plombières—War against Austria. Expulsion of Austria from Italy. The Emperor, at the head of a French army of 200,000 men, to be the Commander-in-Chief of the allied troops. The war not to be commenced before the end of April, and not later than July. In the event of a successful issue of the war, Sardinia to be converted into Upper Italy. Not only were Lombardy and Venice to be given to her, but also Modena, Parma, Romagna, and the Papal Legations. (This was a gain on the preliminaries of Plombières.) The temporal power of the Pope was to be preserved, but to be confined to the city and province of Rome. Mid-Italy was to be organised as an independent state (which was a loss on the preliminaries of Plombières). No mention was made of Naples. Savoy was to be annexed to France.

* Cavour's telegram of January 1st, and his letter of January 8th, 1859, to Villamarina.

The question of the possession of Nice was to be settled after the war.

Bianchi gives these details in his "History of Diplomatic Negotiations," quoting the letter written by Cavour to Villamarina (December 24th, 1858). I only beg to point out that the condition as to the Papal Legations and Romagna does not appear to agree with the proclamation issued by the Emperor at the commencement of hostilities, nor does it agree with what I heard, at the head-quarters of the Emperor in Valeggio, about the answer he gave to the deputation sent by Bologna.* As regards Nice, Cavour positively declared to Pietri and myself, when declaiming against the Peace of Villafranca, that its concession to France had been demanded and agreed upon.

However this may be, although the war was decided upon, the Emperor did not think that he would be able to finish his armaments before the end of April, and till then events proved often so ambiguous that the English proverb, " There is many a slip between the cup and the lip," could fairly be applied to the situation.

Before hostilities could commence a diplomatic campaign, rich in disappointments, had to be fought out. In this campaign Cavour's wonderful sagacity and skill, and his unwearied activity, were of signal service. The

---

* From Bologna, where, after the Austrian troops had withdrawn, a revolutionary outbreak had taken place, a deputation was sent to the Emperor Napoleon, praying him to take up their cause also. According to my informant, the Emperor answered that if they had taken up arms against the Austrians he might have done so, but they had waited till the Austrians had left their town and then broke out in a revolution. Against whom?—the Pope! The French did not come to Italy to deprive the Pope of his possessions.

greatest difficulties were raised by England. Even the Whigs no longer looked with a favourable eye on any territorial alterations in the Italian Peninsula. Starting from the erroneous assumption that the Italian question could be solved by reforms, they did all they could to have these introduced, as has been clearly seen at the Paris Congress, but opposed everything which went further. But when, in 1858, the Tories returned to power, they, still looking upon the arrangement of 1815 as inviolable, spared no pains to prevent the outbreak of war, and to render Austria secure in her Italian possessions. It can be said of them without exaggeration that they displayed a feverish activity all over Europe to secure these ends—in Paris, St. Petersburg, Berlin, Vienna, Turin, Rome, Naples, and the minor courts of Italy—and in their bias for Austria they thwarted the plans of Napoleon more than once.

English diplomacy struck a different chord in every capital. In Paris it conjured up the red phantom of demagogy, which was to assume enormous dimensions in consequence of war. In Turin it ceaselessly asserted that if Piedmont, assisted by France, again took up arms against Austria, she would either be beaten, and for ever lose all chances of a future, or she would become dependent on France, ruin her finances, squander her national resources, and risk her liberal institutions, without winning a single adherent amongst the Italian states, not one of which wished to be annexed to Sardinia. In Vienna, on the other hand, England threatened that if Austria did not cease an armed interference in the Papal States, and if she did not make every exertion to have satisfactory reforms introduced there, as well as in the other Italian states, war would be unavoidable, with incalculable consequences. The answer of Count Buol-Schauenstein is noteworthy, as clearly indicating the bias of the Austrian Cabinet. "We will not abdicate our right of armed interference, and, if asked, will assist with arms the Italian sovereigns. We will not advise any government to introduce reforms. *France plays the part of protectress of nationalities—we are, and will remain, protectors of dynastic right."* *

But in Turin the opinion prevailed that, however strongly England might oppose a war, her Government would not dare to give Austria armed assistance in the face of English public opinion when once hostilities had commenced; but the Emperor Napoleon was not assured on this point, as will be seen below, in the account of the relations that subsisted between him and myself. The English Government at last extracted from him the verbal assurance (given to Lord Cowley, the English ambassador at Paris) that, though he had decided to assist Sardinia if she were attacked by Austria, she could not rely on help from France if she were herself the aggressive party. Lord Malmesbury, the Secretary of State for Foreign Affairs in London, informed the French Cabinet that Her Majesty's Government took formal notice of this assurance given by the Emperor. Napoleon now deemed it necessary to direct Cavour to adopt such tactics as would force Austria to be the aggressor. Cavour did so, and succeeded.

The position of Napoleon was made still more difficult

* Dispatch of Lord Loftus to Lord Malmesbury, Vienna, 15th January, 1859.

by the English Cabinet as regarded his relations with the Governments of Russia and Prussia.

Immediately after the meeting at Plombières, the Emperor Napoleon directed his attention to securing the benevolent neutrality of Russia and Prussia. He sent Prince Napoleon to Warsaw to confer with the Czar. Russia promised to observe a benevolent neutrality, and also to influence the Prussian Government to do the same, but made the promise dependent on certain conditions, one of which was, that *in case Italy should be liberated from Austrian rule, the Emperor should waive every thought of dynastic ambition.* In Berlin the wish was expressed that the Italian question might be settled peaceably by a mutual understanding. However, the envoy of the Emperor left Berlin with the impression that, in case of war, Prussia would not be likely to render armed assistance to Austria.

But the state of affairs became more doubtful as the efforts of England were so fast gaining ground that the Emperor of the French feared the whole matter might get developed into a formal mediation, supported by Prussia, and acquiesced in by Austria, and that it would be difficult under the circumstances not to accede to it.

To prevent this, the Emperor induced Russia to convert the Italian question into a European question, and to propose a congress for its settlement.*

* The diplomatic proofs which we possess of Russia having acted in this matter by request of France, are—1st. The memorandum of Baron Brunnow, Russian ambassador, to Lord Malmesbury (March $\frac{10\text{th}}{22\text{nd}}$, 1859), in which I read as follows:—" Déférant au désire de la France, le Cabinet Imperial a cru devoir prendre l'initiative de cette réunion diplomatique." 2nd. Lord Malmesbury's instructions to Lord Cowley, English Ambas-

Russia did so. The English Tory Government were at first furious at this move, which interfered with their efforts, and proclaimed aloud that they would be no party to a congress in which the stipulations of the Treaty of 1815 would be discussed, and which was convoked to make alterations in the governments of the Italian Peninsula. But they soon perceived that passive opposition was bad policy, and therefore fell in with the idea of a congress, but adapted its objects to their own point of view. In this they succeeded. By the end of March, England had already come to an understanding with Russia and Prussia on the subjects which should form the topics of discussion at the congress. If the congress had met on the basis arranged between these three powers, all the aspirations of Piedmont would have been frustrated.

The means of preventing the congress from meeting were unexpectedly supplied to Piedmont by its adversaries. One of the conditions agreed upon by the three great powers was, that the congress should fix upon the reforms necessary for restoring tranquillity in the Italian Peninsula. It seemed to be a matter of course that the Italian governments could not be excluded from the discussion of these reforms, and it was equally natural that if they participated in the congress, Sardinia alone could not be excluded.

Austria, in signifying her readiness to take part in the congress (but only on condition that nothing should be changed in the territorial arrangements of Italy, and

sador in Paris (May 5th, 1859), in which the following passage occurs:—
Russia informs us that she has proposed the congress at the request of France."

that the treaties between her and the Italian principalities should be considered inviolable), haughtily declared that she would never consent to see Sardinia represented at the congress. But she felt that Sardinia could not be excluded if all the other Italian princes were represented. She therefore turned to the latter, and informed them that she was opposed to having their internal affairs brought forward for discussion at the congress, as this would interfere with their rights as independent sovereigns. She found a willing audience. Ferdinand II., King of Naples, through his minister, Carafa, informed the Government of St. Petersburg (March 30th) that the Great Powers had no right to interfere with his internal affairs, and that he would always protest against such interference. Cardinal Antonelli said that no human power on earth could induce the Holy Father to tolerate such an interference. Tuscany, Parma, and Modena expressed similar views. The Duke of Modena (the same who had intended to settle Slavonians from Austria's military frontier along the French boundary) had already (on March 11th) informed Mr. Scarlett, the English diplomatic agent, that, as the scoundrels (*facinorosi*) under Cavour's protection had tried to stir up his subjects into insurrection, he would trust to Austrian arms. And should war come he would throw in his lot with Austria, as an Italian prince, as well as an Austrian archduke. If necessary, he would perish with Austria, but he would not sever himself from her.

While, on the one side, in consequence of these machinations, the meeting of a congress had become doubtful, on the other the efforts made by England threatened Sardinia with the possibility that the congress might still meet, but with the exclusion of herself and without the presence of the other Italian sovereigns, and on this point Cavour met with hostile inclinations even from the French Government. It is an important fact, and one that the historian of our times must always bear in mind, that the Emperor Napoleon's policy often differed from, and sometimes was opposed to, that pursued by his ministers. They were often not even initiated into their master's policy, nor employed in carrying it out. We Hungarians also were only in communication with the Emperor, with Prince Jerome Napoleon (who, on important occasions, was employed as mediator and executor), and with trusted instruments of the Emperor, who had no political rank. We had nothing to do with his ministers—I at least had never anything to do with them. They were not initiated into our relations—at least not in 1859. Later on, when Thouvenel was Minister for Foreign Affairs, this changed somewhat; but not because the "system" had been altered, but simply because my friend, Colonel Nicholas Kiss, was very intimately connected with Thouvenel, and their families were related to each other; and the Emperor, who knew of this intimacy, found no objection to it. This dualism also existed in Napoleon's relations with the Piedmontese Government. No French minister had any knowledge of what passed at the meeting of Plombières, or of the conditions of the offensive and defensive alliance concluded in December, 1858.

The ministry, with the exception of Prince Napoleon, who at that time was one of their number, did not even know that the alliance existed. But no solidarity existed between him and the other ministers; on the contrary, there was decided opposition, and Prince Napoleon did not sign the secret treaty in his capacity of minister. Generally, the matter stood thus: while adept Italian historians, writing even after Napoleon had lost his throne and was an exile, and when, therefore, their judgment could not have been influenced either by fear or by hope, stated that the fundamental trait of Napoleon's Italian policy was his sympathy for the Italians, produced neither by Cavour nor by anybody else, but of spontaneous growth, the Emperor's ministers did not at all show a friendly feeling towards Piedmont. In fact, at times they evinced sentiments quite of an opposite kind; notably Walewski, who never stood on a cordial footing with Cavour. There was a certain coolness and stiffness between the two, perhaps it would not even be an exaggeration to say hatred.

In this congress question, too, which at the eleventh hour threatened to frustrate the aspirations of the Piedmontese Government, Walewski acted in such a manner that Cavour was obliged to telegraph, on March 20th, 1859, to the Marquis of Villamarina at Paris as follows: "Walewski has written a letter to the French ambassador here, which must cause us either to become disheartened or to resort to desperate measures." When Villamarina spoke to Walewski about this letter, their conversation became exceedingly stormy. "What do you want?" Walewski said, "the Emperor surely will not, must not, carry on a war for no other purpose than that of satisfying the ambition of Sardinia! The matter must be settled peaceably at a congress, and Sardinia has not an atom of right to participate in such a congress."

Villamarina answered, in an abrupt but dignified manner, as follows: " Please to remember, Count, that we shall not submit to an affront like this, which is damaging alike to our interests and to our dignity. Neither policy nor honour would permit us to endure it." " But, left to yourselves, pray what will you do?" asked Walewski." "What shall we do? We will do what our forefathers have done, and what we too have done," replied Villamarina, "we will attack our enemies alone, and you may rest assured that we shall attack them in every way we can think of, and, without having the least regard for anybody, we shall set on fire the four corners of Europe. It is possible that we shall succumb, but we shall succumb in a stream of blood. *However numerically small a nation may be, if it succumb after a gallant struggle, it is certain to rise again, and to be stronger than ever before."* *

Ah! if the destiny of a nation is entrusted to such men, and she can be sure of not being deserted by any one, from the highest aristocrat to the meanest man in the realm, that nation, however small, has a future. Piedmont had a future. Piedmont evolved itself into Italy.

The situation assumed a serious aspect. The Emperor Napoleon summoned Cavour hurriedly to Paris. Cavour reached the French capital on March 25th. On this occasion the first of my memorials was handed to him, a copy of which is given later. He returned home, persuaded that war was imminent; but also with the conviction that Piedmont and Italy would have to undergo great hardships, and

* Letter of March 21st—22nd, 1859, from Villamarina to Cavour.

prepare for gigantic sacrifices.* At the same time he expressed an opinion that war would commence in about two months.

It came sooner. Cavour owed this to Austria, and Austria owed it to two circumstances.

The one was that the Court of Vienna was in a warlike mood. For a long time past it had stood ready for hostilities. It acknowledged that, whatever diplomatists might do, this dissension could only be settled by an appeal to arms. It came to the conclusion that it would be wise to throw down the gauntlet to Piedmont at once, without allowing her army to effect a junction with the French troops. The Court was very confident of victory. It fancied Austria was very strong, the more so as it took for granted (and not without reason) that she commanded a majority in the Diet of the German Confederation, that this majority was resolved to look upon her interests in Italy as the interests of the German Confederation, and that for the defence of Austria the German Confederation would declare war against France, even if Prussia resisted it.†

At the end of March a war on the Rhine was still considered probable, even in Paris. At least Cavour wrote to General Lamarmora (March 29th), that on the Rhine the war would certainly be fought out.

The Court of Vienna endeavoured also to induce Prussia to join it by attacking France on the Rhine. To obtain this assistance the Archduke Albrecht, at

* Letter of Cavour to General Lamarmora of March 29th.
† See Note 4 at the end of this chapter.

that time Governor of Hungary, was sent on a mission to Berlin, where he arrived on April 14th.

"We shall forthwith invade Piedmont," the Archduke said, "to punish it for its bragging. We do not attach much importance to this first move, for we feel certain that we shall annihilate the Sardinian forces before France has time to come to their rescue. The matter is more serious on the Rhine, but even there we shall be victorious if we work together from the commencement of hostilities. Austria will supply a contingent of 200,000 men towards the army of the German Confederation, she will give the chief command to the Prussian Regent (the present Emperor William), and is ready to alternate with Prussia in the presidency of the Diet."

It was a tempting proposal; but the Archduke Albrecht had forgotten that it could not be in the interests of the House of Hohenzollern to have the House of Hapsburg by their side, or to help it to a supremacy in the German Confederation. In 1859 the Prussians were not yet prepared for 1866, but they were thinking about it. Therefore they answered that they would remain neutral, and would only take up arms when they saw that the interests of Germany were threatened.* Austria did not feel much dismayed on this account, feeling that the 200,000 men would be useful in Italy.

Nothing was now wanting for the commencement of hostilities but a pretext, and this was afforded by a second circumstance. Ever since the idea of a congress

* See letters of De Launay, the Sardinian representative at Berlin, to Cavour, dated April 14th and 22nd, 1859.

had been originated, Austria stipulated as a preliminary condition that Piedmont should disarm and should disband her volunteers. Of course Piedmont did not feel the least inclination to do so. In consequence, Austria sent an ultimatum to Turin by Baron Ernest Kellersberg (April 23rd), in which disarmament and the disbanding of the volunteers were demanded in a haughty peremptory way. In case of refusal, hostilities were to be considered as having begun. Three days were allowed for a reply. On April 26th Cavour replied as follows:—"May the responsibility rest on those who were the first to arm, and who put threatening intimations in the place of fair proposals for a peaceful settlement." Cavour telegraphed to Paris, he put the Lomellina (the country along the river Ticino) under water, made preparations to defend Turin, and impatiently awaited the Austrian attack. They did not attack on the 28th. Cavour suspected machinations on the part of England, and he had reason to do so. But, at last, on April 29th, the Austrian Field-Marshal Gyulay crossed the Ticino at the head of an army of 100,000 men. Cavour had gained his end : Austria was the aggressor.

French soldiers commenced to land at Genoa. They found it difficult to effect a landing. English men-of-war stood in the way in the harbour; but still they landed. The Emperor Napoleon landed at Genoa on May 12th.

"*Alea jacta erat.*" * The die was cast.

* See Note 5 at the end of this chapter.

EXPLANATORY REMARKS TO CHAPTER I.

NOTE 1, page 9.

" Before I was better informed, I myself inclined to take this note literally."

UPON more than one occasion I remarked to Mazzini that as the Italian question, in the same way as the Hungarian question in consequence of the events of 1849, had simply resolved itself into the question of national existence, I, in his place, would subordinate republicanism to the interests of such existence; and in order to free Italy from foreign rule, and to unite it into one independent state, I would do everything to come to an understanding with the Court of Turin; for it appeared to me that the King of Sardinia was destined to play the same part in the question of Italian independence as had fallen to the lot of the Transylvanian princes in the question of Hungarian liberty. Mazzini replied that he too would be prepared to subordinate his republican aspirations to the question of national existence, were he not convinced that the liberation of Italy from foreign rule could only be expected from a movement which possessed a republican character. He said that he had taken into consideration every possible contingency, and he could say for certain that the House of Savoy did not even dream of liberating Italy from alien rule. Its utmost aspirations did not go farther than to extend the frontiers of Piedmont, by annexing some Italian provinces; but what it thought of more than anything else was to secure its own throne. To prove this assertion he appealed to the diplomatic note referred to in the text—it was from him I received cognisance of this note—and he further appealed to the fact that it was this note that had lowered the enthusiasm of the Central and South Italian volunteers to the freezing-point, and had thereby made the victory of Austria a possibility.

Mazzini was still of opinion, in 1859, that Italy could not expect from monarchical governments anything satisfactory, and, in consequence, unlike Garibaldi, he remained passive during the war of 1859.

I, on the contrary, always was of opinion that in politics, identity of interests is decisive, and that there are cases, in which identity of interests was to be met with between elements otherwise the most contradictory, as was the case with the interests of the American republicans and the absolutism of France, during the North American war of independence. I, therefore, always said that I should be ready to accept assistance, from whatever quarter it might come, if it would help to regain the independence of my country. I would accept it, as I used to say, *even from the devil*, but I would take care that he should not carry me away. On account of this difference of opinion, all communication between Mazzini and myself was finally broken off, when we Hungarians in 1859 entered into communication with the Emperor Napoleon and the Government of Turin.

However, I fulfil a moral duty, which I owe to the memory of Mazzini, when I quote what Nicomede Bianchi, who, as Director of the Royal Italian Archives, had authentic documents at his disposal, says in his valuable work ("Storia Documentata della Diplomazia Europea in Italia dal 1814 al 1861," vol. 8, page 285).

"Joseph Mazzini has, during the last thirty years, fought with unwavering faith for the idea of the unification of Italy, as the immediate goal of every Italian revolution. It was on his advice that, shortly after the Peace of Villafranca had been concluded, some eminent members of the Republican party put themselves into communication with some of the most prominent members of the Monarchical party, with the intention of concentrating all forces to initiate the unitary revolution in Sicily. These negotiations were then left in suspense, but were not broken off. In March, 1860, they were again resumed. Mazzini, approving of the arrangement, agreed upon then, wrote as follows (March 2nd):—'It is a question not of republic or monarchy, but of national union, to be, or not to be. If Italy wishes to become a monarchy under the sceptre of the House of Savoy, let her; and if, after being freed from foreign rule, she wishes to hail the King, or Cavour, as liberator, or I know not what, let her do so. What all of us want now is, that Italy should be created (*che l'Italia si faccia*).'"

NOTE 2, page 13.

"*The Government of King Victor Emmanuel watched faithfully over the inviolability of the constitution, though in so doing it met with the displeasure of foreign potentates.*"

ORSINI's terrible attempt (on January 14th, 1858) which destroyed so many human lives, was universally abhorred, and it alarmed Napoleon. The enemies of the Cabinet of Turin made use of the opportunity to irritate Napoleon against it. "You see, sire, these are the consequences of the revolutionary agitation carried on under the protection of Cavour," said the Papal Nuncio, when congratulating the Emperor on his escape. And the Austrian Ambassador went so far as to put the question to Napoleon, whether he did not think the time had arrived to come to an understanding with Austria, in order to force Piedmont not to suffer any more, in her territory, the agitation of the Italian refugees and the excesses of the daily press. (Report of Villamarina to Cavour, of January 17th, 1858.) These insinuations did not miss their mark, especially as, about the same time, some incidents happened in Piedmont which did good service to Sacconi the Papal Nuncio, and to Baron Hübner the Austrian Ambassador. One of the Turin daily papers published an article in honour of Orsini, and excusing regicide. Aurelius Bianchi-Giovini, the writer of the article, was prosecuted, but acquitted by the jury. Mazzini stayed several days at Genoa, unmolested; and the *Italia e Popolo*, a Republican journal, published in that town, and Mazzini's party-organ, printed an article, written by this gentleman, in which—hinting at an *eventual* case (which actually happened to occur on January 14th)—instructions were given to the Republicans as to their behaviour.

In consequence of this incident, Count Walewski, the French Minister of Foreign Affairs, forwarded a note to Count Cavour through the Duc de la Tour d'Auvergne, the French Ambassador at Turin (January 22nd, 1858). In this note, without entering on detailed propositions, Count Walewski, in the name of the community of interests of all the governments, called upon the Cabinet of Turin to take energetic measures against the "*Italian demagogues*," for, he said, the governments had not to deal with political views, however audacious and inimical to the political system of Europe, but with the members of a wild sect, with whom regicide and murder is an article of creed, and thereby places itself entirely beyond the pale of the laws of civilised society.

When the French Ambassador read to Count Cavour this note, written in an irritated style, Cavour answered calmly as follows : " The Government of his Majesty will do all in its power to prevent a recurrence of such villainous attempts. We will take care to see the press laws rigorously applied. We will watch the political refugees with even greater vigilance than heretofore, and will not allow one of them to abuse Piedmontese hospitality. But while we are sincerely desirous to satisfy the legitimate demands of the French Government within the limits fixed by the fundamental laws of our country, we, at the same time, deem it our duty to call the attention of the Paris Cabinet to the fact, that there is a continual increase in the number of refugees who come to Piedmont from the other Italian provinces. If it is desired to effect a complete cure, it will be necessary to remove the causes that produce the disease."

Walewski was so much enraged at this reply, that he lost his temper, and said to Villamarina, the Ambassador of Turin, " You must know that we are determined to resort to extreme measures if necessary, and shall go ourselves to countries which do not expel murderers and conspirators, and hunt them out even from the entrails of the earth."

This was a threat indeed from mighty France to little Piedmont ! The threat was followed by four demands. 1. That the publication of the paper *Italia e Popolo* should be prohibited. 2. That the political refugees should not be allowed to write for the papers. 3. That the press offences against foreign potentates and heads of governments should be summarily punished, and not on conviction by a jury. 4. That Bianchi-Giovini and the turbulent refugees should be expelled from the country.

Cavour, taking his stand on the law, said, " No ! To us and to the king the law is sacred. He who commits an offence against the law will be punished by its strong arm. But no threat or interest will induce us to commit a *coup d'état*."

The Emperor Napoleon personally interfered in the matter. To the representatives of Sardinia he spoke of the independence of Italy as the most cherished wish of his heart. He reminded them that the realisation of their hopes depended on an alliance with France ; that from nobody else, least of all from England, could they expect material assistance. He did not use a threat. He spoke with respect of the dignified behaviour of the Sardinian Government. But he begged them to do also something for him, so as not to make the alliance impossible.

But Cavour did not in the least depart from the law. The end of the affair was, that a Bill which had been submitted to the House of Representatives by De Foresta two years before (April, 1856), dealing with conspiracies against foreign powers, with political murders, and with the constitution of the juries for trying press offences, was considered by the Chamber, and also accepted.

The French Government was not in the least inclined to be satisfied with this, but Napoleon was—to his honour be it said. He summoned the Marquis Villamarina, the Sardinian Ambassador, into his presence, and said to him, " I accept with thanks the procedure of the Piedmontese Parliament. I assure you that I shall never forget their loyal behaviour towards my person;" and, as if turning to another subject (while all the time he kept the same end in view), in the manner which was peculiar to him, to convey the idea of great resolutions by a few apparently indifferent words, he asked Villamarina, *"Are the new works of fortification at Casale and Alessandria progressing at all?"* " Sire ! " answered Villamarina, " *we are always preparing for the great day.*"*

With this the impending crisis ended. But I think I must remark that when the altercation, related above, reached its utmost bitterness, in consequence of Walewski's threats and demands, Cavour sent these instructions to Villamarina in Paris, February 9th, 1858 : " Courage ! Continue to represent with elevated head your king and his loyal government. We will never make a compact with disorder, but neither will we submit to the threats of any powerful neighbour. Continue to fight the diplomatic battle with dignity and moderation, but without ever receding a step. Should you have lost all hope of due justice being done to us, you will please return, put on your uniform of a colonel, and, following our King, defend the dignity and honour of our country."

" Charles Albert died in exile, in Oporto, rather than bow to Austria's will. Our young King would go to live and die in America, or would prefer, aye ! prefer a hundred times, to die fighting at the foot of the Alps, rather than dim the spotless honour of his noble race." And so on in the same strain.

In these our times, in which right, and the cherished traditions of nations, have been so little respected, it is refreshing to meet in the golden book of history with such noble figures, among kings and ministers, to whom human rights, liberty, and the sanctity of the law are

* Letter of Villamarina to Cavour of May 29th, 1858.

so sacred. And verily this is also the best policy. There may come, must come, a time when history will know the word "king" only as a tradition of times gone by; but while monarchies exist, the sometimes tardy but always inexorable tribune of the logic of history will always give the verdict that respect for the rights of the subject, and protection of the freedom of the people, is the wisest policy for sovereigns to adopt. For such a policy will surround their thrones with the true love of their subjects, and, verily, I say it is only the true love of a people that will form the rock upon which they can build their thrones, and against which not even the gates of hell can prevail. If built on anything else, its foundation rests on quicksands, which will, sooner or later, be swept away by the vicissitudes of time. How difficult it is to bring this truth home to those in power!

(I have taken the details of this incident from the History of Nicomede Bianchi, already referred to above.)

NOTE 3, page 32.
"*Austria confiscated the property of Lombard-Venetian refugees, who had become Sardinian subjects without any legal proceedings.*"

THIS confiscation was a very despicable part of the Austrian system of government. By an Imperial decree (of December 20th, 1850) it was intimated that all those Lombard-Venetian emigrants who should not return to their country within three years, would be deprived of the rights and released from the obligations of Austrian subjects. In consequence of this decree, many who had been deprived of their Austrian citizenship became naturalised Sardinian subjects, and enjoyed then such rights, with regard to their property in Lombardy and Venice, as other foreigners did. In spite of this, Austria confiscated all the property belonging to emigrants, including the above, without any legal proceedings, in consequence of one of the attempts at insurrection organised by Mazzini. When the Sardinian Government protested, in order to protect the rights of its own subjects, and based its protest on the incontestable maxim of law that property cannot be confiscated unless the owner has been legally convicted of a crime which draws confiscation of property with it, Austria replied, that whether the confiscation was legal or illegal, it made no difference to her; it was sufficient that the Emperor, in the plenitude of his power, deemed confiscation necessary. She did not inquire whether somebody were guilty or not, and did not make any distinction between one emigrant and another. They were all guilty. The more desperate characters among them committed daring acts, the more cautious and moderate watched for their opportunity to gain by those acts. This confiscation of property gave some sort of pledge for the good behaviour of the refugees, and at the same time served as compensation for the damage and cost occasioned by disturbances. If the emigrants were denationalised, Austria did not empower them to become naturalised in other countries. Least of all did she empower their naturalisation in revolutionary Sardinia !

These were the maxims of justice, of Austria's: "*plenitudo potestatis imperialis*," and the Western powers were so anxious that Austria should not be embarrassed in any way, that they did not even dare, courageously and openly, to side with Piedmont in such a matter as this. All they ventured upon was to put polite questions here and there, of course without result. The evil was dragged on from year to year, and Austria pocketed millions upon millions from these sequestrations.

NOTE 4, page 66.

"*Austria considered it certain that the Diet of the German Confederation had decided to look upon the interests of Austria, in Italy, as identical with its own.*"

LORD AUGUSTUS LOFTUS, the English Ambassador at Vienna, sent the following report to Lord Malmesbury (January 27th, 1859) :—

" I am privately informed that Count Buol has received from nearly all the German minor governments the most satisfactory assurances of their entire disapproval of the hostile attitude assumed by France against Austria, and of their alliance and adhesion in the event of a war.

" Count Buol lately expressed to me his great satisfaction at the tone and spirit of the whole German press, and stated, that if the object of the Emperor of the French has been to feel the pulse of the German nation, he had received a most salutary warning, and that any hopes he may have indulged in of disuniting Germany, had been a most signal failure."

Lord Loftus was rightly informed upon the state of public opinion in Germany.

That the minor sovereigns should have allied themselves with Austria is not to be wondered at, but that the German nation, and especially the Liberal party, should have become, all at once, so friendly to the Court of Vienna, that they should even have been prepared to mix up Germany in a war for its defence, this, I say, is a phenomenon which can only be explained by the fact that "national hatred" (of the French) is a passion so strong as to suppress every other consideration, for the German nation in general, and the Liberal party in particular, had many reasons for complaint against the House of Hapsburg. It was chiefly owing to Austria that the agitation for national union and freedom, in 1848, ended in a failure. The Court of Vienna was hated on this account all over Germany up to 1859. But as soon as it became probable that the Italian question might lead to war between France and Austria, hatred of the French suppressed bitter recollections, and the German nation, without distinction of party, considered the interests of Austria, even in Italy, as the interests of the German Confederation. Nearly the whole German press reiterated emphatically, with daily-increasing vigour, the declaration that whoever attacked Austria, even in those of her provinces which did not form part of the German Confederation, attacked Germany. Starting from this marvellous conception in order to fan the martial spirit of the German people, the press had recourse to the insinuation—not at all substantiated —that the Emperor of the French wished to assume the rôle of his great uncle, and to conquer the whole world.

The irritation had increased to such an extent in February, that Jerningham, the English representative at Stuttgard, referring to a remark of Baron Neurath, the President of the Council of State of Wurtemberg, reported to the Foreign Secretary at home that Germany had not been so much agitated during the last fifty years as upon that occasion. The other diplomatic agents of England sent similar reports to their Government.

To give the reader a conception of the state of affairs I consider it sufficient to refer him, amongst all the reports, to the one furnished by Consul-General (at Leipsic) Ward to Lord Malmesbury, March 3rd. I read in it as follows:—

"Recent events have revived the spirit which animated the German people during their arduous struggle against the domination of Napoleon I., during the years 1812 to 1815.

"The Bavarian Chamber of Deputies now sitting at Munich resolved on the 23rd of February, unanimously, and by acclamation, to prohibit

EXPLANATORY REMARKS. 77

the exportation of horses, on which occasion very strong speeches were delivered against the supposed designs of France, and war was pronounced to be inevitable.

"A similar feeling has shown itself in the Diet of Hanover, where a resolution was passed on the 24th February requiring the Government to take measures for resisting any attack upon Austria by the combined forces of the Confederation.

"At Stuttgard thirty-nine deputies have lately published a requisition to the Standing Committee, which sits during the vacation of the Diet, urging, in rather violent language, the necessity of the Wurtemberg Government taking immediate steps for the protection of the Germanic territory against the danger manifest in the French armaments.

"At Wiesbaden the military budget for 1859 has, contrary to custom, been voted, without discussion, and in the midst of acclamation, by the Diet of Nassau.

"In the Diet of Weimar strong sentiments have also been expressed against the French pretensions, and for the adoption of defensive measures by the German states.

"Even here in Leipsic, where commercial views usually supersede all others, at a public dinner lately given to the general commander of the garrison, some rather enthusiastic speeches were made for maintaining the rights of Austria in Italy, and the memory of the late Field Marshal Radeczky and of his successful campaigns in Lombardy, was toasted with great applause.

"The whole newspaper press of Germany, with scarcely an exception, has ranged itself on the side of Austria. The feeling that France is disposed to violate the faith of treaties, and that Austria has the legal right with her, prevails over all other considerations, and even the Liberal party seem in the present conjuncture to have quite forgotten their old grudges against Austria, and to view her no longer in the light of a power which has displeased them by its settled antipathy to political reforms in Germany.

"In these circumstances it is extremely probable that if the efforts for mediation should unfortunately fail, and the preparations for war proceed, the Germanic Diet will eventually pass a resolution adopting the cause of Austria as its own against France. This may be done without waiting for an aggression upon the Federal territory, according to Article XLVII. of the Vienna final Act of June 8th, 1820, which provides that if a Federal state is threatened or attacked in its *non-German* possessions, the Confederation is obliged to take part with and assist or defend such state, provided that a majority of the Diet recognises danger to the Federal territory. Now in the actual state of public opinion in Germany the Diet of Frankfort will find little difficulty in resolving that danger exists for the Confederation in consequence of the Austrian dominions in Italy being menaced by France."

It is noteworthy that this hostile attitude of the Germans, at first at least, did not so much astonish as irritate the Emperor Napoleon.

The *Moniteur*, in its edition of March 15th, in an official article written in a haughty tone, answered to the excitement that prevailed in Germany. This article absolutely denied that there existed even a shadow of hostile feeling against Germany; but this denial was couched in such terms as to imply that Napoleon intended to intimate to the Germans that he did not fear them, and was not to be prevented from carrying out his plans as to Italy by the noise made in Germany.

It will not be without interest to give some of the salient paragraphs of this article *in extenso* :—

" A portion of Germany responds to the most calm attitude of the French Government by the most inconsiderate alarm. On a simple presumption which nothing justifies and everything rejects, prejudices are awakened, mistrust is propagated, passions are unchained, a sort of crusade against France is commenced in the chambers and in the press of some of the states of the Confederation. They accuse her of entertaining ambitious views which she has disavowed, of preparing for conquests of which she does not stand in need, and attempts are made by these calumnies to frighten Europe by imaginary aggressions of which not even an idea ever existed.

" The men who mislead German patriotism in this manner are out of date. Of them it may truly be said that they have forgotten nothing, and learned nothing. They went to sleep in 1813, and they awake after a slumber of half a century with sentiments and passions buried in history, and which are a contradiction to the present time. They are visionaries, who wish absolutely to defend what no one dreams of attacking."

" If the French Government were not convinced that its acts, its principles, and the sentiment of the majority of the German people gave a denial to the suspicions of which it is wished to make it the object, it might reasonably feel hurt; it might see therein not only an act of injustice, but an attempt against the independence of its policy. In fact, the whole movement which is being attempted to be got up on the Rhine on a question which does not threaten Germany, but in which France is interested as a European power, would tend to nothing less than to contest her right of making her influence felt in Europe, and of defending her own interests—even with the most extreme moderation. This is a pretension which would be insulting if it could be looked upon as serious. The life of a great nation like France is not confined to its own frontiers; it manifests itself throughout the whole world by the salutary action which it exercises to the advantage of its national power as well as to the advantage of civilisation. When a nation gives up this duty it abdicates its rank. . . . The French people are susceptible regarding their honour. *Menaces excite them. Conciliation calms them. . . .*"

This certainly was pitched in a high key. I think the reason of this is to be found in the circumstance that the French Government had at that time no cause to apprehend that Prussia shared the martial instincts of the other German states, and they knew that the clamour, without the aid of Prussia, would remain so many empty words. This article in the *Moniteur* actually draws a clear distinction between Prussia and the other German states. It speaks with approbation of the reserved attitude maintained by Prussia, and says—" The reserved attitude of the Berlin Cabinet is certainly more advantageous to Germany than the recklessness of those who, by appealing to the resentments and prejudices of 1813, run the risk of irritating the national sentiments of France."

However, it appears that the contrast thus drawn between Prussia and German public opinion made a bad impression in Germany; and, altogether, the article in the *Moniteur* only enhanced and intensified the agitation in Germany. At least, Sir A. Malet, England's diplomatic agent at the German Confederation, reported to Lord Malmesbury, from Frankfort, March 25th—" The praise bestowed on Prussia placed that country in a false position, and had precisely a contrary effect to that which was probably intended. Though no public declaration of adhesion to the policy of supporting Austria against an attack on her Italian provinces has been given by the Berlin Cabinet, the press has been less reserved. With the exception of the *Cologne Gazette* and the *Elberfeld Journal*, the organs of public opinion assert vehemently that the cause of Austria, even in Italy, is the cause of the German Confederation."

The irritation felt in Germany continually increased, and it appears that some perplexity was caused at the Tuileries by the unfavourable impression the article in the *Moniteur* had created, for the same journal, in its number of April 10th, published a second article pitched in quite a different key.

The key-note of the article is struck where it said that the Emperor of the French is a true friend of the German nation, and is not even hostile to German unity. "The policy of France," it wrote, "cannot have two weights and two measures. What she seeks to make respected in Italy, she will know herself how to respect in Germany. It is not we who would be menaced by the example of a national Germany which would reconcile its Federal organisation with the tendency to unite in one body, of which the principle has been already laid down in the great commercial union of the *Zollverein.*"*

But this second article (written in a flattering strain) as little produced the desired effect as the first, which carried menaces with it. In fact, so little effect did it produce, that Lord Augustus Loftus, English ambassador at the Court of Vienna, wrote on April 21st to the Secretary of State for Foreign Affairs, "Nothing has tended more to produce in Germany a feeling of distrust and suspicion of the plans of France, than that effusive declaration which the *Moniteur*, in its number of April 10th, thought fit to make to the German nation."

Shortly after the appearance of the first of these articles in the *Moniteur*, the idea of a congress, proposed by Russia at the request of France, came to the front. After having undergone many changes, the meeting of a congress might have been considered certain, just at the time when Austria had sent her ultimatum to Turin. The greatest obstacle from the beginning had been the unwillingness of Sardinia to disarm. But on March 19th Count Walewski telegraphed to Pelissier, Duc de Malakoff, French ambassador in London : " Piedmont has accepted the idea of a previous and simultaneous disarmament. This, I must confess, rather surprises me." The meeting of a congress then solely depended upon the question whether Austria would also

---

* This is a very important declaration. Historians will have to pronounce on it. I cannot speak of this declaration without recollecting some words addressed to me by Napoleon III. a few weeks afterwards : " Two Germanies I would not mind ; but one Germany—*ça ne me va pas.*" To which I replied to the Emperor in his own words, " You must never desire the impossible."

It is perfectly true that by the " Zollverein " the foundation for the unification of Germany was laid. Customs union, sooner or later, leads to political union. All doings of the Court of Vienna through three centuries, taken together, have not done so much towards destroying the independence of Hungary as the " Zollverein " entered into, in 1867, by Austria and Hungary. It is really astonishing that Deák and his party did not consider this, though they may not have troubled themselves with the great material losses sure to be caused by the unification of two states, the economical exigencies of which are entirely different.

agree to disarm. Austria, however, would not withdraw the ultimatum she had sent to Turin, though reminded by the Great Powers that if she commenced the war she would be entirely isolated. She would not retrace her steps. The reason of this obstinacy is to be found in the official report of Lord Augustus Loftus, dated 28th April, in which he says :—

" So strong is the conviction here (in Vienna) in the mind of all parties that the Emperor of the French is intent on war, and is only seeking to gain time for his military preparations, that the chief and principal aim of the Austrian Government in the course they have taken is to forestall the French, and to carry out their object of reducing Sardinia before sufficient aid from France can arrive."

Whatever may have been the intention of the Emperor Napoleon, it is a fact that Austria commenced hostilities.

Austria not being attacked, but acting as aggressor, there no longer existed a *casus fœderis* between herself and the German Confederation. In addition to this, the behaviour of Austria had greatly annoyed the Great Powers, and even called forth their distinct disapprobation.

One would think that these considerations would have calmed down the vehement desire to help the Austrians that had taken possession of the German nation and the minor governments. But this was not the case. Consul-General Ward reported to the English Government from Leipsic (March 28th) that it was an undoubted fact that the declaration of war by Austria to Sardinia was approved of, and that Austria's cause had not lost at all popularity amongst the German people. A like approval was reported by Sir A. Malet from Frankfort. Mr. Gordon, the English diplomatic agent in Hanover, reported, on March 29th, that public opinion in Hanover, Brunswick, and Oldenburg, was decidedly in favour of Germany assisting Austria against France, as it was considered certain that the Emperor Napoleon would, sooner or later, attack the Germans, and it would therefore be wiser not to allow Austria, by being defeated now, to be rendered incapable of helping Germany.

The martial feeling in Germany ran so high, and Austria was so firmly persuaded that the majority in the German Diet would vote for the participation of Germany in the war, that the Prussian Government deemed it necessary to inform its diplomatic agents at the German courts, that, as Austria carried on the war as aggressor, and there was no *casus fœderis*, the Prussian Government would not allow itself to be dragged into war by Austria, would resist to the utmost any such attempts, and would not be induced to alter her decision in this respect by any vote it might please the majority of the German Diet to give; that she would be sorry if, in consequence, a rupture were to take place in the German Confederation, but that the responsibility of such a rupture would entirely rest with those who tried to entangle her in a war contrary to her own wish.

Notwithstanding this decided declaration on the part of the Prussian Government, the representatives of the smaller German states agreed, on May 2nd, to move a resolution in the Diet, and to decide by a majority, that Germany should take part in the war on the side of Austria.

The English Tory Government (on whose assistance the Germans thought they could confidently rely) succeeded in preventing this vote being taken, by the equivocal declaration, that if the Germans interfered in the war "at this early stage," they could not reckon on help from England, for, " under existing circumstances," the English Government intended "for the present" to remain neutral, and could therefore neither give assistance to Germany, nor protect with the Navy her coasts from being attacked. (Telegram of May 1st, from Lord Malmesbury to Sir A. Malet, and the Circular of the English Government to its diplomatic agents at the German courts, of May 2nd.)

The historian must know how to read between the lines of diplomatic documents if he does not wish to lose himself in the labyrinth of these events.

The circumspect declarations of the English Tory Government certainly afforded the Emperor Napoleon some reason to be doubtful of the reliance to be placed in England's neutrality, when in the first days of May he availed himself of my services to make sure of English non-interference.

The Court of Vienna reckoned on German help even at the moment it declared war. This is proved by the proclamation addressed by the Emperor Francis Joseph to "*his people*" ("an mein Volk") informing them of the war (April 28th).

In this proclamation it is said that "the glorious history of the Empire proves, that when the dark shadows of revolution had appeared in that part of the world, Providence had often availed (!!) herself of Austria's sword, to suppress by the light of the latter the darkness of the former." (What do the rulers of the world not foist upon "Providence!" What a peculiar phraseology they have at their disposal! There are millions in Europe who know that those shadows, which the light of that sword endeavoured to drive away, were the first dawn of liberty, and that that sword of light was in reality a cloud, which overcasts that dawn. And we Hungarians ever remember the time when that "sword of light" did not suppress, but on the contrary conjured up the phantoms of revolution on the clear sky of Hungary. But this is the way history is forged. And then poor mortals are expected to gather truth from it!)

After having praised the devotion always shown by "his people" to the Imperial family, in which they could serve as an example to the other nations of the earth, and after expressing a conviction that his subjects will stand by the Austrian eagle, which will soar high in honour, aided by that fidelity, devotion, and self-sacrifice of which they have so often before given proof, the imperial proclamation concludes with these words:—

"We hope that we shall not stand alone in the struggle. The fields on which the battles will be fought have been saturated with the blood of our German brethren, when taking those bulwarks of defence (?) which they have retained up to this date. There it is that the vile enemies of Germany always commenced their play when they aspired to break her internal force. That there is such a danger threatening now, is felt all over Germany, from one end to the other, from the hut of the humblest up to the thrones. I speak as a member of the reigning family of the German Confederation, when I call attention to the common danger, and remind you of those glorious days when Europe owed its liberation to the enthusiasm shown by the whole German nation, the respect for which will rise high with the aid of the sons of the people—

'Für Gott und Vaterland!'"

("Für Gott und Vaterland." That meant at that time, as regarded Hungary, that the Hungarians should go and shed their blood, and die for the rule of the Vienna Court over Italy. It was rather too much to expect the Hungarians to look upon that as "the interests of their country." To tell the truth they were rather slow in considering it so. Or perhaps it was "Für Gott?" The third commandment says, "Thou shalt not take the name of the Lord thy God in vain.")

NOTE 5, page 68.

"*The Emperor Napoleon landed at Genoa on May* 12*th.* '*Alea jacta erat.*'"

THE proclamation issued by King Victor Emmanuel ran as follows:

"PEOPLE OF THE KINGDOM!

"Austria attacks us with a powerful army, which, while professing a love of peace, to assault us she has assembled in the unhappy provinces* subject to her domination.

---

* King Victor Emmanuel calls these provinces "unhappy," and it seems that the inhabitants of these provinces thought themselves unhappy too, or else they would not have broken out in revolution, and would not have been in a chronic state of insurrection against Austrian rule, which insurrections would not have given so much to do to the executioner, would not have filled its prisons with Lombardian and Venetian patriots, and these would not have taken refuge by thousands in foreign lands to escape the executioner and the prison, and the confiscation of property without legal inquiry would not have grown into a rich source of the finances of the Austrian Cabinet.

Foolish, unhappy Italians! They did not know how happy, enviably happy they were. You have an official, and therefore, of course, authentic proof of this in the circular of April 29th, announcing that war had broken out, addressed by Count Buol, the Austrian Minister for Foreign Affairs, to the Austrian diplomatic agents abroad, and communicated by them to the courts to which they were accredited.

It is premised therein that Lombardy has been for centuries a fief of the Empire of Germany. Venice was given to Austria in exchange for giving up her Belgian provinces. (" Given in exchange!" By whom? Certainly not by the Venetians, to whom Venice belonged. This and the fact that the proprietors of Venice have not got anything in exchange for themselves are of course matters not worthy to be spoken of.) Thus, therefore, the domination of Austria on the Po and on the Adriatic is *a solid and unquestionable right in every respect.* (What a splendid reasoning!)

After this the circular goes on as follows:—

" But it is not only a legitimate government, it is a just and benevolent one, which administers the Lombardo-Venetian provinces. Those beautiful countries have prospered more rapidly than could have been hoped after the sad fate of so many years of revolution. Milan and other celebrated towns display wealth worthy of their history. Venice is recovering from her profound decline to new and growing prosperity. The administration of justice is regular, manufactures and commerce prosper, science and art are cultivated with ardour. The public burdens are not heavier than in other parts of the monarchy; they would even be lighter if the fatal effects of Sardinian policy did not require that the state should augment its forces, and consequently raise new revenues. The great majority of the people of Lombardy and Venetia are content; the number of the discontented, who have for-

EXPLANATORY REMARKS.

"Unable to support the example of our civil order, and unwilling to submit to the judgment of a European congress on the evils and dangers of which she alone is the cause in Italy, Austria violates her promise to England, and makes a case of war out of a law of honour.

"Austria dares to demand the diminution of our troops; that that brave youth, which from all parts of Italy has thronged to the standard of national independence, be disarmed, and handed over to her.

"A jealous guardian of the ancestral common patrimony of honour and glory, I have handed over to my beloved cousin Prince Eugène the government of the state, while I myself again draw the sword.

"The brave soldiers of the Emperor Napoleon, my generous ally, will fight the battles of liberty and justice with my soldiers.

" People of Italy!

"Austria attacks Piedmont because I have advocated the cause of our common country in the councils of Europe, and because I have not been insensible to your cry of anguish. Thus she has violently broken those treaties which she never respected; thus now all right is on the side of our nation, and I can conscientiously perform the vow made on the tomb of my illustrious father. Taking up arms in defence of my throne, of the liberty of my people, and of the honour of the Italian name, I fight for the rights of the whole nation.

*　　*　　*　　*　　*　　*

"My only ambition is to be the first soldier of Italian independence.
"Turin, April 29th, 1859.
"Viva l'Italia.
"(Signed)　　　　　　VICTOR EMMANUEL.
"(Signed)　　　　　　C. CAVOUR."

***

Napoleon III. addressed the following proclamation to the French people :—

" FRENCHMEN !

"Austria, in causing her army to enter the territory of the King of Sardinia, our ally, declares war against us. She thus violates treaties and justice, and menaces our frontiers. All the Great Powers have protested against this aggression. Piedmont having accepted the conditions

gotten the lessons of 1848, is small in comparison, and would be less than it is without the incessant excitations of Piedmont to increase it."

Behold, what a beautiful picture! Those poor people did not even know how well they were off. What unfortunate creatures!

which should have ensured peace, one asks what can be the reason of this sudden invasion? It is that Austria has brought matters to this extremity, that either her dominion must extend to the Alps, or Italy must be free to the Adriatic, for in that country every corner of territory which remains independent endangers her power.

"Hitherto moderation has been the rule of my conduct, now energy becomes my first duty.

"Let France arm, and say resolutely to Europe: 'I desire no conquest, but I desire firmly to maintain my national and traditional policy. I observe the treaties on condition that no one shall violate them against me. I respect the territory and rights of neutral powers, but I boldly avow my sympathy for a people whose history is mingled with our own, and who groan beneath foreign oppression.

"France has shown her hatred against anarchy; she has been pleased to give me a power strong enough to reduce to helplessness the abettors of disorder and the incorrigible members of those old factions whom one perpetually sees plotting with our enemies, but she has not therefore abdicated her task of civilisation. Her natural allies have always been those who desire the improvement of the human race, and when she draws the sword it is with the purpose, not of dominating, but of liberating.

"The object of this war, then, is to restore Italy to herself, not to make her change masters, and we shall then have next our frontiers a friendly people, who will owe to us their independence.

"We are going into Italy, not to foment disorder, nor to shake the power of the Holy Father, whom we have replaced upon his throne, but to free him from that foreign pressure which weighs upon the whole peninsula, and to help to establish order there upon the satisfaction of legitimate interests.

"We are going, in fine, to seek upon that classic ground, illustrious with so many victories, the footsteps of our fathers. God grant that we may be worthy of them!

"I am about to place myself at the head of the army. I leave in France the Empress and my son. Seconded by the experience and the enlightenment of the last surviving brother of the Emperor, the Empress will understand how to show herself equal to the grandeur of her mission.

"I confide them to the valour of the army, which remains in France to watch over our frontiers and protect our homes; I confide them to the loyalty of the National Guard; I confide them in a word to the whole people, who will encircle them with that affection and devotion, of which I daily receive so many proofs.

"Courage, then, and union! Our country once more will show the world that she has not degenerated. Providence will bless our efforts, for the cause which rests on justice, humanity, love of country, and of independence is holy in the eyes of God.

"Palace of the Tuileries, May 3rd, 1859.
"(Signed)   NAPOLEON."

Strange vicissitude of human fate! Napoleon died in exile. His son fell by the assegais of the Zulus. Even the palace of the Tuileries is but a ruin! *Sic transit gloria mundi!*

The French people felt flattered that their Emperor confided his wife and son to them. My friend, Colonel Kiss, who was an eye-witness of the departure of the Emperor for the war, told me that the artisans and workmen who surrounded his carriage called out to him: "Bonne chance! Allez toujours! N'ayez pas peur! C'est nous qui faisons les revolutions, mais aussi c'est nous qui les empêchons! Allez toujours!"

And like the masses, so were the soldiers. I had often to wait at a railway station whilst another train, filled to suffocation with soldiers, passed through. And the spectacle presented was always the same. In the centre of every carriage stood a drummer beating time to the song of the soldiers. They all sang the same song, the well-known French military song:—

"Mourir pour la patrie."

but on this occasion they had changed it to

"Mourir pour l'Italie
Est la mort la plus belle
La plus digne d'envie."

And many of them died "la mort la plus belle" at Magenta, Solferino; and their death led to Villafranca.

CHAPTER II.

Preliminary Conference of the Belligerent Powers and the Hungarian Exiles—Incidents of the Complication—Endeavours of the English Government to Prevent War—Kossuth's Position—His Invitation to Paris.

AUSTRIA'S armament was complete; and neither in Paris nor in Turin was victory reckoned upon so confidently as to obscure the advantage which would result were the Hungarian nation to rise while Austria was engaged with Italy.

It was still vividly recollected that the Hungarian nation, by its glorious efforts to defend its national independence ten years before, had so rudely shaken the power of the Austrian dynasty, that the latter could not put down Hungary with its own forces.

They saw that the heroic assistance of the Hungarian nation, so much attached to freedom, could all the more be depended upon, as the Court of Vienna had, during the last ten years, not only done nothing to reconcile the Hungarians, but had, on the contrary, carried revenge, oppression, and degradation to the utmost, and done everything likely to rouse the feeling of a deadly offended nation, by abusing the power regained, not by its own strength, but by treason and the armed assistance of the Emperor Nicholas.

The aspirations of the Hungarian nation were personified in the Hungarian refugees, who waved the banner of Hungarian liberty, surrounded by right, justice, treaties, and the nimbus of the history of a thousand years, before the eyes of Europe.

Under these circumstances, the Powers knew that they could influence the Hungarian nation only through the exiles. Through them they also expected to be able to create dissensions in the Hungarian regiments of the Austrian army.

At this time I was still shut out from the continent of Europe.

When, in 1851, I was released from captivity in Asia Minor, and reached Marseilles in the United States frigate *Mississippi*, I communicated to the Prefect that I wished, in order to save my family from the suffering of a long sea voyage, to travel through France to England. The telegraph was set to work, and the end of it was that permission to travel through France was withheld from me.

Later on, when my mother was dying in Brussels, I wished to go there to imprint upon her brow the parting kiss of filial piety. The Belgian Government offered to give me permission for this, only on condition that a policeman should accompany me at every step, even to the death-bed of my mother. I indignantly refused this offer, which would have profaned the sacredness of the dying bed; and my mother died without my being able to kneel before her, and ask for her benediction on my tempest-tossed head.

The Continent was closed to me, but to those of the refugees who lived there, revelations were made about the secrets of the coming war, with intent of communicating them to me, more than a year before the actual outbreak of hostilities, when official diplomacy had not yet suspected anything. In the beginning of December, 1858, I was indirectly informed that war had become inevitable, and that there was a prospect of assistance both in money and arms. But more important than these feelers, on the strength of which no decided steps could be taken, were the personal relations of General Klapka with Count Cavour and Prince Napoleon, who entered into formal negotiations with him.

Amongst these informal feelers is one strange incident which might give material for serious consideration even to the historian.

On December 7th, 1858, my friend and fellow-refugee *Daniel Irányi* (at present a member of the Hungarian Parliament), who was staying in Paris, reported to me that *Mieroslawszky*, an exiled Polish general, came to him with a request from Prince Napoleon to find for him a Hungarian willing to go to Italy to ascertain the strength and feeling of the Hungarian regiments stationed there, as war with Austria had become unavoidable. "The plan is," he said, "that *Piedmont shall cede Savoy and Nice to France, and shall receive in exchange the province of Milan as far as the Mincio. As soon as the province of Milan is occupied, and Austria agrees to its cession, peace will be concluded.* The dismemberment of Austria, and especially the liberation of Hungary, are not included in the plan, but if you (the refugees) could induce the Hungarian regiments to desert their colours, they would be formed into a Hungarian legion, under the command of General Klapka. It therefore depends entirely upon you to divert the struggle into another direction."

The words in italics are the very words used in the treaty concluded at Villafranca seven months later (July, 1859). Is not this astonishing? or was Microslawszky a prophet (if there are still prophets in these days of steam and electricity)? or, again, the historian must ask himself, Was the Peace of Villafranca really made in consequence of the necessity of the situation, more especially the prospect of the armed mediation of Prussia? or was it not the goal steadily kept in view, and suspected by nobody, least of all by Cavour and by Victor Emmanuel, "the first soldier of Italian independence?" To the wish communicated to us by the Polish general, I simply answered, that, *as things now stood*, I did not suppose it would be of any advantage to our interests that we should be used for ascertaining the strength of the Hungarian regiments stationed in Italy. Altogether, I impressed upon my friends, from the beginning, the necessity of proceeding with the utmost precaution and circumspection; lest, without having a sure prospect of real advantage to our country, we should be used merely for causing a diversion to make Austria more inclined to sacrifice Lombardy, by threatening her with the loss of "the most precious jewel in her crown" (Hungary).

For me the idea of the formation of a legion—while nothing more was offered to us in the shape of guarantees—never possessed much attraction. I did not entirely share the opinion that with our legion, even if it consisted of 20,000 to 25,000 men (a number we could scarcely depend upon), we could give the war another direction, in case France, satisfied with Lombardy, stopped her army from advancing further, and left us to ourselves, or even forced us to lay down our arms. We could render assistance to our country, but we ourselves, poor refugees, could not save it—only the nation could do that. But we dared not lead the nation into trouble, dared not abuse the trust the nation reposed in us. In the present case, we could not call our nation to arms unless friendly powers openly identified themselves with the struggle for Hungarian independence, and gave guarantees not to forsake our cause. We should deserve to be shot if, either in the interests of French Imperial ambition or any other alien cause, we used the influence of the Hungarian name, or squandered Hungarian blood simply to make a diversion for another country.

My consultation with General Klapka confirmed my suspicion that we, and through us our nation, were, if possible, to be used only to make a diversion, in order to facilitate the victories of others and secure their ends. General Klapka came to London, on January 17th, to give me an account of what had passed, and to consult with me upon what had best be done. He told me that war was a certainty; that he had had *pourparlers* in Paris with Prince Napoleon, and in Turin with Cavour, and that he also had had an audience of King Victor Emmanuel, which lasted two hours. That the King said most emphatically that he had decided for war, "*coûte que coûte,*" that he knew he risked his throne and the future of his dynasty, "*mais advienne que pourra, je m'y lance,* with my eyes shut. 1st. Because I owe it to the hopes raised all over Italy, and from the full effects of which I can no longer shrink back. 2nd. Because I am bound to revenge the memory of my father. 3rd.

Because I owe it to that hatred of the House of Austria in which I was brought up."

The general said further that the object of the war was not only Lombardy (Cavour declared emphatically that he would not make one step for Lombardy alone), but the total expulsion of the Austrians from Italian soil, and the creation of a North-Italian kingdom; that no change was contemplated with regard to Central and Southern Italy; that the participation of the French Emperor as an ally in the war (and that with a large force, too, of from 150,000 to 200,000 men) had been decided upon, and that as a reward Savoy and Nice were to be ceded to him. Further, that the King wished to commence hostilities at the beginning of April, but that the Emperor was not yet ready, and desired that they should at least wait till the end of May; that all were convinced of the necessity of Hungary taking part also, and that therefore we should receive money, arms, ships for landing, and even a French army corps of from 18,000 to 20,000 men, *but only as an escort, not to penetrate with us into the country*, but to remain in the port to protect our rear. In reply to a question, General Klapka informed me that these promises were made to him by Prince Napoleon, but not officially, and not in the name of the Emperor; that the Prince had also promised to use his influence so that he should speak with the Emperor, but that he (Klapka) had as yet not spoken with him.

From all this I learnt that an army would be given to us not " pour que l'honneur du drapeau français soit effectivement engagé pour la cause hongroise en Hongrie même," but that it should stop near the coast " to protect our rear"—against whom? Everybody can understand, I should think, that if they landed us with a few thousand men, collected abroad, we should be threatened not in our rear from the sea, but in front and on both our flanks; we should have to fight battles before we advanced from the shore into Hungary; we should need assistance in these battles, and support in the country till we had organised the national forces, and arrayed them in battle-order. And the army corps offered to us was to remain near the shore. This meant that, if we were beaten in an encounter before we reached Hungary, we might save ourselves as best we could. If by a flank movement we reached Bosnia, they would leave us there, and conclude peace in Lombardy, stipulating for the cession of Lombardy.

I declared that I would not waste even a single word upon such a basis. I wanted guarantees against the risk of being cast off as soon as done with, and needed support, which could be relied upon, while the nation organised its own forces.

I told General Klapka that what the King, Prince Napoleon, and Cavour said, was very cheering and encouraging, but did not afford a basis on which to rest the affairs of our country. That, in my opinion, the Emperor's intentions alone would turn the scale, but that nobody, except himself, knew what his intentions were, and that very likely he himself did not yet know how far he might go in carrying them into effect. There might be different stages in the accomplishment of his desires.

Thus much was certain; he could not wish to act in such a manner as would provoke a European coalition against him. If he could not secure the active alliance of the other Great Powers, he, at least, must wish for their neutrality. It was possible that this neutrality might be restricted to conditions, and not impossible that one of these conditions might be, that the Austrian power should remain intact, except in its Italian provinces. As the attitude of the other powers was, therefore, still dependent on negotiations, whatever Prince Napoleon, the King, or the King's minister might wish, it was not at all certain yet, whether the Emperor, with whom the decision rested, would consider the use that was to be made of the active participation of the whole of Hungary as fitting into his plans, or whether all he cared for was a small Hungarian legion, organised abroad, similar to the Polish legion of the Crimean war. If the plan had been confined to this only, I would not merely have declined to assist in the matter, but on the contrary I would have hindered it. Even in our defeat we had given signal proof of the vitality of the Hungarian nation, which would be a basis for the future of our country. This we could not throw away. For if the Hungarians were again defeated, because they were abandoned, it would take a century for them to regain their strength a third time. I would not miss making use of any opportunity which might offer itself, but I would also take care that if the interests of our country were not promoted, at least they should not be thrown back. I would not permit the best lives of the nation to be sacrificed in order to make a diversion in the interests of others while it was in my power to prevent it.

Meanwhile, we agreed that General Klapka should

try to speak with the Emperor. From what he said, we should judge whether the matter had sufficient foundation for us to engage in serious negotiations.

The position I took up was this. If there should be a war, in which we were to take part, the liberation of Hungary would have to be considered as one of the main objects of such a war. To secure this, an army would have to be sent to Hungary; not stationed in the port of landing, but sent right into the heart of the country, so that France should stand committed to the defence of Hungary. The appearance of a French army in Hungary would be accompanied by the publication of a proclamation by the Emperor of the French, in which he would publicly identify himself with the liberation and independence of Hungary.

These were my conditions, which I would not alter on any consideration. General Klapka and I were of the same opinion.

The General spoke with the Emperor (February 17th), who promised that he would seriously consider the affairs of Hungary.

I certainly did not find much consolation in this vague promise. There was nothing tangible in it. However, the initiative had been taken, and if a war really took place, there were many important considerations which made the participation of Hungary desirable, so that I did not think it at all unlikely that, after all, it would lead to earnest negotiations. I, therefore, determined to prepare my countrymen in good time for this eventuality. To accomplish this I sent to Hungary the subjoined instructions.

"INSTRUCTIONS TO MY COUNTRYMEN.
"*London, 25th February,* 1859.

1.

"It is probable that in the course of the year (perhaps towards the summer) we shall be able to afford our country an opportunity of fighting out her independence.

"This belief is not merely founded on fluctuating sympathies, but rests upon the solid basis of identity of interests.

"In Turin, as well as in Paris, it is known that the Austrians can be driven out of Italy, but the conquered provinces cannot be securely retained without our assistance. For if, in consequence of the possession of Hungary, Austria remains a first-rate power, she will be strong enough to reconquer what she has lost as soon as circumstances alter a little.

"But it is also known that without the co-operation of Hungary, even the defeat of the Austrians in Italy is uncertain. An army of 150,000 men is an enormous force, if entrenched in a strategical position like the famous Quadrilateral on the Adige.

"To make sure of victory, another seat of war will be required, not only to occupy the Austrians, but also to draw away a much larger force than will compensate the adversaries for the splitting up of their forces.

"The second seat of war can only be Hungary.

"In the past French wars every campaign in Italy was simultaneous with a war on the Rhine. This cannot be done now. Firstly, because it would exasperate Germany. Secondly, because it would not afford any advantage, for to whatever extent the force of Austria would have to be withdrawn from Italy, to the same extent would the army of the other side have to be weakened. This would not be the case were Hungary to be chosen as the other seat of war. Unless we suppose that our nation, which, unprepared and entirely forsaken, completely crushed the Austrian forces in 1849, has become so cowardly as to despair of its future, or so servile as to accustom itself to the foreign yoke; unless we suppose that this is so, it will suffice for the French, in connection with the Italian campaign, to send me and my fellow-exiles with a French army corps of 20,000 men to Hungary, in order to divide the Austrian army and to detach from it not only from 20,000 to 25,000 men, but a whole nation, a nation which in the course of a few months can place 150,000 men in the field, and which has shown that it is able to deal with the Austrians even single-handed.

"On the basis of this identity of interests, I say, France and Piedmont, unless diplomacy should prevent war (which is hardly credible), will ally themselves with the Hungarian nation through me, its chosen representative, designated as such in the declaration of Independence.

"*It is desirable that the nation should know of this.*

2.

"But, however much I may wish to see my country,—and for one hour's existence in my native land, restored to its liberty, I would gladly sacrifice the rest of my life,—I love my country better than my life, and therefore I shall never permit it to be used as an instrument only. Our country, if it fight, must have an object. I will not allow one drop of blood to be sacrificed for the sole purpose of creating a diversion. I will call the nation to arms only if I can appear on the frontier with a force sufficient to allow the national forces to be organised, so that the liberation of the nation may only depend upon its own determination.

"*I therefore warn the nation not to listen to delusive and reckless appeals, but to wait until I call upon it. I shall not carelessly sacrifice any of its blood.*

3.

"The object which I must see ensured before I call out, '*Take up arms and follow me!*' is the independence of our country: neither more nor less. The Declaration of independence says:—'In the choice of a form of government the Hungarian nation is ready to comply with the wishes of Europe.' I shall conform to this, and though I hate the word 'king' (and it would be strange if, after all we have suffered at the hands of kings, I did not hate it!)

I am prepared to accept a king, should it be demanded as the price of our independence that we should elect a king.

4.

"If things go as I wish, the present opportunity will be one more favourable for the regeneration of our nation than centuries may produce again.

"At present, we are not threatened by Russian intervention. Care has been taken to prevent that. Neither need we fear that the English Government will give material assistance to Austria. I am thankful to God that I, a poor exile, was able to arouse such a feeling of sympathy for our country in the bosom of the British nation, that, if we have recourse to arms, no English minister would venture to assist our enemies. The voice of the people of that free country would so unmistakeably manifest itself, that no minister of the Crown would dare to resist it. The English people identify in their sentiments the affairs of Hungary so much with myself that, if I were personally to appear, it would be easy to create such popular manifestations as would secure to us the whole moral weight of England's position, including a speedy acknowledgment of our independence. The material assistance also, which would reach us through private channels, would not be small.

"Add to this the help from France in money, arms, ammunition, and a complete army corps (without which, in addition to the identification of France with the Hungarian movement, I will not allow my influence to be used), and take further into consideration that Austria will be engaged in Italy not in putting down a badly-organised revolution, but in fighting an army of 200,000 men, and, according to human calculation, there can scarcely be any doubt of our success if we remain true to ourselves.

5.

"Not less encouraging than the prospect of victory would be the result of victory. *Our country will be a free and independent Hungary.* Owing to our geographical position we need not dread being turned into a French possession. I shall ensure our country *against treason and ambition.* Rivalry between civil power and military ambition was the cause of our defeat in 1849. For this reason, during the last ten years, I have devoted to the study of the art of warfare every minute not required for keeping alive, all over the world, an interest in the affairs of Hungary. And now I am a soldier, I would not entrust the army to anybody else. Thus the liberty of the people will be secured. Ambition is unknown to me. I yearn for FREEDOM, not for POWER. I can trust myself. I know that I would, on the day of the decisive victory, deposit the sovereignty of the nation intact in its own hands, and withdraw into the modest privacy of my home. Until the day of victory, however, I should know how to protect the nation against all ambition and discord.

6.

"The question therefore is: Does the nation wish to be free, knowing that liberty is a thing not given away like alms, but something to fight for? Or was the great revelation of its youthful strength in 1849 also the *death* of the nation? Did our heroes die in vain? Did our martyrs sacrifice their lives to no purpose? Is there no reason why the Hungarian name is standing in higher estimation, than ever before, in the eyes of the world, in spite of the nation's misfortune? Every thinking man admits that an independent Hungary is destined in the future to form an indispensable part of the European system,—and the Hungarians themselves would resign this existence! Will nobody but the Hungarians themselves believe that they are destined to be the slaves of Austria?—of Austria! as rotten as she is odious, and destitute of vitality.

"I hear it said, 'The people are good, I know.'

"It is also said, 'You have but to appear at the frontier with an army and give out the word of command, and the whole nation will rise like one man.' I believe it, and when the time comes to give the word of command, I shall know how to ensure a response to it.

"But I also know that the more educated classes, absorbed in the race for material wealth, have of late years neglected the national dignity. The Italians, who are not such good soldiers as the Hungarians, dared to refuse to contribute to the forced loan, dared to refuse to humble themselves, dared not to simulate a timid adherence, dared to depend on the 'vis inertiæ,' dared to stand as a living protest before Europe. The Hungarians have submitted like a flock of sheep. For shame! . . . .

"And, even now, is it not always heard in their clubs and other resorts, that it would be disloyal to increase the trouble of Austria; that the Hungarians must be loyal, and that their loyalty will be rewarded by some small concessions?

"This is what is said; and really it is to be feared that, when next in trouble, and when Austria again throws dust in the eyes of Europe, these men will be ready to sell the patrimony of our national existence, like Esau, for 'a dish of lentils.'

"Loyalty! . . Confidence! . . Have the lessons of history been written in vain—in vain for our nation only?

"*Every patriot should consider it to be his duty to prevent the spread of this infection, and to set public opinion against it. The time of responsibility approaches. Condonation for what is past, but responsibility for the present and future!*

7.

"But as things are, it is well for the present that the Hungarian name should stand in the background. It will facilitate our negotiations. It is well that Austria trusts to Hungarian impotence. This confidence must not be changed into suspicion by any rash demonstration.

"I do not recommend conspiracies. If matters go as we may expect, there will be no necessity for conspiracies. In 1848 we did not conspire. It would be a pity to sacrifice even one of those most precious lives; and I also fear that the discovery of a plot would induce Austria, now over-confident, to prevent, at any price, the outbreak of hostilities.

"But though conspiracy is unnecessary, there is plenty of work for every patriot.

8.

"For instance :—

"a. To spread correct views, to stimulate hope, and to impress upon the nation the necessity of showing determination.

"b. To see that everybody endeavours to keep himself ready for the decisive moment, so that as soon as the frontier has been crossed with an army, and a proclamation and the first general order issued from headquarters, all the people who can carry arms shall, in the shortest possible time, collect at the appointed localities to be organised. At the same time, care should be taken to disarm all the smaller forces of the enemy stationed all over the country, and every possible obstacle should be thrown in their way in order to prevent their being concentrated in larger numbers.

"c. To endeavour to be on friendly terms with the soldiery, without distinction as to their nationality.

"d. To enter into close connection with Transylvania, and to spread my views amongst the Széklers settled there.

"e. To dispel the fears of the non-Magyar nationalities, and to induce them, in their own interest, to come to an understanding with the Magyars.

"f. It is necessary now, if ever it was, that a trustworthy patriot should from time to time, if possible one every month, come over to me to inform me of what is going on at home, and to take instructions from me.

"g. To keep me well informed of the numbers and arms of the soldiers, and where they are stationed. This is most important.

"h. I recommend the Croatians to the attention of my countrymen. A great service to our country would be done by him who could induce a Croatian (a lover of liberty, and trusted by his compatriots, especially by those in the Military Frontier) to come over to me to arrange the future position of the two nations, their mutually independent relations, and also the basis and conditions of combined action.

"I again repeat, I wish to entangle nobody in the dangers of conspiracy. For this reason I mention no names. He who loves his country will find means to go to work in the way indicated. The turn of events is so encouraging, and every moment so important, that it would indeed be lamentable if there were none to be found at home who feel the necessity of keeping up with me an uninterrupted communication. This can be done without danger. It is easy to travel, and, once here, interviews can easily be arranged without compromising any one. During my ten years' exile the nation has never assisted me in my arduous task. God grant that the opportunity for the regeneration of our country may not be lost, when the moment of action shall arrive, through the inactivity and indolence of the people!

"If you love your country, and have faith in its future, impress these words well upon your memory, and do whatever patriotism bids you in the directions traced out above. I am loth to believe that there is no friend, or circle of friends, at home to whom you could speak confidentially. If you do no more than make those around you understand the situation, and our prospects, you will have done a good service to our country.

"(Signed) KOSSUTH."

When the star of hope appeared in the heavens of our patriotic longings, like the Zodiacal light, faintly but still perceptibly, there was unanimity and also difference of opinion among the Hungarian exiles. Unanimity as to the ends to be gained, and in readiness for self-sacrifice; difference of opinion as to the ways and means to be employed. Some considered the guarantees laid down by me as indispensable; others would have been ready to be satisfied with help in money and arms alone; and others, again, delighted at the prospect of some fighting, setting aside the counsels of responsibility, were ready to cross the eastern frontier of Transylvania, in the disguise of countrypeople, and to endeavour to stir up the Széklers. Some thought success would be surer, and the nation preserved from a calamity, if I insisted that the foreign powers should negotiate directly with me; others, again, were of opinion that, though I ought to superintend everything, I should keep in the background and allow others to carry on the negotiations, because, being connected with the leaders of European democracy, the powers were estranged from me. As these doings of the Hungarian exiles did not lead to any result, I do not think a narrative of the details would much interest the English reader, and I therefore pass them over. "The earth hath bubbles as the water has," and those were such. They disappeared as soon as war became a reality, and I was invited to Paris.

But though war was becoming more and more probable, the "serious consideration" Napoleon had promised to bestow on the affairs of Hungary went through a good many different phases. The Emperor had to overcome many difficulties, and these caused him to waver more than once.

Amongst these difficulties, one of the greatest, I might say the chief difficulty, was the feverish activity displayed by the English Government to avert war from the head of its " darling Austria," and to preserve to her her Italian possessions intact. Wherever a spark of warlike intention burst forth, England was on the spot, at once, to extinguish it.

Lanza, the Sardinian Minister of Finance, introduced a bill in the House of Representatives, on February 4th, sanctioning a loan of fifty million francs. In submitting the bill he gave as the cause that produced the necessity for the proposed loan the enormous armaments and preparations which Austria had carried out in the Lombardo-Venetian kingdom, and more particularly along the rivers Po and Ticino; and he pointed out the duty of the country to take measures for the protection of the national honour, liberty, and independence.

The loan was voted on February 9th, and Cavour sent a circular to the Sardinian diplomatic agents abroad, in which he justified the loan by the alarming preparations of Austria.

The English Government rushed off to put out the fire, only with this difference, that in Vienna they used a flask of rosewater for the purpose, whereas in Turin they poured water upon it by the bucketful.

To Vienna they wrote: "Count Cavour justifies the loan on the ground of the menacing attitude taken up by Austria on the Sardinian frontier. But Her Majesty's Government think that the Cabinet of Vienna should meet this statement by publicly declaring that Austria, if she be not herself first attacked, has no intention of undertaking any aggressive movement against Sardinia; she might express her willingness to come to such an understanding as would enable both parties to lay aside their mutual distrust, and withdraw their forces from their respective frontiers."*

Similar advice, coupled with reproaches and threats, went from the English Foreign Office to Turin. In the despatch I read: "Sardinia was to blame for the attitude of Austria. If Sardinia had not taken advantage of the feelings with which the population of the Lombardo-Venetian kingdom *was assumed* to be animated as

* Earl of Malmesbury to Lord A. Loftus, February 12th, 1859.

regards the Austrian Government, to raise the cry of Italian liberation, Austria would have had no occasion to take up a *defensive position* on her frontier." Lord Malmesbury most earnestly advised the Cabinet of Turin *" to pause in its headlong career;* to avert the danger which it had so *rashly courted;* to control the passions which it had so *injudiciously excited;* to retract the applications which it had made for foreign support." He admonishes Count Cavour that, in case of war, Sardinia, whether she is aided by a foreign nation or by a revolutionary movement throughout the whole of Italy, will, from the smallness of her resources, soon descend into the position of an auxiliary, and when peace is restored she will experience even a worse fate than that of an ordinary auxiliary, and will find that the interests of the House of Savoy will not be allowed to stand in the way of a new adjustment of the north of Italy, either under a monarchical or under a republican form of government (Malmesbury to Sir J. Hudson, Feb. 12th).

What a different way of behaving! In Vienna smooth like a kid glove! in Turin, how rough! But one thing is certain, that Lord Malmesbury did not prove himself to be a prophet, or anything like one, when he hazarded the opinion that events would go against the interests of the House of Savoy. "*Altro*," says the Italian; and indeed it did come differently.

Always starting from the wrong hypothesis that the cry of Italian liberation would be effectually calmed down by some reforms, these notes formed the commencement of that feverish activity which, while professing to be displayed for the preservation of the "peace of Europe," was really undertaken by the

English Government in the interests of its "darling Austria." One of the most notable incidents of this diplomatic struggle is the confidential mission of Lord Cowley, English Ambassador in Paris, to Vienna. This was doubtless a very clever move to spoil the game of Napoleon, but it found its match in the taciturn man of the Tuileries. The object of this mission was stated in the following telegram :—

"THE EARL OF MALMESBURY TO EARL COWLEY.
 "*Foreign Office, February* 13*th,* 1859.
 " (EXTRACT.)

" The relative situations of France and Austria have assumed an aspect so alarming to the rest of Europe that Her Majesty's Government are earnestly desirous of averting, if possible, the dangers which they threaten.

" The course most likely to produce this result would be an amicable interference on the part of Great Britain to ascertain by the consent of both states how their mutual relations could be placed on a more friendly footing.

" The intimate knowledge your Excellency has of the French Court, its ideas and aspirations, joined to your personal intimacy with Count Buol (the Austrian minister) point you out at once as the most fitting person to carry out this object.

" It would, however, be indispensable to your success that you should ascertain whether the pacific interference of a mutual ally like Great Britain would be agreeable at this moment, and discover what concessions France desires to obtain from Austria, on what is called the Italian question.

" I assume they would include the evacuation of the Papal States by both Austrian and French troops, the amelioration of the law and government of those states, and a guarantee on the part of Austria not to attack Sardinian territory.

" A fourth point would probably be put forward by the French

Government, namely, the abrogation or modification of the treaties of 1847 between Austria and the Duchies of Parma and Modena.

"It would be perhaps pressing the national pride of Austria too much to insist on abrogation, as Austria has a right to make treaties, offensive and defensive, with any independent state; it might nevertheless be possible to induce her and the Duchies to expunge the article which obliges Austria to assist them as against their own subjects.

"(Signed)   MALMESBURY."

NOTE.—The justly obnoxious article of the treaty between Austria and Modena to which the above despatch refers was thus worded:—

"ARTICLE III.—Should circumstances arise within the states of his Royal Highness the Duke of Modena of a nature to cause apprehension that legal tranquillity and order may be disturbed, should such turbulent movements continue to increase, while the means at the disposal of the government were not sufficient to quell them, the Emperor engages upon being required to do so to furnish the necessary military assistance for the preservation or restoration of tranquillity and legal order.

"(Signed)   PR. METTERNICH.
"CL. THEODORE VOLA.
"*Vienna, Dec. 24th, 1847.*"

A similar treaty was concluded with the Duke of Parma.

While the above Article III. rendered the condition of the people of the Duchies hopeless, the second article constituted a standing menace against Piedmont, inasmuch as it accorded to Austria the right of marching troops into, and of occupying the fortresses of, the Duchies, as often as the interest of military precaution required it. This stipulation made of Modena and Parma positively an Austrian dominion not only for defence, but also for attack.

Still Lord Malmesbury was either sufficiently fanciful to imagine, or unjust to pretend, that Piedmont should meekly bear such indignity.

Lord Cowley lost no time in seeing Count Walewski on the subject.

Count Walewski assured his lordship that the Emperor accepted "with grateful acknowledgment" the British proposal, and desired to secure the following points:—

1. Abrogation of all separate treaties.

2. Adoption by all the states of Italy of a system of government which would admit of the taxes being voted by an assembly of some sort.

3. Separate administration of the Legations by a Roman Prince named by the Pope, with Bologna for seat of government; but the Pope not to be forced under any circumstances.

4. Pecuniary aid from all the Roman Catholic states to the Pope for religious purposes, and the consequent reduction of the taxes levied in the Papal States. (Lord Cowley remarked that this question of pecuniary aid to the Pope was hardly a matter on which Great Britain could interfere—of course. Still his lordship tried to interfere, but Count Buol showed not the slightest inclination to come down with Austrian money —of course, of course! Money was rather scarce in the Austrian treasury at that time,—just as scarce as at present. Squeezing the people of their very heart's blood, still struggling with inextricable, hopeless deficits— that is "a system of government" with Austria!)

Upon this Lord Cowley received his definitive instructions, February 22nd (evacuation of the Roman States—reforms—security for better relations between Austria and Sardinia—abrogation or modification of the separate treaties of 1847, with the declaration that the obligation imposed thereby on Austria to interfere with and suppress any popular expression of opinion in the Duchies was particularly obnoxious to the feelings of the British people).

Lord Cowley reached Vienna on February 27th, and reported at some length on the 9th of March to the Earl of Malmesbury the results of his confidential mission :—

" Count Buol has shown a sincere desire to avoid the extremities of war, as far as he might do so without compromising the national honour of Austria. Similar feelings were evinced by the Emperor.

" As to the question of evacuation, the Pope having himself requested the withdrawal within the year of the Austrian and French forces, Austria was ready to comply with the Pope's request, with such caution, however, as was necessary to insure security against possible insurrections.

" With respect to the reforms of administration to be introduced into the Roman States, Count Buol was willing either to resume the negotiations which had been commenced with the French Government upon that subject in 1857, but afterwards allowed to drop by that government, or to fall back on the recommendations made by the five powers to the Pope in 1831-32. He prefers the latter measure.

" Upon the point of security for the better relations between the governments of Austria and Sardinia, Count Buol said that Great Britain must address itself to Turin. It is not from the conduct of Austria that the present critical state of affairs has arisen, but from the ambitious and encroaching policy of Sardinia.

As long as Sardinia remains armed there can be no security for peace.

"On the point of the abrogation or modification of the Austro-Italian treaties of 1847, Austria was naturally more sensitive than on any other. Still Count Buol was disposed to enquire whether they might be replaced, with the consent of the contracting parties, by some other combination, which, while relieving Austria from the necessity of an interference, the responsibility of which is fully felt, would not risk the chance of the Duchies becoming a prey to revolution and anarchy.

"In discussing this question it was necessary to take into consideration the dominant feeling in Count Buol's mind, that the only real danger of revolution to which the Duchies would be exposed would have its source in, and would be supported by, Sardinia."

From this point of view Lord Cowley in the way of cursory conversation suggested either the neutrality of the territory of Sardinia, or a league among the smaller states of Italy for their mutual succour in case of internal disorder. Lord Cowley avowed a strong preference for the idea of neutrality that would cut at once to the root of the existing mischief. Neutral Sardinia being safe from any attack would have no occasion to keep up an army ruinous to her finances. Austria and the governments of Central Italy, on the other hand, relieved from all anxiety as to the aggressive policy of Sardinia, might consent to give up those treaties which have been the cause of so much irritation.

To the objection that Sardinia would never consent to such an arrangement, Lord Cowley advanced the somewhat speculative opinion that the consent of Sardinia, although desirable, was not necessary.

While insisting principally on the four points especially recommended in his instructions, Lord Cowley did not neglect to ascertain Count Buol's sentiments on the other matters suggested by Count Walewski. By this portion of his report we are enlightened on the marvellous mystery until then hidden in impenetrable darkness,—that Austria was sincerely addicted to "reforms;" that her advice had ever tended to encourage *real* ameliorations, only the Austrian Government did not think that *sweeping measures suited the nature of the Italian people.* Besides, the other Italian states were far better governed than it pleased Sardinia to represent them to be.

As to pecuniary aid to the Pope, and consequent reduction of taxes, Count Buol did not evince the least disposition to entertain any proposal of the kind (it is really wonderful how the noble lord could expect to gain over Austria either to the payment of subsidies or to the idea of "reduction of taxes." How green!).

Before closing his despatch he referred to some of the difficulties with which he had to contend in carrying out his instructions. These were such as—

1. The fixed idea that France was determined on war with Austria, and that to make concessions was but to put off the evil day.

2. The pride of Austria naturally revolting at being called upon to make concessions instigated by the animosity and ambition of Sardinia.

3. The attitude assumed by Germany towards France, of which the Austrian Government was naturally anxious to profit.

And, lastly, there being no real question at issue between Austria and France which could fairly be assumed to involve a *casus belli*.

In conclusion, Lord Cowley did not doubt that the Austrian Government would accept, with a sincere desire to bring them to an honest conclusion, any overtures for a reconciliation with France, the acceptance of which would not be incompatible with their honour. But as long as Sardinia was allowed to remain armed he doubted whether Austria would enter into negotiations, since she looked upon the Sardinian army as the advanced guard of France, permitting the latter to take her own time to arm, and would feel no security that peace was intended so long as that advanced guard was in existence. The disarmament of Sardinia was to Austria the gage of the sincerity of France. However, Lord Cowley was disposed to think that the declarations of Austria contained matter which, compared with the professed wishes of France, might be made the basis of an arrangement between the two Imperial Governments.

Lord Malmesbury (by despatch of March 15th) conveyed to his Excellency, by command of the Queen, Her Majesty's entire approbation of the able manner in which he had acquitted himself, and directed him immediately to return to Paris in order to lay before the Emperor the result of his negotiations.

And he went. But what was the end?

The French Ambassador informed Lord Malmesbury, March 18th, that he was instructed to propose that a congress should be held by the five powers to consider the present state of affairs as regards Italy. His Excellency added that the suggestion came from Russia!

"*À coquin, coquin et demi*," say the French.

This was the answer to the famous confidential mission of Lord Cowley to Vienna. The meaning of it is quite clear. The Tuileries stood face to face with the danger of English mediation, which it would have been dangerous not to accept, for the refusal of England's mediation would have supplied this power with a pretext for openly siding with Austria. Mediation was, therefore, warded off by the proposal of a congress. The idea of this congress being started by Russia was a shrewd move; in it there was provision for the unforeseen. For the preliminary disarmament of Sardinia, the question of her admittance to or exclusion from the congress with the other Italian states, and the settlement of the subjects which were to be submitted to the congress were so many rocks on which the idea of a congress might be wrecked. And in fact it was wrecked upon them.

This is the history of Lord Cowley's mission to Vienna.

It shows that the Emperor of the French had to struggle against great difficulties in the carrying out of his plans with regard to Italy, since he was obliged to study the attitude of the European powers, and did not even know by the middle of March which side they would take.

It also demonstrates, first, that those of my fellow-refugees were wrong who thought that the Powers did not (at that time at least) enter into negotiations with me because they took me to be a revolutionist. They maintained a reserve, not on this account, but because they did not think that the time for "serious" negotiations had yet arrived, as war was still very uncertain. As soon as this uncertainty had ceased, they themselves made proposals to me. It further demonstrates that I acted rightly when I did everything in my power to prevent my compatriots from accepting such obligations, and risking such experiments as might, without any compensation, plunge into great misfortune the country which at that time I was still allowed to call "my own."

But it also demonstrates a third moral (one of permanent interest), namely, that diplomacy is a most unscrupulous profession.

By the action of diplomacy we exiled Hungarians were reduced to complete uncertainty as to our prospects, and we watched with intense interest every word and move of those in power in France, to see whether we could not find a clue to the intention and decision of the Emperor. I was continually kept informed of these, as well as of general politics, by Mr. Frederick Szarvady, an exiled compatriot of mine, who lived in Paris. He was closely connected with seventeen foreign papers of different countries, and daily communicated with fifty papers by means of lithographed letters. In consequence of this position he had connections which enabled him to be quickly and thoroughly informed of the latest phases European politics had entered upon.

But even with a thorough knowledge of all the facts and diplomatic incidents, it was no easy matter to keep on the right track, as there were two opposite currents in the policy of the French capital. One was the personal policy of the Emperor, inaugurated by the famous meeting at Plombières, confirmed by the marriage of Prince Napoleon, and embodied in the secret treaty concluded with King Victor Emmanuel. Amongst the men surrounding the Emperor this policy was supported by Prince Napoleon only; he gave it his steady and warm support. The other current (opposite to the former) was the official policy of the ministers, who all, with the exception of Prince Napoleon, together with the deputies and the whole administrative staff, exerted themselves for peace. Amongst these Walewski, the Minister for Foreign Affairs, was the most active—the same man who gave so much trouble to Cavour, and heaped so much insult on injury.

Amidst the difficulties which arose from this movement, the Emperor practised some kind of acrobatic feats by pamphlets, newspaper articles, and official declarations, which have often misled me. I am not ashamed to own it, I am but an ordinary mortal. I could never master the "noble" art of diplomacy, which uses words not to express thoughts, but to conceal them.

Towards the end of January, 1859, appeared the famous pamphlet, "*Napoléon III. et l'Italie.*" Mr. Szarvady informed me that the contents had not only been inspired by the Emperor, but almost dictated by him, and that he had seen the manuscript in which the Emperor had made alterations with his own hand. The object of the pamphlet was to prove to the world that *there was an Italian question,* in refutation of the statement of Austria, *that there was no Italian question, but that there was Piedmontese ambition only*. Diplomatists were unpleasantly affected by the pamphlet, for it furnished them proofs that the Emperor really wished for war, as he expounded proposals quite unacceptable to Austria. Szarvady asked me for instructions as to how to treat this pamphlet, and for general directions about the use of the press.

I answered him as follows (February 7th):—

" 1. As regards agitation to be carried on by the press. As long as every chance has not disappeared of Hungary's being included in one of the combinations now in suspense, so long everything must be avoided in the press which could create a suspicion that the complications will also extend to Hungary. I am rather glad that Hungary has not yet been brought forward. This I particularly wish to avoid; therefore I observe silence here. But when the prospect referred to has gone by entirely, then it will become necessary to agitate energetically and to show that the intentions of the French Government cannot be sincere, as it has entirely left Hungary out of its calculations, and by this omission Austria remains a power sufficiently strong to prevent any *permanent* result from being gained in Italy. Paragraph X. of the famous pamphlet, stating that the Tyrol and the Carinthian Alps are the real fortresses of Austria, is quite true; more so even than the writer seems willing to concede. They would be found to be such not only in case of an Italian revolution, but also in case of invasion by a French army. This is proved by the campaign of 1796, the most splendid of all the exploits of the great Napoleon. He held the whole of Italy, and yet he did not dare pursue thither either the defeated Beaulieu or the defeated Wurmser; he did not dare to do so, though the part of Austria bordering on Germany was occupied by Moreau (and at present the Emperor Napoleon cannot risk such occupation). What gives to the Tyrol and to the Carinthian Alps this strategical importance? The possession of Hungary. Let us take away this, and the former will be nothing but an empty, deserted fortress, without garrison or arms for defence.

" This question cannot now be discussed in newspapers, but it can and must be discussed in conversation.

" What now can and should be done, is to revive the memory of the irrepressible vitality of the young Hungarian nation. An opportunity of doing this is afforded by the historical error in the pamphlet, which divides the population of Austria into Italians and Germans, excluding the Slavs and the Hungarians. A government which proclaims itself the champion of nationalities, and entirely ignores such nations, and does not even acknowledge their existence, must not reckon on the approval of public opinion. And what nations do they ignore? Fifteen million Slavs, the branch of a stock of 75,000,000, and the Hungarians, who have accomplished a few things — who, unprepared, crushed the Austrians in a single campaign; the Hungarians, who defended Europe against the Turks; who, surrounded by three great powers, have been able to preserve their nationality through a thousand years; who have that *unity* for which the Italians only long now, and who, if wounded in the sacred feeling of nationality, will prove on every occasion that they must not be ignored.

"It will be well to lay stress upon the fact that the Hungarian clings firmly to his nationality, in order to show that this feeling is grossly violated by the Austrians. As a notable fact you may quote the letter of Széchényi to the Hungarian Academy of Science (*Tudós-társaság*), (written while he was still detained in a lunatic asylum, as he says, not because his reasoning powers were obscured, but because they were rather too clear). The gist of it comes to this:—'Amidst all the ruin in Hungary this Society remained to represent our nation; this object will no longer be served when the statutes, as revised by the Government, come into force. I did not subscribe my capital to the Society for the object now pursued, and do not mean to pay interest on it either.'

"In the German press the yearning for 'German unity'—the phase it assumed in 1848 is touched upon in the pamphlet—ought to be revived, and it ought to be proved from history that the great obstacle which stands in the way of its realisation is that unnatural conglomeration called the 'Austrian monarchy.' Either this conglomeration must be broken up, which would contribute more than anything else to make Hungary independent, or 'German unity' in its full meaning remains impossible.

"2. The pamphlet entitled '*Napoléon III. et l'Italie*' is most ably written, but whatever ability there is in it, is more of the sort that one would expect from a clever lawyer than from a statesman. A skilful compilation of phrases, supposed to contain history. A good 'pleader,' but without influence on those who, like myself and every statesman, also know what the pamphlet does not say.

"With what object was the pamphlet written? It deprecates war and appeals to public opinion,—and here the syllogism ends. Depend upon it, the Austrians will not withdraw from Italy in consequence of an appeal to public opinion. Coming from a private individual, the pamphlet would be a brilliant feat; but emanating from the Emperor, as we know it does, it says too little to pacify those who fear French supremacy, and too much not to awake susceptibilities. It leaves the impression that the Emperor is afraid, because it can be seen that he has not the courage to speak out the concluding sentence; and because his anxiety to win over the English, Germans, and Prussians is too apparent. Through his anxiety he utterly spoils the good effect which a well-chosen word might otherwise have had; for instance, when he credits the English with having fostered Italian independence; which is not true, for the English Government only recommended the introduction of reforms —moderate reforms—and were even of opinion that the Piedmontese constitution went too far in its concessions. Only the advice given to Austria is real. The rest consists of garbled accounts. He credits Lord Minto with having promised to place the independence of Italy under the protection of England, which is as little true as a good many other statements contained in the pamphlet.

"Will the idea of a 'Confederation' meet with the approval of the Italian nation?* I myself am friendly to the idea of the '*États-Unis de l'Italie*.' I spoke in favour of the idea years ago, but the Italians revolted against it, and I yielded, for I respected their decision, which I believed ought entirely to rest with them in anything that concerned them alone. However, when I spoke of Italian Confederation I did not think of a confederation of the Italian sovereigns. The idea of the 'États-Unis de l'Italie' presupposes a Republican form of government. A confederation of

* The idea of an Italian Confederation was first propounded in this pamphlet. It was again brought forward at the peace negotiations at Villafranca.

monarchies, in the shape either of 'Bundes-Staat' or 'Staaten-Bund,' is absolute nonsense, as proved by the 'Deutscher Bund,' the only illustration of this abortive idea we have in history. Certainly the example has no special attraction for imitation. Börne or Heine (I have forgotten which) says in one place—'Deutscher Bund, toller Hund.' I do not go quite so far, but I affirm that a 'Bund' is not national unity.

"I could say many other things, but what concerns us most is that the pamphlet clearly ignores Hungary. It assures Austria that besides the Italian question there is nothing to be brought against her. If in the Tuileries they nevertheless wish to negotiate with us, the pamphlet tells a falsehood; if it does not, and still they wish to come to an agreement with us, they try to deceive us. It is an instructive fact that when a congress was held for the consolidation of the integrity of the Turkish Empire, Austria was enticed into a bargain with the hope of being compensated by a part of Turkey. We must therefore be on our guard.

"The Emperor (who is the offspring of Revolution) distinctly keeps aloof from all revolutionary elements, and repudiates all revolutionary ideas. We should be revolutionists even if we took part in the contemplated war. I think that it would not have been bad policy to allow one of the craters of European revolution to burn out under European 'control.' If what the pamphlet says is true, he thinks differently. He will see the consequences. If I could find an opportunity for fighting out the independence of Hungary, even under European control, I would not allow it to pass by, for, in the interests of my country, I prefer little but certain to much and uncertain. But if the opportunity is refused to us, if Hungary is ignored, we keep to our old track—*the path of revolutionary solidarity*. We are ready to act, but if necessary, we wait."

This pamphlet was soon followed (February 7th) by the pacifying Speech from the Throne, which only increased the unfavourable impression made upon me by the former. The whole from beginning to end spoke in an astonished and censorious tone of that doubt and alarm which disturbed public confidence without any adequate reason. It forcibly reminded me of the famous "*L'empire c'est la paix*" uttered at Bordeaux. As regards the Italian question it ran as follows:—

"The condition of Italy, and the abnormal circumstance that public order can only be preserved there by foreign arms, have for some time past given well-founded trouble to diplomatists. *Yet this is not sufficient ground for expecting an outbreak of war.* But though there may be some who ardently desire war without adequate cause, and others who in their exaggerated fears are inclined to frighten France by conjuring up the dangers of a new coalition against her, I shall remain steadfast on the path of right, truth, and national honour, and my Government will not allow itself to be carried away or to be intimidated, for my policy will never be either provocative or pusillanimous. Let us therefore pay no heed to false alarms, unjustified uneasiness, or interested apprehensions. *Peace, I hope, will not be disturbed.*"

Influenced by the unfavourable impression made upon me by the Speech from the Throne, I instructed M. Szarvady not to take, at present, any steps which might lead to the suspicion that I had a part, even an indirect one, in the negotiations. If what the Speech from the Throne said was true, that there would be no war, why had the Emperor disturbed Europe, caused damage to his own nation, and deceived the Italians? And if it was not sincere, I could not be too thankful for not having been so quick as others were, in responding to the advances made to us; for what reliance could be placed on the word given to a few exiles by a man who deluded the whole of Europe in this manner?

To this M. Szarvady replied that this identical Speech from the Throne was in Paris held to be as warlike as possible; that the Emperor could not turn up his cards, that he had to combat great difficulties, that the commercial world were alarmed, that the ministers were opposed to war, and, most important of all, that the Emperor had not yet quite arranged with Russia the conditions under which this power would give her consent to the war. Russia wished—1. That the war should be commenced the following year only (this was refused). 2. That the Polish question should not be raised (this was assented to). 3. That some of the points in the Treaty of Paris, rather humiliating to Russia, should be abrogated. The Emperor after a slight hesitation also acceded to this, but Walewski, to frustrate the agreement and to prevent war with Austria, put the whole matter into such shape that Gortchakoff refused to accept it. Admiral La Roncière le Noury was again sent to St. Petersburg. But the preparations for war were carried on with the utmost vigour; the war loan of Sardinia was supported, and war in spite of all difficulties would be waged, because the Emperor wanted war. He wanted it in order to surround himself with the glory of a great general, he also wanted it because he was afraid of the bequest of Orsini, and because the existing state of France could not last. It was necessary to give the French either glory or liberty.

However, though these considerations were calculated to revive somewhat our sinking hopes, the Emperor soon gave us reason to doubt his determination. Early in March a most pacific article appeared in the *Moniteur* declaiming against the "insane world" for suspecting the Emperor of harbouring warlike designs. The article proved by enumerating minute data that it was not true that France was arming, or that any extraordinary activity was displayed in the arsenals, and that the preparations at sea could not be looked upon as alarming, etc. The Emperor had promised to the King of Sardinia that he would defend him if attacked by Austria, *but beyond this he had promised nothing, and everything stated beyond this "was drawn from imagination, untruth, and folly."* The investigation of the questions was now being carried on by diplomacy, and nothing warranted the belief that the result of the scrutiny would not be favourable to the preservation of universal peace.

This article was such a decided disavowal of the policy the Emperor inaugurated at Plombières, that Prince Napoleon, as a warm supporter of this policy, thought it derogatory to his dignity to remain a member of a ministry which could publish such statements. He sent in his resignation. This step justly startled us.

However, Mr. Szarvady soon afforded us relief by the following letter:—

"*Paris, March* 11*th*, 1859.

"By the resignation of Prince Napoleon the situation has not been unfavourably affected; on the contrary, of late it has become rather more definite.

"The Emperor has sent a message to Turin, saying that he has not changed. Cavour is engaged in the elaboration of a manifesto to be published shortly. The King has assured his faithful minister that he will in no case abandon him; that, like his father, he would rather give up his throne than not carry out what the nation expects of him.

"Prince Napoleon, on receiving Ulloa, an Italian general, said to him: 'You are about to return to Turin. Tell them there, and I wish every Italian could hear it, that neither my cousin the Emperor nor I have changed, nor will we change with regard to Italy. But the Emperor—is betrayed by his ministers.' It was usual with Prince Napoleon to refer without reserve in his conversation to the ministers as 'the traitors.'

"When the article in the *Moniteur* appeared, which was extorted by Walewski and Fould, the Prince sent in his resignation. The Emperor refused to accept it, and said that he was ready to insert another article in the *Moniteur* more in accordance with the policy of the Prince, who answered that if the Emperor wished that he should remain in office he would have to part with his other ministers. The Emperor asked for a month to consider the matter, and the Prince answered that in that case he would only re-enter the government after the lapse of a month.

"I assure Your Excellency of the accuracy of all these details.

"War is now more probable than it was ten days ago, but only because Austria is contumacious. Still the situation is exposed to so many influences that we cannot possibly be too cautious. The caution Your Excellency manifests is completely justified.

"(Signed)   SZARVADY."

It cannot be denied that Prince Napoleon had reason to be annoyed by the publication of the article, in which the hand of Walewski, always bitter against Piedmont, and that of the business-like Fould, were distinctly visible.

Prince Napoleon was a faithful and steady friend of the Italians; the Italians knew him to be such, and in the history of Italy he is acknowledged to have been such. He was much too sensible a man not to have understood that the Italian question was one which could not be solved by diplomatic patching. Thus it came about that he was always a trustworthy—often the only—supporter of Cavour in the Tuileries, amongst all the vacillations caused by the many different influences at work there. Being a confidential friend and adviser of the Emperor, and always chosen to the most important missions (such as the mission to Warsaw, the conclusion of the alliance with Sardinia), the Prince was far too much identified with the policy favourable to the national aspirations of the Italians to remain a member of a ministry the ends of whose policy were so entirely different from his own, and who tried to exhibit the policy of France in such a different light, as was proved by the article in the *Moniteur* referred to above. He could not continue to be a member of the ministry without risking his political credit with the Italians. He therefore resigned, and Szarvady was on this, as on most other occasions, well informed when he wrote to me that after the retirement of Prince Napoleon the situation would not become worse.

The reason of this is to be found in the fact that Napoleon III. not only entirely trusted the sagacity of the Prince, but one might even say he affectionately loved him, as I had often occasion to perceive during those few years that I was in connection with them. It was, therefore, perfectly true that with the resignation of Prince Napoleon affairs did not take a turn for the worse, for though not bearing the title of minister, he still was, and continued to be, the *sole* minister of the Emperor in the Italian question, and had also great influence in other matters.

Of this diplomacy England was also aware, as I gathered from a report of Lord Augustus Loftus to Lord Malmesbury (Vienna, January 27th, 1859). In giving his lordship the good news that in Paris affairs had become more reassuring, and that the Emperor of the French had returned to a more peaceful policy, Lord Augustus enumerates several points which materially contributed to this favourable change in the political atmosphere, and amongst them, as not the least important, *the temporary absence of Prince Napoleon from Paris.*

The most amusing part in the affair is that the Prince had just then left Paris to sign (on the occasion of the celebration of his nuptials in Turin) a defensive and offensive treaty in the name of his cousin, the Emperor Napoleon, with King Victor Emmanuel. The object of this treaty was the expulsion of Austria from Italy. At the ratification of this treaty Napoleon showed much satisfaction.* And diplomatists, just at that time, saw peace rising on the political horizon! One almost feels inclined to ask whether diplomatists are worth what they cost the nation.

Every remark made by Prince Napoleon, who took such a great interest in the Italian question, went to show that he completely understood that if it was desirable finally to wrest Italy from the hands of Austria, Hungary must play an important part in the matter. He left nothing undone to win over the Emperor to this view. Of course Hungary was to be utilised only in

* Nel ratificarlo l'Imperatore mostrò di gustare un lietissimo momento di gioja (Cavour to Villamarina, Turin, January 15th, 1859).

case the Italian war became a reality, and this depended almost entirely upon the course the Russian Government would follow. For if England could have succeeded in inducing Russia to side with her, the war would have been an impossibility. Accordingly England did everything to win Russia's support for her views, already aired at the Paris Congress after the Crimean war. These views were, that the discontent reigning on the Italian Peninsula should be removed by the withdrawal of the foreign forces of occupation, by the introduction of reforms, the granting of amnesties, etc. For the English Government persisted in shutting its eyes to the fact that the Italian question was a question of national existence, which could not be solved except by the expulsion of the Austrians. The English Government always liked to reduce the question to one of reforms.

In this sense they wrote to Sir J. Crampton, the English Ambassador at St. Petersburg (January 12th), and declared that:—"Notwithstanding the disposition which the Russian Government has so constantly shown, since the conclusion of the late war, to cultivate the friendship of France, and the unceasing bitterness which characterises its relations with Austria, Her Majesty's Government yet hope that Russia would not refuse to cooperate in their endeavours to preserve the general peace of Europe."

Sir J. Crampton, while communicating this to Prince Gortchakoff, added, that he trusted that Russia, in the interest of the peace of Europe, would lay aside any feeling, favourable or unfavourable, which she might entertain towards either of the two great powers in question. The answer Prince Gortchakoff gave to this communication was as frank as it was remarkable. He said:—

"Russia certainly desires peace, and even requires it for the development of the great measures of internal improvement in which she is engaged (the emancipation of the Serfs). But I must frankly tell you, that we cannot weigh France and Austria in the same balance. Our relations with the former are cordial, with the latter they are far from being so, nor do I see any prospect of an improvement in them.

"Russia was formerly in the habit of offering friendly advice to such of the cabinets of Europe as she had reason to hope would have appreciated her motives in doing so, but it is a policy which she has not found to answer, she has consequently no advice to offer.

"Recollect, that although sincerely desirous that peace should be maintained, I do not tell you that, should it unfortunately be otherwise, we should under no circumstances take part in the contest. We reserve to ourselves entire liberty of action in such a case."

There was no mistake about it—this was clear speaking; little flattering to England, not very pleasant to Austria, but it was "water to our mill."

We had other encouraging signs besides. General Klapka had positive knowledge that the Grand Duke Constantine, and other Russians of high position staying at Nice, had all been unanimous in saying at Turin: "Si vous voulez la guerre, il faut vous adresser aux Hongrois." The Russians have generally shown a very friendly feeling to the Hungarians everywhere, even in official diplomatic circles. Szarvady had very trustworthy connections; and my friend, John Ludvigh (whom during the war we sent to Belgrade as our diplomatic agent), stood on a most friendly footing with the Russian Ambassador at Brussels, who so much liked to converse with "the Hungarian," that when the latter paid him a visit, he was "at home" for nobody else. They chatted together for hours on the past, present, and future.

The Ambassador declared to my friend that it was a positive fact that all over Russia there was a general sympathy for Hungary and contempt for Austria. That the government knew this, and knew it at the time when the Emperor Nicholas gave marching orders to 200,000 men against Hungary, in 1849. That a personage in high position then asked, "Why send such a force there?"; and the Czar himself answered, "Because the war is so unpopular in our country, that it must be over in three months." That no doubt that those Russians who persuaded the Italians to an alliance with Hungary only expressed their personal opinion; but that this was in accordance with the wish of the whole of Russia. That an independent Hungary, as long as it acted with moderation, and did not give support to the Polish question, was not contrary to Russian interests; and that it was also certain that Russia would not again interfere to save Austria, as it was not at all in her interest to keep together the political amalgamation called by that name.

All this was certainly very encouraging, and was not merely idle talk. When, at last, early in May, serious negotiations were entered into with us, the Emperor Napoleon positively assured us that we need have no fear of Russian intervention.

Ludvigh and Szarvady both asked for advice as to

whether they should cultivate these relations. The latter even informed me that if, later on, I should find it necessary to enter into direct communication with the Russian Government, he knew of a Russian in high position who would gladly act as intermediary.

I replied that in politics it is not feeling that decides, but one's interests; and that therefore the connections most certainly ought to be cultivated, but with great caution—we must say as little as possible, but hear and find out as much as possible. To do more than this would be premature, and, for the moment, at least, impossible. Murderers of our country! it did not behove the victim of your crime to take the first step towards reconciliation.

Ludvigh in his conversation with the Russian Ambassador at Brussels had also touched on the Eastern question, but I earnestly cautioned him not to refer to this subject again. Russia was, at present, the only one of all the great powers that leaned towards France; but if there were any cause for her to fear that Napoleon wished to mix up the Italian with the Eastern question, it might have produced such a change in the position of affairs as to cut short our prospects. For Napoleon, who, in 1855, carried on a war to prevent the influence of Russia from extending in the East, could not have been expected, in 1859, to be an open partisan of the extension of Russian power; and of one thing we might be persuaded, that Russia could not be a true friend of any solution or patching up of the Eastern question which would not greatly benefit herself. Any rational solution of the Eastern question pre-supposes an independent Hungary. Without such a country the dissolution of the Turkish Empire would not lead to conferring liberty on the people now under Turkish rule, but simply to an extension of Russian influence. It certainly was not to our interest to call the attention of Russia to this important feature of the Hungarian question, for though Russia might be willing, out of spite against Austria, to overlook the fact that Napoleon was giving us his assistance, I was very much afraid that this forbearance would cease the minute Russia became aware that independent Hungary could become the fulcrum for preventing Russia from becoming the Sun round which the other Eastern people would revolve like so many planets.

I also recommended Ludvigh to make the Russian Ambassador understand that great injustice was done to the Hungarians by confounding them with the "par profession" revolutionary elements. That we did not belong to this class, but that we loved freedom well-regulated by laws; and that this love had been inculcated into us by the history of a thousand years. If not interfered with in our rights by Austria, there would be no nation in Europe less prone to revolutionary spirit than the Hungarian. But that after all the heinous deeds perpetrated on us by Austria, and the revolting events of 1848, Hungary could no longer have any confidence in Austria. Russia could give the Poles at least the *prestige* of a great race as a substitute for the freedom they were deprived of, but Austria could give us nothing. . . . That we desired to become an *independent* state; but that the revolutionary spirit in us did not go beyond desiring the accomplishment of this cherished aspiration.

The past with its dire recollections often formed the subject of conversation between Ludvigh and the Russian Ambassador. Ludvigh asked what was really the object of the Russian intervention in 1849. The Ambassador replied it had no object. Nobody in Russia wished for war, nobody recommended it, and nobody approved of it. It was a whim of the Emperor Nicholas, "une politique de passion," which he regretted later on. There was a great deal of truth in the anecdote told of the Emperor Nicholas, who, pointing to the statue of King Szobieszki, the first deliverer of the House of Hapsburg, said, "imbecile number one," and then pointing to himself, "imbecile number two."

All the same, the Ambassador said that it was a mistake on our part to accept help from the Poles. Ludvigh replied that we had not accepted their help in order to make a demonstration against Russia, which was not at all our intention; but because we were accused of suppressing the Slavs, and because the treacherous revolt of the Croatians, who were in the pay of Vienna, was glorified as a "war of independence" by the Polish refugees in Paris; and that we had to disprove these accusations.

Writing on this subject to Ludvigh, I said, "Your answer is correct, but not complete. They tell me, in vain, that it was the help we accepted from the Poles that provoked the intervention. We are not so foolish as to believe this. There was not yet a single Pole in the Hungarian service in August, 1848, when the Russians invaded Moldavia and Wallachia, and Lord Palmerston wrote to Sir Stratford Canning :—' His Imperial Majesty the Czar has contemplated the possibility of his being called upon to assist Austria in restoring order at Pesth.' The idea of intervention had been accepted by the Congress of Verona (that is, it had been promised) before we were attacked. Jellasich received orders to take the offensive only when the Russians were standing ready close at hand. Vienna did not ask for help in 1849, but only sent word that the promised assistance *was wanted at that moment*. And, then, what did this acceptance of help from the Poles consist in? The number of the Poles in our service never reached 5,000; it was nothing but a small legion. Certainly it did not threaten the Russian Empire, and the Russians knew this very well. They knew also that I did not want to take many Poles into our army; further, that not only did I not wish, but that I decidedly objected to extend the seat of war into Poland; they knew, too, from their experience in Moldavia and Wallachia, how much we respected the rights of neighbouring nations, even when Turkish territory was made the basis of operations against us, in defiance of the law of neutrality. We must not accept too readily the reproach of having done wrong, if others, by such reproaches, wish to cover their own offences and the indignities they have committed against us."

Towards the end of March, 1859, while on the one hand European diplomacy tried to forestall complications by a congress, and Cavour on the other hand did everything in his power to bring matters to a rupture, I received such information as left no doubt whatever that it was intended, in case of war, to instigate my nation to insurrection, without giving any guarantees, and without sending an auxiliary force to Hungary. The scene of the revolution was to be Transylvania—so that, should it be put down, it should still have served to create a diversion. I also heard that among the Hungarian exiles there were some who favoured this project.

I do not think it necessary to trouble the English reader with any further details on this point. Suffice it to say that my suspicions were confirmed by Cavour himself when, in the presence of Alexander Bixio (at one time French Minister of Commerce), a warm supporter of our cause, he positively declared to my friend Szarvady, that the allies could not send an army to Hungary—" Il faut vous entendre avec les Roumains, et agir de ce côté-là " (meaning Transylvania): that they would help us with money and arms, but not with troops (March 29th).

I was terrified to think of the danger that threatened my country. It caused me pain to think that the blood and fate of my nation should be trifled with in this way, to serve, not their own, but somebody else's interest. I considered it a duty towards my country to prevent it if possible. I felt that I could do so. A warning to my friends in Hungary, and a caution published in the newspapers would have been sufficient; but in this case I should have to give up all hopes of future negotiations. I had to choose a way by which not only the danger that threatened my country would be removed, but also one which would prepare the way to an agreement that would serve the interests of Hungary.

To accomplish this, I wrote the subjoined declaration in French, so that the great powers could take cognisance of it as well:—

" DECLARATION.

" *London, March* 25*th*, 1859.

" The Italian question seems to be reserved for one of those congresses which, since 1815, have been the misfortune of nations, because, instead of solving the historical problems of our times, they have confined themselves to patching up accomplished facts, and, by trying to divert the natural course of historical events, have, thereby, rather aggravated the situation. A reaction is sure to set in, and the longer a settlement is deferred so much the more violent will such a reaction be.

"The powers wished for it and they shall have it. The logic of history cannot be belied.

"But as events sometimes take an unexpected course, and as I notice with astonishment that in certain 'high' quarters some fantastic ideas about our country are fostered, I think it advisable that at least my friends and compatriots should be well informed about my views on the subject.

"Allow me first to state the facts of the case:—

"I. It has been clearly demonstrated by our war of independence in 1848-49, that in any war against Austria the co-operation of our nation is not to be despised.

"When the war in Lombardy had come to an end by the surrender of arms at Milan, and when the revolts in Vienna and Prague had been put down, at a time, therefore, when Austria could freely dispose of the greatest part of her forces, she attacked us, the Hungarians, in the most treacherous manner. She instigated the Croatians, Servians, and Wallachians to civil war. These nationalities were reinforced by 40,000 men, recruited from the warlike people of the neighbouring Servia. Three of our most important fortresses were held by Austria. Pressed by the unexpected attack, we were obliged to withdraw behind the river Tisza, and, being deprived of nearly three-fourths of the whole territory of Hungary, were without trained soldiers, arms, ammunition, or money. And still such was the spirit manifested by our nation, and so abundant the resources of our country, that when by the universal consent of our nation I was placed at the head of affairs, a few weeks sufficed to organise efficiently a defence, so that, within a few months, we not only defeated five Austrian armies and drove the enemy from our country, but we also broke the power of Austria to such a degree that she was obliged to have recourse to Russian help, and by taking this step confessed to the whole of Europe that she was not able, by herself, to put down the Hungarian nation.

"And even Russia—the same Russia against which France, England, Sardinia, and Turkey carried on war, and, although employing their united forces, required more than a year to take a single town scarcely fortified—the very same Russia, I say, was obliged to mobilise her whole army, the Imperial Body-Guard included, and to send 200,000 men to combine with the remnants of the Austrian forces against our army, the ranks of which were thinned by our glorious but sanguinary victories; and even this was not sufficient, they were forced to have recourse to treason in order to defeat us.

"I repeat therefore: The co-operation of Hungary, in case of war against Austria, is a help not to be despised.

"II. The advantage of such a co-operation does not only consist in the fact that Austria's power would be attacked at its centre of gravity, and that 15,000,000 of her subjects would be turned into enemies, but also that the unity of her military organisation would be broken up, and her army stationed in Italy more or less dissolved; this army, subjected to strict discipline, would prove a much more formidable adversary than is generally supposed in certain high quarters.

"Fantastic ideas on such points are dangerous.

"Without the co-operation of Hungary, Austria's defeat in Italy is not certain, and still less easy.

"One mistake has already been committed by informing Austria beforehand of the approaching storm. An army of 150,000 to 200,000 men holding that famous strategical position between the Adige and the Mincio (which to-day is quite different from what it was either in 1796 or 1848), and having Verona for its base (which is to-day not a fortified town, but a fortified camp capable of holding 60,000 men, with safe and easy communication with Austria), must prove a powerful adversary not easily dislodged.

"And if, already, victory is neither certain nor easy to gain, the results of victory are very uncertain indeed, while Austria remains a first-class power in consequence of her possession of Hungary.

"There will not always be a large French army of relief stationed in Italy. Political situations may change. And supposing that Austria be driven out from Italy, she will reconquer her provinces upon the first favourable opportunity.

"The Austro-Italian question can only be definitely settled through the independence of Hungary.

"III. I positively state, with that confidence which I gain from the universal wish of our nation as expressed in the Declaration of independence, that the active co-operation of Hungary against Austria can be secured.

"But what is required to secure this co-operation?

"First of all it is necessary that any one who calls the nation to arms should enjoy the confidence of the mass of the people, not of one particular party or social class only.

"Otherwise the nation will not move.

"Napoleon I., at the head of his victorious army, stood at the frontiers of Hungary and called upon the nation to become independent. Not a single man moved. Why not? Because the nation had no confidence in the man who addressed them.

"It is true that many things have changed since that time. But one thing has not changed, which is, that if the man who speaks to the nation did not possess its confidence the nation would not respond. Isolated revolts, perhaps, could be produced (though even that is doubtful), but no revolution. And with regard to isolated revolts and insurrections, the lives of my compatriots would be wasted to no purpose. These lives are much too precious in my opinion for me to allow of their being sacrificed in vain. *I would prevent this sacrifice. It lies in my power to do so; I should consider it my duty to do it, and I would do it.*

"IV. The confidence of the nation being the essential factor of success, the question is, who possesses this confidence?

"I am not ambitious, but I possess the courage of the responsibility of my position, and my intentions are on a level with my duties. Facts remain facts, whether they meet with our approval or not. We must accept them, and acknowledge their philosophy.

"In whom is the confidence of the nation concentrated?

"History supplies the answer.

"The Declaration of independence, and the unanimous assent of the provinces and towns, give it.

"There may be personages who express personal opinions. But they have no right to speak in the name of the nation. Only the nation can give an answer to the question, and it has already done so. It would ill become me to recall the services on which the nation based its confidence. That confidence may or may not be well deserved, but its existence cannot be denied. Until I am physically or morally dead, my words more than those of any one else, can produce a response in the heart of the Hungarian nation.

"Now as regards foreign countries.

"For the last ten years the public opinion of Europe, especially that of England, has been looking upon me as the representative of the affairs of Hungary.

"This, too, is founded on the Declaration of independence.

"The British nation has accustomed itself to identifying my name with the aspirations of the Hungarian nation for independence. The fact is proved, beyond doubt, by the addresses voted to me by 128 towns (amongst them London), by the reception I meet with whenever I appear at a public meeting, and by the resolutions of sympathy and encouragement passed, and still being passed, at a great many meetings.

"If the British nation saw me at the head of a war of independence in Hungary, its sympathy would be assured to us beforehand, and I am in a position to make such popular demonstrations, all over England and Scotland, that there is no ministry which would dare to follow an Austrophile policy in the face of such energetic manifestations of the popular will.

"If, on the other hand, revolutionary attempts were made in Hungary without my participation, the British would look with suspicion upon those who thus trifled with the lives of an heroic nation (as was the case with the revolt in Milan, in 1853). And if, in reply to questions addressed to me, I answered that I considered such attempts as useless, and did not approve of them, the English people would attribute such movements to foreign intrigue, and would meet it with disapprobation, or at least indifference, instead of with sympathy, and would thus allow full scope to its government to follow its habitual Austrophile policy.

"V. I have described the situation, and will now proceed to state my opinions.

"I have often declared in public that whoever may carry on war against Austria, be he Emperor, King, or Sultan, a Christian or a Mahometan, will find me ready to join him and to treat with him in the name of my nation, provided that sufficient guarantees are offered to me that my nation will not be used as an instrument only for the attainment of alien objects that do not touch the interests of Hungary; but that, on the contrary, the independence of Hungary shall be considered to be one of the objects of the war, co-ordinate with the others. Provided, further, that the war is commenced on such a strategical plan and with such a combination of forces as to justify us to arrive at the conclusion that the independence of Hungary, as one of the results of the war, only depends on the energetic co-operation of the Hungarian nation.

"I have also several times stated in public that, though my sentiments are republican (and is it to be wondered at that such is the case, considering what we Hungarians have suffered at the hands of kings?), my country is dearer to me than any theories; and as the independence of the Hungarian nation is the greatest of all my desires, I shall always be ready to sacrifice my personal opinions, and to use all my influence to induce the Hungarians to accept whoever is recommended to them as their constitutional king, if by that means it should prove to be easier, safer, and require fewer victims to acquire, or rather to regain, national independence.

"But, on the other hand, I should be unworthy of the confidence the nation has reposed in me—in fact I should be a traitor to the cause of my country—if I did not watch to prevent the affairs of Hungary from being jeopardised in vain either by excessive confidence misplaced, by credulity produced by impatience, or by political calculations which would not hesitate to sacrifice the lives of a confiding nation without the latter being able to reap the benefit of its sacrifices.

"As far as we are personally concerned it cannot be denied that we are much pained to think that we might be compelled to live still longer in exile and perhaps even to die there; but the sufferings of individuals cannot be considered when the benefit of a nation is at stake. Our nation, however, can wait, for nations do not die.

"Even the defeat of the Hungarians is one of those grand events which augur a safe future. The nation now knows its own vitality. Through this knowledge, through the spirit of the nation, through the geographical position of our country, and through many other joint considerations, Hungary is destined to be an indispensable part of the Europe of the future: always supposing that she will not unnecessarily exhaust herself by wasting her best strength in rash enterprises, and that she will not bring on her own ruin by placing, like paid *condottieri*, her sword and blood at the disposal of men who wish to turn her discontent and bravery to their own account.

"The Hungarian nation must not come to what the Polish nation has come to in our own time, though that had well deserved a better fate.

"I shall, therefore, oppose with all my influence the misuse of Hungary.

"The Hungarian nation must not be used for making a diversion for the benefit of others, without a fair service being rendered to it in return; nor must it be led into ruin by insurrectionary attempts made on the strength of such vague promises as that their affairs will be taken into serious consideration afterwards.

"This must not happen. Should it be attempted I shall prevent it.

"Interest for interest, obligation for obligation. Loyalty is a characteristic of the Hungarian, and we have suffered too much not to find our discretion worthy of reliance.

"The situation is clear enough, and its logic is clear.

" In case of war I can offer, I do not say the only, but certainly the best, chance of securing the energetic co-operation of Hungary. I do not solicit favours, but I offer a service for a return service—help to others for help to ourselves. But I require guarantees for my country. Guarantees, not vague promises which have not the value of firm obligations.

" If it is desired to go without Hungary, let them go, but let it not be attempted to bring her into trouble by intrigues.

" If the co-operation of Hungary is sincerely desired, it is impossible that the giving of guarantees should be objected to, and there is no reason why the services of the very man who could give the best chance of success should be dispensed with.

" If it is wished to dispense with him, it is a sign that the intentions toward Hungary are not sincere. In this case it would be my duty to save my nation from disaster.

" I do not think I am called upon to enter into the details of the conditions which I think indispensable to our assuming obligations as to the co-operation of our country. I shall only point out three conditions, without which I not only could not give my name and assistance for procuring the co-operation of Hungary in the contemplated war, but would even use all my influence to prevent her participation.

" But lest those who do not know me should think that I allow myself to be influenced in my decisions by ambitious susceptibilities (those who know me will not suspect me of anything of the kind), I must give the reasons why I cannot act differently from the course I am determined upon.

" People in Hungary cannot know what was agreed upon at the negotiations, on the strength of which an appeal would be made to them.

" If they, therefore, responded to the appeal they would do so simply because they have confidence in the rectitude and wisdom of their leaders; and because they would believe that their lives would not be sacrificed without the independence of their country having been secured in return.

"My position is such that the greatest responsibility rests upon my shoulders, whether I have a hand in the appeal, or quietly allow others to call upon them to take up arms.

"If the appeal were made through me, the people would rise because they would place their confidence in my rectitude and wisdom. I, therefore, am responsible to them.

"But though I may keep silence, the people will nevertheless think that what happens has my approval, and is done under my superintendence. The responsibility rests therefore, in any case, on me.

"For this reason I am obliged to lay down the following three points as indispensable conditions:—

"1. As the responsibility rests with me, the leadership must also be vested in me. I can assume no responsibility for what others do.

"2. Agreements must be made with me, for, unless I have guarantees in my hands, I cannot be sure that the intentions entertained towards Hungary are sincere.

"3. No attempt to instigate to insurrection shall be made in Hungary until such a force of the allies has appeared there as can inspire reasonable confidence, and, also, can serve as a support till the national forces are organised. The French colours, by their appearance in Hungary, must identify themselves with the cause of Hungarian independence, before the Hungarian nation takes up arms. (This is one of the indispensable guarantees.)

"My friends (General Klapka included) know that I hold these views.

"But I hear with regret that in Paris, as well as in Turin, opinions prevail which are erroneous, to say nothing worse, for it appears they have put a wrong explanation on some assurances which can only have been made without my knowledge, and not in a sufficiently definite form.

"It is desirable that these opinions should no longer be held.

"If the above-mentioned three conditions should not be accepted as a basis of negotiations, which are as much in the interest of the allied powers as in that of Hungary, I should be obliged to think that the intentions towards Hungary are not sincere, and my sense of honour, patriotism, responsibility, and even common morality, would make it my duty to save my nation from the dangers into which it might be drifted.

" (Signed)   Kossuth."

I sent this declaration to my friend, Szarvady, with the request to find means of communicating it to Count Cavour, who at that time was staying in Paris to counteract diplomatic intrigues. With the assistance of Monsieur Bixio, the matter was so arranged that Cavour himself asked Szarvady to read to him my declaration, and when he had listened to the end of it, even asked for a copy of the same.

I give below a short extract of the report that Szarvady forwarded to me of his conversation with Cavour.

"*Paris, March 30th,* 1859.

"Cavour was visibly impressed by our conversation, and by your *exposé*. He finished by expressing himself thus:—' But still I do not see how we could *now* come to an agreement with Kossuth. I do not know whether, if I were a minister of the Emperor Napoleon, I could recommend him to write to Kossuth while Hübner is here. To do so would be a serious matter. As for myself, my position is just as delicate. Kossuth is intimately connected with Mazzini, who is our inexorable opponent; and he is one of those political opponents of mine whose party we might have annihilated, but with whom we could never agree. If Mazzini offered me his co-operation I should feel obliged to refuse it. With regard to Kossuth, I, personally, should be inclined to come to an agreement with him. However, I must point out that he is the editor of one of Mazzini's papers, at least his name figures amongst the contributors. Why does he not maintain a reserve? Why does he not definitely break off his relations with Mazzini? It would be easy enough to assign a reason for the step. He might say that he hopes, with the assistance of Sardinia, to regain the independence of his country, and that he longs for action. Who has done more than we either against the Austrians, or for Italian liberty? Did not the preservation and development of constitutional life in Sardinia inflict more damage upon Austria than all the insurrections instigated by Mazzini? And still Kossuth is hostile to us! So much I say from my own point of view. But please tell Kossuth that I sincerely wish for Hungary to be independent, and will do all that depends upon me to see it accomplished; but I must not forget that we do not stand alone. Mazzini is my political adversary, but of the Emperor he is the most obdurate personal enemy. Against him he sends hired assassins nearly every three months. And he does not even try to conceal this. It is a peculiar kind of madness. Kossuth is said to be Mazzini's friend. What impression would it have upon the Emperor under these circumstances if I spoke to him of Kossuth's intentions.' This is a very delicate matter.

"*Szarvady.*—'Permit me to state precisely the facts of the case. You complain that until now Kossuth has been in opposition to you. I have, only this minute, read Kossuth's declaration to you that whoever advances against Austria will find him ready to join hands with him. You have not yet attacked Austria; all that you have done was to establish and maintain a constitutional government *at home*. Our aspiration being to liberate our country from Austrian rule, we certainly could not consider as a successful attack upon Austria your establishment of a constitutional form of government in Piedmont, and we believed revolutionary means more likely to promote our cause effectually. Our endeavours were not opposed to yours; we might say that they were parallel. You went to work in the way of an existing, acknowledged, and firmly established government; we, on the other hand, could but avail ourselves of those revolutionary means which alone stood at our disposal. However, you have now taken a decided initiative; if it leads to any result, we shall be ready to assist you, provided that we receive proper guarantees. There are no obligations of any kind to prevent Kossuth, or us, or our country from joining you, since now the lines on which you and we work, instead of running parallel, seem to converge. Having spoken so openly and wishing to prevent all misunderstanding, I must also remark that it is not at all on your account that we must so much insist on receiving guarantees. You possess the confidence of all those who are fortunate enough to have the pleasure of knowing you. But you yourself have mentioned that you do not stand alone. We, too, must not lose sight of this. We wish to have it made clear to our consciences, to our countrymen, and before posterity, that we did not recommend our country to make the enormous sacrifices which an insurrection costs without having proper guarantees. Were these not secured, the curse of those who had been so frivolously sacrificed would rest upon us. Your Excellency being a statesman will consider what is best to be done. I deem it my duty also to tell you that there is a party in Hungary (it is true a small party as regards numbers, but not so as regards the position of its members) who would like to benefit by the difficulties which are at present perplexing Austria's statesmen, in order to obtain some concessions. Austria would like to see our nation again playing the same part it played in the time of Maria Theresa. Not long ago a minister* of the Government of 1848 published a pamphlet, justifying the standpoint of this party. This circumstance makes it more important that, if we act, we should do so with all our forces. For this reason it is absolutely necessary that Kossuth should stand at the head of the movement. He can bring together all our forces. Without him any sort of movement will be impossible.'

"Cavour repeated that he quite saw the importance of my communications. He asked me to hand him a copy of your *exposé*, and said that in case I had anything to tell him, I was to write to him direct, and that M. Bixio would hand him my letters.

"I must also state, that in the course of our conversation Cavour also said:—' Before you act you must make sure of the good inten-

* Bartholomew Szemere.

tions of Russia, for you must not reckon now on the Turks. They go with Austria.'

"*Szarvady.*—' I do not think that we have anything to fear from the Russians at present.'

"*Cavour.*—' But bear in mind that the Russians are like the Greeks: it is most difficult to know what they think, whatever they may say.'

" (Signed)   SZARVADY."

In reply to this report of M. Szarvady my answer ran partly thus:—

"What you said to Cavour about the relations subsisting between Mazzini and myself is on the whole correct. I certainly will never disown the existence of these relations; but as a matter of fact I may say that Cavour is not accurately informed. I was never editor of any of Mazzini's papers. My name does not, and cannot appear in the list of regular contributors. My whole connection with the paper in question consisted in my having, at the request of Mazzini, written two articles for publication in it, or rather one article extending over two numbers, under the title of 'Retrospect and Prospect.' That was before the present warlike times, but since these complications have arisen I have not written a single line, and my name does not appear in any list of names. If M. Bixio would be kind enough to inform Count Cavour on this subject, he would oblige me by pointing it out to him that I think it strange that my relations to Mazzini should be brought forward as a great obstacle, for up to the present I have not been fortunate enough to feel that I was under any obligation to Piedmont. In 1851 the Government of Turin refused outright the advances I made to them through the agency of an Englishman. They even made a treaty with Austria for the extradition of our deserters, and, much to my regret, carried it out.

"With no prospect of aid from any of the governments in liberating our country, I naturally sought assistance in the solidarity of European revolution: and nobody would break off his connections without a reason.

"Let the Government of Turin join hands with us, let them assist us to regain the independence of Hungary, and Mazzini himself will find it a matter of course that I accept the co-operation of any one who gives me help towards the accomplishment of our project. I have told Mazzini over and over again that I am always ready to act thus.

"(Signed) KOSSUTH."

With regard to what Cavour said, that it would be a delicate matter to speak to the Emperor about my intentions, he himself disproved the truth of his remark. For there is no doubt that he had spoken to the Emperor on the subject, and spoken so much that when Count Ladislaus Teleki, who had been the diplomatic representative of Hungary in Paris since 1848, and whom I had requested to acquaint Prince Napoleon with my *exposé*, went to see the Prince for this purpose, both the Prince and the Emperor knew it already.

The perusal of my *exposé*, at any rate, made it clear to Count Cavour, to Prince Napoleon, and, through him, to the Emperor of the French, that they would reckon in vain on the assistance of Hungary for the attainment of their own ends only, since it was in my power to prevent it, and I had resolved to prevent it.

Many things have changed since. Hungary has become Cislaithania,—I myself, a refugee before, have now become an outcast—but even now it is a consolation to me to think, that I have been able to save my country from the dangers of falling a prey to foreign interests.

Yet this was only a negative result. I did not expect to become certain as to the attainability of the positive result towards which my efforts were directed, until the question had been decided whether there would be a congress, followed by peace—or whether there would be war.

The latter was so uncertain up to the last moment that even the parties interested did not know what they were about.

Now, when reading the diplomatic documents with that calmness which is brought about by a lapse of twenty years, one cannot but smile to see the different aspects under which the same thing presented itself to different diplomatists—smile to see how positive a fact it is that it is not the custom in diplomatic circles to speak the truth—smile to see how little even those most intimately acquainted with the subject (Cavour himself included) knew what really would happen.

On March 31st Lord Malmesbury telegraphed to Lord Augustus Loftus, the English Ambassador at Vienna, that Cavour had used such passionate and violent language in Paris as to intimate that he would have war in spite of the congress.

On the other hand Sir James Hudson, English Ambassador at Turin, informed Lord Malmesbury on April 3rd that Cavour had returned from Paris in a very peaceable and conciliatory frame of mind, and that he confidently hoped that the congress would go far to put an end to the discontent in Italy. According to Sir James, therefore, Cavour put faith and hope in the congress, the very idea of which he hated, and the meeting of which he made every endeavour to prevent—and actually succeeded in preventing. Sir James also sent the gratifying intelligence to Lord Malmesbury that Cavour was very much pleased that the Tory Ministry had not sent in its resignation, in consequence of the vote of the House of Commons on the Parliamentary Reform Bill,—because, I suppose, he was glad to see the Tories in power, as they were such decided friends of Austria, and made it their leading principle that the possessions of Austria in Italy were sacred and were not to be touched!!

Lest anything should be wanting to the completeness of the diplomatic reports, Lord Cowley, writing from Paris on April 5th, informed his government that Count Walewski had given him the most positive assurances that Cavour had not succeeded in shaking the Emperor in his resolution to preserve peace. Cavour on the other hand had written to General Lamarmora on March 29th:—

" The Italian question was, through mistakes and unfortunate circumstances, as badly introduced as possible. I will explain everything on my return to Turin. Meanwhile, I give you my impressions of the situation here.

" War is inevitable.

" It will be retarded for *at least two months*.

" War will be carried on *not only on the Po, but also on the Rhine*.

" We must make every possible effort to ensure a fortunate issue of the war with regard to Piedmont and Italy. The French, drawn into the war against their inclinations, would never forgive us (Piedmont) if they had to bear the lion's share of the undertaking. It would be unfortunate for us if we were victorious by French help only. In case of a general war, we could save our country only by fighting better, and having more men under arms than the French."

Such was Cavour's view of the situation. As we know, no general war did take place, there were no battles on the Rhine, hostilities were not postponed for two months, the Italians did not fight better than the French—they fought equally well,—nor did they make greater efforts, nor did they put a larger number of men under arms—in fact, they did not put nearly as many. . . Then the result, too, was different from what they had expected. The most peculiar circumstance was, that in spite of all secret treaties, in spite of the proclamations promising liberation to the Italians "from the Alps to the Adriatic," and in spite of the negotiations carried on with us, which indicated an intention of finally breaking Austria's power: in spite of all this, the result of the war was exactly what had been predicted to my friend, Daniel Irányi, as far back as Dec. 7th, 1858, by Mieroslawszky, the Polish general.* A Polish refugee, therefore, discerned the fate of the "personal policy" more clearly than the whole diplomacy of Europe! . . It is thus that great events are produced! It is thus that history is written! And diplomacy is such a trustworthy profession! "Soyons plutôt maçons" we may say with the French.

The outlines I gave of the origin of the war in Chapter I. render it unnecessary that I should continue to reproduce the correspondence carried on during the daily changes in the aspect of political affairs up to the outbreak of hostilities.

At last the war broke out. It must be noticed, however, that the immediate cause for the commencement of hostilities was too trifling to have been foreseen.

When, through the unremitting efforts of the English Government, nearly all the obstacles which

* See p. 90.

stood in the way of the meeting of a congress had been removed, Cavour, in April, 1859, sent the Marquis Massimo d'Azeglio to London.

The English Secretary of State for Foreign Affairs hoped that D'Azeglio might have been sent on a special mission to make such a fair proposal from Sardinia as would lead to the solution of the difficulties.*

He was not a little annoyed, it appears, to find that D'Azeglio had not been entrusted with any special mission, but had been sent only to acquaint himself thoroughly with the feelings of the English Government in general.†

It appears to me that the Sardinian envoy did not think he was called upon to take the English Secretary of State for Foreign Affairs into his confidence as to what the real object was for which he had been sent to London; for his instructions were, not to bring matters to a peaceful issue, but rather to throw difficulties in the way of the congress, the meeting of which had almost become unavoidable owing to the pressure the English Government brought to bear upon the other powers. D'Azeglio was successful in his mission. The greatest difficulty which prevented the congress from meeting was the demand of Austria, obstinately persisted in, that Sardinia should first disarm.

This question passed through several different phases: simultaneous disarmament of Austria and Sardinia ; guarantee to Sardinia against external attacks ; *general* disarmament, including France, &c.

* Malmesbury to Loftus in Vienna, April 14th, 1859.
† Malmesbury to Cowley in Paris, April 21st, 1859.

Cavour, pressed hard on all sides, answered at last (April 17th), by the advice of Prince Napoleon (who, on this occasion also, was a strong supporter of the policy of Piedmont against that of Count Walewski), that, following the example of France, he would accept the idea of a general disarmament, provided that Sardinia should be allowed to participate in the congress on an equal footing with the Great Powers—but not unless.

The English Government also endeavoured to overcome the difficulty by proposing that the disarmament on the part of Austria, France, and Sardinia should be "preliminary, general, real, and simultaneous;" that this disarmament should be carried out by six commissioners, one to be named by each of the Great Powers and one also by Sardinia; that, directly upon the meeting of this commission, the congress should be opened by the five Great Powers and the discussion on the political questions commenced; that the representatives of the Italian states (and of course among them that of Sardinia) should be invited, as soon as the congress was opened, to participate in the discussions on an equal footing with the representatives of the Great Powers, as was the case at the Congress of Laibach in 1821.

This proposal was made on April 19th, and "les télégrammes se succèdent avec rapidité," as Pelissier (Malakoff) expressed it. The French Government accepted the proposal without hesitation (April 20th), and pressed the Government of Turin very much to accede to it also. The Sardinians were forced to yield, but they had one ray of hope still left. Piedmont had about 12,000 volunteers under arms who had flocked thither from all parts of Italy. Cavour instructed D'Azeglio to represent to the English Government that to disarm these 12,000 men and to turn them into the streets would simply mean to give the signal for insurrection in Italy. That this not being a political question, but one of public order and tranquillity, these men should therefore not be included in the disarmament. And this representation had the desired effect upon the English Government, who wrote to Vienna stating categorically that they could not advise Sardinia to agree to the disarmament of these men.

This was like pouring oil on the fire of Austria's passion. The Government of Vienna said that they could not sit down at the same table with Sardinia, and what they wanted was the disarmament of Sardinia without any conditions. *The volunteers must also be disbanded. Austria insisted upon it.* They sent an ultimatum to Turin—and no congress met, but war broke out.

While peace and war were swaying in the balance of fate, as often as the probability of war weighed the scale down, I found that overtures were made to me. I was asked what I was doing? whether I would be inclined to do this or that? whether I would not state my wishes in the form of a note? The communications with Prince Napoleon, through Bixio, were continually kept up, and Bixio kept me always well informed, through Szarvady, how matters stood, and through the same channel kept himself *au courant* regarding my views. On going to Prince Napoleon on April 29th, Bixio met Count Ladislaus Teleki and General Klapka in the waiting-room. Teleki, after having spoken a few words to Klapka in Hungarian, turned to Bixio and said,

" Our differences of opinion are put aside, and we are perfectly ready to act with Kossuth."

Bixio replied with congratulations, and entering the apartment of the Prince, asked him whether he had considered the affairs of Hungary, and whether he did not think that the time had arrived when Kossuth should be invited to come personally to Paris?

The Prince spoke with the greatest sympathy for Hungary. He felt that the decisive moment had come very near, but that he could not yet speak with such certainty as we might wish. He wished to be able to say, not merely that he was doing everything in his power to procure consideration for the affairs of Hungary, but also how far the Emperor was willing to go. On this point, he said, he could not yet give a final answer.

This happened on April 29th, and the result of the kind interest shown by the Prince was that, on May 3rd, Count Ladislaus Teleki, George Klapka, Count Gregory Bethlen, and Nicholas Puky left Paris for London. Teleki and Klapka informed me that, with the consent and knowledge of the Emperor, they were entrusted by the Prince to invite me to a personal conference at Paris.

I conferred with my friends about the conditions on which I was inclined to come to an agreement with the French in reference to the participation of Hungary in the war.

My friends agreed with my views. I accepted the invitation. We started the same evening for Paris.

I travelled under the name of George Brown, and arrangements had been made that I should not meet with unnecessary inquiries or difficulties.

CHAPTER III.

My Journey to Paris May 3rd–8th, 1859—Preliminary Conference with Prince Napoleon on May 5th.

ON my arrival in Paris, I called upon the Prince, accompanied by Ladislaus Teleki and General Klapka. After the customary exchange of civilities we sat down, and the Prince thanked me, in his own name and in that of the Emperor, for having accepted their invitation. He then stated that the decision upon war with Austria was one of great importance; that the Emperor wished the Hungarian nation to avail itself of this opportunity to regain its independence, and that he was willing to help us to achieve that end; that we should therefore discuss this subject without reserve; that I should let him know my views; whether I would be disposed to co-operate in this matter, and, if so, under what conditions. The Prince said that he would report our conference to the Emperor, and trusted that his report might be such as to induce the Emperor to assure me personally that he agreed with my views. He begged me to rest assured that he (the Prince) had the greatest sympathy for Hungary, and that he would feel happy if by his mediation he could, in the interest of the brave Hungarian nation, promote our understanding with the Emperor.

Kossuth.—" I accept with gratitude Your Highness's statement, and express my thanks for the sympathy you have deigned to express for my country; I attach much value to it, for sympathy coming from a man in Your Highness's position may prove a blessing to my country. But permit me to hope that Your Highness will agree with me, that in politics, after all, interests decide. I therefore lay the greatest stress upon the fact that the Emperor, upon his determination to take up the Italian question (the origin of so many troubles) and in order to satisfy the legitimate aspirations of the Italian nation, has decided upon war with Austria; that, in this noble enterprise, our interests meet; and that thus we have an enemy in common. If, by the powerful co-operation of the Emperor, it became possible for the Hungarian nation to resume the war of independence, interrupted by an intervention contrary to all international right, the Emperor would thereby make the campaign much easier for himself, and change the possibility of victory into a certainty. By the independence of Hungary, he would acquire stability for the result for which the war has been undertaken. For even if Austria were driven out of Italy, there is no doubt that on the first favourable opportunity she would return thither, if, by remaining mistress of Hungary, she retained the resources of that country at her disposal for the furtherance of her ambitious designs. The independence of Hungary is as necessary a complement and guarantee of the independence of Italy against Austria, as the war of independence in Hungary is the greatest help in the struggle for Italian independence. I consider our identity of interests as our starting-point; but, just for this very reason, I could only come to an understanding with Your

Highness and the Emperor if I were sufficiently assured that, in the policy pursued by the Emperor, Hungary were to be looked upon not as a means only, but also as an object—a co-ordinate object—of the war. Before I, therefore, proceed in my statement, permit me to ask for an explanation regarding the intentions of the Emperor towards Hungary."

The Prince.—"The Emperor's intention is that Hungary should become an independent state. He entertains no other. He will respect the sovereign right of Hungary to decide upon her own affairs. He does not wish to interfere with her internal affairs. He has only one stipulation, namely, that you should adopt, not a Republican form of government, but a Constitutional Monarchy. As you negotiate and treat with monarchs, I hope you will find this natural."

Kossuth.—"Very natural. Besides, a Constitutional Monarchy quite agrees with the traditional feelings of my nation. The entire past of Hungary has been monarchical, and the events of a thousand years leave a deep impression on the national character. I am a Republican myself, but first of all I am a patriot. I place my country above my theories. My opinion is that interests must be classed according to their importance. The Hungarian question is the question whether Hungary shall exist as a state or not. This is the most important point, to which every other consideration is subordinate. The form of government is a question of minor significance. Guided by this consideration, I myself proposed, in 1849, that our Declaration of independence should pronounce that, as regards the definitive settlement of our form of government, we should conform ourselves to the exigencies of the European situation. This proposal was unanimously adopted by the nation. The exigencies of the European situation, and especially the fact of our alliance with monarchs decidedly point to a Constitutional Monarchy. I, therefore, accept this stipulation of the Emperor without reserve, and can assure Your Highness that my nation will do the same with general consent. Still, to be able to prepare public opinion in our country, I should like to know upon whom the Emperor would most wish our choice of a king to fall."

The Prince.—"The Emperor leaves this entirely to your own discretion. He has no special wish in the matter."

Kossuth.—"Of course the wish to dispose of the crown of Hungary cannot enter our minds for an instant. We have no right to do so. But I know my nation. I know that gratitude is one of their national characteristics. If, as a consequence of our present negotiations, Hungary should become independent, this would be ascribed to the protection of the Emperor, and this again to the mediation of Your Highness. I cannot refrain from expressing my conviction that my nation would offer the crown of St. Stephen to Your Highness."

Upon this the Prince, who sat with me at a small table, rose, and making a deep bow said,—"I am sensible of the honour you do me, and thank you very much. But I must request you not to mention this again to me, or to the Emperor when you will speak with him. We Bonapartes have learnt much from the history of our uncle. We have learnt not only what we must, but also what we must not, do. We know that members of our family must not accept foreign thrones, for that might lead to a European coalition against us. Permit me to say that the French Imperial throne is such as not to allow us to risk its possession to our family even for the sake of the illustrious crown of St. Stephen.* Therefore do not let us mention the subject again; let us leave it and pass on to practical subjects. Tell me what you wish, what you require to put the Hungarian nation under arms again, in order that they may make use of the Italian war to resume their struggle for national independence?"

Kossuth.—"Well, I obey Your Highness's commands. Let us leave the cares of the future to the future. Let us consider the practical side of the question. Permit me to state, Monseigneur, what my position is, in order to make the situation quite clear. My past, I believe, is sufficiently well known to Your Highness to make it unnecessary for me to prove that, without my co-operation, although isolated outbreaks might be attempted—but only attempted—in Hungary, it would be impossible to induce people to rise in sufficient numbers to give the movement the force of a national revolution. This is the natural consequence of past events, which I could not alter even if I wished. And while I live, and do not nullify myself politically or morally, the question of Hungarian independence is, and will remain, so completely identified in the feelings of the people of Hungary with my name and person, that if, without my assent, they were called upon to take up arms, the summons would doubtless be received by the masses with hesitation and distrust. People would say,—'The thing is suspicious.

* See note at the end of the chapter in reference to this subject.

Why does not Kossuth take part in it? It cannot be right. Let us await what he says to it.'

"That such is the situation is also the conviction of my friends who are present, and who have initiated the negotiations with Your Highness and the Government of Turin. I do not think I am wrong in my supposition that I owe it to the right conception of the situation that I—to whom the Continent has been shut up until now—have at this moment the pleasure of conferring with Your Highness in Paris.

Your Imperial Highness will but accord me justice in believing that, having no personal motives to gratify, I am far from being so ambitious as to long for the position I hold; on the contrary, I consider it a heavy burden, because of the responsibilities it carries with it. Yet I consider it my duty, as an honest patriot, not to hesitate in accepting this position; for I am convinced that until somebody else will succeed to my place, as the man in whom the people repose their confidence, nobody else will be able to gather so much strength round the banner of independence as I can.

"After having said so much to make the situation clear, I need hardly add that this state of affairs throws a heavy responsibility upon me. If there is anybody in the world who must not frivolously risk the lives and fate of my nation, it is myself. It would be unpardonable villainy on my part if, simply to gratify the natural aspirations of an exile, I were to abuse the confidence placed in me by my nation and bring disaster upon my country. It is my imperative duty to save my nation— which has suffered, and is still suffering, so much—from being dragged with no palpable object into such a movement as would only increase its sufferings, and from an unsuccessful insurrection that might compromise its future for a long time to come—possibly for ever. I could only give my assistance for creating a revolution in Hungary if I could in good faith say to my nation: 'See, we have so arranged the situation for you, and have procured you such favourable chances, that the attainment of your independence depends solely upon your own determination.'

"My friends Teleki and Klapka entirely concur in this view. And, therefore, to the question of Your Highness as to what we wish and what we require in order to induce our nation to participate in the war against Austria by resuming its struggle of independence, I answer, in my own name, as well as in that of my friends who are here present, and, further, in the name of all the Hungarian exiles—I may even say in the name of the whole Hungarian nation—that, first of all and above everything else, we want a material guarantee that the instigating of Hungary to insurrection is not solely intended to make a diversion in order to weaken Austria's force in Italy and thereby to facilitate victory in that country; we want a guarantee that the Emperor and King Victor Emmanuel look upon the independence of Hungary as an object of this war co-ordinate with the object of Italy, and that they should give proof of it by deeds before God and the world; we want an assurance that if Hungary takes up arms against Austria on this understanding she will not be left in the lurch, and that in case of victory no peace shall be concluded with regard to Italy without

Hungary being liberated from the rule of Austria and made an independent state.

"We must look upon these assurances as a condition *sine quâ non*, and deem it our patriotic duty to state to Your Highness that this is our irrevocable resolution. Only on this condition can we offer to co-operate so far as to induce our nation to rise in arms against Austria.

"Should the Emperor think that he cannot give us these guarantees, we should be very much grieved that we were not allowed to make use of this opportunity, but, retiring into the obscurity of our exile, we shall find consolation in the knowledge that, though we may not have been able to assist our country, at least we saved her from being drawn into misfortune for alien objects."

Teleki and Klapka declared that they entirely concurred in what I had said.

Prince Napoleon listened with the greatest attention and with apparent emotion, and, after a short pause, replied, "The feelings to which you have just given expression do honour to your patriotism, but I must remind you of what I have already stated—that it is the firm intention of the Emperor that this war shall also lead to the independence of Hungary; and I think that if the Emperor personally assures you of his intervention that will be sufficient to alleviate your scruples."

Kossuth. "It certainly would, if it were a personal question only. We would, without hesitation, place our fate in the hands of the Emperor. But the question is that of our country. We must consider the interests of our country, and to do this we need facts which may induce our nation to share in our acquiescence. We are extremely glad to be assured of benevolent intentions towards Hungary by such a powerful monarch as the Emperor of the French; but we cannot help remembering that in the history of the Hungarian wars of independence similar good intentions of the Tuileries are not unknown, but that they have never been realised, and this not because the intentions were not sincere and firm, but because the altered circumstances were not considered favourable to their realisation. The same thing might happen now. Nobody can foresee what turn events will take. But it would be a terrible misfortune to our country, not only grave in its effects at the present, but seriously compromising to its whole future, if on the strength of these intentions we were to open the floodgates of revolution, and then, when the torrent could no longer be arrested, the situation should change so far that the Emperor could not find it prudent to engage in the realisation of his noble project. It rests with His Majesty the Emperor to consider whether he can engage in such a realisation. What we wish, and what we also consider our duty to urge, is that we should be called upon to initiate revolution in Hungary only at the moment and on the condition that the Emperor thinks the time has arrived for carrying out his benevolent intentions towards our country, and does not meet with any difficulty in giving to our country proper guarantees on those points which I have had the pleasure of enumerating."

The Prince. " And what are those guarantees ? "

Kossuth. " They are—

" 1. To unfurl the French flag in Hungary in

company with such a military force as the Emperor shall judge strong enough to protect the honour of that flag.

"2. In connection with the appearance of this flag and army the Emperor shall publish a proclamation to the Hungarian nation, in which he shall say that, being at war with Austria, and having accepted the Hungarians as his confederates, he sends an army to Hungary as a friend and ally. He does so to help the Hungarians to carry into effect their Declaration of independence of 1849, which—though its operation may have been temporarily suspended by an intervention, undertaken against all international law—the Emperor of the French, who is proud of the fact that his own throne rests on the will of the people, considers as being in full force, since the Hungarian nation, after a glorious war (by which it clearly demonstrated its capacity to exist as an independent state), making use of its sovereign will, unanimously declared that the House of Hapsburg had lost all claim to the throne, and that Hungary had become an independent state. The proclamation should further say that this declaration has never been revoked by any other declaration of the people.

"These are the conditions on the acceptance of which, alone, we can offer our co-operation. We can assure Your Highness that if these guarantees were given to our nation, we would lead into Hungary, provided we received permission and means to do so, under the protection of French colours, and accompanied by French troops, an army composed of Hungarian refugees, prisoners of war, and those who have deserted on Italian soil. And on the strength of the Emperor's proclamation we would call our nation to arms. In a short time (for we have some little experience in rapid organisation) we should be able to co-operate for the Emperor's success with an army of some hundred thousand brave and enthusiastic men, backed by a whole nation. This rising would be the decisive blow to our common enemy, even independently of the fact that the rise of our people would cause dissolution in the Austrian ranks.

"With these guarantees we could calmly look forward to all contingencies, not only because the powerful Emperor of the French and his Italian ally had identified themselves, in the face of the whole world, with the question of the independence of Hungary (and this identification would animate our nation to wonderful exertions, and would place our struggle *ipso facto* under the protection of international law), but, also, because in such a case—but only in such a case—we should quickly be enabled to place Hungary in such a position that she could say, 'Come what may, we are masters of our own destiny.'

"One thing more, Your Highness. In a proclamation which we should issue with reference to the Emperor's proclamation, we should of course inform the nation that until a government could be formed (and we should invite them to constitute one) the administration of the country would be carried on by a commission, under the presidency of the man whom the nation, in its declaration of independence, appointed Governor of Hungary. For practical reasons, in case our proposals should meet with acceptance, it would be desirable that this should also be mentioned in the Emperor's proclamation."

The Prince. "It appears to be not only desirable, but even necessary, that this should be done in the event of your proposals being accepted. But I must mention that the Emperor would not like to have to deal with a numerically large commission, for, of course, the matter must remain confidential, and I, therefore, hope that we shall only have to do with you three. Have you any other wish?"

Kossuth. "It would greatly contribute to dispel our apprehensions to know that we have nothing to fear from foreign intervention."

The Prince. "I think that you have nothing to fear on this score. Certainly not Russian intervention. Care has been taken of that, I can positively assure you."

Kossuth. "What remains for us to request is material assistance, in the shape of money and arms. We are poor refugees, and cannot, in our present position, have recourse to the money market. If the Emperor decides to let my nation participate in the war on the basis I have laid down, I believe he himself will find it desirable that we should come forth as thoroughly equipped as possible. I must confess that we want help in money and arms, not only to enable us to organise a force abroad, but also for the equipment of our national army, which we would organise at home, and also for its maintenance at the beginning of the campaign, until we should be enabled to avail ourselves of the resources of our country. Of course assistance given to us under this head would form a national debt, and its settlement would form part of the details of our agreement. While we throw ourselves on the benevolence of the Emperor in this respect, I will only mention that for the success of our preparations we may want the protection of the Emperor not only in Piedmont (where difficulties might be thrown in our way by the administration), but also in the states on the south-eastern borders of Hungary. I mean in Servia and Moldavo-Wallachia. I need not explain to Your Highness the importance these states have in our eyes."

The Prince. "If we agree on the chief points, I do not think there will be any difficulty with the rest. I shall now at once make a report of our conference to the Emperor. I need hardly say that my report will not only be correct but also sympathetic. If the Emperor is inclined to accept your views he will certainly wish to speak to you, and if so, most likely this evening. Where are you to be found?"

Kossuth. "I dine with Colonel Nicholas Kiss, in the Rue St. Dominique, and shall also spend the evening there. I shall there await Your Highness's commands."

The Prince. "I know where Colonel Kiss lives. If the Emperor wishes to see you I will come myself to fetch you, and will introduce you to him."

He did so. At about 11 o'clock at night the Prince came for me to the house of Colonel Kiss, and we drove together to the Tuileries. In the salon which is decorated with trophies, in the form of banners, and opens into the study of the Emperor, the Prince hurried forward a few steps to announce me. The Emperor at once came to the door to meet me, cordially shook hands with me, adding the usual "charmé de faire votre connaissance." We all three sat down, (the Emperor, the Prince, and myself); orders were given to the door-keeper not to allow anybody to interrupt us; and we talked together for nearly two hours.

Conference with the Emperor Napoleon III. in the night of May 5th, 1859.

The Emperor commenced the conversation by saying that I perhaps still felt hurt because when I returned from Asia Minor he did not permit me to disembark at Marseilles, and to travel through France. He begged me to believe that it caused him pain, but that he was obliged to act as he had done, because there was just at that time a general excitement in the country, and perhaps hundreds of thousands might have followed me to Paris, and some of them might have used the opportunity to create unpleasant disturbances.

I assured the Emperor that I had long since forgotten that little unpleasantness. It did no harm to my country. Altogether it had no other effect than that of making me a little sea-sick, which was my own fault. Why was I such a bad sailor? As we talked of the past I asked to be permitted to say, that greater than this was the pain caused to me by the frustration of the patriotic hopes which I had attached to the late Eastern war. This disappointment, however, belonged to the past, hope to the present. What did not happen then might come to pass now, in consequence of our apparent identity of interests; and the Emperor might be assured that if I should have the good fortune to behold in him the deliverer of my poor, suffering country, he might always reckon on the most sincere and thankful devotion, not only of myself, but of every Hungarian.

The Emperor. "I trust with all my heart that

I may be able to realise your patriotic hopes. I have such intentions, and assure you that I shall do everything in my power to bring about what you wish. But much depends upon circumstances. In politics we must take these into consideration. The Prince has reported your views to me. I understand that you promise the co-operation of Hungary in the war on two conditions. One of them is, that I should extend the seat of war from the banks of the Po to those of the Danube and Theiss. The other is, that the appearance of my troops in Hungary should be heralded by a proclamation, in which (referring to the Declaration of the independence of Hungary in 1849) I should, as friend and ally, call upon your nation to realise its declaration, by taking up arms against our common foe. Have I rightly comprehended your views?"

Kossuth. " Precisely, Sire, and I am sure that His Imperial Highness was too conscientious an interpreter of the motives which lead me to these conditions to render it necessary that I should repeat them."

The Emperor. "It is not necessary. The prince was your true interpreter; he was more, he was your advocate, '*Il a plaidé votre cause chaleureusement.*' I appreciate your motives. I have considered the matter. As regards the proclamation, there will not be much difficulty in that, if the other point, the sending of an army, is fulfilled. The thing is not without a precedent in the history of my House." (He stepped to the table and took up a parchment-roll.) "Here is the original draft of the proclamation addressed by my uncle to the Hungarian nation in 1809. Do you know it?"

Kossuth. "Yes, indeed! Almost by heart. ' L'Empereur d'Autriche, infidèle à ses traités, méconnaissant la générosité. . . . .' "

The Emperor. "That is right. You have a good memory.—I, therefore, have a precedent to go by, and I shall take no exception to the fact that this proclamation led to no result at that time. Circumstances were different then. What happened in 1848-49 has entirely changed the situation. Besides, I should have the support of Hungarian patriots who are trusted by their nation. My uncle did not enjoy this advantage. We could, therefore, consider this point as settled, if the other question, that of sending an army, were settled; on which, of course, the former entirely depends. And I must confess that this question of sending an army presents great difficulties to me. The chief obstacle is England. The Tory Government now in power manifests a decidedly hostile attitude towards my enterprises even as regards Italy. They cling to the treaties of 1815, which others besides myself have torn to tatters long ago. For, you see, those treaties proscribed the Napoleons, and I am here at this moment. However, they are good enough to serve as pretexts to conceal evil intentions. You may imagine what the Tories would do were I to extend the war to the Danube, if they behave in the way they do while there is a question of Italy only. To extend the war so far would mean to strike out for ever the Austrian dynasty from the list of the Great Powers, and the English Government clings obstinately to that dynasty. The antiquated notion that the existence of the House of Hapsburg as a Great Power is essential to the maintenance of the European equilibrium is one of the traditional maxims of English policy. I have reason to believe that England would even be capable of actually intervening against me—and that I cannot risk. Please take this into consideration."

The Prince (interrupting). "But, sire, could we not win England over to our side? England has great interests in the East. Say, if we were to offer her the prospect of the possession of Constantinople?"

The Emperor (lighting a cigarette over the lamp). "Il ne faut jamais vouloir l'impossible."

Kossuth. "And that really is 'impossible;' besides, I do not think we want it. Excuse the question, Sire, but what is it Your Majesty desires of England? Do you wish that she should be your ally, as in the Crimea, and actively participate in the war?"

The Emperor. "No, I do not dream of it; I only wish that her neutrality could be made sure of."

Kossuth. "I presume, Sire, that as soon as matters had been brought to a crisis by the Austrian ultimatum (which reads like a declaration of war), Your Majesty's Government took steps in London to ascertain what position England intends taking up, in case your Majesty should participate in the war. May I ask whether your Majesty has not yet received some reassuring official reply from England?"

The Emperor. "No; no answer has as yet arrived to such a note of my Government as you refer to."

Kossuth. "No doubt the present English Government would very much like to help Austria. Having regard to English public opinion, however, they cannot well go so far as to lead England into war out of pure friendship to Austria; at least not until they can point to an actual violation of some direct interest of their country. For this reason I should not be at all surprised if the English government in their reply were to hold out a prospect of neutrality."

The Emperor. "I myself think that this is likely to happen. But, considering the aims they pursue by their policy, I shall not feel satisfied as long as England's policy remains in the hands of the present Government."

Kossuth. "Your Majesty's distrust is well founded. The problem therefore would be, to overthrow the ministry of Lord Derby, and to do so just on the question of its foreign policy. The place of the Tories should be taken by the Whigs, on such an understanding as would entirely secure the neutrality of England. As your Majesty wishes only this much from England, permit me to declare that I will take upon myself the task to carry this into effect."

The Emperor. "What do you mean? Do you really think that you can do this?"

Kossuth. "Yes, Sire, I believe I can. Pray do not regard my words as mere extravagant boasting. I am only a poor exile, whose sphere of action is very limited, and certainly do not dream of being able to direct England's policy, but I know the position of the parties; I am on a friendly footing with the personages who can bring this about; and I hope I shall be able to persuade them to do it. With your Majesty's permission I shall say how I mean to go to work.

"First of all, I beg leave to state that public opinion in England is very favourable to my country. Perhaps

I myself have contributed a little to this. In any case, it is so. I can affirm as a fact, that the late Eastern war, at the time of its declaration, was only popular in England because people believed and hoped that the Poles and the Hungarians, especially the Hungarians, would profit thereby.

The Emperor (interrupting). " That was so, I know."

Kossuth. " It is really no exaggeration on my part, Sire, to say, that if I could ·go and say to the English people: ' Behold, the powerful Emperor of the French has taken pity on my poor and unfortunate country, and has decided to assist Hungary to become free and independent, but we have also need of English help. Here is an opportunity to give proof of the sympathy which you have so often and unmistakably expressed for us. Do you also have compassion upon my poor compatriots, and help them too!'— if I could say this, countless petitions would be sent by the people to the Queen, the Government, and Parliament, declaring that they were ready for any sacrifice in this matter. And if I said, ' I do not want you to spend a drop of English blood, or a single shilling of English money, nay, I even wish you to preserve them both for your own benefit; I only want you not to stand in our way, but to remain neutral, for by this you would do a great service to Hungary ' — if I could say this, there is no doubt that ' neutrality' would be the general outcry from Land's End to John o' Groat's.

" Your Majesty knows that public opinion is a great power in England. Not because those who hold the reins of government would refrain from disregarding public opinion, if they considered it their interest so to do, but chiefly because it is a great support in case the Government finds it suits them to appeal to it.

"I would therefore commence by persuading the Lord Mayor of London to preside in person over a great meeting. At this meeting I would ask the public to pronounce in favour of neutrality. I would continue to rouse public opinion in some other large cities, and I would do so in public meetings, which would be free, and, consequently, enormously crowded. There is no doubt that everywhere resolutions favourable to my wishes would be carried, and these would call forth an enthusiastic response from the press and from all parts of the country. Making use of this agitation in the public mind, the leaders of the Whigs, if they had a majority at their disposal, would be enabled to defeat the Tory ministry on this question of its foreign policy. However, the Whigs have no majority. The problem therefore is, to procure a majority for them on condition that they will observe a benevolent neutrality. I think that I can manage this.

"The two great parties—the Tories and the Whigs—are about evenly balanced in the Lower House. Measured accurately, the Tories have a majority of a few votes. It is true that the Tory ministry at the beginning of April was left in minority by thirty-nine votes on the question of parliamentary reform, but the majority on that occasion was not composed of Whigs alone, but of independent members, most of whom belonged to the so-called 'Manchester School' under the leadership of Cobden and Bright. This party stands quite independently between the two great parties of the state, and the Whigs cannot always depend upon them, though occasionally, as on the parliamentary reform question, they vote together. Lord Derby believed his position so little compromised by that adverse vote, that he did not resign, but appealed to the constituencies. I do not believe that the Whigs will win in the elections which are now progressing. On the contrary, from the results, in so far as they are known, we may anticipate a gain to the Tories of about twenty seats. This is sufficient to enable them to hold their own against the Whigs, unless the latter can acquire a majority by the support of independent members. The independent party commands about ninety votes in the Lower House, and is therefore not strong enough to form a ministry, but nevertheless it was, and will remain on the present occasion too, master of the situation. If only two-thirds of their number vote one way, the majority of the House will be on that side with which these two-thirds have thrown in their lot. The existence of any government depends upon their goodwill. They are masters of the situation in every question on which the Tories and Whigs are opposed to each other. One of the political doctrines of this party is, that England, except perhaps so far as she is obliged to protect Belgium, should not mix herself in any Continental wars. Lord Palmerston knows this, and he also knows, that if he decides to observe neutrality on the question now pending—and he must decide on neutrality, or else he has no chance of coming into office—the independent party will vote with him on principle, and that therefore, though his own party be in decided minority, he could defeat the Tories at any moment. Lord Palmerston also knows, however, that unless he came to a preliminary understanding with the bulk of the independent members, he could not remain in power for a fortnight, for he is much disliked by the Manchester School, especially by Cobden, the powerful leader of the masses. I possess a most interesting letter from him on this subject. This explains why Lord Palmerston, though thoroughly tired of being the leader of 'Her Majesty's Opposition,' did not propose a vote of want of confidence in Lord Derby's government; though the ministry were defeated in a vote a few weeks ago. The minority of the Tories on that occasion did not mean a majority of the Whigs.

"Thus stands the situation.

"Your Majesty may find it strange; nevertheless, it is a positive fact that I stand in the most intimate relation to Cobden's party, though this party wants peace at any price, and I sigh for war, because I believe the liberation of my country can be accomplished in no other way. I venture to say that the members of this party will readily do anything I may ask of them as a politician, as long as it is not opposed to their political convictions. Fortunately in the question before us, after what your Majesty has been pleased to state, our interests entirely coincide with their principles; and I, therefore, think I can safely reckon upon their assistance.

"If I should be fortunate enough to receive your Majesty's authority to do so, I would confidentially inform some of those who are my most trusted friends, as to how the situation really stands, and would request them, as soon as the public opinion of the country had sufficiently manifested itself in public meetings, &c., to go to Lord Palmerston and assure him of the votes of the majority of their party on two conditions; one of them being, that he, as well as the ministerial colleagues he should designate for a future Liberal administration, should pledge themselves in writing that the English Government shall even then remain neutral in this war, if Your Majesty, with the object of establishing the independence of Hungary, should extend the seat of war to Hungary; the other being, that in order to ensure that this policy is carried out, one or two members of the independent party should enter the new Cabinet, on the understanding that in case his lordship should violate the neutrality, in spite of the engagement he gave to them, these two members would leave the Cabinet, and thus overthrow his government.

"I should think myself fortunate if I succeeded in convincing your Majesty that this procedure seems to promise success. I feel so far sure of success, that I would not mind promising that shortly after the meeting of Parliament (which may be expected to take place early in June), the Whigs will come into power, and I may have the pleasure of showing to your Majesty, in writing, the engagement of the new ministers to observe neutrality. And as the change of ministry would take place on this understanding, I am of opinion that it will be easy for Your Majesty's Ambassador in London, in his conversation with the Prime Minister, to hint at the convenience of Her Britannic Majesty assuring your Majesty of the benevolent neutrality of England, in an autograph letter."

The Emperor. "What you have said is most interesting and most important. We beg you to proceed forthwith with your scheme; and be convinced that in securing the neutrality of England you will have removed the greatest obstacle that stands in the way of the realisation of your patriotic hopes."

After this I took occasion to recommend warmly the affairs of my country to the Emperor. Amongst other things, I mentioned that the peace of Europe could only be put on a normal basis if the questions of historical necessity were solved. I spoke of the glory which history would award to that power which, by taking in hand the solving of these questions, would inaugurate a new illustrious epoch in the history of Europe. These are phrases, and I therefore do not repeat them in full, and only mention them because they furnished the Emperor an opportunity of making a remark, which I think deserves to be noted down. Hastily reviewing the state of Europe, I happened to mention the question of *German unity*, when the Emperor interrupted me and said, smiling : " Ah, quant à cela, ça ne me va pas, passe pour deux Allemagnes, mais Allemagne une, ça ne me va pas, nullement." I replied by simply repeating those words of the Emperor, " Il ne faut jamais vouloir l'impossible." The inevitable evolutions of history may be retarded, but not prevented, and to endeavour to suppress them may prove dangerous.

In our conversation I, of course, brought forward the question of foreign intervention, and said that this question was of the very greatest importance to us; that I did not receive a single letter or message of any sort from home in which the question was not put whether we were quite sure that Russia would not nterfere against us.

To this the Emperor replied, in the most positive

manner, that we need not in the least fear Russian intervention. Russia would not only not interfere against us, but on the contrary was so much annoyed with Austria that she would be glad if Hungary were liberated; but, of course, she expected that we should not complicate the Hungarian with the Polish question. The Emperor recommended great precaution in this respect, whereon I instantly assured him that we would be cautious. As regarded Prussia, the Emperor remarked that so far he had no reason to fear that the Cabinet of Berlin intended, either directly or indirectly, to help Austria; that the appeals made by the Court of Vienna had been decidedly refused; that he (the Emperor) would do all in his power to confirm the Cabinet of Berlin in this resolution, and he hoped in his endeavour to be assisted also by Russia. "Besides," continued the Emperor, smiling, "if, contrary to my expectations, the Prussians were to interfere in the struggle, they certainly would not select Hungary as their seat of war. But I hope they will not interfere."

When I thought that the end of our conversation was drawing near, the Emperor made a remark, which might have been meant as much an inquiry as a request, that "after all we might perhaps be able to organise at once a small insurrectionary movement in Transylvania, amongst the Széklers."

I decidedly refused to hear of it, and begged the Emperor to divest his mind of any such ideas. I impressed upon him that the Hungarian character was not suited for secret conspiracies; that before a small force could be organised amongst the Széklers, the movement would be suppressed. That the small force which

Austria left in Transylvania would be sufficient to secure this result; and, in consequence, we should also lose the assistance of the Széklers when we took up arms in earnest. That it might even happen, that if they saw no respectable force, but only a small movement, there might be such desperate characters amongst the Transylvanian Wallachians, as would, by their robberies and other excesses, make it possible for Austria, in a measure, to repeat the atrocious deeds she perpetrated in 1849. "No, Sire," I said, "this would be in strong contrast with the stand-point which I considered it a duty to my country to take up. I shall not trifle with the lives of my countrymen."

The Emperor. "*Eh bien!* let us change the subject; *n'en parlons plus.* Have you any knowledge of the number of Austrian troops garrisoned in Transylvania?"

Kossuth. "Yes, Sire; there are 4,500 men along the valley of the Olt, where the chief points are Csikszereda, Brassó, and Szeben; 3,000 men in the valley of the Maros —chief points, Marosvásárhely Medgyes, and Gyula-Fehérvár, and Déva, a detached fort; finally, 4,500 men scattered round about Besztercze, Deés, and Kolozsvár. In all 12,000 men, with one fortress (Gyulafehérvár), and one fortified town (Nagyszeben)."

I had to show the Emperor the places named on a large map of Austro-Hungary, which was hanging up against the wall of his study.

The Emperor ended our long talk by saying: "*C'est donc entendu.* I assure you that I shall make use of the co-operation of Hungary in the war, on one condition only, namely, if I can give you the guarantees you require, not otherwise. It is my intention to leave nothing undone in order to give you these guarantees. Return to England, and endeavour to secure England's neutrality. If you succeed in this a great difficulty will be overcome. I authorise you to inform your friends discreetly how matters stand. Meanwhile it will, of course, be advisable to think of making preparations. While you are occupied with your important enterprise in England, your colleagues may go to Italy, collect those of the Hungarian refugees who are able to carry arms, and look to the organisation of the forces. The Government of Piedmont will be duly instructed, will provide money, arms, and the selection of Hungarian prisoners of war. Senator Pietri will be entrusted with all details. You will have to confer with him.

(Turning to the Prince) "Ask Senator Pietri to come to you to-morrow. Inform him of the nature of his trust, and put him in communication with these gentlemen, that the matter may be proceeded with at once."

(To me) "Of course you will take care that public opinion in Hungary is duly prepared. I believe you will find it necessary to send trustworthy agents to Bucharest and Belgrade. Tell them to call upon our diplomatic agents in those towns, who will receive the necessary instructions. When you have accomplished your enterprise in England, pray hurry to Italy. Inform us, through Pietri, of your arrival. We shall let you know where we can meet and—à revoir en Italie."

I thanked the Emperor for his affable reception and

the hope which he held out to my country, and asked permission to be allowed—as a parting remark—to remind him that the Napoleons had a heavy account to settle with the Austrian dynasty, and that I thought, by my proposals in the name of my nation, to give him an opportunity of definitely settling the account. As an honest and unassuming man I begged the Emperor to be convinced that if we should succeed in inscribing his name in the annals of our history as the liberator of the Italian and of the Hungarian nations, he would secure the devotion to his House of two grateful nations, upon whom he might depend under any circumstances; that he would prevent the possibility of those trials, which may come sooner or later, in face of the representatives of the doctrine of "divine right," between whom and the Napoleons there may be an armistice, but never a sincere and cordial peace.

With this we parted.

The night was delightfully clear. Coming out from the Tuileries the Prince offered me a cigar, and asked me to stroll with him along the river-side. "I can say," said the Prince, " that this interview justifies great hopes. You may be satisfied with the result. The Emperor was much more positive in what he said to you than I had expected. For he hesitates a long time, and does not easily decide upon anything, but when once he has decided he is as firm as this granite" (he struck the parapet with his fist). "We do not always agree. At the time of the *coup d'état* we did not agree either. *Vous savez je suis un peu républicain.* I disapproved of the *coup d'état.* Not that I am indifferent to the possession of power, but because I do not think anything of the title under which one possesses power. President or Emperor—where is the difference? And I believe, with a little patience, the title would have come of itself, without a crime. However, his *entourage* was impatient. I was so much annoyed with the matter that, at personal risk, I apprised some of the most eminent Republicans of the danger when there was still time for preventing it. *Mais que voulez-vous?* Sentimentalists are not men of deeds. *A propos* of the republicans—what will your friends Ledru and Mazzini say to all this?"

Kossuth. "Certainly they will not be pleased with it. But I have often told them there is a great difference between France and Hungary. France till now has only made revolutions for a form of government, and the same object will instigate her to all her future revolutions. Hers is a domestic quarrel. It was never a question of national existence. With us it is a question of, 'To be, or not to be?' a question not of political theories, but of existence. And then, in France revolution is nothing but a short series of street-fights, decided one way or the other in a few days; for the very reason that it is only a question of form of government. It is different in Hungary. We must defend our national existence against a power, not only in possession of all the strength in our own country, but also at the same time a foreigner, having a foreign army and foreign finances at disposal against us. What they call revolution—which, however, is not revolution, but a struggle for existence—means with us war, a great war with a foreign power. Therefore, I should be a bad patriot, a very bad patriot indeed, if, in deference to the political doctrines I hold, I were to hesitate to grasp the hand, no matter whose it be, which offers to assist my country in this great war, in this struggle for existence. Republican America has in a great measure to thank absolutist France for her independence. I have often said to Ledru and Mazzini, that I would contract an alliance for this purpose, not only with an emperor, king, sultan, or any other despot, under whatever name he may be known, but even with the very Devil himself! *Seulement je prendrais garde qu'il ne m'emporte pas.*"

Our cigars were nearly out. The prince gave me a rendezvous for the next day, to introduce us to Pietri, and drove me back to the house of Colonel Kiss, where I narrated the salient points of my conference with the Emperor to my friends, who were impatiently awaiting me.

The following day I went with Teleki and Klapka to the Prince. Pietri soon appeared. The Prince undertook to inform him on the subject in our presence, and he did so with such accuracy and scrupulous exactitude, that when, after having finished his explanation, he asked me whether he had told everything, and told it rightly, I could only reply that I had not a word to add or to alter.

Thus we were put into communication with the man who was entrusted by the Emperor with the conduct of our affairs.

We three, the same day, constituted ourselves into the "National Hungarian Directory," and held our first meeting, the minutes of which were taken by Teleki.

After having arranged the most urgent matters with

Pietri, I returned to London to take in hand the accomplishment of England's neutrality, intending, after having attained my object, to go to Italy, where Teleki and Klapka would have already commenced to organise the army.

NOTE to Page 159.

"*Prince Napoleon :* '*We have learnt from the history of our uncle . . . that the members of our family must not accept foreign thrones.*'"

In the war of 1859 Prince Napoleon was commander of the 5th French Army Corps, which was ordered to Tuscany to push on thence to the Po (from Sarzana over the Apennines towards Parma). This move had a strategical importance of its own. It induced the Austrians to evacuate not only Ancona, Bologna, Ferrara, but also the fortress of Piacenza (June 11th).

But Italian historians generally state that this expedition of Prince Napoleon was undertaken in the interest of his dynasty. It is said that it was intended to found a kingdom for the Prince in Central Italy. Cavour himself appears to have suspected this, for as soon as he had been informed by telegraph that the Prince had been ordered to Tuscany, he hastened to Alessandria to the Emperor, to dissuade him from this step. The Emperor was not to be dissuaded, and on Cavour reminding him that the presence of the Prince in Tuscany at the head of an army corps would create suspicions and jealousy in the councils of the Great Powers, the Emperor only answered: " It is not my intention to place a French prince upon a throne in Central Italy ; and, if necessary, I shall give assurances in this respect to the Great Powers, through the usual diplomatic channels."

I am decidedly of opinion that the Emperor Napoleon really did not have such an intention. He could not have had it, for he was too cautious a man to be inclined to provoke a European coalition against himself. It is a fact that he did not like to see Tuscany united to Piedmont; it is equally true that in the final distribution of Italy he wished to secure French influence; but, just for these reasons, he did not wish for a united Italy. I am firmly convinced that what Prince Napoleon told me of the "moral brought home to them by the history of his uncle" was not merely a well-turned phrase, or simply an expression of his personal views, but contained the well-considered policy of the House of Bonaparte.

Nicomede Bianchi says distinctly in his excellent work ("Storia Documentata," vol. viii.) that Prince Napoleon—much to the indignation of Walewski—pleaded warmly that Tuscany should be united with Piedmont. But Bianchi also seemed to share the view that the expedition of the Prince to Tuscany covered a desire for a throne, for he adds, that the Prince became only a pleader of that unity when "he became convinced that his presence in Tuscany did not create such sympathy as might have been considered the forerunner of future hopes."

I believe that the eminent historian has fallen into an error in this instance. I am convinced that Prince Napoleon did not dream of speculating on a throne in Italy.

To prove that my conviction is correct, I refer, first of all, to the Prince's reply, when I held out to him the prospect of the crown of St. Stephen, in the event of the liberation of Hungary becoming an accomplished fact:—

"We have learnt from the history of our uncle that the members of our family should not accept foreign thrones, for this might lead to European coalitions being formed against us—and our family cannot feel inclined to risk the French throne even for the glorious crown of St. Stephen."

These words stated a fact, and did not express an individual sentiment. Sentiments and intentions leave room for the question being put, whether they are sincere. But when somebody thus points to a given situation, and appeals to a fact, the reality of which cannot be doubted for an instant, his words carry such weight with them, as to invest them with a value independent of the individual.

In the second place I refer to the proclamation addressed by Prince Napoleon to the Tuscans from the port of Leghorn on May 23rd, in which I read—

"My mission is purely military, I must not and will not occupy myself with internal affairs. Napoleon III. has declared that he has no other ambition than to lead the sacred cause of liberty to victory, and that he will not allow himself to be guided by family interests."

By these words he entirely disowned every ambitious intention, and he was certainly too shrewd a man—in case he had fostered such an ambition—to consider it a good way of winning sympathy, to say anything, in the first moment of landing, which would have laid him open to the charge of having told a falsehood.

Yet it must be admitted that generals occasionally do publish strange proclamations. The Austrian General Gyulay also published a proclamation, when he invaded Piedmont, in which he told the people that he had come to "liberate Piedmont from the oppression in which it was held by a revolutionary party." And he commenced his pious work by robbing the people of all the food they had. In consequence of this "liberation" the price of bread went up 500 per cent. in Vercelli. And lest the people should be troubled by the cares of having to wash their linen, his soldiers dragged the sheets even from underneath the sick as they lay in the hospitals.

It is evident, therefore, that proclamations do not always tell the truth, but the truthfulness of the Prince's proclamation is guaranteed by the decisive circumstance that the declaration of the Emperor, to which this proclamation refers, possessed binding force towards the European powers, not to adhere to which would have been equivalent to provoking the Powers to interfere as enemies, and they were only too anxious to find a pretext for so doing.

Finally, I refer to the fact that Russia, which of all the powers was the only one which acquiesced in the Italian enterprise of the Emperor Napoleon, made its consent entirely dependent on the condition that, in the case of Italy being liberated from Austrian rule he would not think of filling thrones.

I therefore believe that those historians are mistaken who state that Prince Napoleon wished by his expedition to Tuscany to pave the way for occupying a throne in Central Italy. He did not even dream of it.

CHAPTER IV.

The Question of Neutrality in England—Speeches at Public Meetings—
Change of Government.

I.

I WAS back in London from Paris on May 8th. The parliamentary elections were just then in full progress. None of my English friends were in London, and it depended entirely on their help whether I could redeem the promise I had given to the Emperor Napoleon. Much to my regret, Cobden was not even in England at the time. He was travelling in North America, and was not expected to return till towards the end of June. I was therefore obliged to do without his invaluable assistance. Charles Gilpin, M.P. for the borough of Northampton, was, therefore, the anchor of my hope.

I cannot mention the name of Gilpin without paying to his memory a tribute of the deepest respect, sincerest affection, and warmest thanks. Gilpin was one of the noblest characters I have ever met with in my life. He was honour itself, charity and human love personified, an example of social virtues, a comforter of sufferers, an indefatigable supporter of those who were forsaken. Such he proved to be to the Hungarian refugees, towards whom he manifested an especial sympathy. I never knew a man, not himself an exile, who could so thoroughly feel what sufferings and what claims on Christian sympathy the words "without a country" contain. I never knew a man who carried out more consistently that sublime command of Our Saviour, "Love your neighbour as yourself;" and this man bestowed a friendship upon me such as is seldom met with in this world. He was my friend before he had seen me. It was on his motion that the Common Council of the City of London, of which he was a member, lifted its voice against our detention in Asia Minor. It was to him I owed the enthusiastic reception with which I was honoured by the municipality of this great city, which was the commencement of such an expression of sympathy as has never before been shown to the defeated cause of any nation, or to any exile in a foreign country. And during our separation he still remained my friend until his death, through all the changes of my ill-fated life. He was a faithful and sincere friend. A sincerer man, a man of truer heart, there could not be. Blessed be his memory!

I communicated to him, in confidence, what had passed between myself and the Emperor; he gave me his word that he would help me to attain my end, and he redeemed his word.

We talked over the *modus operandi*. He approved of my suggestion that we should commence with public meetings; but was of opinion that we must wait a few days until the elections were over, lest I should lay myself open to the charge of trying to interfere with them, though a foreigner; that, besides, it was necessary to know the result of the elections, according to which we should have to arrange our future proceedings. It was expected that the elections would be over by about May 14th; five or six days would be sufficient to let the excitement calm down, and to give time for the people to take an interest in something else. Accordingly, we had only about ten days left in which to hold public meetings; for parliament would very likely be opened on the last day of the month. We decided that meetings should be held in London, Manchester, Bradford, and Glasgow. Gilpin took upon himself to make the necessary arrangements for the meetings in London and Manchester; to induce the Lord Mayor to preside over the London meeting, and to use his influence that the Manchester meeting should be convened under the auspices of the "Free Trade League." I was to think about Bradford and Glasgow, while Gilpin was to arrange at once with the Lord Mayor, and then to start for Manchester to make the necessary arrangements there; afterwards he undertook to confer confidentially with the most important members of his party, and to secure their co-operation towards the attainment of my object. We agreed that I should at once set to work to prepare at least two well-considered speeches for the meetings in London and Manchester, treating of the question in all its aspects.

On May 13th a proclamation by the Queen was published, in which it was clearly stated that the Government of Great Britain *wished to observe a strict neutrality all through the war.*

My position was undoubtedly aggravated by this declaration. Some of my compatriots were of opinion that there was no further need for agitation, as what the Emperor of the French had wished for— the neutrality of England—had been officially proclaimed. But remembering that the Emperor Napoleon had decidedly declared that he did not think he could trust to England's neutrality while the ministry of Lord Derby was in power, I myself did not think that the obstacle, which, according to the Emperor, stood in the way of sending an army to Hungary, had been entirely removed. I therefore did not consider my object gained. I thought that the situation had changed so far only as to compel me to commence the agitation on a different basis than would have been the case had the proclamation of neutrality not been issued.

The subjoined speeches will show how I thought it best to acquit myself of my task.

II.

Public Meeting in the Great Hall of the London Tavern.

London, May 20th, 1859.

The Lord Mayor of the City of London took the chair. There were present on the platform V. Cooper, M.P., C. Gilpin, M.P., J. White, M.P., Professor Newman, Mr. Nicholay, and others. Long before the proceedings commenced every corner of the spacious hall was filled to suffocation.

The Lord Mayor, in opening the meeting, stated that the subject which had brought together the large assemblage of gentlemen whom he saw before him, had that day occupied the attention of the Common Council of the City of London, which had heard with satisfaction that the Queen had issued a proclamation of neutrality. So far from fearing that the meeting over which he had the honour to preside would not endorse the opinion of the Common Council—that England should not be mixed up in the war—he was firmly convinced that he only expressed the opinion of those present when he uttered the wish that the neutrality of England should be maintained over whatever part or province of the Austrian monarchy the war might extend. After expressing a hope that the war now being carried on would serve the interests of the oppressed races, the chairman called upon the "last legitimate ruler of Hungary," whom he introduced to them with the hope that the national rights of his country would be acknowledged, and that he might return to his birthplace amidst the enthusiasm of his victorious countrymen.

I was received with loud and long-continued cheering, and, after thanking the meeting for the enthusiastic reception accorded to me, I proceeded to deliver the following lecture:—

"My Lord Mayor! the cloud called *the Italian question* has at last begun to discharge the electric fluid with which it has been overcharged for more than forty years.

"It is a momentous event, likely to mark an epoch in the history of Europe.

"What is the position which England ought to take in this critical emergency? is the question which naturally suggests itself. Your lordship, whose opinions carry with themselves a threefold authority, that of an independent English patriot, that of a tried and consistent friend of liberty, and that of the exalted representative of this great commercial metropolis of the world—your lordship has answered the question.

"The position which your lordship says England ought to take, and from which she ought not to depart, is that of *honest neutrality and strict non-intervention*.

SPEECH AT THE LONDON TAVERN. 193

"I feel greatly honoured in being permitted to take part in the proceedings of this evening, though after what has fallen from your lordship I know that my humble opinions in my individual capacity can pretend to no weight with this assembly.

"But though by the stormy waves of national adversity I have been cast a homeless exile on the shores of this happy country—the happy home of the free and the sanctuary of the oppressed—the municipality of this great metropolis has deigned to receive me as the representative of the Hungarian nationality. Upwards of one hundred cities, boroughs, and corporations have followed in the wake, and the liberal instinct of the people of England and Scotland has vouchsafed to make me the depositary of the tokens of their sympathy for my native land.

"Thus it has fallen to my lot to stand prominently identified in public opinion with the cause of my oppressed nation and of European liberty in general. Such being the peculiarity of my individual position, I for one cannot help deriving corroborative persuasion from the coincidence that the conclusion at which your lordship arrived from an English point of view, is exactly the same as that at which I have arrived from a European point of view.

"As an exile, as a Hungarian, as a member of an oppressed nationality, as a man identified in all his aspirations with the cause of my country's emancipation, I cannot but repeat as an ardent prayer, what your lordship advanced as the well-matured opinion of an English patriot—that England should deliberately adhere to the policy of honest neutrality and of strict non-intervention.

"If in consequence of this concurrence of opinions I were to be asked whether I anticipate that the war which is just commencing may eventually result to the advantage of the cause with which every aspiration of my heart is identified, I should unhesitatingly declare that I do anticipate such an eventual result provided England does not direct the natural course of events into a wrong channel by interfering in the war.

"This anticipation does not flow from the excitement which recent events must naturally have produced on my feelings.

Adversity is a great teacher, my lord, and the icy finger of time is a mighty disenchanter. I have suffered much in the last ten years of my tempest-tossed life, but in compensation I have learnt something. I have learnt not to clutch with eager impatience the fleeting forelock of illusory hopes. I have learnt with calm reflection to trace the law of concatenation between cause and effect, which presides over the logic of history.

"I rest my anticipations on the incontrovertible axiom that the difficulties of the oppressor may become a chance of deliverance for the oppressed.

"I see Francis Joseph of Austria, the murderer of my nation, engaged in a great war. I reflect on the relative position of the contending parties, and on the strategical necessities which must develop themselves in the course of the war, and I come to the conclusion that at no distant time emancipation will be within the reach of some of those nationalities, the oppression of which by the House of Austria is the great European nuisance; without the removal of this, patchwork arrangements may be devised, calculated to disguise for a little while longer the rottenness of the political structure of Europe; but a permanent peace and a settled condition of the European community are utterly impossible.

"Your lordship has appropriately alluded to the royal proclamation by which Her Majesty's Government have entered on a public pledge to abstain from taking any part directly or indirectly in the war which has just commenced on the Continent, and to maintain a strict and impartial neutrality.

"This certainly is a move in the right direction.

"Condign credit is owing to Her Majesty's Government for the constitutional spirit which they have displayed in showing due regard for the demands of public opinion manifested with more than ordinary emphasis both from the hustings during the election and by numerous meetings held since.

"So far, so good.

"I make bold to say that if it be desired that the proclaimed neutrality should assume the character of a settled rule, not subject to eventual modifications, it is now more than ever necessary that the expression of public opinion should not relax—nay, that it should be made even more explicit than hitherto, in order that no room should be left for any doubt as to the sense in which the people of these realms desire the proclaimed principle of neutrality to be understood, and as to the consistency with which it ought to be acted upon.

" Diplomacy, my lord, is a very slippery business—and prevention is the only cure.

"Neutrality is a general expression, yet it implies a special meaning, the bearing of which cannot be fully fathomed, unless we have it clearly understood with which of the contending parties Her Majesty's Government would side if they were not to remain neutral.

"Now I do not remember to have heard of one single ministerial declaration which has left the impression on my mind that if Her Majesty's Government were not to remain neutral they would side with Sardinia and France against Austria, whereas I have heard of many declarations forcibly leading to the inference that the alternative was either neutrality or support of Austria.

"It has been always universally admitted that England was to remain neutral in the beginning, but it was added that she should watch what turn events would take, and should arm in the meanwhile, so as to be prepared to do—— What, pray? Perhaps to repel any aggression on her territories, colonies, or dependencies? Of course that should be done, that would be done, and gloriously too.

"'Come the three corners of the world in arms——' You know the rest of the proud, bold strain. But this has nothing to do with neutrality or non-neutrality; this is a question of attack and defence, and the plainest common-sense reflection will show that England will not be attacked in *this* war if she does not run into it herself. England, therefore, should not arm to repulse an attack, but she should arm, it was said, in order to be prepared to *protect her interests*.

"Again I should say, so far so good. Only that *interest* is a very vague word. It may mean nothing, or it may mean anything, to suit the fancy of the moment.

"But we *have* been vouchsafed a foretaste of what it *might* mean—we have been told that if a French fleet should enter the Adriatic, it *might* be the interest of England to oppose it; we have been told, and on high authority too, that if Trieste were to be attacked, it might be in the interest of England to defend it; nay, the ministerial candidate for the West Riding of Yorkshire even told the electors that it might be in the interest of England to protect Venice. To protect Venice from what? Of course, from the great misfortune of getting emancipated from the detested yoke of Austria.

"Thus, turn it as we may, the alternative is this: either England remains neutral, or else she will be brought to support Austria. If in this war England were to depart from the principle of strict and impartial neutrality, you would be in danger of seeing the colours of England nailed to the mast of Austria; in the history of the oppression of nationalities you would have the fair name of Britannia coupled with that of Austria, the despotic power and personified oppressor of national rights.

"This feature of the case—viz., that departure from the principle of neutrality means in this instance support of Austria—should never for a moment be lost sight of; it will convince every Englishman that, though the proclamation of neutrality is deserving of unreserved approbation, there is much left to be watched, to be cleared up, and to be controlled by public opinion.

"The important question, which ought to be satisfactorily answered, is: What is the world to understand by the assurance that the English Government are purposed and determined to abstain from taking any part in *this* war? Is this declaration made under the tacit proviso that England will remain neutral provided the war remains restricted to Italy? Or is it meant to intimate that England will adhere to the principle of impartial neutrality and strict non-intervention although, in the natural course of events, the area of the conflict may happen to be extended to other parts of the Austrian dominions?

"I wish this assembly to come to a proper conclusion on this subject. I shall, therefore, with your leave, enter on a brief examination of certain preconceived ideas—I might well call them prejudices—which, if they are not emphatically repudiated by public opinion, will be likely to carry England into the war, in spite of the prospects held out by the proclamation of neutrality.

" 1. These prejudices turn upon the radically erroneous interpretation of what is called the Italian question.

" 2. Upon the undue regard which we hear professed on the part of England for the treaties of 1815.

" 3. Upon what diplomatists call the localisation of the war; and,

" 4. Upon that greatest of all imaginable misconceptions, that the integrity of the Austrian Empire is essential to the maintenance of the balance of power.

" May it please your lordship to allow me to make some remarks on each of these points.

" First, as to the real merit of the Italian question.

" There are commotions which owe their origin to maladministration and misgovernment. These may be put to rest by seasonable concessions, improvements, and reforms.

" But ill-governed as Italy, with the exception of Piedmont, is, the Italian question is not of this character. The problem imperatively claiming its adequate solution in the Italian question is not between this or that form of government, this or that abuse or grievance, demanding this or that improvement, concession, redress; no, the Italian question is a question of national existence; and because it is a question of national existence, the first and foremost point in its practical solution is, the total and definitive expulsion of Austria from Italy; her expulsion in such a manner that she should not be able ever to go back again.

" Many political questions may admit of a compromise, but this is one of those which can admit of no compromise. Either Austria is finally ejected from Italy, or else, do what the powers of Europe may, the Italian question will recur again and again. No administrative reforms, no readjustment of provincial frontiers can conjure it away, and no terrorism can stifle it. Nothing short of the utter extermination of the Italians could secure the rule of Austria in Italy. And a nation of 26,000,000 baffles extermination. Well wrote Lord Napier to Viscount Palmerston in 1848—"The Italians may be crushed, but will not be extirpated. The enthusiasm of hope will kindle, and the broken thread will be knit again and again."

"It was owing to this state of the Italian question that, as far back as 1846, when the Papal dominions were even worse governed than they are now (and to say this is to say much indeed), the moderate Liberal party, I say the moderate party, declared to the Papal Commissaries—' That however dreadful, however insupportable, were the particular sufferings of the Roman people, their questions with the government had for them but a secondary interest—the principal question was Italy—that what revolted against their feelings more than anything else was that the Papal Government had made itself the slave of Austria in Italy; and that whenever an opportunity for fighting the Austrians offered itself, the Romans would join in the fight with all the energies of a harassed and indignant people, because the life of all Italy was elevated into the sentiment of nationality.

"It was likewise owing to this state of the Italian question that, when Venice and Lombardy had risen in 1848, the whole of Italy united with them in a crusade against Austria.

"The same state of the Italian question explains the fact that when—from fear lest the French might enter Italy—Austria, in 1848, offered to the provisional government of Milan the unconditional independence of Lombardy, with power to dispose of themselves as they might please, the Milanese rejected the offer with the declaration that they would never separate themselves from their Venetian brethren, and that they fought not for Lombardy, but for Italy.

"It is equally owing to this state of the Italian question that we see at this very moment the people of Piedmont, though happy and contented with their own condition, cheerfully accept all the sacrifices and sufferings of a great war, that King Victor Emanuel, having inscribed on his banner the independence of Italy, sees a great number of republicans rallying around him, just as the monarchists would have rallied around the banner of Italy if the republicans had unfurled it with a reasonable prospect of success; it is from the same cause that Tuscany threw itself into the arms of the King of Piedmont, that volunteers from all parts of Italy flock to the banner of the king; that the most extraordinary measures of rigour have to be resorted to by the King of Naples to prevent his people from joining also; and last, not least, to the same cause is it due that we see the French received with joy and enthusiasm in Italy.

"Now, my lord, it does strike me that in all the transactions preceding the declaration of war by Austria, there was this shortcoming in the policy of England, that the Italian question was not viewed as a question of national existence, but was viewed as one that might be solved on the basis of Austria retaining her Italian possessions if she would only consent not to interfere with the rest of Italy.

"I shall not now enter on an exposure of the strangest of all strange misconceptions—that Austria could be left in possession of Venice and Lombardy, and be bound by any treaties, by any arrangements, not to exert the preponderating influence of her position on Central and Southern Italy, in the direction of that principle of unmitigated despotism in which the House of Austria lives and moves and has its being. To show this I should have to refer to diplomatic documents which ought not to have escaped the attention of contemporary statesmen, but which would carry me to a greater length than I can afford on the present occasion to go.

"Therefore, I will only remark that, unless it be explicitly understood throughout Europe that the maintenance of Austria in her Italian possessions does not enter into the intents and schemes of England, no proclamation of neutrality will prevent your country from being, sooner or later, swept into the war, in consequence of entangling alliances, for which it is manifest that mighty influences are at work.

"It is a strange sight which one sees going on now in Germany; that the German nation, which hardly ever was united in any single purpose, should appear ready for once to sink all dissensions in the determination to resist an anticipated rush of the French on the Rhine; this, my lord, if the Germans really had to fear such an intention on the part of their French neighbours, would justly command the approbation of every sensible man. There is, however, much of a false alarm at the bottom of the agitation in Germany, for it is perfectly absurd to suppose that the French Government, having already a big war on hand, could meditate an attack on the Rhine, an attack which could not be directed against Austria, but could only aim at Prussia and the confederated minor German states—an attack which would be sure to put a mighty European coalition in battle array against France. The fact is, that there are influences at work to turn the patriotic feelings of the German nation to the profit of the House of Austria, in order to set Austria's foot firmly on the neck of other nationalities which have as much right to an independent national existence as the Germans themselves.

"But, believe me, gentlemen, in spite of the prevailing artificial excitement, the noble instincts of the German nation could never be deluded into the disgraceful part of being made the '*valet de bourreau*' (hangman's assistant) of the House of Austria for enslaving other nationalities; unless it were supposed that England sympathised with Austria, and that the Government of Great Britain wished to maintain Austria in her Italian possessions.

"It cannot be denied that the Government of this country have given the Germans reason to believe that such was their intention with regard to Austria, for unfortunately we have heard it proclaimed in Parliament by the official organ of England's foreign policy, that Austria has strong claims on your sympathy because she is kindred in race to Anglo-Saxon England.

"Well, I am bound to remark, in all humility, that this pitiful appeal to your commiseration happens to be a very unfortunate display of proficiency in ethnographic studies. The unnatural compound of heterogeneous elements formed by a long series of usurpations, which goes by the name of Austria, is so far from being German, and therefore so far from being kindred to the

Anglo-Saxon stock, that though, at the last census of 1851, the Government of Austria employed both artifice and terrorism to establish for their dominions the character of a German nationality, they found it impossible to raise the number of their German subjects higher than to about seven millions, out of a population of thirty-seven millions. The fact is, Austria is the only power in Europe which has no national character: it is of no country, of no race; it is just a dynasty, and nothing more; it is simply the House of Hapsburg—no, not even that, for everything in that House is usurpation, down to their very name. They are not Hapsburgs, they are Lorrain - Vaudemonts, 'rebellious Crown officers of France,' as Napoleon I. used to style them. The Lords Denbigh, of the House of Fielding, are the only Hapsburgs on earth, not they.

"However, since such declarations of sympathy, coupled with recognitions of the pretended rights of Austria, have gone forth in an official manner from the English Government, it is not to be wondered at that the impression prevails throughout Germany, and throughout the Austrian dominions, that, in spite of the declaration of neutrality, England will come round by and by, and in one way or another will find out some pretext for either directly supporting Austria, or for assisting Germany in supporting her.

"This impression exerts a detrimental influence on the spirit of the oppressed nationalities, such as I am sure every liberal-minded Englishman will lament. On the other hand, it causes Germany to take a false direction, which, if not checked in time, will sooner or later first entangle England in untoward combinations, and then, under some eventual pretext, sweep her into the war.

"I think it therefore urgent that, while approving of the policy of impartial neutrality and strict non-intervention, the public opinion of the English nation should emphatically repudiate the idea of ever lending, under any circumstances, support to Austria, against the emancipation of the nationalities oppressed by her.

"I now come to the pretended inviolability of the treaties of 1815.

"It is the more important to have the mist of prejudices cleared away in this respect, since it admits of no doubt that, should it so happen (which God forfend) that England were to depart from the principle of neutrality, it would depart from it in favour of Austria, and on the ground and under the pretext that England is bound to preserve the treaties of 1815 intact.

"It is woeful to remember, my lord, that the Sovereigns who, on pretence of asserting the liberties of Europe, induced the nations to shed their blood in streams for nearly a quarter of a century, and to waste the prosperity of generations for no other purpose than for the preservation of certain dynasties, requited the deluded nations at the Congress of Vienna by selling and bartering them like cattle, and by treating Europe like an allodial farm. Thus it is that Lombardy was dealt with, thus it is that Venice, the fairy city, robbed of its glorious independence of thirteen hundred years' standing, was tossed over like a cricket-ball into the grasp of the House of Hapsburg.

"The history of Italy during the last forty years is nothing but a record of groans, of ever-growing hatred and discontent, of ever-recurring commotions, conspiracies, revolts, and revolutions, of scaffolds soaked in the blood of patriots, of the horrors of Spielberg and Mantua, and of the chafing anger with which the words 'Out with the Austrians' tremble on the lips of every Italian. These forty years are recorded in history as a standing protest against those impious treaties. The robbed have all the time loudly protested, by words, deeds, sufferings, and sacrifice of their lives, against the compact of the robbers.

"Yet, forsooth, we are still told that the treaties of 1815 are inviolable.

"Why, I have heard it reported that England rang with a merry peal, when the stern inward judge, conscience, led the hand of Castlereagh to suicide; and shall we in 1859 be offered the sight of England plunging into the incalculable calamities of a great war for no better purpose than to uphold the accursed work of the Castlereaghs, and from no better motive than to keep the House of Austria safe?

"Inviolable treaties, indeed! Why, my lord, the forty-four years that have since passed have riddled those treaties like a sieve. The Bourbons, whom they restored to the throne of France, have vanished, and the Bonapartes, whom they proscribed, occupy the place of the Bourbons on the throne of France.

"And how many changes have not been made in the state of Europe, in spite of those 'inviolable treaties'? Two of these changes—the transformation of Switzerland from a confederation of States into a Confederated State, and the independence of Belgium—have been accomplished to the profit of liberty. But, for the rest, the distinctive feature through which those treaties have passed is this, that every poor plant of freedom which they had spared has been uprooted by the unsparing hand of despotism. From the Republic of Cracow, poor remnant of Poland, swallowed by Austria, down to the freedom of the press guaranteed to Germany, but reduced to such a condition that, in the native land of Guttenberg, not one square yard of soil is left to set a free press upon, everything that was not evil in those inviolable treaties has been trampled down, to the profit of despotism, of concordats of Jesuits, and of benighting darkness. And all these violations of the inviolable treaties were accomplished without England's once shaking her mighty trident to forbid them. And shall it be recorded in history that when the question is, how to drive Austria from Italy, when the natural logic of this undertaking might present my own native country with a chance for that deliverance to which England bade God-speed with a mighty outcry of sympathy rolling like thunder from John o' Groat's to Land's End—that deliverance for which prayers have ascended, and are ascending still, to the Father of Mankind from millions of British hearts —shall it be recorded in history that at such a time, that under such circumstances, England plunged into the horrors and calamities of war—nay, that she took upon herself to make this war prolonged and universal for the mere purpose of upholding the inviolability of those rotten treaties in favour of Austria, good for nothing on earth except to spread darkness and to perpetuate servitude?

"There you have that Austria in Piedmont carrying on war in

a manner that recalls to memory the horrors of the long bygone ages of barbarism. You may read in the accounts furnished to the daily papers by their special correspondents that the rigorously disciplined soldiers of Austria were allowed to act the part of robbers let loose upon an unoffending population, to offer violence to unprotected families, to outrage daughters in presence of their parents, and to revel in such other savage crimes as the blood of civilised men curdles at hearing, and the tongue falters in relating.

"Such she was always—always! These horrors but faintly reflect what Hungary had to suffer from her in our late war. And shall it be said that England, the home of gentlemen, sent her brave sons to shed their blood and to stain their honour in fighting side by side with such a *soldatesca* for those highwayman compacts of 1815 to the profit of that Austria?

"No! let the people of England raise aloud their mighty voice. Let them thunder forth the forbidding word: *No, this shall not be!*

"Let them give to the government of the nation the pillar of the nation's clearly expressed will to lean upon, remind them that they are the ministers of England and not of Austria, and fortify their national position against the influence of foreign insidious whisperings.

"There is danger, I tell you, men of England, there is danger before your doors! Do not blindly confide in appearances. The wooden and iron bulwarks of England went forth to the Mediterranean with *sealed secret orders*. What if those silent papers should have had something to do with the ship *Orion* moored athwart in the port of Genoa so as to impede the disembarkation of French troops, and refusing to move an inch out of the way? It is rumoured that the indignation of the Genoese was loud, that England's naval officers were obliged to stay all night ashore, as even the poorest gondolier refused to row them to their ship for any price. What if you should hear of the recurrence of petty annoyances—may be by chance, may be by design—but at all events calculated to annoy the French and Italians, and so provoke some untoward collision, upon the ground of which you may then hear *England's honour* talked of in stirring variations, and as you have been appropriately warned by the *Times*, you may go to bed one evening believing yourselves at peace, and may wake on the morrow to find yourselves at war. And all this for the glorious purpose of vindicating the inviolability of the precious treaties of 1815.

"Let the people's voice keep England out of war till Parliament meets. Parliament will keep her safe when it shall have met. The hustings gave a guarantee for this. But if the people relax in watchfulness the evil of an *accomplished fact* may intervene which even Parliament may find it difficult to redress.

"The third point which I have to elucidate is what diplomatists call the localisation of the war.

"If this expression has any meaning at all, it means that the war shall be fought out on Italian territory.

"Well, my lord, I apprehend those who say so talk absolute nonsense.

"They have not consulted the most elementary principles of strategy.

"If the war is to have any issue at all, the Austrians must not only be ejected from Italy, they must be ejected in such a manner that they shall not be able to go back again.

"Tactical victories without a strategical result may have led to armistices, but have never finished a war, nor ever will.

"Now, in the rear of the fortified defensive position of the Austrians between the Mincio and the Adige, and at a little distance beyond the Tagliamento, is the frontier line which separates Lombardy and Venice from the other dominions of Austria. Well, imagine that the Austrians attacked in front, in that famous position, despair of holding their ground, and retire behind the Tagliamento. Does England mean to say that France and Piedmont shall be forbidden to follow them? Does England mean to say that Austria, being at war, should enjoy all the advantages of neutrality on her seas and on her own territory?—that Austria has only to retire beyond a certain line, there stop and mock her enemies, because these would be obliged by the localisation principle not to overstep the Italian territory?

" Why! this is absolutely preposterous.

" We in our own war of independence ejected from our territory three armies in succession. They fled across the frontiers of neighbouring Turkish territory, and we did not follow them, from respect for the neutral rights of our neighbour. But Turkey did not disarm the ejected Austrians, as by the law of nations she ought to have done, and the result was that they came back and attacked us again.

" However, in that case they retreated to a territory which was not their own, and therefore was under the rights and duties of neutrality, but in the present case it is pretended, upon the principle of localisation, that Austria, though belligerent, should enjoy all privileges of neutrality in her own seas and on her own territory.

" She does not confine her means of warfare to those resources which she might draw from Italy. No, she uses every nook of her dominions, whether connected with the Germanic Confederation or not, for raising armies and drawing every implement and supplement of warfare from everywhere; yet it is pretended that the powers with whom she is at war should hold her territory beyond Italy inviolable; it is pretended that she may be belligerent, but should be thought neutral too.

" Again I say, this is absolute nonsense.

" There is yet another consideration. The strategical position of Austria in the famous square between the Mincio and Adige, with its four fortresses on its four corners, is not what it was in the famous campaign of 1796. It was like an embryo then, it is like a giant now. Verona is no longer a mere fortress, but is a fortified camp, capable of sheltering 60,000 men. And diplomacy comes with its idea of localisation, and claims from France and Piedmont that they should be content with a front attack, content as it were with running their heads against a wall, and that they should abstain from taking the power of Austria in flank and rear, either by sea or by land, on any other point of her dominions. Why, the pretension is absolutely monstrous! never heard of, and without precedent in the history of warfare. If that is the boasted 'impartiality' of English neutrality, I should like to know what you call 'partiality.'

"It would be utterly vain to speculate upon what England would have to do if France were to dash at the Rhine and occupy Belgium, or attack Germany, because no man in his senses can think that the Emperor of the French can be extremely anxious to get Prussia and Germany to turn upon him while he has Austria on hand. If he be attacked by them, he will of course defend himself, and will not, I imagine, be without allies. But that he should intend to attack them—is idle dreaming. Therefore, you ought to consider the war such as it is—Piedmont and France on the one hand, and the house of Austria on the other. And on this ground I should ask, Are you willing to guarantee with your blood and money the privileges of neutrality for her non-Italian possessions to belligerent Austria? Are you willing to have your country plunged in war for the purpose of protecting Austria from such military operations as, consistently with the laws of nations, her antagonists may think fit to direct against her outside of Italy?

"If you are not prepared to do this (as I trust you are not), well, then do not rest satisfied with vague declarations, but go straight to the practical point, and let it be clearly understood by the Government that, whether the battle-field be confined to the Po, or may extend to any other portion of the Austrian dominions, you wish England to maintain a strict and impartial neutrality, and that you will as little vote one penny of subsidy, or sacrifice one drop of English blood, for the safety of Austria in the Adriatic, on the Danube, or on the Theiss, as you would for her safety on the Po.

"I think it both urgent and important, my Lord Mayor, that public opinion should be explicit in its manifestations, because I cannot forget that some distinguished members of Her Majesty's Government hinted at the possibility of England's flying to the rescue of Austria if she were to be attacked in the Adriatic.

"And I ask what is this Austria to you that you should hug

her to the protecting bosom of your Britannia, at the cost of rivers of your blood, and hundreds of millions of your money, at the cost of bringing incalculable confusion into your commercial relations, inflicting deep, perhaps incurable, wounds on your prosperity, checking your progress, and arresting the course of your peaceful reforms?

"What, I ask again, is the House of Austria to you? Is its existence very advantageous to your commercial interests? Why, just consult the latest returns of the Board of Trade, and you will see that your commerce with small but free Belgium is nearly six times as extensive as with the big but enslaved Austrian Empire; Uruguay nearly equals it; the Philippine Islands, poor Norway, and little Greece rank each before Austria. But I know that when the heterogeneous compound of that European nuisance is once dissolved your commercial intercourse with Hungary alone must be ten times as extensive as it is with the whole Austrian Empire now.

"Or is it true, as some are accustomed to tell you, that Austria is a useful ally, both faithful and true?

"Useful indeed! I know that the House of Austria was the insatiable pensioner of England, that she was the bottomless sack into which England poured millions from the life-sweat of her industrious people. I know that in the late French wars you gave them the little snug sum of 17,000,000 pounds sterling, which, according to the value money then had, was a handsome sum, but what advantage you have got from her in return is not yet recorded in history. I know that you have saved the House of Austria, but I do not know that you are indebted to her for your safety, for your rank amongst the nations, for your prosperity, or for your freedom.

"A dear ally she was to you, forsooth! Only too dear. But in what sense useful? That I have yet to learn.

"Austria, your ally, faithful and true! Why, gentlemen, remember the Crimean war! Cast your eyes on the gloomy burial-ground before Sebastopol. It was faithful Austria, that pale phantom of death, which sent your heroes to die in vain on that barren field, while she stood by idly, without firing a shot, without raising a finger in return for your generosity—a generosity ever to be regretted—which, out of regard to Austria, forced Poland and Hungary into inactivity, and in consequence rendered the war barren of results, alike to the security of Europe and to the freedom of nations.

"But if I can find no answer to the question, 'What is Austria to England?' I could tell you a tale of horrors about what Austria is to the great birthright of mankind—liberty; what she is to freedom of conscience; what she is to culture and enlightenment; what she is to everything that good men prize.

"No, England cannot, England will not load herself with the reproach of oppressed millions by stepping between Austria and retribution, for which she appears to be marked by the finger of long-forbearing but just Providence.

"And why, I ask, why should England plunge into the calamities of war for keeping *that* Austria safe? One answer is given to this question, and it brings me to the last chapter of my remarks. It is said that the integrity of the Austrian empire is necessary to the maintenance of the balance of power.

"Oh, this expression '*balance of power*,' all spectre as it is, that cannot stand the light of common sense!—this expression is a terrible Moloch, to which right, justice, political morality, freedom, and the existence of nations have been immolated as so many holocausts. Enough! Let it not be said to the disgrace of England, that she increased the number of the victims and persisted in perpetuating the sacrifice.

"I would trespass upon your forbearance were I to enter now on an analysis of the origin of the idea of 'balance of power,' or the different changes it has undergone at the hands of diplomacy, till at last it became at the Congress of Vienna such a cabalistic abracadabra,—but unlike that of the olden Syrians, creating the diseases which it is intended to cure. I shall restrict myself to asking one question. Against what kind of preponderance is the integrity of the Austrian Empire meant to constitute a barrier? Diplomatists make no secret of their answer. They say against Russian and French preponderance. They do not mention Prussia, for the rivalry existing between the Prussian and Austrian dynasties only turns upon the supremacy in the German Confederation. Their efforts are directed to prevent something from happening—namely, that Germany should not be united. But as to who should be the head of united Germany: I do not believe that any English diplomatist would think it desirable that Austria, preserved in its integrity, when there are scarcely seven millions of Germans amongst a population of thirty-seven millions, should be the first power in united Germany. Were Austria to occupy such a position, the principle of the 'balance of power' in Europe, as rightly understood, would be exactly reversed, besides being contrary to the independence and freedom of the German nation. Prussia can therefore be dismissed from our minds. English diplomacy does not think of Prussia when it says that the integrity of Austria is necessary to the European equilibrium. It evidently thinks of Russia and France.

"Well, as to Russia: there you have the indisputable evidence of history. Russia has long been an extending power, and by its extensions has long since threatened the independence and liberty of Europe. Can any one give me a single instance of Austria's having resisted Russia from extending any farther? Nobody can cite me a single instance from the whole history of these extensions. But, unfortunately, history records that Austria joined Russia in her conquests, and divided the spoils with her (Remember the case of Poland); that she played the part of receiver of stolen goods (I refer to the circumstances under which Bucovina was given to Austria); also that she assisted, absolutely assisted Russia in upsetting the European equilibrium. Of all this you will find records in history; but you will find no record of Austria's having resisted the encroachments of Russia. And why not? The reason is simple. Russia is a Sclav power, and there are seventeen million people belonging to the Sclavonic race in the Austrian Empire, all of them discontented and oppressed; and some of them form not only nationalities, but nations, who have a separate past history as a nation, and who see and hate in the Austrian rule the extermination of their independence. Such is Austria's position, and as far as Russia is concerned it has its logic, to which the Czar Alexander gave expression when he instructed Admiral Tsitsakoff to say, if he found Austria playing fast and loose, ' Ye seventeen millions, rise against the oppressor of your nationality! Here I am to help you!'

"Consider this, and you will understand the reason why France and England, in spite of excessive flattery, persuasion, and courting, were not able to induce Austria to draw her sword against Russia in the Crimean war.

"And English diplomatists call this Austria a barrier against Russia? Impossible! Gentlemen, that is not blindness, but deception; deception of the English public, little versed in foreign politics.

"Now let us turn to the relation of Austria to France.

"On the 19th of November last I read a paper at Glasgow, in which these words occur: 'In any war in which France stands on the one side and Austria on the other, France has but to advance to the frontiers of any of the nationalities oppressed by Austria and say, "Here I am to help you; rise and throw off the yoke of Austria!" and they will hail the invitation with enthusiasm.'

"I said this six months ago, when war had not yet been mentioned, and behold! my anticipations are already realised in Italy. And you may see the anticipations by-and-by realised in other quarters, too, if the French wish it. It only depends upon them: I can answer for my nation.

"No, gentlemen: the power which is called Austria is not a factor in, but a hindrance to, the equilibrium of power—she is not a barrier but a high road; not a guarantee of peace, but a sword of Damocles suspended over the tranquillity of Europe; she is a cavern from which the European volcano is fed. She is an artificial agglomeration of which the component parts possess no organic cohesion, and cannot be brought into affinity by any possible means. The very existence of such a power constantly opens new questions and provokes war. You have proof of this before your eyes. If Austria did not hold Italy in her grasp, there would be no Italian question.

"Those who state that Austria is a powerful factor in what is called the system of the balance of power, show that they have not the faintest idea of the nature of Austria's power. The artificial compound commonly called Austria is a fictitious power, which possesses only the outward show of a great power; it is a tree which has bark outside, but is empty inside. This is so because the Austrian dynasty cannot rule in the interests of a nation, and therefore cannot rule beneficially. Austria can adopt no national policy, for she cannot be German, Hungarian, Sclav, and Italian at the same time; she can satisfy one nationality only at the expense of the others; she can realise the aspirations of one solely by oppressing the others, can make one contented only by making the others discontented. Austria can display power only within her own dominions by instigating her own subjects of different races to oppress each other, and even this can only be done until she meets with strong resistance (as for example in 1848 and 1849). Excepting the one instance under Maria Theresa, when, thanks to the chivalrous assistance of the Hungarian nation, strength was displayed, Austria was never strong against an outside foe. Never! She was always beaten. Whenever she was at variance with a foreign power she could not extricate herself by her own strength; she was always obliged to have recourse to foreign help, for the Austrian soldiers do not fight with the courage which the knowledge that you fight for your 'country' imparts.

"The nations agglomerated into the artificial compound called Austria certainly contain very considerable elements of power; but that does not make the Austrian monarchy powerful. Restored to themselves, those nations would doubtless form a strong barrier against every undue extension of power, for they would have something to defend,—their liberty and independence would be dear to them. But, bound together by force, they are not a barrier, but the vulnerable point in Europe's peace and security, and an encouragement to war; for every power knows that whoever attacks Austria can reckon upon the assistance of one or another of these nationalities—maybe on all of them.

"I have thus endeavoured, my Lord Mayor, to elucidate four

points which I beg the meeting well to consider, because it is on the view which the English nation will take of these points that the policy of England will eventually depend.

"There is one point more to which I desire to advert.

"It is said that if the Italians or the Hungarians would act alone, England would not feel tempted to intervene, but that the French intervention alters the case materially; that the Emperor of the French cannot be actuated by any other but ambitious views; that he means conquest, and this England could not allow; nor ought those oppressed nations to assist in the exchange of one taskmaster for another.

"These are grave considerations, and here is my answer to them.

"It is easy to say that the oppressed nationalities should act alone. Unity of will and harmony of design are not everything, especially when the task of liberation possesses the character of a formidable war. The forces must be collected and organised, and action must be combined on a preconcerted plan, and before that combination can be arrived at the disciplined army crushes the unorganised popular masses, and the hangman and the scaffold do the rest. This is the key to the mystery that with a couple of hundred thousand soldiers millions of brave, liberty-loving people may be held in bondage for ages. Rare are the instances in history in which deliverance from oppression has been achieved without foreign assistance. The United States of America had the assistance of despotic France in establishing their independence. Even England, heroic and brave, had the 15,000 Dutch grenadiers and the Dutch fleet of 500 sail brought by William of Orange to the rescue of the liberties of England. We Hungarians, we achieved our independence without foreign assistance; but it was by foreign intervention that Austria was enabled to enslave us again.

"What a curious change has suddenly come over the minds of governments and aristocrats, that they raise a hue and cry against what they call the intervention of the French in Italy.

"Why, my lord, for about forty years we scarcely have heard of anything else than intervention against liberty. There was intervention in Spain, at Naples, in Piedmont, in Sicily, at Rome, in Moldo-Wallachia, in Hungary, in Baden, in Sleswick-Holstein, everywhere intervention against liberty. And I do not know that England ever had drawn her sword to forbid it. Sometimes a tame remonstrance may have been offered, but in the case of my own dear native land nothing was done. The English Government even said that they had not a word of observation to offer. Well, here at last is a case, when a chance for emancipation from the yoke of Austria is presenting itself by an intervention (if intervention it be), and a hue and cry is raised against it, principles are invoked in favour of oppression which were never invoked in favour of the oppressed. It is discreditable hypocrisy!

"Let Austria be replaced in the position to which the heroic arms of my nation hurled her in 1849 before foreign intervention raised her up from the dust, and be sure of it, neither Italy nor we shall want any assistance; but if England permitted Austria to be saved, and the rights of nationalities to be crushed by foreign intervention, let it not be recorded that when it might have turned to the advantage of the oppressed nationalities, then only was it first opposed by that England which was so much indebted herself to foreign assistance for deliverance from oppression.

"Besides, in this case there is not intervention exactly. There is war between established governments. Austria has declared war against Sardinia, which is the ally of France; and France helps her attacked ally. That one or more nationalities may take advantage of the opportunity,—this, I should think, is not exactly a proper reason for England to throw, Brennus-like, her sword into the scale in favour of Austria.

"What may be the especial motives which induced the present ruler of France to engage in this war, I do not pretend to know; but I know what can *not* be in his interest, and therefore cannot be in his intentions.

"It cannot be in his interest to enter on the career of a conqueror, because that would be positive ruin to him, as it was the ruin of Napoleon I. Nay, I say more, that great Captain was certainly an ambitious man, but if he were to rise this day from his grave, I feel perfectly certain that, with all his towering ambition, not even he could enter now on the career of a conqueror. At certain times certain things are impossible, and conquest is one of them. Furthermore, I know that it cannot be in the interest of the Emperor of the French—nay, it is positively against his interest— to aim at the oppression of nationalities. It was the irreverent disregard for the sentiment of nationality which sent Napoleon I. to die, a fettered eagle, on the scorching rocks of St. Helena. It is the same irreverent disregard of the sentiment of nationality which will shatter to atoms the tottering throne of Austria.

"And certainly it does strike me that Napoleon III. is not exactly the man to repeat the fault by which Napoleon I. fell. He knows that by doing good to the oppressed nationalities he may earn great moral advantage; by doing them harm, he could not earn anything but ruin to himself.

"In forming my opinions, I take *interests* for a starting point, and knowing that, in matters where so great interests are at stake, men are not likely to do that which is against their interests, I dare trust to the soundness of my conclusions.

"After all, there is some guarantee also in the force of circumstances. Suppose the logical development of the present war should offer my own nation, not an incitement to hazardous desultory riots (that I should sternly advise her to avoid), but should offer her such a chance as would with reasonable prospects place her independence within the reach of her own determination, would you advise her to reject the chance because, under the mysterious dispensation of Providence, the chance would have come to her from a Bonaparte? Why, she would be a fool to reject it! It is clear that Hungary can never be made a French Department. If her strength alone would not suffice to prevent this, her distance places her beyond that danger.

"And even as to Italy. Hated as Austria is by every Italian, the iron rod of Austria was strong enough to prevent Italy from organising and arming the nation. Thanks to the assistance of France, the Italians can do this now. Let them be wise enough to take advantage of the occasion, and having been helped to deliver themselves from the foe, if they do not know how to secure their future independence from the friend, they do not deserve to be free.

"When the fate of nations is trembling in the scale, woe to the man who, loving himself more than his fatherland, would allow himself to be guided in his judgment by his personal sympathies and antipathies rather than by what he owes to his country. I love my fatherland more than anything on earth, and, inspired by this love, I ask one boon, one only boon from England, and that is, that she should not support Austria. England has not interfered for liberty; let her not interfere for despotism.

"The only boon I ask is impartial neutrality, and this, too, I should not ask if I were not certain in my conscience that England's interference in the war would bring incalculable calamity on this your free and happy country, without any possible present profit or future compensation.

"I owe, and gladly profess to owe, eternal gratitude to England. I should feel it much like a misfortune befalling my own native land, should England inconsiderately rush into a calamitous course by uniting her destiny with that of the House of Austria.

"The English nation has mighty destinies in her hands. I beg you to remember this: No war can be thought to have assumed European proportions unless Germany and Russia become parties to it. Now, my lord, I am of opinion that, though the German nation is uncommonly excited, Germany will not fly into the war to the rescue of Austria unless Prussia abjure the policy of Frederick the Great, which raised her to the position of a first-rate power. Considering such a case I, for one, cannot think that the Regent of Prussia will risk such danger, unless he be sure of being supported by England. Thus it evidently depends on the resolution of England whether or not this war is to assume general European proportions, because if Prussia, from reliance upon England's support, plunges into the war on the side of Austria, it is more than reasonable to anticipate that France in that case will be supported by Russia.

"Let Her Majesty's Government therefore ponder well the consequences of a rash, inconsiderate step. Let them well weigh the immense responsibility of their position.

"The course which the national interests of England recommend is very clear. Keep yourself out of harm, develop your own freedom, advance your prosperity, go on steadily on the road of progress, to your own advantage as well as to that of humanity at large and of civilisation, and allow me to hope that if, under the merciful dispensation of Providence, a chance of national emancipation should arise from the present complications for any of the nationalities whom Austria holds in bondage, the good wishes and hearty prayers of this free, generous nation will be not with the oppressor but will be with the oppressed,—that England will not be backward in cheering the endeavour with her approbation, and in encouraging it by her sympathy."

Mr. Dakin proposed, and Professor Newman seconded, the following resolution :—

"This meeting, having heard with satisfaction of the official declaration of neutrality, expects that Her Majesty's Government will not violate the neutrality, either directly or indirectly, and that no treaties, or the exigencies of allies, which might draw England into difficulties, will be made a pretext for violating the neutrality."

It was further decided that this resolution should be handed to the Prime Minister by a deputation headed by the Lord Mayor. This deputation waited upon the Premier on May 26th, and was introduced by the Lord Mayor. Mr. Gilpin read the resolution of the meeting, and Lord Derby, in reply, stated that he was glad to be able to say that the views of the Government entirely coincided with the wishes expressed by the meeting.

III.
Meeting at Manchester.

On May 24th, 1859, the large Free Trade Hall at Manchester was filled to suffocation. The object of the meeting was to agitate for England's neutrality in the war that had just commenced in Italy.

I had received an invitation from the committee of management to take part in the proceedings, and to convince the inhabitants of Manchester, by a statement of my views, that it was absolutely necessary for the English nation indefatigably to watch the proceedings of the Government, so as to prevent any deviation from the declaration of neutrality.

On entering the Hall, I was greeted by the thousands present with enthusiastic cheers.

The meeting was presided over by the chairman of the Anti-Corn Law League, Mr. George Wilson. There were present on the platform many members of Parliament and members of the Town Council, whose presence rather enhanced the importance of the meeting.

The Chairman, after having briefly stated the object of the meeting, thanked me for my presence there that evening, and, amid hearty applause, assured me that as this was not the first occasion on which Manchester had accorded me an enthusiastic reception, so in future I might be certain that while I stayed in England I could safely rely on a second home, and true and faithful friends. With this he declared the meeting opened, and I, being called upon, spoke as follows:—

"Mr. Chairman, I am deeply impressed with the sympathy

SPEECH AT MANCHESTER. 219

which you, Mr. Chairman, and this important gathering have done me the honour to show to me.

"For ten long dreary years I have borne not only my own adversity, but the concentrated pangs and sorrows of my downtrodden nation.

"I have done my best to bear them with meek resignation, but have not borne them without confident hope.

"Every beating of my heart during these long dreary years was a prayer to Him who rules the destinies of nations and weighs the tears of the oppressed in the balance of retribution, who, long-suffering but just, brings the day of judgment upon those who have sinned, and forgiveness to those who have repented, that He would look down in mercy on my native land.

"But all I prayed for was only that He might grant to my fatherland one wink of a favourable opportunity, which would place the reclamation of the indestructible rights of independent national existence within its power.

"It is but rarely given to human wisdom to create opportunities, but it is given to the sense of duty to make the best of them.

"It appears as if the ray of opportunity appeared in the horizon.

"I have grown old under the weight of sorrowful years, but not too old to do the duty of a patriot. I take new strength for the performance of this duty from the sympathy you have shown to me. I will take it as a remembrance to be given to the unknown heroes of my nation, who—if God wills as we will—may shortly be called upon to take up arms and regain the independence of our country.

"The Emperor of Austria, the oppressor of the Hungarian nation, has a great war on his hands. The war commences in Italy, but it will be utterly impossible so to circumscribe it that it shall not extend to other portions of the Austrian dominions. For if Austria had but to withdraw behind a certain line, in order to prevent her antagonists from following her retreating army, or attacking her in flank and rear from other non-Italian points, the war could never be brought to an end, nor could it result in anything except useless spilling of blood.

"Therefore, since from a strategical point of view it is impossible not to anticipate that the war will by-and-by extend to other portions of the Austrian dominions, you will, I trust, agree with me that it is natural I should look upon this war as a dispensation of Providence which is likely to place the emancipation of Hungary within the reach of her own determination.

"I have ventured on these preliminary observations, Sir, because I have seen it remarked in certain papers that the policy which England might think fit to follow in the present crisis is a domestic affair of yours, with which I ought not to interfere.

"Now, I have never interfered with your domestic affairs, but the English people are much too just not to say that I am right in stating that this is much more a domestic affair of Hungary than of England.

"Why, Sir, I accept the invitation to meetings in favour of neutrality all over England for this very reason, that I might warn the English people that unless they send forth their veto, their government will interfere in our domestic affairs, and thus mar the prospects which a merciful Providence seems to have prepared for us.

"Standing on such ground, I appear here before you to-day, and ask, Is not this legitimate ground for me to stand upon?

"Well, sir, to enter at once on the subject, I shall begin by saying that I have read with great satisfaction the royal proclamation by which Her Majesty's Government publicly pledge themselves as firmly determined to abstain from taking any part in this war, and to maintain a strict and impartial neutrality. Now, so far as words can go, this is indeed a wise and patriotic determination. I defy any man to point out any present gain, moral or material, or the prospect of any future compensation, which England could derive from plunging into the horrors and calamities of war on the present occasion. The declaration of Her Majesty's Government has besides the merit of corresponding to the interests of England, and also that of being a constitutional tribute paid to the will of the nation, because I can state without fear of contradiction that there scarcely ever was an instance in matters of foreign policy when the public opinion of this country was more unanimous than we have seen it to be as manifested around the hustings during the recent elections, and in the numerous meetings held since.

"However, Sir, if it be the desire of the nation that the principle of neutrality already proclaimed should have the character of a settled rule; if it be desired that independently of the varying chances of the initiatory struggle the principle of neutrality should be acted upon with unwavering consistency, and that the professed impartiality should not degenerate into a screen for partial manœuvres calculated under some specious pretext to clear the way for intermeddling first, and intervention afterwards; if, in one word, you wish to be assured that, going one evening to bed with the idea that you are at peace, you shall not wake next morning to find yourselves at war, it is of extreme importance, gentlemen, that the manifestations of public opinion should not relax—nay, that they should be made even more explicit and universal than hitherto. For in the first place, if the proclamation of the Queen has responded to the will of the nation, it is proper that the manifestations of public opinion should respond to the proclamation of the Queen. In the second place, the situation is too grave to allow of any doubt that mighty influences are at work, some of them, I fear, not exactly of a constitutional character, for getting England into entangling alliances which, if not prevented, must eventually sweep England into war, and for purposes, too, which, while they have nothing in common with your national interests, are, I am sure, of a character utterly repugnant to your feelings.

"On this point I trust you will agree with me if you will but inquire into the exact purport of England's neutrality in the present case.

"Neutrality, gentlemen, does not only signify that you keep yourselves out of harm; it also signifies that you do not lend your support to one or another of the contending parties. I say one or another of the contending parties, because if the principle of neutrality were to be departed from, it would of course be done in favour of one party only. Therefore, that a full estimate of your neutrality may be formed in this case, it is necessary to consider with which of the contending parties Her Majesty's Government would be likely to side if they were not to remain neutral.

"Now, gentlemen, it is to official declarations and to acts that we must look for an answer to this question.

"In the first place, then, I, for one, cannot remember to have heard of one single ministerial declaration which had left the impression on my mind that Her Majesty's Government would side with Piedmont or France, if they were not to remain neutral. But I have heard of many, many declarations, which forcibly lead to the inference that, if the government were not to remain neutral, they would support Austria. We have heard Her Majesty's Secretary of State for Foreign Affairs declare openly in Parliament that Austria had strong claims on your sympathy, though (I feel bound to remark) the ground assigned for this claim—namely, affinity of race with Anglo-Saxon England—happens to have absolutely no foundation. Then we have heard it repeated in every possible variety of phrase that Austria ought to retain her Italian possessions, because she holds them by the right of the treaties of 1815, which (oh! strange oblivion of facts!) are declared inviolable. We have heard it said, that if a French fleet were to enter the Adriatic, it might be in the interest of England to oppose it; but we have not heard it said that England might oppose Austria if she were to do this or to do that. We have heard it said, that if Trieste were to be attacked, it might be in the interest of England to defend it; but we have not heard it said, that if Genoa, or Nice, or Leghorn were to be attacked they might be defended by England. Nay, the defeated Ministerial candidate for the West Riding of Yorkshire even went so far in his inspired open-heartedness as to tell the electors that it might be in the interest of England to protect Venice. To protect Venice from what? Why, of course, from the lamentable misfortune of getting emancipated from the detested yoke of Austria.

"Thus, gentlemen, the official and semi-official declarations make it only too evident that all the leanings, all the sympathies of the aristocracy, and all the inclinations of official influential quarters are turned towards Austria; so much so that if the principle of neutrality were to be departed from one fine evening, you would next morning find yourselves fighting, not for Italy, but for Austria.

"So much as to official declarations: now again as to facts. We have before our eyes the display of a vast armament, which will cost you a vast deal of money, to be sure. However, England can never do too much for the preservation of her exalted rank amongst the maritime powers of the world. To preserve this is a commendable ambition. But, Sir, it is a curious fact that just when neutrality has been proclaimed, the nation is called to arms, riflemen are called upon to form, as if some Hannibal were actually before your very doors. The navy is being manned with an energy far surpassing that which we witnessed either at the time of the Crimean war, or when India broke into a terrible conflagration. Well may you ask, What does all this mean?

"Does it mean that the government anticipate an invasion, and desire to be prepared to repel it? Why, gentlemen, the most ordinary reflection will suggest that unless it be supposed that the ruler of France is entirely out of his senses, he not only cannot be anxious to provoke, but he must be very anxious to avoid a conflict with England, since he has already one great war on hand.

"He lived in your country long enough to know that yours is not a people to be trifled with. He knows well what resources— almost inexhaustible resources—England could command for a defensive war; he knows that every country of Europe might be stripped of its last shilling, and might be exhausted to its last nerve, before the defensive resources of this sea-girt island could be so much as shaken in their solid foundations. And he knows something of the spirit of your people too. He must know that whoever would embark on an attack upon this country would have to deal not with an enemy only, but with a nation each man of which would prove every inch a hero in defence of his native land. No fear about that. 'This England never did, nor ever shall, lie at the proud foot of a conqueror.' You were not attacked when the mighty war of India burst upon you like a thunderclap from a cloudless sky. Your army and navy were far away, but your people were at home, and therefore England was safe. If you were not attacked then, it is sheer nonsense to suppose that you are in the danger of invasion now. No! England will not be attacked in this war, unless she chooses to plunge into it of her own accord.

"Then what do these armaments mean? What does it mean when you are told that England must arm in order to be prepared to defend her territory, her colonies, her dependencies, from aggression? Why, gentlemen, it evidently means that there is some intention somewhere to make England provoke that aggression in order to be able to say that government was obliged to repel it, and in order thus to get a pretence for launching into the war in support of despotic, priest-ridden Austria, whose very existence rests upon a series of acts which, as Professor Newman says in his pamphlet on 'The Sins of the House of Hapsburg,' even in the ancient heathen times were regarded as hateful to gods, and deserving of no defence from men.

" In this tendency to seize upon or create some pretence for flying to the rescue of Austria, there is a danger, gentlemen, which threatens to sweep you into the incalculable calamities of war without present gain or the prospect of any future compensation. That this is the 'true truth,' as our honest Conservatives are in the habit of saying, becomes perfectly evident from concomitant facts.

" It is pretended that England arms in her own defence, yet the fact is that ship after ship is dispatched from these shores,— to the Mediterranean, and to the Adriatic. Let nobody say that there are British possessions in that part of the world which England might be called upon to defend. Yes, there are British possessions—Gibraltar, Malta, and the Ionian Islands; however, this time there is not the slightest chance of their being attacked. But it is a notorious fact, that your ships were sent on their errand with *sealed secret orders*, and I have yet to learn that English admirals either require, or are accustomed to receive, sealed secret orders, to be opened on the high seas, only to teach them that it is their duty to protect English colonies and dependencies from aggression. What are the exact contents of those silent papers? I, of course, do not pretend to know, but facts will sometimes shed much light on the darkness of mysteries, and no sooner do those sealed secret orders make their way to the Mediterranean than we meet with very significant facts. We find that the English ship *Orion* was moored athwart in the port of Genoa, so as to hinder the disembarkation of French troops, just at the moment when the Austrians were on the offensive against Piedmont; consequently every minute of delay in landing the French troops might have become fatal to Italy. This fact may have been purely accidental, but, if so, I must own the accidents that befall impartial England are very partial indeed to Austria.

"We find another English ship refusing to salute the flag of Tuscany. The Grand Duke of Tuscany deserted his country, and went over to the enemy of Italy, but Tuscany remained and joined in the work of the emancipation of Italy. Was this a good reason for the British Government to refuse the commonest mark of international civility to the flag of Tuscany, which is not the flag of the Grand Duke, or of one government or another, but is the flag of Tuscany, just as the flag of England is the flag of England, and of nobody else? The English Government has undoubtedly the right to entertain, or not to entertain, diplomatic relations with the Government of Tuscany, but it is another thing to refuse to acknowledge the existence of Tuscany as an independent state, because that is not a fact open to controversy; it is a fact acknowledged by European public law. I do not know that such an open mark of disrespect for a nation with whom England is at peace could form part of the protection which the British Government owes to British subjects in any nook or crook of the habitable globe; but I know that the act strongly savours of a decided partiality for Austria, and is one of the many provoking annoyances and petty vexations offered to the enemies of Austria, which look much like a predetermined plan.

"Again, the public papers report that the English Government addressed a formal demand to France to the effect that 'the shores of Dalmatia in the Adriatic from Fiume (which is a Hungarian port) to Cattaro should be invested with the privileges of neutrality.' Now, gentlemen, those shores are in the possession of Austria, and Austria is at war with France, therefore the demand means nothing less than that Austria, though at war, shall enjoy the advantages of a neutral party. Nay, it means even more. Austria has an army of from thirty to forty thousand men in Dalmatia, which, from reasons into which I shall not enter now, forms the most vulnerable point of Austria. Were Dalmatia endowed with the inviolable character of a neutral territory, Austria, of course, would immediately send those forty thousand men with all their accompanying equipment to reinforce her army in Italy. Thus the proposition of the English Government just means as much as if they proposed to send an auxiliary English army of forty thousand men to the rescue of Austria in Italy. Now, gentlemen, this certainly is not impartial neutrality. It is positive intermeddling with the war in favour of Austria. It is using the great weight of England's moral power, backed by the material power of your formidable Mediterranean fleet, for the double purpose of increasing Austria's means of resistance in Italy, and of keeping her safe beyond Italy.

"In my individual position as a Hungarian, I cannot but view with deep sorrow and anxiety this conduct of the English Government. Its ultimate aim is to put a distance between the conflict and Hungary, and thus to deprive my down-trodden nation of that chance of emancipation which Providence in its wise dispensation appears to be preparing for her in the logical course of these retributive trials which are at last descending upon the crime-burdened House of Austria.

"That is preposterous, Sir. It is with regret that I use such a word; but, gentlemen, it is an absurdity, an absurdity unheard of in history, that England should throw the weight of her powerful position into the balance, in order to secure to belligerent Austria the advantages of a neutral party. It is reported in the papers that this monstrous pretension has already led to an angry correspondence ;—it may yet lead to war if the people's voice does not check the perilous course in time by a clear and emphatic manifestation of its determination not to allow the brilliant escutcheon of England to be stained by helping the House of Austria to secure their impious foot on the neck of oppressed nationalities.

"I could remind you, gentlemen, of many more equally significant facts, but I shall cut short this rehearsal of unpleasant details by saying with the *Daily News*, that 'a systematic warfare of petty provocations, vexatious and officious meddlings is pursued, dictated by a partial and unequal spirit,' and that 'not an order to an admiral, not an instruction to an ambassador, not an article in a ministerial organ, but exposes or suggests a fretful impatience of preserving even the decencies of neutrality.'

"Upon all these grounds, upon this concurrent evidence of official declarations and of facts, I repeat my assertion, that if the English Government were to depart from the principle of impartial neutrality, they would not support Piedmont and France, they would not support Italy, but would support Austria.

"I may have been too prolix, and perhaps tedious, in dwelling on this feature of the case, but I take it to be the important point around which the whole question is turning.

"Imagine that no Austrian leanings existed in official quarters; imagine that no affection or sympathy for the House of Austria, no solicitude for the safety of that curse of nations animated some influential portions of English high life. There would then be absolutely no danger of England's being drifted into the war, because there is not the slightest chance that the Government of England would feel tempted to shake the mighty trident of these realms in favour of the independence of Italy or any other of those nationalities to which the logic of the present complications might promise chance of deliverance.

"No, this is out of the question. It may cause a pang to some, but it is out of the question. The only alternative is between neutrality and war in support of Austria.

"Now, gentlemen, if war is a dreadful calamity under any circumstances, in what light would England—free, constitutional England—appear before the tribunal of political morality, before God, before history, before the opinion of civilised mankind, if from remissness of public spirit, if from too confident reliance on vague declarations, she should allow herself to be plunged into the calamities of war for such an iniquitous object as the preservation of the House of Austria, and because for the preservation of this house, therefore for the stifling of the aspirations of freedom, and the destruction of returning life in oppressed nationalities?

"I am conscientiously convinced that the people of England utterly abhor the idea of lending their help to such a wicked object. But, Sir, it is not sufficient to feel abhorrence; it is of vital importance that the people's voice should make itself heard in an explicit manner. Because as long as the grim drama of war is played exclusively on Italian territory, there is no longer any fear of your government taking a part in it. As far as that goes, neutrality is a settled rule. The danger of your getting involved in the war will commence when the war extends, as extend it must, to other portions of the Austrian dominions, and thus may present my own dear native land with a chance of emancipation.

"To prevent this, by threats, and even by armed intervention if need be,—that is the point for which powerful influences are at work, and therefore if the people are not willing (as I trust they are not willing) to let England's purse and England's sword be used for retaining in bondage the nations whom Austria oppresses, it is of extreme importance to have the Government understand, that the people of England are firmly determined that England shall remain neutral, whether the war be restricted to Italy, or extend to other portions of the Austrian dominions, and that the people of England are as little willing to pay one penny of subsidy, or shed one drop of English blood for the safety of Austria in the Adriatic, on the Danube, or on the Tisza, as they would be willing to expend money or blood for her safety on the Po. This, and this alone, is the all-important point on which everything depends.

"I do not ask you to fight for our cause; I only ask you not to allow that England should fight the battles of our enemy. Remain at peace, and keep your country out of harm.

"But you are told, there is no freedom on the other side either Suppose it were so: the greater reason for you to stand aloof. England has no business to prop one despotism against another.

"The objection might be understood if the question were, whether you should fight for French despotism; but that is not the case. I ask you not to fight at all, but to leave alone.

"Suppose there were really no other choice left in the case but the exchange of one taskmaster for another. Then I should say to you, Let the nations who are interested decide on that; it is their business, not yours.

"What could the Austrophiles answer if they were told from the banks of the Po, that despotism in France was personal, and therefore temporary, while Austrian despotism was a permanent, hereditary system; that despotism in France was a mere form of government, but Austrian despotism was murder of national existence; that, whatever may have been the form of government in France, there was always a nation besides the government, and that nation was, and is, one of those focuses from which the light of civilisation has radiated over the world, whereas Austria is not a nation, but a mere dynasty, which will be while it exists, as it was always, and actually is, the focus from which political, religious, and intellectual darkness is shed?

"But, Sir, woe to the man who, when the fate of nations is trembling in the scale, would allow himself to be guided in his judgment by his personal sympathies and antipathies, rather than by what he owed to his country. I am not one of those men who are led away by passion; I have calmly reflected on the situation; I have consulted the interest of the parties concerned, which, after all, is the definitive regulator of intents and purposes; and I have come to the conclusion that what the war turns upon is not the exchange of one taskmaster for another, but the liberation of nations. This conclusion rests, first, on the incontrovertible axiom that the difficulties of the oppressor are always a chance of deliverance for the oppressed. Next, the conclusion rests on the fact that

I defy fate itself to make the condition of Italy or Hungary worse than it is, and when things cannot be made worse, every change is for the better. In the third place, as to Italy, we must not forget that France and Austria are not the only parties in the war; there is the King of Piedmont likewise, and he, whatever else he may be, is certainly not an impersonation of the principle of despotism.

"The Italian question is a question of nationality.

"The London *Times* calls the feeling of nationality a sickly fancy, a ridiculous illusion, and a crack-brained dream. It really gives one pain to see that a respectable mouthpiece of public opinion should adopt the axiom which Milton puts in the mouth of Satan, 'Evil, be thou my good.'

"The Italian question is not a national question! There is no national question, for national feeling is a fancy, an illusion, and a product of a diseased imagination, says the *Times*.

"Why, Sir, the question of nationality means that Italy should be left to the Italians, Hungary to the Hungarians, Germany to the Germans, England to the English, and that none should be kept in bondage by a foreign power. Is that a dream?

"There was a time, gentlemen, when the distressed powers sought refuge in an appeal to the feeling of nationality, now despised, and preached to the people that this feeling should be satisfied. They did so especially in Italy; and not only England did so, but also the House of Austria, in whose favour national feeling is now trodden down.

"This nefarious hypocrisy reminds me of three proclamations issued at the time of the great war which at the beginning of the present century cost you also so much blood and treasure.

"One of these proclamations was issued by the Austrian Archduke John, and countersigned by Field-Marshal Count Goess. It was addressed in 1809 to the Italians, and in it they are called upon '*to liberate themselves from the foreign yoke! to become Italians! to become an independent Italian nation! not to suffer the annihilation of their national existence, but to bestow upon themselves such a political organisation as will exclude every foreign element from the Italian Peninsula.'* Appealing to the sacred word of the Emperor Francis of Austria, the Italian people are assured in the same proclamation *' that the House of Austria do not wish for conquests in Italy, but only wish to insure the national independence of the Italians.'*

"The second proclamation was issued by General Nugent, Commander-in-Chief of the Anglo-Austrian army, under date of Ravenna, December 10th, 1813. In it England and Austria spoke thus to the Italians: *'People of Italy! You must all become one independent nation!'*

"The third of the proclamations I wish to call your attention to was issued by General Bentinck (Leghorn, March 14th, 1814), and in the name of England called upon the people of Italy to follow the example of the Spanish nation, and become an Italian nation! to take up arms to fight out their national independence! England was ready to help them if they wished it, and did not expect anything of them, except that they should enforce their national rights and become a free and independent nation.

"These three proclamations are in strong contrast to the contempt with which the Italian national feeling is now treated.

"The Italians do nothing else now than what they were called upon to do by England and Austria: they ask the House of Austria to respect the sacredness of the word of the Emperor Francis, which, however, was so unscrupulously violated.

"The Italian question is a question of nationality, and because this is so, the first and foremost point in its practical solution is the complete and final expulsion of the Austrians from Italy.

"On this point the aspirations of the Italians were concentrated for nearly half a century. Yet they could not accomplish it, brave, death-scorning, and liberty-loving as they are. And why could they not accomplish it? Merely because it was an impossibility for them to develop, organise, and arm their national forces. If the whole of Europe were in a blaze, as it was in 1848, and Austria engaged in every corner of her Empire, the thing might be done. But without this, and by narrow localised conspiracies, it cannot be achieved. To drive Austria completely from Italy is not an undertaking which can be accomplished in a couple of hot days from behind barricades. That undertaking is a war, for which the enemy draws its forces and its resources from abroad. Therefore to free Italy from such a foe would have required the combined action of the whole nation on a preconcerted plan; that combination could not have been extended to the whole nation without disclosure, and the slightest disclosure would have resulted in the disciplined army of Austria crushing the unorganised masses—and the hangman doing the rest. Such was the condition of Italy. She remained the slave of Austria, because she could not organise and arm the nation. Now I have long doubted whether the King of Piedmont would ever unfurl the banner of Italian independence. My doubt rested on this ground, that since Austria was not engaged anywhere else, the King of Piedmont alone, with his own army, could not worst Austria, unless backed by the whole Italian nation, armed, ammunitioned, ready to fight; but before this could be brought about, the superior forces of Austria would have crushed the Piedmontese army, and this crushed, the popular masses could not have arrived at a compact organisation. Therefore I doubted whether the King of Piedmont would unfurl the banner of Italian independence, because I knew that he did not dare to do it without foreign assistance. But he has got that assistance at last, and a mighty assistance it is. Thus assisted, he not only presents Italy with a chance, nay, with a certainty of getting rid of Austria—he presents the Italians besides with the important advantage of being at last enabled to range the whole nation, organised and armed, around the banner of independence.

"Now I ask, in the name of common sense, is not that a chance for Italian liberty? Why, Sir, let the Italians be wise enough to profit by the occasion, and having had foreign assistance for getting rid of the foe, if they should not know how to secure their independence from the friend, theirs would cease to be national misfortune, for it would be national impotence.

"But what foreign assistance! assistance coming from Napoleon! That is held up before your eyes as a powerful motive which should induce you to do—what? Ally yourselves with Piedmont? Join the Italians, and thus make their chance of independence doubly secure, both against friend and foe? Oh, no; there is no chance of your government drifting England into war for that object. The argument that the Italians should distrust the Emperor of the French is held out to you as a proper motive for England's helping Austria to rivet her chains around Italy. What a marvellous logic that is! Why, in the assistance of France there is at least a chance for Italy, but the salvation of Austria is certain thraldom for Italy.

"I am not exactly the man to guess what thoughts and purposes are likely to have entered into the determination of the present ruler of France, to throw the sword of his gallant army into the scale of the destinies of Italy. Maybe, having much to retrieve in public opinion, he thought it his interest to do good in a good cause—maybe he thought a helping hand to Italy would best insure his safety from personal attacks—maybe he saw that Italy was a volcano that was sure sooner or later to explode, and he thought it best to open a safety-valve himself—maybe he thought he would consolidate his position at home by assisting in the work of emancipating Italy, which has so many claims on the fraternal affection of the French nation, because it must be owned, and ought gladly to be owned, that there is much of a noble instinct in the impressionable heart of the French nation. All this may be or may not be; I cannot tell; but what I can tell is, that interests the most antagonistic in character may often meet in one common point. It would not be for the first time that a despotic ruler of France helped a foreign nation to independence. You remember the history of the United States of America. You know how much they are indebted for their independence to the assistance of despotic France. Be this as it may, I find it safest to take interests, not men, for a starting-point in my reasonings. Standing upon this ground, I made bold to say in the speech which I delivered in London the other day, that I know what cannot be in the interest of Napoleon, therefore cannot be in his intentions. I showed by appealing to the history of his illustrious predecessor Napoleon I., that the *rôle* of conqueror or oppressor of foreign nations is against the interests of Napoleon III., and that therefore it cannot be his intention to assume it. And I am of opinion that the Emperor of the French has learnt something from the history of his uncle; he has learnt what to beware of.

"And after all there is a kind of security in the force of circumstances, too. National emancipation is not a word that, once inscribed on a banner, can easily be blotted from it. There are spirits which, once conjured up, are difficult to lay.

"While these considerations are sufficient, on the one hand, to allay any misgivings the Italians may have about being exposed to the danger of exchanging one taskmaster for another, in case they accept help from the French, you must, on the other hand, never lose sight of the fact that the Italian question is not simply a question of a change in the form of government, but a question of liberation from foreign rule, the carrying out of which presupposes a great war. This is of such decisive importance that it would really be nothing short of foolishness on the part of the Italians if they subordinated the great interest of national existence to personal antipathies, and did not accept foreign help by whomsoever it is proffered.

"But with regard to Hungary these considerations are of greater importance still.

"Looking seriously at the strategical exigencies of the war that has just commenced, it is impossible not to think it most probable that the Austrian yoke will be shaken off elsewhere than in Italy, provided England does not by her interference prevent the natural course of events. Suppose that the logical development of the present war should offer my own nation a chance for regaining her national independence, to which the history of a thousand years entitles it, and which was taken from it ten years ago only by intervention, undertaken against all public law. I ask, would it not be madness on our part if we were to reject the chance, because under the mysterious dispensation of Providence the chance had come to us from a Bonaparte? Even suppose that the Emperor of the French were prompted by a desire of conquest : surely we Hungarians cannot run any risk of being annexed to France! Distance alone places us beyond that danger.

"Such is the estimate of chances, Sir, which has led me confidently to anticipate that the present complications will result to the advantage of the nationalities whom Austria holds in bondage, provided the English Government does not rush to the rescue of Austria.

"If anything had been wanting to confirm me in the opinion that there is a chance of liberty, I should have found it in the exertions made to sweep England into the conflict in support of the House of Austria. You may be sure, gentlemen, that we should see no such exertions if the oppressed nationalities had not a chance of liberation. The aristocrats of England dread the words : *liberty of the people*, and that is the reason of all the exertions we witness.

"I beg you now to consider what course this war is likely to take in case Her Majesty's Government adhere to the proclamation of neutrality, and what course it must take if they interfere.

"If they do not interfere, the war will remain restricted to the Italian Peninsula and the rest of the Austrian dominions. Italy in the first place ; Hungary, in the due course of events, may get a chance for emancipation. Now, however the aristocracy may view such a consummation, I feel sure it is not an issue which the people of England would wish to thwart. Besides this, it is just possible that there may arise internal commotions in Turkey. Perhaps the Christian population of Turkey, finding their unwelcome protectors otherwise engaged, may wish to improve the occasion by rising for their independence. Such, at least, is the opinion which your government appears to entertain. Now, Sir, I know that England is pledged to assist Turkey in repelling foreign invasion, but I do not know, nor should I think it in keeping with the principles and opinions of the people of England, that you should draw your sword for the protection of Austria, in order to prevent the Christian nations of European Turkey from endeavouring to assert their independence.

"Such, then, are the prospects of the war if England remains neutral. If, on the contrary, England takes part in the conflict —as she would only be likely to do on the side of Austria—then, Sir, the prospect will be a long and general European war. Germany, excited as she is, will certainly not risk the danger unless Prussia takes the lead, and Prussia, situated as she is in the close neighbourhood of Russia, most assuredly will not plunge into the war unless she be certain of the support of England. On the other hand, if England lends her support to Prussia for the preservation of Austria in this war, nothing more certain than that Russia too will step in—but on the opposite side. She will side with France. And there you have a long terrible European war with every corrupt interest, with every sordid ambition brought into play, with nations set against nations, brothers against brothers, and Europe once more exposed to a repetition of that dreadful epoch in which you poured out your life-blood like water, and loaded your country with 800 millions of an eternal national debt, for not so much profit, either to yourselves or to mankind, as would balance a straw in the scale. It was the fear of the liberty which was then commencing to dawn over Europe that actuated the ruling classes of those days to involve you in those terrible wars. And is the experiment to be repeated again and again, for no better purpose than to mar the chances of national liberty by propping the rickety throne of Austria?

"Oh, I can tell, if any man on earth can, how warmly this people feels for the cause of liberty all over the world. I am a living witness of its generous instinct. I can say that I rested my tempest-tossed head on its protecting bosom for many long years. It allowed me to lay my hand on its heart during the days of hopeless adversity, and to derive consolation from feeling the pulsations of its sympathy. I came to this country a poor homeless exile, illustrious in nothing but the faintly-reflected light which fell on my undeserving head from the fact that it had fallen to my lot to be prominently connected with the struggle of my country for emancipation from Austrian oppression. Those men and those parties who this day would fain sweep England into the calamities of war for keeping their pet Austria safe—they turned the cold shoulder upon the poor exile, they opened a willing ear to the calumnies which malice heaped upon him, and treated his very name with scorn, derision, and contempt, and all this because I fought for liberty against Austria, because I was instrumental in shaking her infernal power until it was laid low in the very dust, and nothing short of 200,000 Russian bayonets could lift it up again. But what with them was a motive for hatred and antipathy was with the people a motive for love and sympathy; it cheered my sad heart with a brother's consolation; it bade me to trust and not to despair; it bade God-speed to my good cause, and showered such popular honours on my undeserving head as the most exalted despots with all their might could not command, and with all their gold could not purchase. And all this precisely because I stood before the people as a living protest against the usurpation of Austria, against her iniquitous supremacy founded on oppression of right, on contempt of the laws of humanity, on political servitude, on impious encroachments even on the inmost treasure of man's soul, the liberty of adoring God according to the dictates of conscience.

"And, behold! the hour of retribution is approaching. The Lord in His inscrutable dispensation is calling forth the dawn of emancipation from a quarter whence human wisdom could not have expected it. But dawn brings light with it. Let us bow down and adore Him who holds the designs of men in the hollow of His hand.

"And at this critical moment, which may reverse the current of long-flowing desolation, you see those who hated me, because they loved Austria, you see them again what they always have been. You see them using the mighty influence of their political power, and of their social standing, for preserving that Babylon of abomination called Austria. What if your blood be shed in streams, what if your money be spent by hundreds of millions, what if incalculable convulsion be brought into your commercial relations, what if deep wounds, maybe incurable wounds, be inflicted on your prosperity, what if your progress is checked, what if your peaceful reforms, what if the development of your free institutions be arrested—if only Austria be saved, though saved with England's money and with England's blood!

"But, gentlemen, if the English protectors of Austria remain the same as of yore, the people of England likewise remain what they always were: witness the reception I have been honoured with here this day.

"About two years ago, when the stain of an Austrian alliance menaced the bright escutcheon of England—here in this very hall, the glorious hall of England's commercial freedom, here I saw 4,000 Englishmen rise like one man and repudiate the stain of an Austrian alliance, with three hearty groans for Austria, three such hearty groans as shook the walls and, propagated on the wings of your free press, made themselves heard in the recesses of Downing Street; and the stain was averted. The danger recurs again, only that then it threatened only a stain, now it threatens national calamity—it threatens the horrors and miseries of grim war.

"Beware of illusions, men of England. As you are sure of your life, you can be sure of the fact that if the position of neutrality be departed from, England will be made to shed its blood and to waste the life-sweat of her people for no better purpose than to keep the House of Austria safe.

"No! that cannot be! No! that will not be! Let the people raise loud their mighty voice, let them thunder forth the forbidding cry—'No, this shall not be!' Give to the government of the nation the pillar of the nation's clearly-expressed will to lean upon; remind them that they are the Ministers of England, and not of Austria; fortify their national position against the influence of insidious whisperings, and let them be made clearly to understand that if you, who feel a brother's love and sympathy for the cause of Italian independence, and for the cause of Hungarian emancipation,—if you, from regards to what you owe to your country, are content not to take an active part in the war in favour of liberty, you certainly will not allow England's blood to be spilled, and England's money wasted, for the safety of Austrian oppression, whether it be in the Adriatic, on the Danube, on the Tisza, or on the Po. [The whole meeting rises to its feet, and by waving of hats and handkerchiefs, and cheering, gives expression to its unanimous approval of what fell from the speaker.]

"Let Austria be forsaken by England, and she will be forsaken by God.

"Keep your country out of the miseries of war; that is the best, the only practical service which, under present circumstances, you can render to the dawning prospects of the cause of national emancipation.

"This is the only prayer I have to make, and for my parting word, maybe the last parting word which I address to you in my life, I invoke the blessing of the Almighty upon your country—a blessing that will last to the consummation of time."

The meeting showed its sympathy by cheering me heartily. When quiet had been restored, the other subjects before the meeting were proceeded with.

What followed after this is reported in the *Times* of May 25th, 1859, as follows:—

"Mr. Bazley, M.P., said that he observed with infinite pleasure that Her Majesty's Ministers had replied to the memorial which had recently been transmitted to them from this city on the subject of non-intervention, to the agreeable effect that they regarded that memorial as supporting their own views and opinions. He hoped, therefore, that when the news of the present demonstration reached the ministerial ears, their feelings would be that the policy of non-intervention was doubly supported by Manchester. He moved the following resolution: 'That the past interference of the English Government in the disputes of Continental states has not secured that visionary object, the 'balance of power,' nor has it promoted the freedom of the nations of Europe; that its main result has been to load the industry of England with enormous debt and oppressive taxes, to impede the progress of reform, and lessen the comforts and happiness of the people.'

"Mr. Harvey (Mayor of Salford) seconded the resolution, which was carried unanimously.

"Mr. Hadfield, M.P., moved :—'That this meeting, fully confiding in the patriotism and energy of the people of England to repel any aggression upon their territory, expresses its satisfaction at the official declaration of neutrality, as embodied in the royal proclamation of the 12th inst., pledging Her Majesty's Government to abstain from taking any part, either directly or indirectly, in the war which has just commenced on the Continent, and to maintain a strict and impartial neutrality; and urges upon the government a rigid adherence to the principle of this proclamation, whether the present conflict be or be not confined to the Italian Peninsula.' Mr. Hadfield said he deeply sympathised with the country which had produced such a man as Louis Kossuth. He sympathised with the man himself, and he trusted that the desire of his heart would be accomplished, and that the noble people to which he belonged would take that position among the nations of the earth to which they were so well entitled. (Mr. Kossuth here rose from his seat and shook Mr. Hadfield warmly by the hand, amid the hearty applause of the audience.)

"Mr. J. A. Nicholls seconded the resolution in a very able speech.

"Dr. Watts supported the resolution.

"The motion was carried unanimously.

"Mr. T. B. Potter moved the next resolution :—'That this meeting expresses its thanks to Governor Kossuth for his presence here this evening, and its admiration of his noble conduct during his residence as an exile in this country.'

"The Rev. Marmaduke Miller seconded the resolution.

"Mr. S. Pope, in obedience to the call of the audience, briefly supported it, and it was carried with the utmost enthusiasm.

"Mr. Kossuth returned thanks.

"Mr. Kossuth then proposed a vote of thanks to Mr. Wilson for his presidency over the meeting, which was seconded by Mr. Potter, and carried with three cheers."

IV.
Public Meeting at Bradford.

The next evening (May 25th) I delivered a speech at Bradford, on the same subject.

The inhabitants of Bradford have always shown great kindness to me. Mr. J. Mitchell, managing·partner of the Bradford branch of the large Manchester firm of Henry—of whom the *Times* used to speak as the "Merchant Princes"—lived in Bradford. Mr. Mitchell was one of my truest and most active English friends. Whenever I delivered a lecture, it was he who always secured me a sympathetic audience at Bradford. And whenever it was necessary, in the interest of my country, to carry on political agitation, a simple word to him was sufficient to organise, within two or three days, one of those monster public meetings which form so distinctive a feature in the active life of free England.

It so happened, also, on this occasion, that, in accordance with a wish expressed by me in Bradford, as in other towns, the Town Council first passed a resolution in favour of neutrality, and then I received an invitation to be present at a meeting to be held on May 25th. This meeting rivalled that of Manchester in point of numbers.

The speech I delivered at this meeting was chiefly devoted to the Philo-Austrian agitation in Germany, as may be seen from the subjoined extract:—

Speech by Kossuth, delivered at Bradford, May 25th, 1859.
"Were Her Majesty's Government to abandon their neutrality, they certainly would not tell you that their reason for doing

so was their irrepressible sympathy for the House of Austria. No, they would not say so; but they would appeal, as they have always done, ever since the present complications arose, to the inviolability of the treaties of 1815; they would say that the territorial integrity of Austria forms an essential part of the balance of power, and that this equilibrium must be maintained; and they would further point out to you, that the extension of the area of hostilities as far as Dalmatia might have a disturbing influence on the internal tranquillity of the Turkish Empire.

"I have gone fully into these subjects, partly in the speech I delivered yesterday in Manchester, and partly in that which I delivered last Friday in London—as far as it is possible to treat such an extensive subject in one speech. My speeches have obtained publicity through the daily press, and the interest with which you watch the present complications makes me believe that you have paid some little attention to them; therefore I will not trespass on your patience with a repetition of those arguments. I only wish to express my firm conviction, that though the treaties of 1815, the balance of power, and the internal tranquillity of Turkey, may be very often mentioned in diplomatic correspondence, in statements, and in manifestoes, yet the danger of England's becoming implicated in the war does not come from these quarters : the danger that threatens you most comes from Germany.

"It is notorious that the Germans—and the fact is really astonishing—even those of them who belong to the Liberal party, have worked themselves up into a feverish enthusiasm for Austria. They are ready to rush into war to preserve the territory and power of Austria intact. That whoever attacks Austria, even in her non-German possessions, attacks the German Confederation; and further, that the German Confederation must defend Austria in all her Italian possessions also;—these are postulates that you will find reiterated daily by nearly every newspaper in Germany, and urged in the German Chambers of Representatives with the eloquence of Demosthenes. The impression created by these tidings is entirely confirmed by the diplomatic reports which I have had an opportunity of perusing.

" The matter went so far that, though Austria was the aggressor, and thereby deprived her German partisans of the opportunity of looking upon her trouble as a *casus fœderis*, yet the artificially-fostered martial feeling ran so high, that it was actually decided that at the meeting of the German Diet, on May 2nd (therefore after the Austrian Army had invaded Piedmontese territory), a resolution for a declaration of war against France, on behalf of Austria, should be carried by a majority of votes.

" This did not happen, however, and I must admit that it was partly due to the protest of the English Government that these measures, fraught with danger, were not resorted to.

" But I must request you to direct your attention to two circumstances. The first is, that the English Government took exception, not to the fact of the Germans helping Austria in this war, but only to their wishing to do so *at this early stage* of it. Lord Malmesbury stated this distinctly, in his instructions to the English diplomatic agent at Frankfort. The other circumstance is this, that your Government have not at all given the Germans to understand that, if they interfere in the war, they cannot reckon on England's assistance, because England will remain neutral. They have only told them not to expect English support if they interfere at this early stage, because *at present, under existing circumstances*, the English Government wish to remain neutral.

" Therefore to you they talk of neutrality, but in official diplomatic correspondence England's neutrality is spoken of only as a thing in force for *the present* and *under existing circumstances*.

" These are very alarming signs, gentlemen; for it is sophistical and contrary to all common sense to say that events might take a turn that would oblige England to relinquish her neutrality, in order to defend her possessions. This supposition is sheer nonsense, unless England join of her own accord in the war; therefore, the contingency of such a change in the *existing circumstances*, under which your Government forestall the eventual possibility of their not maintaining their proclaimed neutrality, can only refer to the case of the present war not remaining confined to Italy, but extending to some other non-Italian possession of Austria.

"Gentlemen, what fills me, as a Hungarian patriot who daily prays for the deliverance of his oppressed country with the greatest alarm is this stipulation as to the neutrality of England. For, as I have shown in my former speeches, the extension to other Austrian dominions of the war now commenced in Italy is such a strategical necessity, that without it no satisfactory result can be come to, however many battles may be won.

"I must, therefore, candidly confess that I so confidently hope that the extension of the seat of war will bring a chance for the liberation of my much-suffering country, as to believe that anybody who opposes this extension will dash from the lips of my nation the cup of liberty held out by Providence, which manifests itself in the favourable turn of events.

"Well, gentlemen, I appeal to my past history to prove that I have always been a staunch sympathiser with aspirations for the German people's liberty, and that I have done everything in my power to maintain friendly relations between my country and the German nation. This was rendered desirable, not only by the solidarity of the cause of liberty, but also by the many interests we have in common. Therefore I am sincerely sorry that, in the present instance, the Hungarian and the German nations are ranged under opposite standards, in consequence of their wishes and aspirations.

"Still I can say without hesitation, that if I could be sure that the warlike excitement of the German nation would not draw England into the war, I should not believe that the incomprehensible sympathy of the Germans for the House of Austria would be able to give affairs such a turn as to afford me reason for fear that my patriotic hopes would be frustrated. I do not believe it, because the Royal Prussian Government has declared categorically and officially, that, unless Germany is attacked, Prussia will not allow herself to be dragged into the war for the particular interests of the Austrian dynasty, in spite of a majority of votes of the German Diet; though she may by this decision run the risk of causing a rupture in the Confederation. And I believe that this declaration of the Prussian Government may be safely relied upon, for it is not at all in the interest of the Hohenzollerns that the position as a great power of the House of Hapsburg, or rather of Lorraine-Vaudemont, should come out unimpaired from the present calamity. On the contrary, it is in their interest that Austria's power should be considerably reduced; for otherwise they themselves would sooner or later have to take in hand the work of humiliating the arrogance of the Court of Vienna. Add to this, that if Prussia, against all expectations, should let herself be persuaded to take up arms for the defence of the Court of Vienna, this result would doubtless, considering the constrained relations between the Courts of St. Petersburg and Vienna, lead to Russia's taking part in the war on the opposite side. When we regard the geographical position of those countries this is a circumstance which makes it improbable that the Prussian Minister of War, who, in his sympathies for Austria stands conspicuously alone among his colleagues, should soon become the leading man in the Berlin Cabinet. It may be taken for granted that, in that case, the Government of Berlin would only be tempted to interfere with arms for the protection of the family interests of the House of Hapsburg, if Austria in return were to desist from competing for the supremacy in the German Confederation, and leave the House of Hohenzollern in undisputed possession of it. Now if anything is certain in this world, it is that the proud House of Austria will never do this, unless she is driven out from Germany by force.

"As the sympathy for Austria so artificially kindled in the bosom of the Germans cannot reckon on support from Prussia, I am firmly convinced that if every prospect of help from England were also excluded, the Germans would not join in the war, in spite of the excited state they are in; or, if they did, the armed interference of one part of Germany, split up into parties herself, could neither prevent the war from spreading to the banks of the Tisza, nor there become dangerous to the Hungarian nation's just aspirations for independence.

"But the matter assumes an entirely different aspect if you come to consider that it is just the martial enthusiasm of the German nation that may furnish a pretext, or, if you like, an opportunity to your Government for dragging the English nation into the war in order to save Austria. In such a case it would be English interference which would snatch the cup of liberation from the lips of my nation, and which would preserve Austrian rule even in Italy.

"Gentlemen, I am afraid, and not without reason, of the possibility of English interference. I am not an alarmist, nor do I conjure up dangers; I simply look to facts.

"From trustworthy private sources I hear that Russian diplomatists state unhesitatingly that there really exists a treaty between Austria and the English Government.

"I do not go quite so far as to make a similar statement. However, it is a fact, confirmed by the confidential mission of Lord Cowley to Vienna, that your Government has assured Austria of their assistance, if the Viennese Cabinet will give their sanction to the introduction of some reforms in the public administration of Italy.

"That the Italian question is nothing else than a question of national existence, which cannot be solved by some paltry reforms, everybody in Europe knows except your own Government, who persistently shut their eyes to facts clear as daylight. And why do they shut their eyes? Because they pertinaciously start from the assumption that the aspirations of the Italians for national independence cannot be entertained for a moment, and that the Court of Vienna must be preserved intact in all her possessions. This is the reason why the English Government, ever since the commencement of the present complications, have displayed such feverish activity in order to avert the danger of war from Austria. This activity of the English Government stands in such close connection with the agitation in Germany, and it is, further, so self-evident that this agitation in Germany was intended to discourage the French and Sardinian Governments from commencing hostilities, that I should not be at all surprised to hear, when once the secrets of diplomacy are unveiled, that the English Government had a hand in those matters which we witness with surprise in Germany.

"It is a notorious fact that the Emperor of Austria, in his manifesto of April 28th, in which he informed his 'peoples' of the outbreak of hostilities, expresses a decided hope that he will *not stand alone;* and he clearly states that he bases his hopes on the Germans. But the Germans, in discord with Prussia, cannot dare to join in the war in favour of Austria, unless supported by England. I can also tell you, gentlemen—and I take my information from the reports of the English diplomatic agents in Germany—that the Germans assuredly expect assistance from England. If you add to this that the English Government notoriously cling still to the assumption that Austria must emerge from the present calamities without loss of territory; if you add the facts I enumerated in my London and Manchester speeches, which leave no doubt that the English Government is manifesting great partiality towards Austria; if you add that by making the observance of neutrality 'at present' and 'under existing circumstances,' dependent on conditions, a loophole for eventual interference has been purposely kept open; if you add further—and on this I lay especial stress—that your Foreign Secretary has forwarded to the French Government, through Lord Cowley, a note bearing date 5th inst., in which it is clearly stated that the English Government expect that hostilities will be confined to the Italian Peninsula: it is impossible, gentlemen, that you should not perceive that, while the reins of the government of England remain in the hands of the present Philo-Austrian Ministry, you are exposed, in spite of the neutrality laid down in Her Majesty's proclamation, to the danger of being mixed up in the war for the benefit of Austria, should hostilities not remain confined to Italy.

"This danger can be averted from England solely by an energetic manifestation of public opinion. There is all the more necessity for this, as your Government are either quite mistaken as to the true nature of the feelings of the English public, or they wish to mystify the French, who have taken up arms to fight for the independence of the Italians.

"You have clear proof of this in what Lord Malmesbury says in his note of May 5th, to which I have already referred :—

"' *The British nation* almost unanimously *disapproves of the present war;* it wishes to prevent England's participation in its continuation, and earnestly hopes *that the war will be confined* to the *Italian Peninsula.*'

"Now, gentlemen, of all these statements, this only is true—that the British nation wishes to remain neutral in the present war. It is not true that it disapproves of the war, or that it wishes to have it confined to the Italian Peninsula. On the contrary, I can state from my own personal experience, that the British nation rejoices that the present war opens a prospect to the Italian nation of liberating their country from the Austrian rule, and that the English people wish from the bottom of their hearts that hostilities would extend to the other dominions of Austria, and lead to the liberation of the other nationalities, especially of my own nation, groaning under the yoke of Austria. I possess too many signs of your sympathy for my country to doubt that this statement of mine will be borne out by this crowded meeting.

"It is now nearly eight years, gentlemen, since I first set foot on this free and happy island, and from that moment up to the present day I have had, and still have, so many proofs that the British sympathise universally and genuinely with Hungary's struggle for independence, that I may safely affirm that, however much the Government of Great Britain may wish to preserve the rule of the Court of Vienna over Hungary, there is no ministry that would dare propose to the British nation to take up arms in order to prevent Hungary from becoming free, and that there is no parliament that would vote a single man, or a single penny, for carrying on a war expressly undertaken for obtaining such an avowed object.

"In order, therefore, to enable the present Government of Great Britain to interfere in the present war for preserving the sway of the Austrian dynasty over the nationalities groaning under Austrian yoke—to do this, I say, an opportunity, not to say a pretext, is required which, it may be supposed, will not meet with such decided opposition from the British nation.

"For this reason I have told you, gentlemen, that the danger of your being implicated in the war comes from Germany; for if the German nation interferes in the war, and by this interference extends the scene of hostilities to the Rhine, your Government will say that surely France does not fight there for liberating nationalities, as she does on the banks of the Po, or might do on the banks of the Tisza, and that it is in the interest of England not to allow of any territorial change on the Rhine, or any kind of curtailing of the independence of the German nation.

" But I assure you, gentlemen, that the present war does not threaten either the territorial integrity or the independence of Germany. The agitation in Germany is only the result of an excitement got up by artifice, the sole object of which is to preserve the integrity of Austrian power, so that it may continue to serve as a support to different petty German despots and aristocrats, in their endeavours to suppress all aspirations for German liberty.

" It is most desirable that the British public should not be misled, through the great clamour which is made about the agitation in Germany, as to what the nature and meaning of it is; and as I understand that your town, which is extending and rising in importance very fast, is closely connected with Germany in a commercial as well as in a social respect, I think it would not be inappropriate for me to enter, with your permission, a little more fully into this German question.

" I admit, without the least hesitation, that I perfectly understand that the Bavarian, Suabian, Hessian, Nassau, Reuss-Schleitz and Gleitz-Lobenstein princes, *et hoc genus omne*, are anxious to rush to the rescue of that Austria upon which they look as the chief support of the security of their diminutive thrones. I can also understand that the Metternichs, the Schwarzenbergs, the Wittgensteins, the Windischgraetzes, and other similar celebrities whose names appear in the Almanac of Gotha, are quite ready to range themselves under the banner of Austrian despotism. However, I do not believe that they will find much sympathy for their particular family interests among the liberty-loving British people.

" But I must admit that I am at a loss to understand by what process of reasoning the German people, more especially the German Liberals and the German democrats, can have arrived at the conclusion that it is in their interest to assist Austria in any part of the globe, and especially to try to maintain her power in those of her dominions which do not form part of the German Confederation.

"For it is a historical fact that the German princes who now instigate their nation to rush into the calamities of a great war for the defence of Austria, have for half a century so much oppressed their subjects that the yoke has become quite unbearable, and has led to armed resistance.

"The German nation has fought with admirable patience and untiring perseverance for liberty and unity; first in the press, afterwards in the Diet, and finally with arms.

"And who was it that instituted political inquisition in Mayence in 1819? Who induced the Diet to pass a resolution against the liberty of the press, against the right of free association, and even against the colours symbolic of German unity?

"Who was it that filled the prisons with patriots, and populated the distant wildernesses of America with noble-hearted German democrats?

"Who was it on whose assistance the German princelings could always rely in the work of oppressing their subjects?

"Austria! always Austria! Not Austria the people, those participators in the sufferings, but Austria the Court of Vienna. This was the source of all the evil that during long years befell Germany.

"Now, therefore, I ask, is it not strange that the liberal-minded Germans are in a state of feverish excitement about the danger in which Austria is placed, and are ready to sacrifice their lives for the preservation of that power, the annihilation of which they ought to hail as the beginning of Germany's regeneration?

"When the representatives of the German people met in 1848 at Frankfort, in the Church of St. Paul, and gave unanimous expression to the universal wish of their constituents that Germany should become united, was it not an Austrian Archduke who first misled them by his artificial trickeries, and, later on, silenced them and imprisoned or exiled those who had elected him Governor of the Empire?

"Was not the ambitious opposition of the House of Austria

the rock on which the patriotic aspirations of the German nation were wrecked?

"When the Germans of Schleswig-Holstein, wishing to remain Germans, took up arms against the policy of centralisation pursued by Denmark, was it not an Austrian army which surrendered them to their enemies?

"When the Hessians, having exhausted every means for the preservation of their lawful institutions, and following in the footsteps of William Penn, had recourse to passive resistance against their perjured ruler, was it not an Austrian army that overcame their resistance?

"Wherever a spark of the aspirations for liberty of the year 1848 was left, it was trampled upon by the armies of Austria.

"Again I ask, is it not strange that the freedom-loving German people should now wish to preserve intact the tyrannical power of those whom, a short ten years ago, they hated as the personified curse of Germany, and who up to this moment have done nothing in any way to remove this well-deserved hatred?

"Is it possible that the German democrats can forget that the hand which now pretends to uplift the banner of Germany, a country neither attacked nor threatened by any one, is the very hand that is stained with the blood of Blum and Trütschler, and that, in Germany, has oppressed liberty as well as unity?

"Is it possible that the friends of Robert Blum should accept Windischgrätz as their leader? that Guttenberg's nation should rally round the banner of Metternich? and that the people of Schleswig-Holstein should follow a Schwarzenberg?

"Extraordinary aberration! An Eastern saying tells us that if we are doubtful what to do for the best, we should notice what our enemies do. If we do the opposite, we may be certain that we are doing right. The German nation need only bear this simple maxim in mind to come to the conclusion that the support of Austria, for the very reason of its being so much in the interest of the celebrities of the Almanac of Gotha, cannot prove a profitable policy for the German nation.

"But let us examine a little whether the Germans have any

reason to fear that the war now going on may at present, or in the future, threaten the territorial integrity, nationality, or independence of Germany.

"As regards the present, it would be superfluous to say a word to prove that, unless the Germans attack the French, these will not attack Germany in the present war. To dream of such a thing is an absurdity which even the Court of Vienna did not dare hint at; though it has done everything to excite the Germans against the French.

"The paradox of the late General Radovitz, long since exploded, that the Rhine must be defended on the banks of the Po, has been notably revived.

"The Emperor of Austria is a cunning man. Neither the Emperor of the French, nor anybody else, has attacked him, as a 'member of the German Confederation:' he was attacked on account of keeping the Italians in Italy under foreign yoke. Yet in his proclamation issued at the commencement of the war, as a reigning member of the German Confederation, he addresses himself to his '*German brethren,*' and reminds them of the '*Italian bulwarks*' which his '*German brethren have taken at the expense of their lives.*'

"Is this, then, Radovitz's paradox—'The Rhine must be defended on the Po;' or, in other words, 'Germany cannot feel secure unless Italy is kept under the Austrian yoke?'

"This need only be expressed in so many words to elicit its own refutation. Besides, it is a historical mis-statement. Those 'Italian bulwarks' might have protected Austria (I need now stop to inquire when and if they have ever done so), but they never could, and never did protect Germany. No French general was ever such a fool as to cross the Alps and then re-cross them, in order to attack the Germans, his next-door neighbours along the Rhine. That is therefore an exploded prejudice which deserves no consideration.

"Agitation in Germany is kept up, not by this prejudice, but by Austrian intrigues, which have succeeded in impressing it upon the minds of the Germans that the Emperor of the French is endeavouring, by his campaign in Italy, to assume the *rôle* of his uncle as a conqueror of the world ; that, if Austria is defeated, he will attack Germany, and that therefore it is in the interest of Germany to preserve the integrity of Austria's power, so as to enable her to defend Germany with the Italian, Hungarian, Croatian, and Polish bayonets thus retained.

"To this I have only to say that whoever or whatever the Emperor of the French may or may not be, it is certain that he is not a lunatic. Lunatic he would be if he cherished the idea of becoming a conqueror of the world. Half a century ago the ambition of Napoleon I. sent him to St. Helena to die. Since then the world has progressed. Love of freedom, and feelings of nationality have grown, and the people have become stronger. The *rôle* of Napoleon I. would nowadays be an anachronism, a thing which has no place in history. Were it not that an inclination to transcendentalism is one of the peculiarities of the German character, it would indeed be astonishing that such an educated and enlightened nation as the Germans are should be caught in the net of Austrian intrigue, and pursued by a chimera of this kind—should be ready to rush into the calamities of a great war, and put the whole of Europe in flames, for no other object than to enable Austria to continue to rule her non-German possessions, by which alone the House of Hapsburg is able to suppress the German people's national aspirations for freedom.

" I must add that if for the establishment of their security, which is at present threatened from no quarter, the Germans calculate on the Italian, Hungarian, Croatian, and Polish bayonets of the Cabinet of Vienna, their calculation is disgraceful, unjust, and inaccurate.

" It is disgraceful, because the Germans thereby plainly admit, to the discredit of their nation, that they are not capable of defending themselves, with their own strength, against a foreign attack. Really, I am astonished that German self-respect does not indignantly repudiate this degrading insinuation.

" It is not only disgraceful, it is also unjust. For what does it mean, but that the Germans wish to secure the Austrian yoke over the Italians, Hungarians, Croatians, and Poles, in order to enable the Court of Vienna, in return, to protect the Germans, who have despaired of their own vitality?

"It means simply that the Germans wish to establish their freedom on the servitude of others; their independence on the enslavement of others. It means that the Germans demand for themselves what is included in the words 'Fatherland, national existence, and freedom,' but refuse it to others, who are as much entitled to its possession as the Germans themselves. It is written in the law of the religion that teaches us to love our neighbours : 'Do unto others as ye would that they should do unto you.' I do not believe that this meting with two different measures—this refusal to do what is just, right, and charitable— will call forth a response from your freedom-loving hearts, or be rewarded by the sympathy of the British nation.

"And, finally, I say that this disgraceful and unjust calculation is also inaccurate. For argument's sake, let us suppose the impossible; let us suppose Germany threatened by a foreign conquest. The subjugation of Germany would be so dangerous to the freedom and independence of the other nationalities, that, in such an emergency, the Germans could safely rely on the assistance of the nationalities liberated from the Austrian yoke. On the contrary, if it were by the interference of Germany that the liberation of the nationalities was frustrated, all these nationalities would become so many enemies of Germany; their hatred of Austria would extend to Germany also, in the same way as the horror of the hangman extends to the hangman's assistants. Even if those nationalities, oppressed by Austria with the assistance of Germany, were led into battle for the protection of Germany, they might ponder over the matter; and it is quite possible that the very bayonets on which the Germans had relied for their safety might become a danger to them.

"A free man does not voluntarily pass under the yoke, but a dissatisfied servant easily changes masters. To him who has nothing to lose every change is a hope.

"Let the Germans beware of forcing other nations to proceed on this path.

"However, I must tell you, gentlemen—and I wish that the Germans would not, on account of my own insignificance, refuse to give their unbiassed attention to my words, in case they should be brought to their knowledge—I say, that if I were a German, I would look for the safety of Germany, not in the compulsory military service of the nationalities oppressed by the Court of Vienna, but in the realisation of the aspirations inspired by the national genius of Germany, which has been handed down as an inheritance from one generation to the other ever since the times of the last of the *Hohenstaufens*, but which still lives only in the hearts of the people:—I would look for the safety of Germany in her unity.

"If the German nation does not look forward to the future with such fearless confidence as by her strength and self-esteem she would be justified in doing, it is only because she is not united —it is because Germany, like Italy, is only a geographical expression; the abode of a nationality, not of a nation—simply of a nationality, which can become a nation only by unity.

"A united German nation would feel as safe in the arms of unity as a babe in the arms of its mother.

"This unity can be realised in two ways only: either in the form of a republic, like that of the United States of America, or in the form of a monarchy.

"It does not become me (moreover, this would hardly be the place) to analyse the merits of the two different systems, but it comes within the scope of my observations to point out to you that the *chief obstacle* to German unity in the form of a republic, and the *only obstacle* to it in the form of a monarchy, is presented by the House of Austria — that same House of Austria for the integrity of which the Germans exhibit such enthusiasm.

"Doubtless every German prince is hostile to a republican union; this is but natural. But, after all, the chief obstacle is presented by the Austrian dynasty, for the other princes can only oppose to the aspirations of their peoples the armed force recruited from among their subjects; while, on the other hand, Austria also has at her disposal the armed force of 30,000,000 non-German people, drawn into her service against their own will.

"To the realisation of the aspirations for unity in the form of a monarchy the House of Austria is the only obstacle, as is proved by the events of 1848. The German nation offered the imperial crown to the King of Prussia, who accepted it on condition that the other German princes agreed to its acceptance. All agreed, except Wurtemberg. Of course the dissension of this state alone would not have proved a bar. What, then, prevented the German people from carrying out its warm wish and decision? The opposition of the House of Austria. It could not happen otherwise; for Austria, as long as she has the position of a great power, will never resign herself to the humiliation of allowing somebody else to rule as Emperor over her. If the Germans were to succeed in preserving the Austrian rule over her non-German dominions, and then, forgetting the hard lessons of the past, were to select the ruler of Austria as German Emperor, the consequences would be either that German unity would again be frustrated, because Prussia refused to acknowledge as German Emperor a ruler in whose heterogeneous possessions but 7,000,000 of Germans are to be found, or Germany would possess an Emperor who, with the forces drawn from among his 30,000,000 non-German subjects, would keep the Germans in subjection, and in turn, with the Germans keep in subjection those 30,000,000.

"I ask, therefore, is it not a great blunder on the part of the Germans, to be ready to shed their blood for the preservation of Austria as a great power, when it is clear as daylight that, if they were to succeed they would thereby sacrifice either national unity or liberty?

"These considerations, I believe, are sufficient to convince anybody that the movement in Germany is not of such a nature as to deserve that the British nation should allow itself to be dragged into the war by it; on the contrary, the more friendly you are to the German nation the more you must endeavour to prevent such a course being taken.

"The fact is, powerful influences are at work to make Germany play the part of hangman's assistant in the oppression of other nationalities; but you may be sure, gentlemen, that however much the Germans may be blinded for the moment by passion, they will not rush into the danger unless they believe they can rely on England's alliance and assistance.

"Therein lies the danger for you, gentlemen, and this danger can only be removed by the British nation making it unmistakably understood, to those who govern the country here, and to those who carry on intrigues on the Continent in order to mislead the public opinion of this country, that Great Britain is firmly determined to observe a strict neutrality, whether the war extend to the other provinces of Austria or not; and that this liberty-loving people will not sacrifice a drop of British blood, or a penny of British money, for the preservation of the ambition and power of the Austrian dynasty, either on the Adriatic, the Danube, and the Theiss, or on the Po and the Mincio.

"I beg you to interest yourselves in the incidents of the struggle, so that if it happens, as I hope it will happen, that the sacred cause of the liberation of nationalities is enabled to profit by the present complications, it may not be recorded in history that England failed to encourage the oppressed, in their struggle for liberty, by her approval, and to cheer them up by her sympathy. But, beyond this, do not interfere in the war; and, of all things, beware lest those in power should make England an accessory to the crime of Austria. There are men in England, possessed of the confidence of the people, who avow peace as their principle. They must know that, whoever supports Austria supports the unavoidable repetition of continuous wars, and stamps himself as a champion of darkness and despotism. This is not a *rôle* that would suit England's character or exalt her interest. Let those, therefore, whom it behoves take care that the inclinations of the counsellors of the Queen shall not be opposed to Her Majesty's proclamation of neutrality.

"And, with this, I bid 'Good bye' to you. As these words pass my lips, my heart is moved with deep emotion, for I remember the hearty sympathy with which you have honoured me in the past. Permit me to hope that my humble name will not entirely pass from your memory; but, above all, I request you to preserve a kind remembrance of my dear country. We live in troubled times. Who knows what the morrow may bring? Whatever it may bring, a sense of duty will make us do what reason recommends. We are not professional revolutionists: we are patriots, and will do our duty as such. You will hear no reports from Hungary of senseless insurrections and light-minded playing with the lives of the sons of a noble-hearted nation; but, if God wills as we will, you may possibly hear that my nation has risen with the full right gained by its history of a thousand years; and when you hear that the banner of national independence has again been unfurled on the soil of my country, saturated with the blood of martyrs, oh! let me hope that you will include my country in your prayers at the Throne of Grace, and let me believe that such expressions of sympathy from the liberty-loving British nation will re-echo all over this happy island, as will preserve us from the misfortune and you from the disgrace of England's Government lending to Austria for our suppression the weight of Great Britain's power."

V.

Termination of my Tour of Public Meetings, at Glasgow.

After London, Manchester, and Bradford, only Glasgow* remained to finish my tour of public meetings.

* In speaking of Glasgow the scenes of the past are recalled to my memory.

If the gratitude which I owe as a man and as a patriot to the people of Great Britain in general allowed me to make any distinction between different places according to the duration of the kindness I received, I should have to say that in Scotland I felt as if in a second home, and that there I was received as a son, and never repudiated. And in my second home the liberal-minded public of Glasgow especially were what, as a patriot, I might call my "*stronghold;*" and, as a bread-winning father of a family, I looked upon it

The public meeting at Glasgow was held immediately after the one at Bradford (May 26th or 27th).

as my reserve bank, the door of which was always open to me. In the latter respect only Edinburgh could compete with it. With regard to what I said of Glasgow, that to me as a patriot it was a "stronghold," the same thing could be said by Garibaldi, by Mazzini, and by many others whose names are connected with the struggles for liberty on the Continent.

The chief national characteristics of the Scotch are constancy and unwearied perseverance. These qualities made that dreary and barren land a home of prosperity, a flourishing paradise. Those who see with envy that Scotchmen go anywhere, take to anything, are always and everywhere happy, are in the habit of saying that you may bury a Scotchman in the bowels of Vesuvius and he will find a way out. It is meant for irony, but is the greatest compliment that can be paid to a nation. And that perseverance which is afraid of nothing, is in a special degree a characteristic of the inhabitants of Glasgow. It is only necessary to look at their harbour to be convinced of this.

Glasgow is situated on the banks of the Clyde, some twenty-two English miles from the sea. The Clyde was formerly such a small rivulet that there are people still living who have "jumped" over it at Glasgow; at the beginning of this century, even at high tide the depth of the water was never more than $3\frac{1}{2}$ feet. And out of the bed of this rivulet the perseverance of the inhabitants of Glasgow has, at a distance of twenty-two miles from the sea, built an enormous port, comprising an area of fifty acres, which is crowded with a whole forest of masts: along the quays (the total length of which is 1,400 feet) hundreds of ships lie, three deep, including some of the largest steamers afloat, which carry thousands of travellers and the products of Scotch labour to America, India, and Australia. The annual revenue from customs dues collected at Glasgow amounted to £470 at the beginning of this century, and between 1850-60 it had already risen to £700,000 per annum.

This steady perseverance, which has wrought such wonders of material progress (setting an example to those who consider and take counsel for years while slowly carrying out some trifling undertaking!), does not belie itself in respect of political sympathy and faithfulness to principles. When once a Scotchman has become somebody's friend, he steadily remains his friend. When once he has taken up any matter, he does not drop it again through good or evil report. His interest is not like a fire of straw, but like that of the gathering coal which he burns on his hearth.

As such I found the kindness of my Glasgow friends in the past, and such I find it now, after an absence of nineteen years: they have not yet excluded me from their kind remembrance. Let them accept my grateful thanks, sent from my distant retreat. More especially I owe thanks to Mr. John MacAdam, who holds the first place amongst my Glasgow friends.

Its arrangements had been taken in hand by the greatly-esteemed committee of the Parliamentary Reform Association. The members of this committee were present on the platform, and in consequence the importance of this political demonstration was greatly increased. It was an imposing sight to see the vast expanse of the City Hall crowded to suffocation. Of my speech, which I could only improvise, in consequence of the great exertions I had undergone during the preceding few days, I find, besides the headings of the subjects, only the following extracts amongst my notes :—

"*Introduction :* Once more, very likely for the last time in my life, do I appear before you in this hall, the walls of which have so often re-echoed your expressions of sympathy for the poor exile, and for the exile's oppressed country.

" When I see friends before me and around me on this platform who have faithfully stood by me in the days of affliction when there was no ray on the dark horizon of my patriotic hopes— friends who have consoled me like brothers when my heart was overwhelmed with sorrow, who have encouraged me when I was disheartened and when my hopes had dwindled away, and have taught me to trust to Him who weighs in the balance of retribution the tears of those who suffer: I am possessed, Mr. Chairman, by the thought that I may never again see these friends in this life, and by the remembrance of all the kindness which has been bestowed upon me on so many occasions in this hall, and I feel that I do not possess that self-possession which is necessary to me to discharge, I do not say satisfactorily, but only passably, the task which, on the invitation of the much-respected committee of the Parliamentary Reform Association, I have undertaken on this occasion, when I am talking to you for the last time in my life. The last time, I say; for whether the hopes which I attach to the present complications are fulfilled or frustrated, I do not think it probable that I shall ever again be able to see this city.

"If ever it was necessary that I should have a most tranquil mind, it is at this moment; not only on account of the importance of the subject before us, but also because I have not been able to appear before you with a paper prepared at my leisure; a circumstance you will not find extraordinary if you will be good enough to take into consideration how much I have been occupied during the last few days.

"Let your indulgence be my shield this evening, gentlemen. I cannot deliver a well-considered oration; at the utmost, I can give some information on one point or another, and that only in an informal manner, as good friends are wont to do in the hour of parting."

VI.

Overthrow of the Tory Government.—Neutrality assured.

With the speech at Glasgow my round of public meetings was brought to a termination.

I had reason to be satisfied with the result. The English people had come to the conclusion that in spite of the Queen's proclamation of neutrality, the impartial neutrality of England could not be considered safe in the hands of a Tory Cabinet; and that, if it remained in power, England's whole political, and in case of need also, material weight, would be thrown into the scale in order that the Court of Vienna might come out of the struggle unimpaired in its possessions, or at least with as little damage as possible.

My speeches were reprinted in all the English papers without party distinction. The publicity which they in consequence attained, the facts to which I called the attention of the public, the active exchange of ideas which, through my speeches, originated in the English as well as in the Continental press, and finally the resolutions which were carried at the public meetings, no doubt shook the foundation on which the Tory Cabinet was based, apparently securely, through the proclamation of neutrality. The "Thunderer of Printing House Square," as the *Times* was then still called, could not, of course, resist the temptation of directing a sharp attack against me. Spite against me had become as natural to the writer as bragging cowardice to Falstaff; but these bitter attacks, which at other times have threatened me with injury, on this occasion did me good service. For as it could not be denied that the best policy for England to pursue was to remain neutral, the writer, in order to attack me, was obliged to have recourse to such misrepresentations of my statements and such deductions therefrom that the intentional and malicious distortion could not be hidden. This gave me an opportunity, and even an undeniable right, to protest in the columns of the *Times* itself against those misrepresentations. In consequence my views were accepted in those circles which were accustomed habitually to take their inspiration from the columns of that paper, which was still considered a power. They were accepted, for however high party feeling may run in England, it always remains a great feature of the English character to insist upon fair play, and to turn away from those who, in order to damage their adversary, have recourse to imputations and misrepresentations of facts.

The decisive moment was near. It was expected that Parliament would meet on May 31st. I hurried back to London to be able to confer with my political friends as to our procedure.

The elections had changed little in the proportion of the numbers of the different parties. What change did take place was in favour of the Tory Ministry, who had gained twenty-six seats. They were still in a minority as compared with the total of the other parties, but compared with the Whigs they were in a decided majority.

The papers put the numbers of the different parties as follows:—Supporters of the Government, 302; Opposition (taking all the different shades together), 353; together, 655. Only 654 members sit in the House of Commons. The difference of *one* vote arose from the two candidates for Aylesbury having polled the same number of votes, in which case, according to English custom, both members enter the House and vote in the election of the Speaker, and afterwards the question is decided by a new polling. According to these figures the Government would have been in a minority by 51, had the Whigs, the members of the Independent party, and those members belonging to no party, voted together; but as compared with the Whigs alone they could command a majority of 39, for of the 353 members forming the Opposition, 90 did not belong to the Whig party.

The situation was, therefore, such as I had described to the Emperor Napoleon. On this occasion, too, the Independent party, which had so often decided the fate of ministries, was master of the situation.

Parliament actually met on May 31st. The election of Speaker was not turned into a party question. John

Evelyn Denison was unanimously elected. The Speech from the Throne was expected to be read on June 7th.

In the last days before the opening of Parliament, it was doubtful whether the Whigs would be able to agree amongst themselves, because both Lord Palmerston and Lord John Russell aspired to the leadership of the party, and therefore, in case of victory, to be Prime Minister. Neither would yield (*vanitas vanitatum!*); until at last they agreed that, whichever should be called upon to form a new Cabinet might rely on the subordination of the other. When this difference had been arranged, the leaders of the Whig party, relying on the fact that the Independent members had voted with them at the beginning of the previous April (when the Government had been defeated in a division on the Reform Bill), felt so sure that they would now unconditionally vote with them again, that they announced in their papers that in the debate on the reply to the Speech from the Throne, a vote of want of confidence in the Government would be moved. However, Lord Palmerston was advised to calculate first the strength of the Opposition, lest he should be defeated, and expose himself to ridicule. He counted the votes, and arrived at the conclusion that, unless he succeeded in winning over the Manchester Free Trade party, he could not reckon upon a majority, especially as some of the members who belonged to no party (for instance, Mr. Roebuck, member for Sheffield) had declared that they would vote for Lord Derby, in opposition to Lord Palmerston. When this unpleasant discovery was made, the papers of the Whig party announced that no vote of want of confidence would be moved on the debate in reply to the

Speech from the Throne, but that the decisive battle would be fought later on, on some other question!

Now the moment had arrived to bring to a practical issue what I had implored my friends to do in the interest of the liberty of Hungary and Italy. My late lamented friend, Mr. Charles Gilpin, took the matter in hand. He was in constant communication with me, and once more conferred upon the conditions with the more influential members of his party, notably with Mr. John Bright, who, in the absence of Mr. Cobden, was the leader of the party; and, in accordance with their mutual agreement, he assured Lord Palmerston of the support of his party on these conditions:—

1. That the Tory Ministry should be overthrown expressly on a question affecting foreign politics.

2. That Lord Palmerston, as well as Lord John Russell, and any other member of the future Cabinet whose selection might have been already determined upon, should each address a separate letter to Mr. Gilpin, binding themselves that the basis of their foreign policy would be the absolute neutrality of England, not only while war is confined to Italy, but also in case it should extend from the Po to the banks of the Danube and Theiss.

3. That, in order to ensure this neutrality, two members of the future Ministry should be chosen from the party on whose behalf Mr. Gilpin was negotiating.

Lord Palmerston accepted these conditions, and next day he, as well as Lord John Russell and the other three members of the new Cabinet whose selection had already been decided upon, handed the letters referred to in the second point of the agreement to Mr. Gilpin (*who immediately handed the originals of the letters to me, authorising me to make discreet use of them, and more particularly to show them to the Emperor Napoleon* **); and Lord Palmerston also declared in his letter that, in conformity with the third condition, Messrs. Richard Cobden and Milner Gibson would be nominated members of the future Ministry. Accordingly Mr. Gilpin and his political friends, as well as myself, were perfectly satisfied; though I, knowing the feelings Mr. Cobden entertained for Lord Palmerston, doubted whether the former would accept a post in the latter's Ministry. My anticipation was realised: he did not accept it.

So far, the matter had been arranged as I had wished. All the members of the different shades of the Liberal party were summoned to a conference, to be held at Willis's Rooms on June 6th. The circulars already bore, together with the signatures of Palmerston, Russell, and others, that of Milner Gibson.

---

* It is a considerable drawback to the present work that I cannot communicate these letters. I took them with me to Italy, and showed them at Valleggio to the Emperor Napoleon, who read them all, but I cannot find them among my papers now. I either left them with the Emperor, or they were added to the minutes of the "Hungarian National Committee." I do not remember exactly what became of them. It is a great pity also that the minutes are not in my possession; the loss of them is even more to be regretted than the loss of the letters, as they are an official source of the history of the refugees. I requested Messrs. Daniel Irányi and Nicholas Puky, who have taken part in the deliberations of the committee (the former as recorder of the minutes, the latter as cashier), to let me know whether the minutes were in their possession; and if not, who is likely to have them. Their reply was that they were not in their possession, and that they remembered as little as I to whom they were confided for safe keeping. It is a loss much to be regretted. No doubt they will turn up some day. Still, there is no use denying that I deserve censure for not having remembered, all through my public career, to bestow some little care upon the preservation of these documents, which might supply some facts concerning contemporary history.

The votes which could be safely relied upon showed, though not a large, still a clear majority. It was decided that the Government should be overthrown on the debate on the reply to the Speech from the Throne, and it was entrusted to the Marquis of Hartington to move the vote of want of confidence.

The Government, on the other hand, also made strenuous efforts to meet the struggle, and did everything to be ready to receive the onslaught with a firm phalanx.

In the Speech from the Throne with which the Queen opened the already-constituted Houses of Parliament on June 7th, the foreign policy was referred to as follows:—

"I have directed that papers shall be laid before you, from which you will learn how earnest and unceasing have been my endeavours to preserve the peace of Europe.

"These endeavours have unhappily failed, and war has been declared between France and Sardinia on one side, and Austria on the other. Receiving assurances of friendship from both the contending parties, I intend to maintain between them a strict and impartial neutrality; and I hope, with God's assistance, to preserve to my people the blessing of continual peace.

"Considering, however, the present state of Europe, I have deemed it necessary to the security of my dominions and the honour of my crown to increase my naval forces to an extent exceeding that which has been sanctioned by Parliament.

"I rely with confidence on your cordial concurrence in this precautionary measure of defensive policy."

It happens but rarely in England that the debate on the reply to the Speech from the Throne decides the fate of the ministry. No doubt in the course of debate the policy and the acts of the Cabinet are commented upon, and the standpoint which the Opposition intend to take up is fixed; but as a rule the reply is only an echo of the Speech from the Throne, and is mostly accepted without an amendment being moved or a division taken.

It so happened on this occasion that in the House of Lords the reply to the Speech from the Throne was moved by Lord Powis (a supporter of the Government), and seconded by Lord Lifford (of the Opposition), who, however, stated that the Opposition did not consider the foreign policy of the Cabinet reassuring, and intended to attack it.

During the debate which ensued some noteworthy statements were made.

Lord Malmesbury, Secretary of State for Foreign Affairs, reminded their lordships that what was then (1859) happening in Italy was the direct consequence of the policy pursued in 1848 by the Whig Ministry of Lord Granville, who had such an opportunity of liberating Italy from the despotism of which Austria was accused as would perhaps never again present itself.

Lord Normanby called the attention of the House to the intrigues of Sardinia, of France, and especially of Russia—a power endeavouring to extend its influence to the Mediterranean, while one of the objects of the Peace of Tilsit had been to keep away from that sea every power which did not border on it. England must prepare to thwart those intrigues. His lordship called upon the Government to resist every attempt at obtaining universal power, and, considering what happened in Parma, Modena, and Tuscany, he decidedly disapproved of the sympathy which Lord Palmerston had expressed for the Italians.

Lord Brougham declared the pretext that war was being carried on in the interests of liberty to be false. Nobody desired more than he did that the Austrians should be driven out from Italy, but he did not wish that the Italians should simply change masters.

Lord Derby, the Prime Minister, said that if there was a question of either the Italian *or any other nation* liberating itself from an intolerable yoke and introducing a system of government similar to the English, every Englishman would be induced to sympathise with the movement. But in the present instance this was not the case. " I cannot approve," the noble lord continued, " of the policy of Austria, and do not feel any sympathy either for Austrian rule or for the Austrian system of government, but I must say that the present war has been brought about by false pretexts. The war was undertaken, not for the liberation of Italy, but for the extension of Sardinia, and thus it is proved that a constitutional form of government does not at all supply a guarantee against the adoption of an aggressive and expansive policy, which is stated to be a special characteristic of a despotic form of government." I believe that the noble lord need not have gone far to find a proof of this elsewhere—the belt which England has put round the world demonstrates that truth sufficiently. He finished by saying that under the existing complications England must observe an *armed neutrality.*

The reply to the Speech from the Throne was adopted without a division.

A different course was pursued in the Lower House. The reply to the Speech from the Throne was moved by Mr. A. Egerton, and seconded by Sir J. Elphinstone, both supporters of the Government. Thereupon Lord Hartington (of the Opposition) moved, as an amendment, that the House should state in the reply to the Speech from the Throne that it was absolutely necessary that the ministry should possess the confidence of the country and of the House, and that the present Cabinet was not in possession of this confidence.

Lord Bury seconded the amendment, stating that he wished for the observance of a complete, perfect, and absolute neutrality, and that he did not believe the present Government would be sincerely friendly to such a policy.

An animated and prolonged debate ensued, which terminated only late at night on June 10th (or rather early in the morning of June 11th).

Bright (the leader of the party whose co-operation ensured a majority) spoke on June 9th in favour of the amendment. He laid special stress, in his speech, on the circumstance that the proclaimed neutrality was not real and sincere, as it was accompanied by such warlike preparations as were not at all justified by a defensive policy. The proclamation of the Queen, earnestly calling upon the people to enlist for service in the navy, had been read in the streets to the sound of music. At that present moment as many men had enlisted already as would man twelve men-of-war; and there were more soldiers in the country than ever before. It was impossible that all these extraordinary war preparations should not create the suspicion among the French that they were directed against them, and were only intended to support Austria, as England could not be threatened by any attack in the present war. He mentioned that the universal opinion prevailing in Germany was that England was preparing to assist Austria, and this opinion was justified by the statements the Government had made, and by the armaments, which went much beyond what was required for the defence of the country. The people of England wished to be sure that they would not be dragged into the present war; this was the incontestable will of the nation, and it was therefore necessary that the reins of government should pass into such hands as would remove every doubt that might be entertained abroad as to the neutrality of England, and would reassure the people of this country that it would not be drawn into the war against its will.

The next morning, June 11th, I received the following letter from my friend Gilpin, addressed the previous night to me from the House of Commons:—

"*House of Commons,*
"½-*past* 1, *Morning, June* 11*th.*

" MY DEAR FRIEND,

" I have not been able to 'catch the Speaker's eye' this evening, but have again spoken to Lord John Russell, to Sidney Herbert, and to Sir Charles Wood. Again and again they confirmed the declarations contained in their letters you have in your hands. Nothing could possibly be more unequivocal than the answer they *all* give that no insurrection in Hungary, whether independent of the present war, or in connection with its extending to Hungary, *could justify or even excuse the intervention of England.*

" Lord John Russell treated the suggestion—in the hearing of

Bright, Sidney Herbert, and myself—as wholly beyond the scope of possibility, and declared plainly that while the treaties of 1815 might appear to some to give *the shadow* of a justification for interference in Italy, there could be no such ground, no such pretext, with reference to Hungary.

"The weight of this argument was fully admitted even by Seymour Fitzgerald, the actual Under-Secretary of State for Foreign Affairs, who told me besides that he meant in his speech of yesterday to convey to the fullest extent the impression that Government held themselves bound to the strictest neutrality in the present war *under all circumstances.*

" Sidney Herbert (probably our future Minister of War) and Sir G. Cornewall Lewis (the late Chancellor of the Exchequer, and probably the future one, or else Minister of Home Affairs) fully share the opinion of Lord John. Sir Charles Wood treated the possibility of our interference in the war to discourage a revolution in Hungary as palpably absurd. Sir Benjamin Hall is of the same opinion, and I believe both these baronets (ministerial candidates both) would not only deprecate and denounce any adverse interference on the part of England in such case, but would strongly sympathise with the Hungarian people.

" I tried to induce Lord John to say in his speech what he repeated in conversation to me in reference to Hungary, but he said that as yet there was no revolution in Hungary; it would not do for him to anticipate it, else he might be considered to *suggest* it; and I think there was some weight in this reason for not making the statement publicly.

" We are just about to divide ($\frac{1}{2}$-past one, Saturday morning.) You will probably see by the time this reaches you if we are successful or unsuccessful. I hope victory.

" Ever truly yours,

" C. GILPIN."

And truly they did carry off a victory. Lord Hartington's motion of want of confidence was carried by a majority of 13 (323 members voted for, 310 against the motion; 21 were absent). It was a small majority. I, however, looked upon this as rather a favourable circumstance than one to cause me anxiety, as my friends remained masters of the situation, for without them the Whigs could not remain twenty-four hours in power.

The Derby Ministry handed in its resignation, which was accepted by the Queen. After some unsuccessful attempts by Lord Granville, the task of forming a new Cabinet was entrusted to Lord Palmerston.

What the Emperor Napoleon had wished for had come to pass. England's neutrality was secured. The obstacle which stood in the way of the cause of my country's freedom being taken up had been removed. Thanks to the assistance of my English friends, I had redeemed my promise.

The formation of a new Administration took up a few days. It entered office on June 18th. I did not think it necessary to stay in England till this had taken place. My colleagues of the National Hungarian Committee (Ladislaus Teleki and Klapka), and my compatriots who had assembled in Genoa, had for weeks past solicited me to come to Italy as soon as possible, as important affairs required my presence there.

I left England on June 16th.

Let a letter from my lamented friend Gilpin, which I received at Genoa, stand here as a conclusion of this chapter.

CHARLES GILPIN TO KOSSUTH.

"*London, June* 18*th,* 1859.
"MY DEAR FRIEND,
"You will find here enclosed a full list of the new Ministry.

"I have to acquaint you with a change in my position which you will be quite as much surprised in hearing of as it was unsought and unexpected by me.

"Lord Palmerston sent for me yesterday, and offered me a place in his Government. He spoke so frankly and so cordially, that though I never sought a position in the Ministry, nor ever thought of accepting one (as you well know), I took the subject into my consideration, and this evening accepted the offered post of Secretary of the Poor Law Board. The post is of course a subordinate one in a political point of view: still I thought my accepting it will contribute towards strengthening the standing of our party in the Ministry, and will besides enable me to do some good to my fellow-men.

"I availed myself of the opportunity to have a very full conversation with the Premier on the subject of non-intervention. I mentioned that, several members of the Ministry not having been privy to what has passed between us in that regard, he will find it natural that, *in the interest of those concerned,* I felt extremely anxious to know whether we can rest assured that the principle of non-intervention will be rigorously adhered to, even in the case of the war extending to Hungary; and above all, that England will not *in any case* assist Austria.

"Palmerston replied that he felt as strongly on the subject as I did. The principle of non-intervention in the present war constituted the fundamental principle of the policy of the Ministry; and he added that, unless the independence of Belgium were threatened—of which he had not the slightest apprehension—he did not fear our being mixed up in the war. As to the emergency of the war extending to Hungary, and the Hungarians possibly profiting by it, that was a contingency that would in no way alter

England's policy of non-intervention, since the war would still remain confined to the territory of the belligerent parties, and Kossuth was perfectly right in maintaining that Austria, being one of the belligerent parties, cannot claim the privilege of neutrality for any portion of her dominions, least of all for the territory of the crown of Hungary, which does not belong to the German Confederation. He could therefore give me the fullest assurance that 'my Hungarian friends' could set their minds perfectly at ease with regard to the conduct of England.

"You will please use this information cautiously, as it took place at a private interview, and is therefore of a confidential character; but of course you are at liberty to communicate it to the Emperor if you please.

"I spoke again with Lord John Russell also. He told me that, as regards Hungary, he was quite prepared to go as far as myself.

"I have given you the views of the leading statesmen in our new Ministry. The Premier's views only were wanting, and these I now supply. I wish you could have *heard* them. *They satisfied me!* so you may suppose they were pretty full and unequivocal.

"Now when we add to this the letters you have in hand, and the explicit declarations of several prominent members of the Ministry, especially those of the Secretary of State for Foreign Affairs; when we add to it that, in conversation with several influential members of the Conservative party, including Seymour Fitzgerald, the late Under-Secretary of State for Foreign Affairs, I received assurances and expressions of opinion quite as explicit and unequivocal as those from Lord John Russell; when we add to it the fact that a very large number of the House of Commons warmly sympathise with the movement for Hungarian nationality; and when we take into consideration the further fact that—as you well know—the whole people of England and Scotland ardently endorses that sympathy, I think we may regard it as *absolutely impossible.* that, in the event of Hungary taking up arms for the re-vindication of her independence in connection with the present war becoming extended to your country, there would be any departure from the strictest—and, I will add, benevolent—neutrality on the part of England.

"And, after all, Cobden and Milner Gibson will sit in the Cabinet; and you know, as I know, that *they would rather break up fifty Cabinets* * than allow England to go to war for Austria in such a cause.

"Now taking all in all, certainly no influence could possibly outbalance weight like this in the councils of the nation: so I feel warranted to tell you that, in this regard, you may proceed with perfect tranquillity of mind in your burdensome career.

"And now, whether it be in the ordering of an all-wise and often inscrutable Providence to open the way for your return to your own loved country, or whether exile must be still your lot, God bless and prosper you wherever you go !

"I am, and shall be as long as I live,
"Your true and faithful friend,
"CHARLES GILPIN."

* *Cobden*, who was travelling at this time in America, did not—as I have mentioned already—accept a post in the ministry; but Milner Gibson, with the party that was master of the situation backing him up, was strong enough alone, if necessary, to "break up fifty Cabinets." In England they knew this from experience. The *Times*, in reviewing the careers of the new Ministers, wrote about Milner Gibson as follows:—"Mr. Milner Gibson, who has already broken up so many Cabinets, will at last preserve the *present one*." A man who is thus spoken of is a power.

CHAPTER V.

EVENTS THAT HAPPENED IN THE INTERIM.

The Hungarians at Genoa—Organisation of an Army—Agreement with Prince Couza and explanation of this relation—Conference with Prince Michael Obrenovics—Mission to Belgrade.

WHILE I was occupied in England with securing English neutrality, the Hungarian exiled officers commenced to assemble at Genoa. That town had been selected as the headquarters of the Hungarian National Committee. The organisation of an army proceeded from thence, and was carried on amid difficulties. Only on June 16th was the first general order issued from headquarters. In the interval I kept up a brisk correspondence with the members of the Hungarian National Committee and my other compatriots, who were all waiting anxiously to have work allotted to them. This correspondence mostly referred to various matters connected with the formation of an army, and to the anxiety incidental thereto. As the organisation of the army is treated of at some length in the first of the notes annexed to this chapter, I do not think it necessary here to produce the correspondence of that time having reference to that subject, or that which refers to the domestic troubles of the community of refugees.

I arrived at Genoa from England on June 22nd, two days before the great battle of Solferino (June 24th), which was preceded by the victories of Montebello,

Palestra, Casteggio, and Magenta. The struggle was sanguinary. The superiority of the allies in tactics was brilliantly demonstrated. Meanwhile, General Klapka, my colleague in the Committee, in one of his letters to me, expressed the opinion that the possibility of an untoward turn of events on the Mincio was not excluded; the Austrian soldier was becoming accustomed to warfare, and might sooner or later acquire a knowledge of the French method of attack, and then decision would simply rest with the superior numerical strength. These apprehensions, no doubt, weighed also upon the Emperor's mind, and we might, therefore, hope that he would readily assist us in our preparations. He stood in need of men who would be under an obligation to him, and where could he find such more willing than in Hungary, provided he lent us assistance?

Theoretically, this view was not without foundation, but in practice our affairs had not made any progress in this direction. Beyond the preliminary steps towards organising an army, and the arrangements for providing money to meet the current expenses, scarcely anything had been done in our affairs; certainly nothing to clear up our political situation.

The victorious progress made by the allied forces was in itself sufficient to prevent my colleagues from being able to communicate directly with the Emperor. They had not even once the opportunity of speaking to him personally during all the time that I was detained in England. Prince Napoleon, who might have been a strong support of our cause, was at the head of the 5th French Army Corps in Tuscany, and therefore parted from the Emperor. The statesmen of Turin, on the other hand, considered that everything in the matter depended upon the Emperor, and in this they went so far, that for whatever I had laid down as a condition for creating a revolution in Hungary, we could reckon upon finding ready support in Turin, but we could not count upon a decisive resolution. This uncertainty reacted even upon the most insignificant details in that sphere of action to which my colleagues at this time still confined their efforts. At every step they had to overcome difficulties. In his letters to me, General Klapka ascribed this to our friends being so much occupied with their own concerns, that one or the other circumstance might easily escape their notice and inflict damage upon us; but he did not think that he could complain about want of goodwill on their part. So far from allaying my apprehensions, this explanation rather alarmed me. The line of separation which our friends had drawn between their own troubles and our cause did not seem to indicate to me a very reassuring conception of the mutuality of our interests. What increased my fears was that Count Ladislaus Teleki plainly confessed to me, in his letters, that he noticed a great deal of wavering in the behaviour of the Allies towards us, and that they (Teleki and his colleagues) could not make any progress. They certainly did not progress in the direction upon which the hope of the liberation of our country depended. The Allies had continually laid the greatest stress upon the friendly neutrality of England. Prince Napoleon openly said to my friend, Colonel Nicholas Kiss, that England's policy was so unfriendly that, unless I succeeded in effecting a decided change in it, events might take a very unfavourable turn. And when I commenced agitating, and when English public opinion pronounced more and more powerfully in favour of a sincere and absolute neutrality, and there was a prospect of a change of government, Teleki lost no time in informing Prince Napoleon and Count Cavour personally, and the Emperor, through Pietri, of my activity. They received the news with great satisfaction, and expressed their desires that their thanks should be conveyed to me, but they never hinted that in case of a successful issue of my mission we might reckon upon the seat of war being extended to Hungary; still less did they take such practical steps as could be looked upon as preparation for an action in this direction. Nearly every letter which I received from Italy gave me the impression, to begin with, that all efforts were being concentrated in trying, through the Hungarian refugees, to influence and create dissension among their countrymen fighting in the Austrian ranks, without the Allies, as a return service, identifying themselves with the Hungarian cause. It appeared to me that by yielding to such incitements my friends at Genoa were being drifted into a false position. I therefore never ceased to enjoin upon them the necessity of never losing sight of the fact, that every step we took, whether important or not, must have the object of forcing the Allies to identify themselves publicly with the cause of our country. Unless this object were previously attained, the secession of Hungarian soldiery would be against the interest of our country, as in case it were successful the victory of the Allies would thereby be made easier, and might make the espousal of the Hungarian cause superfluous.

To serve simply as *condottieri* of a legion in the interest of others was not a rôle we could permit ourselves to assume. I begged them to beware lest we should be squeezed like a lemon, and thrown away afterwards. A little service had been pressed out of me—I ought not to call it a little service—I mean, the agitation for neutrality in England. It was a great sacrifice which unpleasantly disturbed old friendly relations, to which I got used. I knew that it would be a sacrifice, but I found consolation in the fact that it would only be a personal sacrifice. If we went a step further, unless the powers identified themselves with our cause in return, the sacrifice would fall upon our country, and this we could not allow. I had no reason to doubt the good intentions of the powers, but it appeared to me that they (mistakenly) attached more importance to the difficulties thrown in their way by the diplomatists of other countries than to the advantage which would accrue to them by taking our cause into their hands. The interests of Hungary demanded of us that we should be possessed of the consciousness of that advantage. We were negotiating parties, not suppliants. And it was not to be supposed that this patient acceptance of a false position, this coaxing, this hushing, this submission to all the petty humiliations of being put aside, would by-and-by advance our cause and smooth over the difficulties of our position. On the contrary, we should thereby be thrown back dissolved, and at last find ourselves where, in consequence of their pliability, the poor Poles found themselves in the Crimean war. Interests would decide. If the interests existed we could imperil nothing by invariably making every step we took in the interest of the Allies, dependent upon their identifying themselves with the cause of our country; and if there were no interests, or if they were of less importance than other counter-considerations (the most weighty of which, the constant difficulties raised by the secret diplomacy of Downing Street, I hoped to remove), we compromised ourselves by concessions, and only raised false hopes in our country.

To this and similar warnings I invariably received as an answer from all sides that I should hurry to Italy, in order that my presence might bring unanimity and uniformity into the now widely divergent activities. This entreaty to hurry to Italy runs through the whole bulk of letters I received at this time. Ladislaus Teleki particularly was nervously impressed with this necessity, so much so that he wrote to me from Genoa, under date of June 5th: "I daily pray that God may bring you here as soon as possible. Laying my hand on my heart, I affirm my belief that never in your life were you wanted anywhere so much as you are at present here. God bless you! My hand trembles. I cannot write more, though I should like to continue to implore you."

For my English readers I deem it sufficient to say as much as this about the correspondence of that time, and without reproducing the letters themselves, I pass to those subjects appertaining to the period the details of which may possess some historical interest. These subjects are:—

1. The Organisation of an army.
2. The Agreement of General Klapka with Prince Couza.
3. My Conference with Prince Michael Obrenovics

(son of Milos), Prince of Servia, and the mission of John Ludvigh to Belgrade.

I.

Organisation of an Army.

We expected to receive the necessary forces for the organisation of an army, excepting a small number of refugees, partly from the prisoners of war, ready to take service, partly from those men of the Hungarian regiments of the Austrian army who would by their own free will come over to our side.

To facilitate recruiting from the former, the Emperor of the French, as Commander-in-Chief of the allied troops, issued an order that from the prisoners of war the Hungarians were to be selected, and those of them who wished to serve under our standard placed at our disposal. In order to be able also to communicate with those prisoners of war who were not sent towards Genoa, the National Hungarian Committee sent two colonels and one captain to the French and Sardinian headquarters to ask authority to communicate anywhere with the prisoners of war taken from Austria, in order to persuade those who were of Hungarian nationality to enlist. These officers were cordially received, both by the Emperor at Volta, and by the King at Rivoltella. A separate written authority was given to each of them, signed on behalf of France by Major-General Martinprey, and on behalf of Sardinia by Lieutenant-General Della Rocca, chief of the King's general staff.

But, in making the selection from those prisoners of war who were sent in the direction of Genoa, a difficulty arose from the authorities making the "tight-fitting trousers" (*pantalon collant*) the distinctive mark of Hungarian nationality, while the Austrians had artfully mixed all the nationalities together. The Hungarian regiments, who wear tight trousers and *bakkancs*,* were filled with men belonging to all sorts of different nationalities.† All these were selected for us, as they wore tight trousers and bakkancs. On the other hand, amongst the prisoners of war taken from Bohemian, German, and other regiments, there were many Hungarians. These swore in vain that they were Hungarians, and entreated in vain to be allowed to join us. They did not wear tight trousers and bakkancs, and were therefore transported to France and Africa. Such is the effect of doing things in a slovenly manner. It took a long time to alter this abnormal state of affairs. This selection produced some curious scenes. On one occasion 1,400 prisoners, Italians from Lombardy, were transported by the French from Genoa to Africa. They enthusiastically desired to enter the Piedmontese army,— but in vain; and when they saw that only the Hungarians were retained, they declared, even when on board the ship, that they too were Hungarians. Many Croatian and German prisoners who happened to wear

* Boots laced outside the trousers.
† By this confusion of nationalities, now and then some Poles found their way into our ranks. The Russian Ambassador at Turin officially protested against this. He declared to Cavour that if every Pole were not sent away from the Hungarian army, he must not count upon Russia's benevolent neutrality. We were therefore obliged to be most particular in the elimination of the Polish element from our army.

tight trousers declared that they too were Hungarians, and it was only upon examination that they were excluded.

As regards the bringing over of men from the Hungarian regiments, the subject was brought forward in our conversations, and the question was put whether it would not be advisable first of all to issue an anonymous proclamation about the formation of a Hungarian army, and endeavour to distribute it among the Hungarian regiments of the Austrian forces.

As soon as I had returned from Paris to London, on May 8th, I protested, in my letter to my colleagues of the National Hungarian Committee, against the issue of an anonymous proclamation. " What is it we want ?" I wrote. "Why, what we want is that the Hungarians in the Austrian army should know that those who join us, or are taken prisoners, will not be treated as deserters or prisoners of war, but preserving their rank or being promoted to a higher one, they will be formed under the Hungarian standard into a distinct Hungarian army. More effectually than by the issue of an anonymous proclamation (which, from its being anonymous, does not offer any security, and has therefore no weight) the object in view would be attained if King Victor Emmanuel were to issue an order to his Minister of War, in which, referring to the oppression of Hungary, and to the community of interests between the Italian and Hungarian nations in the present war, he expressed his conviction that there were doubtless many amongst the brave Hungarians who, serving Austria only under compulsion, felt that their place was on the side of the Allies at war with Austria, and not under the banner of the oppressor of their country; and for this reason, finding it necessary to see that those noble Hungarian soldiers who entertained such ideas should receive such an organisation as would give clear proof of the sympathy the King had for the Hungarian nation, the King commanded his Minister of War to take such necessary steps that Hungarian deserters, and those who might desert thereafter, as well as those Hungarians who were taken prisoners of war, and were ready to enlist, should be formed into a distinct corps, having their own Hungarian standard, Hungarian organisation, Hungarian word of command, and placed under the command of Hungarian officers; and that the officers, preserving the rank they then held, should be furnished with the necessary money for equipments, while the non-commissioned officers and privates should receive the bounty-money.

Such a decree should be issued by the King, published in the official gazette, and then, printed on loose sheets, it should be distributed among the Hungarian regiments by the secret Italian committees which existed in the kingdom of Lombardy, Venice, in the principalities, and the Romagna. Such a procedure would promise success, and would also afford us a guarantee that the Hungarian contingent was looked upon as an ally, and not as a body of hirelings, and that its national character was also preserved in the organisation. But an anonymous proclamation would neither promise success nor afford such a guarantee, and might therefore work mischief.

My colleagues (Count Ladislaus Teleki and General Klapka) approved of my view of the matter. They thought the issue of a royal decree, as proposed by me, very desirable, and lost no time in communicating our plan to Count Cavour, who promised that he would recommend it in the *spirit* I had wished; "only" (as Klapka wrote in reply to me) "the Government, with due regard to their position, will have to moderate their expressions to a certain degree," "and therefore" (as Teleki put it in his letter to me) "the decree will be couched in a somewhat more bureaucratic style, but its fundamental idea will remain the same."

Well, as far as the bureaucratic style was concerned, we might have acquiesced in that, but, unfortunately, when the decree for the formation of an army was issued at last, it did not in the least correspond with the spirit of my proposal. My colleagues were obliged to make strong representations in order to bring matters into a more satisfactory train, and when I arrived in Italy, after having brought to a conclusion the agitations for neutrality in England, there remained plenty for me to repair, complete, and arrange.

It was towards the end of May that Count Cavour, in his capacity of Minister of War, informed my colleagues that the decree was ready, but that he thought it more advisable not to publish it until we had at least a corps of some hundred men, lest, in case no volunteers arrived and no prisoners of war were willing to enlist, the Government of Sardinia should be compromised by the unsuccessful decree. Ladislaus Teleki called this mode of arguing a *circulus vitiosus*, for the decree was wanted for the very purpose of procuring soldiers.

While the publication of the decree was being delayed by this difference of opinion, the first elements for the formation of an army began to assemble. The National Hungarian Committee, in their order of June

5th, gave instructions for the organisation of these elements. Colonel Ihász (my steadfast and faithful friend, and the sharer of my fate in exile up to the present day) was entrusted with the collection and organisation of the forces.

One of the forts which surround Genoa, the loftily-situated "Forte Castellaccio," was assigned to them as barracks. The better places had been already occupied by the French. Our force, just forming itself, was transferred to Acqui on June 12th. We commenced our organisation with 120 men. (When the news of the Peace of Villafranca fell among us like a thunderbolt from a clear sky, the number exceeded *four thousand*.) The men, and the three Hungarian officers who had been employed from the commencement, received the same pay and rations as their Sardinian comrades: the other officers, who were waiting to be put on active service, drew their pay from the National Hungarian Committee. At this early stage in the formation of our forces, nobody at Genoa knew anything about the contents of the royal decree, the publication of which was promised to us; but the mere fact that, in the official correspondence with reference to the formation of these 120 men into a corps, they were spoken of as a "legion," gave us offence and cause for apprehensions. The Hungarian refugees were of opinion that, in the modern sense of the word, "legion" is understood to mean a force which, without having a national aim of its own, simply engages itself to fight, on certain conditions, for the interests of the state by which it is paid. "If," they said to themselves, "we are a legion, we do not fight for the interests of our country. This state of things alarms us immensely, for Hungarian refugees are ready for any sacrifice in the interest of their country, but *only in the interest of their country.*"

Entreaties *en masse* were sent to me in London, begging me to use my influence to obtain an assurance that the national object of our forces then in formation would be kept in view.

But if the title of "legion" already alarmed my compatriots, their apprehensions were turned into an exasperation which threatened us with utter dissolution, when they came to know the contents of the royal decree, which, though dated May 24th, was not published before June 10th, and was signed by the Duke Edmund of Savoja-Carignan, who had been appointed Regent during the time the king was occupied with the command of the army.

This decree, couched in the customary official terms used in connection with the formation of all sorts of volunteer troops, simply ordered that *in the Royal Sardinian army a Hungarian Legion should be formed*, in which the non-commissioned officers, corporals, and privates would be enrolled for the time of the present war, besides those Hungarian volunteers who wished to take part (*intendono concorrere*) in the war against Austria. Beyond this, the decree simply mentioned that the same regulations would apply to the formation of this legion as were issued with reference to the organisation of *the other volunteer forces* in the previous April, when there existed no agreement as to a Hungarian army, nor had a Hungarian army been even mentioned!

These were the contents of the decree which had been looked forward to with so much impatience.

Simply a mercenary legion, in the service of Piedmont, engaged for the time of the present war! Of a Hungarian national object, not a single word! Not even a Hungarian standard! Nothing that would have presented a Hungarian national character! In short, there was only this difference between our force and the Italian volunteer troops, that the organisation (*ordinamento*) of our battalions and squadrons was to be the same as in the Hungarian army of 1848-49.

The exasperation in our ranks caused by this decree was indescribable. Everybody agreed that we could not submit to this. The staff and other officers declared that they would not serve on these conditions. Fortunately affairs did not remain long in this unsatisfactory state. My colleagues, Count Ladislaus Teleki and Klapka, hastened to Turin, and obtained permission that our army should have a Hungarian standard and a Hungarian national character, and that its national object should be clearly stated in the oath taken by the men, and in the pledged agreement of the officers.

Count Cavour, in agreeing to these stipulations, only requested us not to speak too ostentatiously of them, as diplomacy was very jealous of us. These things having been arranged, with the general order of June 16th, issued by General Klapka, who by a special decree had been nominated Commander of the Hungarian army, the formation of the army was taken in hand with all the requisite official formalities.

In the general order it was clearly stated, in order to dispel all apprehension among the troops, that the government had openly declared that all obligations towards the King of Piedmont which the Hungarians entered into by their enlistment in the legion would lose legal force and cease to be binding the moment the legion entered on Hungarian soil, and accordingly the oath would be so worded that all those who took it would already swear fidelity to Hungary and obedience to the Hungarian National Government which was to be formed for the recovery of Hungary's independence, and that they would only swear allegiance and obedience to King Victor Emmanuel for the time they remained on Italian ground.

In order to leave no doubt in the minds of the men, it was stated in the general order of June 17th that the legion would, on and after the next day, be called "The Hungarian Army in Italy."

I arrived at Genoa on June 22nd. We had then about 1,000 men at Acqui, divided into two battalions, under the command of Ihász.

On making myself acquainted with the details of the arrangements, I found that the formation of the army was not being carried out according to proper regulations; that besides the concessions my friends had already obtained from the Government of Turin, much else remained to be desired. More particularly, I thought we ought not to be hampered by red-tape tardiness in the formation of our army. I stated my opinions on all these subjects; they were discussed, and the result of the discussion was passed as a resolution. To my regret, the minutes of this committee are not in my possession. I have, however, before me the Hungarian original of the Note, which I worked out on the subject a few days later at Parma, at the express wish of Prince Napoleon, and of which I handed the Prince a translation in French.

Note of Kossuth on the formation of the Hungarian Army in Italy (made by Prince Napoleon's own desire, and handed to him at Parma on June 28th, 1859).

" Seeing that the restoration of Hungary's independence might possibly be taken in hand in conjunction with the present war, permission has been obtained for the formation of a Hungarian national army in Italy. The National Committee, which was entrusted with the conducting of this affair, can only hope to bring their labours to a quick and successful issue if they are provided with the means for organising the forces on a Hungarian national system; not only in the matter of tactical organisation and division, but also in that of equipment.

" We can only count upon the enthusiastic eagerness of those men who have already joined us, and the secession of the greatest possible number of men from the Hungarian portion of the Austrian army, on the following conditions :—

" 1. That they be assured by the Hungarian National Committee that their organisation and military service in Italy is only a means to make it possible for them to fight in the course of the present war on their native soil for the liberty and independence of their country.

" 2. That, in connection with this conviction, they be organised and equipped in a manner which allows them to feel that they are in all respects a Hungarian national army while they are still on foreign territory.

" They will not be able to feel so, and they will not bear the stamp of Hungarian soldiers which would stimulate their enthusiasm to an incalculable extent, if, in their equipment, we are confined to such material as can be supplied to us by the Piedmontese military depôts,—these, besides, being already nearly empty.

" As regards the tactical organisation, we must not lose sight of the important consideration that the Hungarian army which will be formed in Italy can only become such an important factor in the present war as will enable us to throw a large, perhaps decisive, weight into the balance for attaining the object of the present war, if it is organised on a system which, in case of the war being transferred to Hungary, will afford a ready framework for enabling us to bring the whole military force of Hungary into efficiency with the least possible delay.

"Hungary, with its dependencies, counts fifteen million inhabitants, and, according to our experience of 1848, can easily put an army of 160,000 to 200,000 men into the field (among them some 20,000 to 25,000 cavalry).

"If the strength of the army we organise here can only be brought up to 8,000 or 10,000 men, it would be possible to bring the whole military force of Hungary into efficiency in six or eight weeks, provided that the organisation has been carried out on our own system.

"But, on the other hand, if we adopt, for the organisation of our force in Italy, the Piedmontese system—which is very excellent in its way, but does not correspond with our customs and requirements—this would not only not facilitate the future work of organisation at home, but would, on the contrary, throw difficulties in our way; for instead of simply filling up our ranks to the required strength with the forces at our disposal at home, we should have also to re-organise the corps we took with us from Italy.

"The consideration that a soldier should not be made to leave off a habit once contracted, induced us, in 1848, to retain much of the Austrian military system, which we, perhaps, did not approve; and we obtained good results by this precaution. The consequence of forcing the Piedmontese system upon us would be, that our soldiers would first have to forget the Austrian system and become accustomed to the Piedmontese, and then again have to forget the Piedmontese and accustom themselves to the Hungarian.

"The Piedmontese battalions are numerically weak; this may be a judicious arrangement in the army of a well-organised government, which keeps the supply of reserves in good working order; and with weak battalions, two officers and one drummer to each company may be sufficient; but we could not fill up the gaps in our ranks with the same ease, and we must, therefore, turn out strong battalions, so that, until we can better develop our system of supply of reserves, our battalions shall, in spite of battles and forced marches, form efficient tactical units. With strong battalions, however, two officers and one drummer to each company are not sufficient.

"With regard to clothing, I need only mention that the Piedmontese military depôts cannot supply us with Hungarian uniforms.

"As there is a want of officers, we ought to endeavour to select them from among the refugees staying in Turkey, England, and America, and assist them with money to defray their travelling expenses.

"A pension has already been promised in the royal decree to the wounded, but the other officers ought also to be assured that, in case we cannot reach our country, they will be transferred to one or other of the allied armies, still preserving their rank, or that they will at least receive a gratuity, consisting of a year's pay, including all other allowances. The most sacred duties also oblige me to ask what provision would be made for the rank and file in the unfortunate eventuality of peace being concluded without the independence of Hungary having been secured? To send them out into the world as beggars, unprovided for and homeless, is so dreadful for me to contemplate that my conscience would not permit me to encourage them to enlist, if no provision were made for them. The least which humanity itself demands is that peace should not be concluded without its being made a condition that they may return home without molestation—provision being made for the faithful execution of this condition. Some gratuity also will have to be provided for the men.

"While, therefore, soliciting a decision in this respect with regard both to the officers and to the men, I would at the same time, for the reasons enumerated above, submit the following proposals with reference to the mode of organisation :—

" 1. The organisation shall be carried out on our own system, an outline of which I will send in as soon as I return to Genoa.

"2. The appointment and promotion of officers shall be made upon the recommendation of the Hungarian National Committee.

"3. The officers shall receive the necessary means for their outfit, and money shall be advanced to the men.

"To provide these things is so much a custom with us at home that the Hungarian National Committee has been obliged to supply them out of funds placed at their disposal by His Majesty the Emperor of the French. As those funds were intended for another purpose, we beg that the advances thus made may be refunded to us.

"4. The Hungarian National Committee shall appoint a Council of Administration which, in conjunction with, and under the control of, a military Commissioner, to be nominated by the Piedmontese Government, shall carry out the equipment in the shortest possible manner. The accounts of such council to be audited by the Commissioner.

"5. The Hungarian National Committee will, through this Council of Administration, and on the system of organisation laid down in point No. 1, first submit an estimate of costs for the equipment of 4,000 or 5,000 men, and as soon as it is passed by the military Commissioner of the Piedmontese Government, the whole sum of the estimate shall be placed at the disposal of the Hungarian National Committee, in order to enable them to carry out the equipment speedily and efficaciously through their own army contractor, under such control and audit as mentioned in point No. 4.

"If some pieces of clothing—cloaks, for instance—can be supplied by the Piedmontese military depôts in kind, their price shall be deducted from the estimate of costs.

"6. All money spent on this organisation to be considered a loan to the Hungarian nation, which will have to be repaid hereafter.

"7. In consequence of the victorious progress of the war, Genoa is no longer a suitable seat for the Hungarian National Committee, which therefore, together with their chief depôt, ought to be transferred to Milan. Such a course seems to be all the more advisable as, on account of the prolonged stay of the Austrians in the above town, it is hardly possible that no workmen could be found there who are acquainted with the sort of work required for the equipment of Hungarian troops. No such men are to be found in Genoa.

" 8. As soon as a battalion is equipped it might be sent to do garrison duty at Piacenza, Pizzighettone, or Cremona; or if their employment at the seat of war should be considered necessary, it is desirable that the Hungarian forces under Hungarian leaders—subordinated, however, to the commander of the respective army corps, should be employed on the right wing of the allied troops in such a way as Garibaldi's force on the left wing. This would be desirable in order to rouse the enthusiasm of the Hungarian troops by convincing them that every step is directed to bringing them nearer home.

" 9. It is absolutely necessary that they should be assured, through me, that the object of their service is that they may be led home into their native country in order to take part there in the struggle for regaining the independence of their nation. Unless they possess this conviction, I not only cannot hope to induce the Hungarians to desert the Austrian ranks and come over to us in great numbers, but I cannot even guarantee that those who have already enlisted will feel inclined to take the oath.

" 10. As the thought that they will be obliged to fight against their own countrymen in a foreign land may create in many of them a justifiable reluctance, I take the liberty of pointing out what the commanders should be chiefly guided by in the employment of the Hungarian troops—namely, the fact that the greatest service these troops can render to the allied forces is not to promote victory here in Italy by their active participation in the war (of which the invincible allied forces are not in need), but to create disorder and dissolution in the ranks of the enemy by the display of the Hungarian standard. I beg to direct careful attention to the consideration of this matter.

"11. Lastly, as the Austrians have of late enrolled many Hungarians in foreign regiments, directions would have to be issued not only that should the prisoners of war belonging to Hungarian regiments be placed at the disposal of the Hungarian National Committee for selection, as has been the case hitherto, in consequence of which several hundred Hungarian prisoners able to fight have been sent to France,—but that this regulation should apply to all soldiers coming from countries belonging to the Hungarian Crown, without distinction of nationality. For keeping in view the possibility of an advance on Hungarian territory, I cannot possibly overrate the importance of the organisation of one Croatian battalion or more.

"These proposals are, to a great extent, the same as those which I have authorised General Czetz to submit to his Excellency Count Cavour.

(Signed) "KOSSUTH,
"President of the Hungarian National Committee."
Dated Parma, June 28th, 1859.

From Prince Napoleon at Parma I went with Senator Pietri to the Imperial head-quarters (at Valleggio).* On this occasion the Emperor Napoleon expressed a wish to see his army joined, as soon as possible, by one or two Hungarian battalions wearing the tight trousers. To this I replied that I could gratify his wish in nine or ten days (as we possessed some practical experience of speedy equipment) if our hands were not tied,—if we could proceed with the equipment according to our own system, and if we had the necessary funds placed at our disposal, subject to supervision, and on condition of having the accounts audited, instead of being obliged to take the circuitous way of corresponding with the Sardinian War Office about the smallest detail. I remarked

* This visit will be referred to under Chapter VI.

that the required oath of allegiance to Victor Emmanuel had created some apprehension among the men, in regard to its wording. That apprehension was undoubtedly without foundation; still it existed. It could be silenced, but it would be difficult to eradicate it; and as it was desirable that the enthusiasm which the men have evinced in their readiness to serve should be kept as high as possible, it would be well if we could be exempted, for the time at least, from taking the oath.

The Emperor replied that as the Hungarian army had a national object of its own, he did not believe in the necessity of this oath, and was convinced that we should be able to maintain discipline and subordination in the army even without it; perhaps better without it, since the omission of the oath of allegiance to the King of Sardinia could but strengthen their faith in the national destination of our army. He also authorised me to use his name and to acquaint Count Cavour of this opinion. Count Cavour agreed with the Emperor's views. He relinquished the oath, and only required the signature to a pledged agreement. He was even prepared to omit the name of King Victor Emmanuel entirely from the agreement, which was to be restricted simply to a pledge of obedience to the military laws.

With respect to our having more liberty in the equipment, in order to accelerate its completion, the Emperor approved of its being accorded to us, all the more as it was undeniable that there were no tight trousers, or *bakkanes*, or laced Hungarian coats to be found in the Piedmontese military depôts. The Emperor then turned to Senator Pietri, who had been present at our conversation, and said to him, "Please accompany

Mr. Kossuth to Turin, and in my name tell Count Cavour that I wish him to allow Mr. Kossuth and his colleagues total freedom in the equipment of the Hungarian army, as I consider it important that we should as soon as possible see a Hungarian force, in their tight trousers, with our army. If Cavour should find any difficulty as far as money is concerned, you will please see to it that the matter is not retarded on that account."

Our difficulties thus having been removed, it rested with us to show that we could proceed speedily. At that time the number of our men exceeded already 4,000. By telegraph I asked my colleagues of the Committee, the staff attached to this Committee, the generals, and the two colonels in command of our brigades, to come to Turin. We held a meeting on July 4th, and decided upon the details of organisation and equipment, and, without loss of time, settled the terms with some manufacturers of Turin for the supply of complete equipment for two battalions within eight days. By the side of the Commander-in-Chief of the army, General Klapka, a committee of equipment was appointed under the presidency of General Czecz, who, at the same time, was delegated to superintend the instruction of the troops. We systematised our further procedure; we handed to Count Cavour a report detailing the whole organisation. This report corresponded to the one referred to above, which I handed to Prince Napoleon, and on its basis we arranged everything with Count Cavour the following day (July 5), to our mutual satisfaction.

We had already two brigades, five battalions of which were quite complete. The first brigade was commanded by Colonel Daniel Ihász, the second by Colonel Nicholas

Kiss. We flattered ourselves that, in a short time, we should be able to lead home a Hungarian army of considerable strength; and that we should see the whole nation flock around this nucleus and fight, as ten years previously our "nameless demi-gods" had fought for country and liberty; and that they would once for all fight out the independence of Hungary.

Alas! from the clear sky of our hopes fell the thunderbolt of Villafranca.

There was an end to our hopes, and, with them, to the organisation of an army.

"Habent mortalia casum."

II.
Agreement with Prince Couza.

General Klapka, in his letter of May 22nd, communicated to me the subjoined agreement, which on his tour in the East he had concluded with Prince Alexander Couza, the Prince-Elect of Moldavia and Wallachia.

Agreement A.

"Prince Couza gives permission to the Hungarian patriots to establish depôts for arms in the valley of the Szereth, in Bakau, Roman, or other places still nearer the frontier of Transylvania, like Okna, and Piatra.

"The Prince shall ask his Majesty the Emperor of the French for 30,000 firearms, of which 10,000 shall be used for arming the Moldavo-Wallachian army, and 20,000 shall be placed at the disposal of the leaders of the Hungarian and Transylvanian insurgents. The Prince shall ask for these arms at once, considering the threatening aspect of the situation, and the time which is required to transport them from the Mediterranean ports to the spot.

" Subsequent consignments of war material, which will have to be divided between Hungary and the Principalities, according to their respective requirements, shall form the subject of an agreement to be concluded hereafter.

" Besides the arms demanded of the allied governments, application shall be made to the Servian Government for a certain number of guns. Some of these guns will be placed at the disposal of the Hungarians by the Moldavo-Wallachian Government.

" On the other hand, General Klapka shall exert himself to the utmost in Paris and London to have, not only the arms and necessary ammunition dispatched immediately, but also those articles of equipment which are necessary to enable the Moldavian, Wallachian, and Hungarian troops to take the field at once. He shall further exert himself to secure in Paris, or elsewhere, the services of a sufficient staff of surgeons, and some engineer and artillery officers, who will have to organise these two services of the army.

" The General shall act in all these questions in harmony with the Prince's diplomatic agent at Paris.

" Hungarian agents shall be sent to Jassy, Bucharest, and Galatz in order to keep up constant communication with the government of his Highness the Prince.

" The agents at Belgrade shall take care to keep the Moldavo-Wallachian Government informed of everything that is going on there.

" As soon as the war breaks out in Italy, the Moldavo-Wallachian Government shall place at the disposal of the Hungarian military commander all that is necessary to enable him to send the arms, ammunition, &c., to the frontier.

" The Hungarians, in their turn, offer the most active assistance to enable the Moldavo-Wallachian Government to occupy Bucovina, and to overcome all the difficulties which may arise from circumstances and possible complications."

Agreement B.

" It is important to the success of the insurrection in Hungary that the Hungarian, Wallachian, and Servian nationalities should put aside all party spirit, all ideas of separation, and all those animosities which caused such deplorable results in 1848-49.

" They should remember that Austria may again have recourse to those vile instruments which, at the time referred to, she used to instigate the nationalities, who at that time were still rivals, against each other, in order to keep one in servitude by means of the other, and in this way all of them.

" The Hungarians are convinced beforehand that the sympathy of the Wallachians is assured to them. In Paris it is also expected of the Government of the Principalities that, led by its own interests, it will use its influence with that part of the population of Hungary and Transylvania which belongs to their race to bring about a reconcilation.

" In return the Hungarian patriots will, as soon as hostilities have commenced, state that the following principles will be embodied in their constitution :—

" 1. Oblivion of all past dissensions, and complete reconciliation between the Servians, Wallachians, and Hungarians.

" 2. Equal liberty and right to every inhabitant of Hungary, without distinction of race or creed.

" 3. Self-administration of the commune and county. The people inhabiting the same district, and speaking different tongues, will amicably settle between themselves their official language.

" 4. Complete independence regarding the different creeds and nationalities in the administration of public worship and instruction.

" 5. The Servian and Wallachian forces to be organised separately and commanded respectively in the Servian and Wallachian languages. The qualification for the different offices in the whole army to be the same for everybody.

" 6. After the war is over an assembly, called together in Transylvania, will decide about the administrative union of that province with Hungary, and in case the majority should decide that

Transylvania should resume its ancient separate administration, this will not be opposed.

"7. It is necessary that the principle of fraternity should guide us all. This alone can lead to the goal towards which we all are straining; and this goal is, the confederation of the three Danubian States—Hungary, Servia, and Moldo-Wallachia."

The readiness of Prince Couza to ally himself with the Hungarian nation against Austria requires an explanation.

The contents of Paragraphs XXII. to XXVII. of the Treaty of Paris of 1856, which disposed of the fate of Moldavia and Wallachia, may be compressed into the following three points :—

1. That the Principalities, placed under the joint protection of the contracting powers, should not in future be exposed either to the " protection " of Russia or to the interference of Austria.

2. That the suzerainty of the Porte should be preserved, but that the Principalities should have their privileges and liberties guaranteed, and should have their own independent national administration, complete liberty in religious, legislative, commercial and shipping affairs, and should also possess their own national armies.

3. That though the definite organisation of the Principalities should be decided upon by the contracting powers, and put into operation by a *hatti-sheriff* of the Porte, the organisation should be such as would correspond to the wishes of the people.

With regard to this last point the contracting powers decided that the Porte should in each Principality call together an *ad hoc* divan, on such a basis that the interests of all classes of society should be represented, and in this way it would faithfully interpret the wishes of the people. A European Commission, with the assistance of a Commissioner of the Porte, was entrusted with the consideration of the wishes of these two divans, and with the enunciation of proposals as to definite organisation. The final decision in the matter was reserved to a conference of the powers which was to meet at Paris for that purpose.

For the realisation of the intentions of the peace-makers it was above all necessary that the two *ad hoc* divans should be so constituted that they should fairly represent the public opinion of the principalities.

But the overwhelming majority of the inhabitants wished that the two Principalities should be united. This was generally known. It could not, therefore, be doubted that the two divans would decide in favour of the union, provided that, in conformity with the intentions of the Treaty of Paris, they were so constituted that they could safely be looked upon as representing public opinion.

. The Porte, however, was firmly determined to oppose the union, and was supported in her opposition by Austria. The question of union had already been brought forward at the peace negotiations in Paris, and if, in spite of the support of France, Russia, and Sardinia, it was not decided upon, this must be ascribed to Austria's having succeeded in inducing England to alter her opinion on the subject and adopt Austria's view.

In accordance with the treaty, the Porte was obliged to communicate to the representatives of the powers the firman calling together the divans. The Russian, French, a Sardinian representatives determinedly opposed the publication of the firman, as it appeared to them that it was intended to make a declaration in favour of union impossible. In consequence of this opposition the question of convoking the Divans was discussed at a conference of ambassadors under the presidency of Rcsid Pasha, in which Thouvenel the French, Redcliffe the English, Prokesch-Osten the Austrian, Wildenbrock the Prussian, and General Durando the Sardinian, ambassadors, took part. The meetings of this conference were as stormy as they were protracted, in consequence of the obstinacy manifested by Austria against the union. They came to an end only on January 7th, 1857, and the firman which had been agreed upon was of such a construction as to leave a manifestation in favour of union a possibility. The Porte and Austria then had recourse to all sorts of pressure and briberies to make the elections turn out adverse to union. In this they succeeded in Moldavia with the help of Vogorides, the Kaimakan of Konak. The French, Russian, Prussian, and Sardinian ambassadors, demanded that the elections—gained by tyranny, violence, fraud, and bribery—should be annulled. The diplomatic struggle which ensued, and in which England supported Austria, first led to the abdication of the Turkish Ministry, and, later on, on August 6th, 1857, brought about the rupture of diplomatic relations between the Porte and the four Powers named above.

Meanwhile the Emperor Napoleon was anxious to preserve his alliance with England at any price. He paid a visit to the Queen of England at the beginning of August, and on this occasion made a compromise with the English Government, according to which England would join the four Powers which insisted upon the nullification of the Moldavian elections, while France, on the other hand, would not press the Principalities to unite *at once.*

In consequence of this agreement the Porte yielded. The Moldavian elections huddled up by Vogorides were cancelled, and the Divan constituted by fresh elections was in favour of union. The same was the case in Wallachia, and the two Divans expressed their wish that the two Principalities, united into one state, should be ruled by a Prince with the right of succession, to be chosen from among the princes of the reigning houses of Europe.

Taking into consideration this general wish of public opinion, the European Commission prepared their scheme for the organisation of the Principalities; for the final settlement of which the ambassadors of the signatory powers to the Treaty of Paris met at Paris, on May 22nd, 1858, under the presidency of Count Walewski, the French Minister for Foreign Affairs.

At this conference the two opposite parties had heated, irritated, and obdurate altercations. It occupied eighteen long sittings, till at last, on August 19th, the political constitution of the two Principalities was decided upon, but this in a manner which satisfied nobody, neither those who wanted a union, nor those who did not want it. A regular absurdity, it is referred to by Cavour, in his letter to the Marquis Pes de Villamarina (August 22nd and 30th, 1859) in the following terms: " In the matter of the Principalities, the Powers have cut an awkward figure (*hanno fatto una brutta figura*). Instead of making peace they have sown the seeds of revolution."

The chief points of the constitution thus agreed upon may be shortly recapitulated as follows :—

The Principalities will assume the title of the " *United Principalities of Moldavia and Wallachia.*"

They will have an autonomous government of their own, which will be entirely independent of the Porte.

Each Principality will have a *separate National Assembly*, constituted by election.

A *native* Hospodar will stand at the head of the executive power in each Principality, and he will govern with responsible ministers.

The two Hospodars, to be elected by the *National Assemblies*, will be tributary to the Porte, and will take their investiture at her hands.

The two Principalities will have *a common* Central Committee, which will point out to the *two Hospodars* the reforms to be introduced, and will prepare the more important Bills; they will besides have *one common* High Court of Justice, and *one common* Court of Cassation.

The militia of the *two* Principalities will form *one* army, and be subject to *one* commander.

Such was this masterpiece of European diplomacy. Confusion; a mass of contradictions. Too little for a blessing, too much for a curse.

The Emperor Napoleon III., in the Speech from the Throne with which he opened the French Senate and Corps Législatif, on February 7th, 1859, refers in the following terms to this matter, in connection with foreign affairs :—

"The Cabinet of Vienna and my own, I am sorry to say, have often been at variance (*en dissidence*) about the most important questions, and a great deal of conciliation (*esprit de conciliation*) has been required to solve these questions. Thus, for instance, the reorganisation of the Danubian Principalities could only be accomplished with many difficulties—difficulties which have done much *to prevent the complete attainment of their very justifiable wishes;* and if I were asked what interest France has in those distant provinces on the banks of the Danube, my answer would be that France has interests wherever where there is a question of leading to victory a righteous and civilising cause."

This solemn statement of the powerful Emperor of the French explains much. It explains on the one hand the animosities of the inhabitants of the Principalities towards the Cabinet of Vienna, which was held up to the world as "a bar to the satisfaction of their most justifiable wishes"; it explains, on the other hand, their inclination to enter into an alliance with us, upon being reminded of the desirability of it from a quarter whence they received in such a solemn way the assurance that the powerful Emperor of the French regarded the victory of their righteous and civilising cause as an interest of France.

The readiness of Prince Couza to join hands with the Hungarians against Austria is still further explained by the history of his election, a short account of which I feel I must give here; first, because it always gives me pleasure to bow with reverence before the spectacle of patriotism which suppresses party strife and self-interest, wherever I may meet with such a spectacle in history; and, secondly, because of the consideration that if the lessons of history, so much praised, but so seldom turned to account, were not written in vain, the instance which I quote here might induce all those in whose sphere reigns the foul infection of party interest and corruption, the enemy of all citizen virtues, to turn to them and repent.

In Moldavia Colonel Alexander Couza was unanimously elected Hospodar by the forty-nine members of the National Assembly, on January 17th, 1859, though, according to a Constantinople newspaper, he did not possess the two following qualifications—ten years' service and an income of 30,005 zechins.

The Wallachian National Assembly met for the election of a Hospodar at Bucharest on February 3rd.

Great animosity reigned on the one hand between the two parties, and on the other between the Left and the Kajmakam, who, amidst passionate outbursts of feeling, was accused of having exercised an unlawful influence upon the elections.

The verification of credentials, and with it the constitution of the Assembly, had for two days given occasion to such stormy scenes as, taken in connection with the excitement of the populace which had gathered in thousands round the building where the Assembly held its sitting, commenced to assume an aspect vividly reminding the spectator of the scenes of the French Revolution.

On the third day Boeresco, a young deputy of the Left, moved that the Assembly should continue the sitting with closed doors in order to listen to what he had to propose. The motion was carried, and Boeresco, while expressing deep regret at the passionate antagonism which existed between the two parties of the Assembly, showed that what provoked all this antagonism was the question of the election of the head of their state, as every one believed that the victory of his candidate would bring his party into power, and consequently every one found the idea that the other party's candidate should be victorious unbearable. Hence the rivalry which, by dividing the parties, threatened the country with anarchy, and therefore with foreign occupation. This could only be avoided by their coming to an understanding about the election. A person could not form the subject of such an understanding, because every one had his individual candidate to whose election he clung, in opposition to the election of all others. But there was a principle about which, without having regard to personalities, they could all agree, which was the principle of *union*, for without party distinction they all felt that only by union could the Roumanian nation be regenerated. Placing himself, therefore, on this standpoint, he moved that the two Principalities should have one Prince. Moldavia having already elected her ruler, Wallachia should place her confidence in the same man. This would not clash with the Paris Convention, which, though it provided that the two assemblies should elect separately, did not prohibit their both electing one and the same person; and only if they so fixed their choice would it be possible to effect harmoniously the other provisions of the convention, which with two distinct heads of the state could only produce friction. "Accomplished facts," if resting on right, carried great weight with them. Let the members of the Assembly elevate their minds from the low level of party interests to the loftier consideration of laying the foundation of their country's existence, and let them place the union before the Powers as an accomplished fact.

The speech of Boeresco produced a deep impression. With one heart and one voice the deputies exclaimed, "Long live Alexander Couza, our Prince!" This exclamation was heartily re-echoed by the multitude collected outside. The Metropolitan (the President of the Assembly) knelt down, and, in a voice trembling with emotion, thanked God for having enlightened the representatives of the Roumanian nation; he begged the Almighty to let the spirit of patriotic concord reign amongst them and lead to good results, and called upon the representatives to pledge themselves by oath to preserve concord, and to support, without party distinctions, the sole Prince of the United Principalities. "We swear!" shouted the representatives. The minutes of the sitting were prepared upon the spur of the moment, and all signed them. George Stirbey, the member for Krajova, expressed regret that his father (a late Hospodar, and then a member of the Assembly) was prevented by illness from being present, and begged that the minutes should be taken to him to his sick-bed for signature. G. Bibesco (Duke Brancovano) stated that his father (who had been Hospodar from 1842 to 1849), not being a member of that Assembly, could not affix his signature to the minutes, but that he approved of it with all his heart. The representatives returned to the Assembly room. There were no "sides" of the House, no parties. They went through the process of verifying the votes without debate. There was nothing to debate upon, as patriotism, suppressing personal interests, had with self-denial anticipated all debate. Prince Alexander Ghika and Rodolph Golesco themselves had already declared that they acknowledged their elections to be illegal; and these and four others (Mano, Balliano, Hagiadi, and Plechoiano) were struck off the list of representatives. The other sixty-six had their credentials verified; of these two (Prince Stirbey and Slatiniano) were absent on account of illness. The sixty-four members present were summoned to a secret vote, and the Metropolitan, holding in one hand the Cross and in the other hand the Gospel, took the following oath, which the representatives repeated after him:—" I swear that in the vote I am about to give I shall not be guided by personal interest or by alien suggestion, or by any other consideration than that of the public welfare." After having taken the oath the representatives proceeded to vote. Sixty-four members voted, and on opening the ballot papers it was found that all the sixty-four votes had been given to Alexander Couza. By secret ballot he had been elected unanimously. The bells began to ring, and the people's shouts of joy rang through the air. The enthusiasm that prevailed defies description.

This is the spirit which a people needs to create a country; or, if it is lost, to re-conquer it.

The Wallachian National Assembly, by this able as well as patriotic step, realised what the Conference of Paris, chiefly in consequence of the opposition of Austria, did not concede, but what the Emperor Napoleon in his Speech from the Throne called the very justifiable wish of the nation; and Prince Couza ascended the throne at Bucharest on February 20. However, there remained the doubtful question of the investiture by the Porte and the approval of the guaranteeing powers. The Porte protested against the election, and appealed to the signatory powers of the Treaty of Paris to decide about it. Again a conference was called together.

It does not come within my province to enlarge upon the animated discussions and various events of this conference. Suffice it to say that in the end the 'force of "accomplished facts resting on right" carried off the victory, but for months it seemed probable that the question would have to be decided by an appeal to arms, in consequence of the opposition of the Cabinet of Vienna, which called the double election of Prince Couza an evasion of the provisions of the Paris Conference, and an insult derogatory to the dignity of the guaranteeing powers. Austria opposed the union of the Principalities with no less determination than the Porte herself, and was also supported in her opposition by the English Tory Government. The Porte concentrated a considerable army in Bulgaria. The Wallachian Government, about the middle of May, raised a loan of eight millions, and drew up 20,000 men along the Danube. The excitement in the East was extreme, and the newspapers stated that Austria had offered an offensive and defensive alliance to Turkey. This alliance, in the extent which Austria wished to give to it, was not accepted by Turkey, but still there could scarcely be a doubt that if it came to an armed conflict between the Porte and the United Danubian Principalities, the Cabinet of Vienna would side with the Porte, and that the Principalities might expect the armed interference of Austria.

This explains the readiness of Prince Couza to ally himself with the Hungarians. Our interests met. It was in the interest of Prince Couza to see Austria occupied in Hungary in a way which would prevent her from meddling with arms in Wallachian affairs, and it was our interest to put Transylvania under arms, and in our organisation to be able to depend upon freedom of action and support from that side, and further to stand on such a footing with the Danubian Principalities as would exclude the apprehension that a repetition of the atrocities of 1848–49 might occur again, and that our war of independence in Transylvania would be complicated by civil strife.

There is another point in the agreement entered into by General Klapka which also calls for some little explanation: I refer to what is said about Bucovina.

Of course this condition was made on the supposition that the question of union might induce the Cabinet of Vienna to interfere with arms in the Principalities; and starting from this supposition it is impossible not to see the reasonableness of Prince Couza's intention eventually to occupy, or more correctly speaking, to reoccupy Bucovina. For Bucovina once belonged to Moldavia; it had been torn from Moldavia, and the way by which it came into the possession of the Court of Vienna is one of the most disreputable intrigues recorded in history. The possession of Bucovina by Austria does not even rest on the right of conquest. It is a very disreputable affair altogether. When Kaunitz and Galiczyn negotiated about the partition of unfortunate Poland, Kaunitz was dissatisfied with the Austrian share of the booty, whereupon Galiczyn answered: "We shall make it up by taking away the territory of somebody else—the Turk—who has plenty." And it happened as he had said. Russia attacked Turkey, occupied Moldavo-Wallachia, and in 1774 presented a part of Moldavia (the Bucovina of the present day), which was not its own, to the Court of Vienna, as an addition to the Polish booty. No wonder if Prince Couza were to remember this, in case of a war.

So much for the better understanding of the agreement entered into by General Klapka.

But it is with regret that I must state that, though in the memorable sitting of the Bucharest National Assembly of February 5th, on an appeal from the Metropolitan, all the members had sworn to maintain concord and to support the Prince, in whom was personified the principle of union, this oath, and the identity of interests under prevailing perils, and the still more important, because permanent, consideration, that the Roumanian nation, surrounded by a sea of Slav races, is, in the interest of its independence, and through its geographical position, clearly forced to an alliance with the Hungarian nation—all these considerations, I say, did not possess sufficient weight to disarm the hatred nourished towards us by those Roumanians who cast an eye upon Transylvania, under some fictitious pretensions which rest on a state of things that existed in times prior to the migration of the nations, and are besides mere legends only, and who in their fanaticism forget that if the formation of states in Europe were proceeded with on the basis of what existed before the migration of the nations set in, not only would nine-tenths of the nations of Europe lose their claim to existence, but for the Roumanian nation itself there would be no place in the beautiful country they now inhabit. A nation is only produced by history.

These fanatics, full of subversive tendencies, hotly opposed an alliance between the Roumanian and Hungarian nations.

The question of the election of a Prince was in suspense. The Porte and Austria step by step defended the standpoint they had taken up against union. Even towards the end of May, when it was no longer possible for them to refuse the acceptance in principle of accomplished facts, they threw many difficulties (partly of formal and partly of essential character) in the way of granting the investiture, all of which were designed to frustrate the importance of Couza's double election for the accomplishment of a union. First, it was declared that the investiture would be granted in two separate firmans in order to preserve the principle of "non-union"; at another time, one firman was conceded, but under the reservation that, in future, Moldavia and Wallachia should not be allowed to elect the same Prince. Couza considering this (and with perfect right) a violation of the Principalities' right of self-government, addressed a letter to the Emperor Napoleon; and entrusted its delivery to Mr. Bal . . . no, charging him also with the representation of the affair of the union, and also the execution in Italy of the practical details of his agreement with us.

Mr. Bal . . . no, a warm supporter of the policy of Prince Couza, manifested the most friendly disposition towards us, to which I bear testimony with gratitude. Meanwhile, one of the most eminent and influential statesmen of Wallachia, who, during the time he spent as a refugee abroad, had there also contracted important connections, a Mr. Br . . . no, thought it wise to go about this time on a journey to the West, and though he had no official position, he endeavoured to utilise his own personal influence in making politics on his own account.

Mr. Br .... no has proved himself our sworn enemy, and did everything to prevent the agreement initiated by Klapka.

The following data, bearing upon this subject, deserve to be recorded here:—

COUNT LADISLAUS TELEKI TO KOSSUTH.

"*Genoa, June 29th,* 1859.

" The enclosed letter has to-day reached Strzelecky* from Bal ... no. I send it 'pour l'acquit de ma conscience.' I know that you are well informed as to how the whole matter stands, and you know best what can be done with the Roumanians. Br ... no himself is an individual not easily convinced; I know him as such, but still I venture to hope that the steps to be taken hereafter may have success.

" (Signed)   LADISLAUS TELEKI."

The letter to Strzelecky referred to, ran as follows:

" I have returned from Genoa, and expect that the rising or falling tide of the sea of politics may carry me to the Emperor, or take me out into the open sea (which after all I should not mind).

" From this you can see that I do not yet know what I shall do, or when I shall leave here.

" Cavour has returned from headquarters, but I could not yet see him. All this is very disagreeable, and if I were not afraid of the success of Br ... no's intrigues (I met Br ... no here), I should consider my mission accomplished with the delivery of Prince Couza's letter to the Emperor.

* Strzelecky was a very intimate friend of General Klapka, and specially well versed in Eastern affairs.

"Br . . . no wishes to return to power again and, as he has done before, he will make use of the Emperor, Cavour, and Prince Napoleon, in order to accomplish his wish. If he succeeds (which is the only thing that I fear) *there will be an end to our affair*. Br . . . no and his party are inveterate enemies of Hungary.

"(Signed)   BAL . . . NO."

GENERAL CZECZ TO KOSSUTH.

"*2nd July*, 1859.

"I have the pleasure of communicating also the following from my last conversation with Count Cavour, held by desire of your Excellency:—

"Count Cavour stated openly to Mr. Br . . . no, the day before yesterday, that if he and his party were even to moot the Transylvanian question, he (Cavour) would listen to nothing more about Wallachian affairs.

"In consequence of this statement Mr. Br . . . no started the same evening for Paris. Therefore he will not go to headquarters to see the Emperor.

"Mr. Bal . . . no will start this evening for Genoa, there to await your Excellency.

"(Signed)   CZECZ."

The explanation of Count Cavour's statement, referred to above, is supplied by a note which I found in the same packet with the letter; and which (translated from the French) runs as follows:—

BR . . . NO'S STATEMENT.

"I do not believe in the liberal professions and moderation of the Hungarians. They use them as a mask solely calculated to mislead the Emperor. I know that they are more exclusive than ever, and I do not believe in Hungary . . . . But even if it were otherwise, we can never come to an understanding as regards Transylvania, which we cannot concede to Hungary under any title. The

Roumanians beyond the Carpathians wish to be united with us; we have promised to support them; it would be treason if we conceded them to Hungary. The historical right to which Hungary appeals is a farce."

It is much to be regretted that such feeling can be entertained. I can only wish that Mr. Br . . . no, who since then has exercised great influence over the history of his country, may have been led by the practical sphere in which he has been active as a statesman, to views more just to the Hungarian nation, as well as fairer to the rights of existing states, and more accurate regarding the interests of his own country.

The Peace of Villafranca also prevented General Klapka's agreement from being carried out, but did not put an end to the apparent relation between the two. The second volume of my " Memories " will speak of its unpleasant continuation, and will supply an explanation of the word " apparent."

On this occasion nothing happened, except that I made an agreement with Mr. Bal . . . no, the confidential agent of Prince Couza, about the 30,000 arms, which had been sent to the East on our account. According to this agreement, one part of the fire-arms was to be held at our disposal in depôts, the other part was to be placed at the disposal of the Roumanian Government; on condition, however, that upon three months' notice at any time they should place the same number of arms at our disposal.

Of course the original donors had also a word to say in the matter, in consequence of which the question of arms went through different phases, which, however, belong to the history of the next few years, and ended with a letter of thanks, dated Warsaw, May 17th, 1863, which commences, "Le Gouvernement national polonais, à M. L. Kossuth," and bears as signature a seal in which the Polish eagle is surrounded by these words, "Rzad Narodowy. Równósc, Wolnósc, Niepodleglosc." (The National Government. Equality, Freedom, Independence.)

III.

Conference with Prince Michael Obrenovics.—Mission to Belgrade.

Servia also, as in 1839 and 1842, made a revolution at the end of 1858, to change her sovereign. On the last occasion she did so without difficulty and without making a noise over it. On Dec. 22nd the Skuptshina sent a deputation to inform Prince Alexander Karagyorgyevics that he had been dethroned, and that in his place Milosh Obrenovics (father of Prince Michael) who was already more than 80 years old, had been re-elected. Prince Alexander protested, and sought refuge in the Turkish fortress of Belgrade; but not meeting with any support at Constantinople, he sent in his resignation early in January; and Milosh Obrenovics (his election having been confirmed by the Porte, Jan. 14th, with regard to his own person and with exclusion of the right of inheritance) again became Prince of Servia after an exile* of twenty years.

* I take this opportunity to narrate a little anecdote of 1848, which, so far as I know, has not been published anywhere before.
I was President of the Committee for the defence of the country, when, in the autumn of 1848, a man of gentlemanly appearance who (unless my memory

General Klapka, in the same letter in which he communicated to me the agreement he had entered into with Prince Couza, informed me that he had also conferred with Prince Michael Obrenovics, the son

deceives me) gave his name as Petrovics, called on me with a few lines from a well-known statesman of the Obrenovics party. In the letter I was informed that the bearer thereof came to me on a very important but strictly secret mission, and requested a private interview. I received the man, who, however, only spoke Servian, while I, unfortunately, did not understand his language. We were in need of an interpreter. On looking round the anti-chamber, I perceived Duschek, whose self-sacrifice, integrity, and truly patriotic services have since been rewarded with so much calumny. I asked him whether he did not know some trustworthy and honest patriot who could act as interpreter between myself and the Servian, who alleged he was sent on an important mission. Duschek, after a little reflection, recommended the orthodox Greek Bishop of Buda at that time, who was known as an honest patriot who had openly joined the movement of 1848, and whose son held an appointment in the Ministry of Finances. After having acquired information from other sources as well, as to the reputation the right rev. gentleman enjoyed as a patriot, I found him acceptable, and requested his presence for the following day. He acted as interpreter, after having given his word of honour that he would keep secret what he was about to hear, whatever this might be.

As interpreted by the bishop, the Servian envoy made the following statement :—

"Not a little inconvenience is caused to you by those Servians who flock over from Servia by thousands to fight against you. I am entrusted by the leaders of the Obrenovics party to propose to you that on my wishes, which I shall proffer, being acceded to, we shall relieve you of that anxiety."

To my inquiry as to how they intended to effect this, he replied: "We are tired of the rule of Alexander Karagyorgyevics; we wish to make a revolution to dethrone him, and recall the aged Milos. If revolution breaks out in Servia you may be sure that my compatriots will flock back in haste from Hungary in order to join their respective parties." To my further inquiry, as to what they wanted from us, he replied : "We want two things; first, some thousand ducats [not a large sum; if I remember rightly, he mentioned six thousand]; secondly, that you send somebody to Munich to Prince Milos to inform him, that as his partisans deem it necessary that he should be in the neighbourhood you offer him a hospitable home on Hungarian territory, and will be pleased to see him. If you do this much we will make a revolution, upon the news of which all the Servians will return home; and the House of Obrenovics, having to thank you for your assistance in its restoration, will certainly take care that these shall not return again to your country."

22

of Prince Milos, on the basis of that agreement. Prince Michael having thus received intelligence of our affairs in Paris, was struck with the thought, that as the Emperor Napoleon was not disinclined to take up the

> I replied that there would be no difficulty with regard to the second point, but with respect to those ducats, the whole affair did not appear to me to be very serious, as he asked for six, and not sixty, or six hundred, thousand; that I did not believe they could make a revolution with six thousand ducats. But the envoy stated positively that it would be enough for them, and also explained the reason why. "We only want money," he said, "to bring the country notabilities of our party to Kragujevacz, with a proper retinue, in order to pass a resolution for the dethronement of Prince Alexander, in the Assembly there. The rest is our own business. After the deposition has been resolved upon, a provisional government, of course, will be proclaimed, which, if Prince Alexander surrenders, will meet everywhere with ready submission; if he resists, in those districts at least which join the movement against him, the provisional government will all the more easily be able to defray the further expenses of the revolution, as in our country every man is armed, and there is no expenditure under this head in case of revolution." To my further remark that in no case could I consider the statement of a stranger a sufficient basis, the envoy said that he considered that quite natural; so much so, that even if I were inclined to hand over to him the demanded six thousand ducats, he would not accept them. But he requested me to instruct the commander of the fortress of Pétervárad to send a trustworthy person to Belgrade (the envoy told me where he could be found, and by what pass-word he might be recognised), whom he would take to the chief men of their party. The money would only be appropriated if these confirmed his (the envoy's) statements; it would have to be sent to Pétervárad, and would be received not by him, but by the person authorised by the leaders to take it.
>
> I followed the matter up, and being convinced of the correctness of the statements of the envoy, I thought the affair was worth a trial. I sent Mr. (later Colonel) Emerich Szabó to Munich to inform Milos, who at once repaired to Agram. The transmission of the six thousand ducats to Pétervárad, and their payment to the Servian agent I entrusted to the same orthodox Greek Bishop of Buda who had acted as interpreter at our interview, and was therefore let into the secret.
>
> The right rev. gentleman took the ducats, gave his word of honour that he would faithfully carry out his mission, and started—not, however, for Pétervárad, but for the camp of the insurgent Servians, to whom he handed over the money. He himself remained at Ujvidék—as Bishop!
>
> The House of Obrenovics returned to the throne of Servia only ten years later.

cause of Hungary in connection with the Italian question, he might also, perhaps, be persuaded to take up the Eastern question at the same time. With this intention in view, he started for Paris, in May, 1859, and had a conference with the Emperor shortly before the latter left for the seat of war in Italy.

The Emperor gave Prince Michael a decided refusal. He said it would be a dangerous thing to mix up the Italian question with the Eastern question. Hungary's case was entirely different. A war in Hungary was still confined to the Austrian dominions, and as he (the Emperor) was already at war with Austria, the extension of the scene of war to Hungary (which did not form part of the German Confederation) was not a matter to supply a plausible pretext for a European intervention, and still English diplomatists had so far talked themselves into the principle of the localisation of the war, that even the extension of hostilities to Hungary entirely depended upon the ability of Kossuth to secure the neutrality of England. Kossuth had hope of his success, but if the war were further complicated by the Eastern question, England would certainly not remain neutral, and the matter would lead to incalculable complications. Therefore, the Eastern question could not be even thought of. "But," continued the Emperor, "you no doubt understand, Prince Michael, that the independence of Hungary is in the interest of Servia. That this is the case is so clear, that on this ground alone I deem it just to invite you to facilitate and support in Servia the preparations of the Hungarian patriots. I am very desirous that an understanding on this point should be arranged. You would do well just to pay a flying visit to London, and to confer with Kossuth."

This is what Prince Michael narrated to me. He went to London in company with his private secretary, Mr. Zu—cs. He considered it wise to keep our meeting secret, lest it should come to the ears of the Tory Cabinet, which was already suspicious enough. My late friend, Mr. John Ludvigh, having been selected by me for the mission to Belgrade, I invited him to come over from Brussels to London to receive his instructions. He and Mr. Zu—cs arranged my interview with Prince Michael. We met at Ludvigh's lodgings by night.

Prince Michael, after having informed me of his conversation with the Emperor, stated that he had always sympathised with our cause, and that he was also bound to us by family and personal ties. His wife was a Hungarian lady (daughter of Count Hunyady), and he had spent the greater part of his long exile in Hungary (at Ivánka), and owed us gratitude for the Hungarian hospitality extended to him. He would be glad if he could be of use to the cause of my country, and was prepared to do everything which his position permitted him to do without imperilling the interests of his own country.

I thanked the Prince for his sympathy and goodwill, but as interests decide in politics, I wished to hear what was his understanding of the identity of interests of Servia and Hungary, so that on this basis we might come to an agreement; for I had such a high opinion of his love of justice, as to be convinced that he would not make his support, on which I placed great value, dependent on conditions concerning either Servia herself or the

Servian population of Hungary which would be opposed to the integrity or unity of Hungary, and would in consequence be unacceptable to us.

Upon this the Prince declared that he did not even dream of such conditions. He started from identity of interests, and found this in the following circumstances:—

"First of all," said the Prince, "though we Servians, in consequence of our having been kept in subjugation by the Turks for centuries, are backward in civilisation and unpolished, we are a young nation conscious of our own vigorous strength—a nation not content with the semi-independence which was wrested from the Turks under the leadership of my father, and confirmed by the Treaty of Adrianople of 1829. Our aim is to be a perfectly independent nation such as our ancestors were. The tributary relation in which we stand to the Porte and the investiture which we must beg for at Constantinople offend our national self-respect; and that Turkish Pasha there in the fortress of Belgrade, the Turkish guns, with their muzzles directed against our capital, the Turkish soldiers bragging about in our streets—all these things cause our feelings to revolt, and remind us at every step that we are an enslaved nation. We wish to be an independent state, and trust to ourselves to be able to measure our strength with that of the Turks, as we did under George Cserni at the beginning of this century, and in 1816, and afterwards under my father; and we are the more able to do so now that we have a settled government of our own, and are therefore capable of being organised. Only we must wait for the opportune moment. But our misfortune is that we have the Austrian power in close proximity, and the whole world knows that Austria aims at the extension of her territory towards the East, and considers the Eastern countries an eventual booty in which she hopes to share; therefore she is always ready to interfere whenever there is a movement among her neighbours opposed to her ambitious aims. There is no doubt that as soon as we unfurl the banner of independence, the Cabinet of Vienna will infallibly intervene, unless we take up arms under the protection of Russia, in which case the Court of Vienna would not occupy Servia, for it is afraid of the Russians. But we wish to be a free and independent nation, and we know that to throw off the Turkish yoke by Russian help would mean to be independent in name only, but in reality to be dependent upon Russia—in a word, simply to change masters. We therefore see in the vicinity of Austria the greatest impediment to our independence. By this vicinity we are doomed to be either Turkish tributaries, with the prospect of an eventual Austrian dominion, or to be vassals of Russia. Every inhabitant of Servia instinctively feels this as much as I do. Hence that deep-rooted hatred, bordering on fury, which we feel towards Austria. I beg you to recollect the diplomatic note of Garashanin, with which, at the time of the Crimean war, when Austria offered to occupy Servia too, as she had occupied Moldo-Wallachia, Europe was officially informed that the Servian nation hated Austria, as the personification of insatiable, greedy ambition, as much as they hated the devil himself. This is true to the letter. It therefore lies in our interest to have the Austrian power removed from our vicinity, and this can only be attained by the independence of Hungary. It is in our interest that Hungary should be independent; not because we expect or wish that Hungary should fight for the attainment of our independence—this we desire as little, I presume, as you desire that Servia should fight for the independence of Hungary" (I, interrupting: "We certainly do not desire that")—"but the independence of Hungary is in our interest because we know that an independent Hungary would not foster any ambitious schemes against us; in fact, could not, as it would be clearly against her national interests so to do. Nor could an independent Hungary be an enemy of our independence, because, as the situation stands, unless Servia becomes independent by her own strength, she will sooner or later be taken in tow by Russia, and Hungary has every reason to wish that this should not be brought about. We are, therefore, convinced that in independent Hungary we should possess a neighbour who would not only prove no obstacle to our independence, but would be a sincere friend of it in her own interest. This is one point in which our interests meet in agreement.

"The second point consists in what you have repeatedly laid stress upon in your speeches delivered here in England during the late Eastern war—namely, that the smaller nations can only protect their independent national existence from being swallowed up by the Great Powers, by allying themselves for mutual protection against an attack from without. We entirely share this view. We are aware that if we fought out our independence, it would be very difficult to retain it without such an alliance. In this respect our interests are common—we are dependent on each other; and, as in your agreement with Prince Couza (which has been communicated to me), you say yourselves that you consider the defensive alliance between Hungary, Moldo-Wallachia, and Servia, or the so-called Danubian Confederation, the goal towards which it is your wish to strive, I shall only say, without enlarging further on this subject, that I entirely agree with you.

"There might be also a third point in which our interests meet. Though it depends rather on conjecture, still I mention it, as I wish the relation between us to be sincere, and for that end frankness is indispensable. I do not know what you think about the future of the Turkish Empire. I believe that its dissolution is merely a question of time; but I feel certain that you must wish as much as we wish that, in case of its dissolution, it should fall a prey neither to Russia nor to Austria, but that a liberated people should obtain its inheritance. This latter is impossible while Austria is in possession of Hungary, for Austria lies in wait for prey. But there is another aspect of the question. If, in the case of dissolution, that part of the Turkish Empire which is inhabited by Slavs should be split up into several small states, these would inevitably come under the influence of Russia. This, again, is a matter that is opposed to your interest; and it also clashes with ours, for we should not like to be surrounded by the preponderating power of Russia. This can only be avoided if the Eastern Slavs form themselves into such a compact mass as will impart self-supporting vitality to their existence as a state. Well, I must say that I believe, not that the Croatians, but that we Servians, are appointed to form the nucleus of this eventual formation. The Croatians are on the periphery; we are inside the circle. Their religion, the characters of their alphabet, and their history are quite different from, while our religion, characters, and history are the same as, those of the other Eastern Slavs. But I say this only by way of parenthesis; it does not belong to the subject now before us. What belongs to it is that we may consider our interests to meet in the prospect of such an eventuality, as it is our joint interest that in case the Turkish Empire should dissolve, its heir should be not Russian or Austrian ambition, but Servia's liberated people. This consideration, as well as that of the acquisition of independence, and the preservation of the acquired independence, induces me to wish Hungary to be independent, and to be all the more ready to assist you in your struggle as far as I can do so without imperilling my country, since the independence of Hungary is desired also by the Emperor of the French, to cultivate whose sympathy is for my personal interest as well as for that of my country."

I assured the Prince that I considered the keen perception of the identity of our interests, to the explanation of which I had just had the pleasure of listening, as a pledge of the future independence of Hungary and Servia, and availing myself of the opportunity offered to me by that passage of the Prince's speech in which he mentioned that he did not know what I thought of the future of the Turkish Empire, I declared that, as I also owed personal gratitude to the Porte, I wished with all my heart that, conforming herself to the requirements of the age, she might succeed in the regeneration of her Empire, in order to make its preservation possible. "I was always so much of the opinion that, after those acquisitions of self-government which were already secured by treaty to Servia, as well as to Moldo-Wallachia, the absolute independence of these states would be in the interest, not only of us Hungarians, but also of the Porte herself, that I am really astonished that Turkish statesmen did not see it to be so. The retention of the nominal supremacy over Servia and the United Danubian Principalities is a source, not of strength, but of weakness, to the Porte, for it wounds the national self-respect, and makes the Servians and Roumanians enemies of the Porte without giving her compensation, by some perceptible advantage in a material or political respect, for the danger and damage arising from the present situation. The paltry tribute is not worth mentioning. The whole suzerainty is mere foolish vanity for which the Porte will have to suffer severely, sooner or later, if she continues to cling to it. While I was the guest of Turkey, first as a fugitive, and later by detention, I endeavoured to make Turkish statesmen understand this; but, I am sorry to say, in vain. The word of a poor exile, who has no power in his hands, does not carry much weight with it; I believe, however, that if Hungary became independent and tendered similar counsel, backed up by power, she might expect to be listened to." I only mentioned this as I wished to convince the Prince that my declaration that we Hungarians were with heart and soul friends of the independence of Servia, was not merely inspired by the necessities of our present situation, but emanated from a deep and serious conviction, based on a conception of the highest interests of my country, to which the sense of gratitude I owed to the Porte was not opposed either.

"With regard to the eventual dissolution of the

Turkish Empire in Europe, I cannot deny that, as the Turks came to Europe at a time when the countries which they conquered were inhabited, no longer by heterogenous, undeveloped races, but by historically-formed, real nations, this historical basis, in connection with the religion and intensity of national feeling, has produced such contrasts as cannot very well be reconciled. I myself therefore consider the eventual dissolution of the Turkish Empire very probable; and I only express my conviction when I say that, in the logic of history, the matter of greatest importance to my country, and, I might even say, to Europe, is not that the Christian nationalities of the Turkish provinces should remain under Turkish rule, but that they should come under neither Russian nor Austrian dominion, nor within the sphere of their power, and that, as you have rightly remarked, the freedom of the people should be the heir of Turkish rule.

"The preservation of the Turkish Empire, to which, as I have already stated, the independence of Servia and the United Danubian Principalities is not at all opposed, has until now been accepted as a maxim of European diplomacy, not because the liberation of the Eastern Christian nationalities was opposed to the interests of Europe, but because the integrity of the Turkish Empire was considered a barrier to the extension of the power of Russia, in combination with the eager desire on the part of the House of Austria to share in the booty; but it cannot be denied that this barrier may also be found, and be found with more permanent security, in the freedom of nations. I am persuaded that a defensive alliance between independent Hungary,

Croatia, Servia, and the Danubian Principalities would form a securer bulwark for European peace and independence against all undue extension than the present one. I do not believe that the state-system of Europe could ever be brought to a normal settlement in the East without that confederation and the re-establishment of Poland. If we now start from the hypothesis that national freedom may become the heir of Turkish rule, it should be left to the respective nationalities to decide whether they will think it safer for their freedom closely to unite in one or more compact bodies, or to resort to an alliance, preserving their national individuality. Considering the intense national feeling perceptible in Bulgaria, Montenegro, and Bosnia, I should think an alliance more probable, but this is mere conjecture; I only desire to convey the assurance that, in case of a dissolution of the Turkish Empire, I should consider it as little dangerous to Hungary that the Eastern Slavs, if it so pleased them, should form one state, as I consider the regeneration of Slavonic Poland, there in the North, dangerous, a thing which, as a friend of freedom, and as a Hungarian, I really desire with all my heart. The essential matter for us is that the Southern Slavs should not, when the Turkish Empire crumbles to pieces, be taken in tow either by Russia or by Austria, but should remain free and independent, after the manner they think most fit."

After having thus mutually explained the basis on which we agreed, we passed on to the practical details of the work we had to do.

1. The foremost and most important was that we should come to some arrangement with the Croatians and the Croato-Slavonian population of the Military

Frontier. This was most important, because we had made it a condition of our participation in the war that a French army should advance from the Adriatic into Hungary, and it would be a great obstacle if the French were not well received in Croatia. We were even prepared to grant to Croatia complete and absolute independence if she did not wish to preserve her connection, of 800 years' standing, with the crown of Hungary. As we could move there freely, we thought Belgrade the most convenient place for these negotiations, and for this purpose determined to send Mr. John Ludvigh there. The French and Sardinian diplomatic agents at Belgrade would be instructed to protect him, and to support him in his mission. But to make this negotiation possible it would be necessary to send into Slavonia, Croatia, and the Military Frontier a qualified person from Servia who knew the country, could move about freely, was acquainted with the situation, and had social connections. His task would be to enter into confidential relations with the most influential patriots and leading personages, and to induce them to go to Belgrade to treat with Ludvigh, who would have the necessary power and instructions. The choice of a proper person to be sent on this errand was a very delicate matter, as interests of infinite importance were attached to it. We were therefore obliged to have recourse to the wisdom of the Prince, and to claim the support of his good offices. The Prince promised to procure such a person as would in every respect answer our purpose.

2. If we came to an agreement with the Croatians, the Allied Powers, of course, would provide them with the necessary funds for armaments. However, as it was

probable that the contemplated mission to Croatia, the journey of the Croatian patriots to Belgrade, &c., would cost more than we could lay hands upon in this primitive stage of our undertaking, I inquired whether we might reckon on the Prince's benevolent assistance in case of need with an advance of money, the repayment of which we should look upon as a sacred duty. The Prince promised this with the greatest readiness.

3. We hoped that on this occasion the Servians living in Hungary would join us. In the matter of nationality we were prepared to go as far as was at all consistent with the territorial integrity and political unity of our country. I communicated to the Prince my views on the subject.* I mentioned to him that we had already called upon, and would continue to urge, the leaders of the movement at home to come to an understanding with our Servian compatriots on this basis, and I begged the Prince to support such an understanding by his powerful influence.

The Prince considered our concessions perfectly satisfactory, and gave his word that he would do everything to promote the understanding, and speaking with positive knowledge, assured us that we should not meet with any difficulty in this respect.

4. Arrangements had already been made for forwarding arms to the East, and more arms would be forwarded in case the assurance of English neutrality should lead to the extension of hostilities to Hungary. The consignments up to this time had been directed to Moldavia. As it was our intention, however, to arm at the proper

* These will be given below with communications sent home from Genoa (June 22nd).

time the countries bordering on Servia, we asked permission to send arms also to Servia, to be stored away there until wanted. Whether we might forward the arms directly to Servia or bring them over from Moldavia; whether by water or by land, and if by land, which would be the safest road to send them by; and whether Belgrade would be the more convenient place to store them away in, or Maidenbek rather, where I knew the Servians had at this time extensive government buildings standing empty—all these questions were details to be settled on the spot. I only asked for his consent *in thesi*, and his support and assistance in overcoming the difficulties of transport, and, further, for his permission, that at the proper time, the individual entrusted with the transport of arms should be allowed to present himself to the Prince, and receive his orders.

The Prince acceded to this.

5. I said I was informed that His Highness possessed twenty batteries, of six guns each. If I was not mistaken, steps had been taken by Prince Couza, both in his and in our interest, to induce His Highness to a grant of a part of them. It would be a great relief to me to know that those steps had met with a favourable reception, and I should consider it a special favour if we should receive a few guns for the army to be organised on the Lower Danube.

The Prince replied that arrangements had already been made for compliance on the first point, and also held out to us the prospect of compliance on the second, but remarked that as the guns had been manufactured in Servia, it would be wise to have their utility tested by experts, and that we ourselves should have to procure the necessary artillery horses.

6. We had fixed our choice upon Lieutenant-General Vetter, as Commander of the Forces on the Lower Danube. As soon as the French expedition had been definitely decided upon, he would have to go to Servia and direct from there the organisation of an army in our country, and collect a little force of Hungarian volunteers who would join him, and then, at the opportune moment, cross over into Hungary. I asked whether we might hope to obtain permission for such an organisation, and if so, whether the Prince had any objection against the person of Vetter?

The Prince said he had none at all. He also agreed to the contemplated organisation on Servian territory, and did not even object, in order to give proof of the brotherly feeling between the two nations, that Vetter should engage some hundred volunteers in Servia itself, whose presence in the Hungarian camp, he thought, would have a good effect upon the Servians in Hungary. But he stated clearly that Lieutenant-General Vetter could go to Servia only when there was no longer any doubt about a French expedition being sent, that he was also obliged to make this a condition *sine quâ non* of his permission for the organisation of an army, since in case we were not supported by France, and made revolution only on our own account, he would consider it a very risky matter for Servia to give us room for the organisation of an army—without mention of the fact that he himself would be exposed to endless troubles. It was not forgotten that he himself was not the ruler; the ruler was his father, who was too much grieved by the remembrance of his exile to be persuaded to take any risky steps. The appointment of Mr. Ludvigh, the mission to Croatia, the transport of arms, were all such matters as could, if conducted with proper precaution, be carried out without coming to the knowledge of the gossiping *entourage* of the old Prince. Therefore Mr. Ludvigh must be cautious that his mission was kept a profound secret—at any rate, until an arrangement was come to with the Croatians; he should not attract attention, nor make his presence in Belgrade known in Hungary, lest the assembling of Hungarians in large numbers there should arouse the suspicions of the Austrian consul; nor should he confer on the subject with any one except with those whom he (the Prince) would point out to him. All this was essential, but when once it came to the organisation of an army, that could not be carried out without the knowledge of the old Prince, for should he hear of it he would be so enraged at the idea that such things were ventured upon without his knowledge and consent, that he would summarily put a stop to everything. It would therefore be necessary to obtain his approval, which the Prince would take upon himself to gain, but only on condition that he could point to the fact that we were backed up by the Emperor of the French.

Such was my interview with the Prince. Ludvigh was careful to be duly informed about the situation in Belgrade. He embarked at Marseilles early in June, of course under an assumed name. On June 22nd he sent an envoy from Belgrade to Croatia, but before this envoy could do anything towards the object of his mission, the Peace of Villafranca put an end to everything. Therefore the letters from Ludvigh do not possess much political importance, but they throw some light on the situation of those times, and therefore I think some extracts from them deserve publication.

Extracts from the Letters addressed by John Ludvigh, while on his Mission to Belgrade, to Kossuth.

1.

" *Belgrade, June 22nd,* 1859.

" Our man has started only to-day. I had expected that they would have at least procured a proper person by the time I arrived, but, alas! they have done nothing. Garashanin was not even informed on the subject. It is true, he has been ill, and nobody else can fill his place. The few words which I communicated in your name to him, as the foremost statesman of this country, much pleased him, because they came from you.*

---

* I did not know Garashanin personally, but during the time I was staying at Shumla and Kutahia I exchanged several letters with him. I found him to be a far-seeing statesman of deep sagacity and liberal principles. He always manifested great cordiality towards myself and my family, and has put me under a special obligation by the kind attention with which he arranged everything for the personal safety of my poor wife, when, hotly pursued and amidst a thousand dangers, she fled from our country to Belgrade.

During the Russo-Turkish complications, the Czar Nicholas used my name as a pretext to force Garashanin, who wished the Servians to be a free nation and not the servants of Russia, from his ministerial post. In the English Blue Book the following note may be found:—

" Colonel Rose to Lord John Russell. Constantinople, March 11, 1853.— Mr. Nikolajevics, the Servian diplomatic agent, called upon me yesterday, and informed me in an excited manner that a few days ago Prince Menchikoff enjoined him to inform the Prince of Servia that he must at once dismiss Mr. Garashanin, as he is a disciple of Kossuth and Mazzini, and that a Russian embassy had categorically informed him that if the Prince did not comply Russia would produce a revolution or some other great catastrophe in Servia! Mr. Nikolajevics declared that Garashanin was quite innocent of what he had been accused of."

" I should be proud of such a disciple, but unfortunately I cannot boast of this. But this is the way in which holy Russian autocracy " rules."— Kossuth.

"Our man is a native of the country to which he has gone, and will, therefore, be better able than anybody else to find out the proper persons.

"As far as I had the opportunity of travelling with different people, Austrian consuls, military officers, &c., and conversing with them, under cover of my assumed name, I have gained the impression that Austrian chauvinism only exists in the German newspaper press. I met with an aide-de-camp of the Czar of Russia, but from him I only heard what we already knew—namely, 'Nous n'aimons pas les Autrichiens.' The Austrian consul at Odessa, on the other hand, said to me: 'Unsere Stellung ist, in Russland, eine hoechst unangenehme, doch haben wir bei Hof eine freundliche Partei' ('Our position in Russia is a very unpleasant one, but we have a friendly party at Court'). I should have liked to know which was that 'friendly party;' and as he did not mention any names, I am forced to suspect that the 'friendly party' exists only in imagination.

"I saw two steamers belonging to the Imperial Navy on my way. One of them was the *Schlick;* the name of the other one I did not ascertain. The *Schlick* had a transport-ship in tow up the river, with sailors on board. We stopped at Gyurgyevo, and a thorough-bred Austrian officer stepped on board our ship; and after having favoured us with all sorts of ridiculous rhodomontades of Austrian victories, he recommended the volunteers on the transport ship in tow of the *Schlick* to the care of the captain. To this our captain answered, 'These are not volunteers; they are sailors who are about to return home.' 'Herr Hauptmann,' answered the officer, 'they are volunteers;' and then turning to the captain, he repeated, 'And you will take care of these volunteers.' Thus I came to know that, in consequence of the suspension of navigation, the sailors had been thrown out of employment. They were offered a free passage home; and when they came on board the ship, the Austrians turned them into volunteers.

"In Galatz, as well as in Orsova, I convinced myself personally that with fifty able *honvéds* every one of these transport-steamers could be captured, which would be most advantageous for the organisation of the insurrection on the Lower Danube and the Save. I told G. to speak about this to your ally, the young Prince.

"The old Prince wishes to know everything, and they would fain not let him know anything, because he talks before he carries out anything. He does not like Garashanin, who is, however, the only man who is able to effect anything. This explains the great pains that were taken in London to keep everything secret, even when there was no need for it. They are afraid, not only of Austria, but of the old gentleman. The Italian diplomatic agent has made a good impression upon me. From him I know that the presence of the old French diplomatic agent is a serious calamity, as he plays the *rôle* of the Austrian rather than that of a French agent. The Italian is dissatisfied that the *nervus rerum gerendarum* is wanting, and his new French colleague has not arrived yet. He finds the time hang heavily on his hands, as I do, and still we cannot see much of each other. It is stated that the town swarms with Austrian spies. I am tired of hearing this daily repeated, but the Italian agent also gives another reason for this endless fear of Austrian spies. He was told that if the old gentleman came to know the object of our presence here, he would send us both away without ceremony, not to oblige Austria, but because we do not tell him everything.

"There were some Hungarians in the crew of the steamer. One of them said, in a mixture of broken German and Hungarian, 'We know that Kossuth already has a regiment : would to God he were coming !' I asked him whether his comrades thought so, too. 'How could they think differently?' was the answer. And as, in order to propagate the intelligence, I had told him one thing and another, which I pretended I had heard on my way, or read in the papers, whenever I appeared on deck, the young fellow came up to me to enter into conversation.

"More such incidents cheered my dreary journey. But I had also to hear quite different things from the lips of Austrians, which, however, did not annoy, but rather amused me. In one case I was very near losing my temper. I made a remark about the good German spoken by a woman living in Servia; that I scarcely expected to hear such pure German spoken by a Servian woman, and conjectured that, perhaps, she had not even lived in Servia before. 'I live in Carlowitz,' she replied. 'So you are Hungarian?' said I. 'No, I come from *Austrian Servia*,' was her answer. The 'Hungarian Banat,' therefore, was 'Austrian Servia' for her.

"I live in the same hotel with a Viennese banker. He is a Francophobist; and I, of course, am to him an Austrophobist Frenchman. We had a discussion about Austria; and he, who is an enemy of revolution, confessed to me that he fears an insurrection will break out in Vienna, as the labouring and artisan classes—in a word, the poor and lower middle classes of the population—are very dissatisfied.* And amongst other things he also said that he himself with a business in Constantinople, a factory in Bohemia, and a bank in Vienna, only pays as much in taxes as any poor mechanic.

" (Signed)   LUDVIGH."

* This dissatisfaction reminds me that the Viennese, in their "satisfaction" with the ministers Bach and Bruck, Cardinal Rauscher and Grünne, the Emperor's aide-de-camp, amused themselves with the following epigram:—

Wenn's *Bach*—erl vertrocknet,
Und's *Bruck*—erl bricht,
Wenn's *Rauscher*—l verstummet,
Und's *Grünne*—verschwindet,
Kommt's Glück—Eher nicht.

When Bach (brook) has dried up, and Bruck (bridge) has broken down, when Rauscher (roaring noise) has become silent, and Grunne (green) has disappeared, then will come happiness, and not before. All these things took place. And yet where is the "Gluck"? Well, there is Bosnia! and that *is* a "Gluck!"

While I write these lines, the papers bring the news that there is a movement perceptible in the Vienna Reichsrath to make a reduction in the standing army. By this intelligence I am reminded of another epigram. Shortly before the outbreak of the war in 1859, Minister Bruck proposed that to the words of the Austrian national anthem, "*Gott erhalte unser'n Kaiser*" (May God preserve our Emperor), may be added these words, "Und unsere Armee" (And our army also). For, unless God worked a miracle in support of the army, it would perish, as the country was not able to perform this duty. That is how matters stood twenty years ago; and how do they stand now?—
KOSSUTH.

2.
"*Belgrade, July 9th,* 1859.

"I have not had any report yet from my man, which causes me anxiety, although G—— considers the silence natural, and is not at all doubtful as to the result of his mission.

"On the news of the victory of Solferino becoming known here, all the Servian officers stationed in the town conveyed their congratulations to the French as well as to the Sardinian diplomatic agent. The French consul, in his joy, threw money into the street among the people standing about in the darkness of midnight. The clinking of glasses roused the martial spirit of the Sardinian diplomatic agent too, and the next day he demanded of me why we should wait any longer and not strike at the Austrians at once, and occupy Zimony. The rest would come of itself. Merely for the sake of continuing the conversation I refrained from taking exception to his warlike mood. 'Let us strike,' I said. 'I know that there are 1,800 men in Zimony, and amongst them numerous old Honvéds; in Pancsova there are 2,400 men. In any case, it is safer to commence with the smaller number.'

"In the course of this conversation the warlike Sardinian undertook the office of speaking to the young Prince, and of asking him for a loan of 40,000 florins. I encouraged him the more in his intention as I wished to find out what the Prince would say. His answer was that if a French army did not come to Hungary, he would not support the Hungarian movement. 'We join you if you prove the stronger,' holds good here also.

"The Servian hates the German, but a large part of Belgrade, like the Servians on the other side of the river, likes to be able to chat in German. If the Hungarians had a national government, Hungarian might be heard here, too, instead of German. It is really a question of national existence to free the Hungarians not only from German rule, but also from German literary and social influence.

"LUDVIGH."

3.

"*Belgrade, July* 13*th*, 1859.

"The government here, and the relation between father and son, are best illustrated by the following incident :—A few days ago some official, perhaps at the risk of his life, whispered in the ear of the young Prince that an order from the government was about to be sent at once to the authorities in I do not know what border village, to execute without delay three individuals, who had not been summoned, or examined, or prosecuted, or condemned. The young Prince went to the old gentleman and put a question on the subject, to which the latter replied, 'That is no business of yours.' The young Prince : 'It is just because it is no business of mine that I wish to leave this place, for such proceedings cannot end well; nobody can be sure of his life if to be accused by any intriguer is sufficient for putting a man to death.' The old Prince replied, 'It so pleases me, and I thus wish it.' The young Prince then threatened to leave the country, a step of which the old father is afraid; and only this fear saved the three men from being hanged.

"On the 12th of this month, while the young Prince was staying at S——, the old man took it into his head to order the arrest of eight distinguished men, most of them old senators. Why, nobody knows. Garashanin says he does not believe they are implicated in anything, and that if they had been arrested he himself would not have felt safe from meeting with a similar fate, were it not for the old man's belief that he (Garashanin) has a good reputation with, and is liked by, the Emperor of the French; this belief was his safeguard.

"It is a fact that the odd, capricious rule of the old Prince has created much dissatisfaction. The young Prince himself attempted to bring about a change of ministry, but his feeble representations will remain without result in the face of the obstinacy of the old man, as long as there is nobody who speaks with the authority of the French Emperor. I cannot sufficiently insist that it is high time Lesseps should at last come. Only when he speaks up energetically in the name of the Emperor of the French, can we expect to see the present situation changed, and the promises of Prince Michael fulfilled. True, the old Prince himself hates the Austrians so much, that I should not at all be surprised to hear, one fine morning, that he has given orders to attack the Austrians. However, the next day his valet may concoct some story, and the third day we may wake up and find ourselves attacked. It is a most wretched state of affairs, which must be changed. Lesseps ought not to delay.

"It is only cowardice and fear that induces the inhabitants of Hungary to offer voluntary contributions, and then only to small amounts. The appearance of a little French army will sweep the land clean of Austrians. The Servians living along the frontier do not dream of a national question. It is the same with the Croatians; at least, so I am told. Everything depends upon the first success.

" (Signed) LUDVIGH."

As soon as the Peace of Villafranca had put an end to our hopes, I instructed Ludvigh not to send me any more reports, but with a view to the future, to confirm the understanding with Servia, to arrive at an agreement with Croatia, and to make arrangements for keeping up communication with both; for though I looked forward to coming events without hope, by the abnormal peace the state of Europe had become still more abnormal than it was before. Great questions were thrown up, but nothing was solved, nothing was durable, and the turn events might take was incalculable. As soon as the understanding had been established, or he (Ludvigh) saw that it could not be arrived at, he was to return home—What do I say? Home! we have no "home"—return into exile at Brussels, and may God comfort us all!

He returned. We met at Paris, and he verbally reported to me all about his proceedings. I have no notes on the subject. From Brussels he sent me the following additional report, which I think of sufficient interest to lay before the reader.

4.

LUDVIGH TO KOSSUTH.
"*Brussels, September* 25*th*, 1859.

" As a supplement to my verbal report, and to the reports I sent you while on my mission, it may not be superfluous to give you some more particulars which I think may contribute to a just appreciation both of the situation in the East and of individuals :—

" 1. With regard to the Servians.

" In no class of the population did I find an anti-Magyar feeling. The name 'Magyar,' which the German newspapers used by way of mockery instead of 'Ungar,' in order to instigate a rupture, and to create irritation, now produces a feeling of respect among the Servians, as if 'the noble and brave' were added to it.

"The Germans, on the other hand, are contemptuously called 'Suabians,' and this name they extend to all those who stand under Austrian protection, even if they are Servians; but the Magyar, even under Austrian protection, remains a Magyar.

" With reference to the events of 1848, it is certain that the question of nationality did not much trouble the mass of the people; they were incited more by an appeal to their religious feeling, and the first volunteers who crossed into Hungary did not concern themselves about anything else but pillage.

" No doubt it might have sounded disagreeable in the ears of the Servian leaders that we should call them 'bands of robbers,' and I say that if we refer to past events, either in the press or in speech, we must, for the sake of the future, beware of the use of such epithets. But the fact is true, very true, and it has in Servia an historical basis. The disposition and character of a nation must be studied from its history; and for this reason you were quite right when, even before your conference with the Prince, you refused on principle the mode of armed assistance which had been proposed.

"In spite of its good intentions, we can confide in the present government only with circumspection. The past, not the present, warns us to be cautious. I mentioned that it would not be at all difficult to persuade the present government to attack Austria, but this was not very advisable even under the extremely favourable circumstances of last July, nor will it ever be so. We want nothing else of the Servians than to be allowed to move about freely in their country, and that they should keep a sharp eye on the Austrian spies. In a short time it would be possible, in some out-of-the-way place, to organise a little army recruited from Hungarian and Bulgarian emigrants living along the frontier.

"When Milos Obrenovics dies his son will change his government, if it is not changed sooner by a revolution or a conspiracy. But there is suspicion of the character of the son too; it seems to have infected the blood of the nation. A great part of the men at present and formerly in power, are uneducated, like Milos himself, old pandours and valets. But there are many young men who have studied at Pesth, Vienna, Paris, &c., and these mostly follow a military career. It is very likely that the Prince will take these into his Ministry. There is not an atom of sympathy for Austria in these young men; on the contrary, they feel the burden of Austrian interference. Garashanin will become his factotum. For I had occasion to perceive during my stay in Belgrade that the young Prince has disclosed his innermost thoughts only to him, but still the shadow of mistrust follows him, as it does his father. It looks as if his father had instilled into him the suspicion that Garashanin aspires to the throne.

"The whole science of statecraft in the government consists in —conspiracy. The last government persecuted the people from fear of conspiracy, and was overthrown by conspiracy. The present government was called into existence by conspiracy, and seeks its vitality in conspiracy. It will do no harm to tell you who are the men who govern Servia.

"Milos I have sufficiently described. He is a living example of a knight of good fortune. Without even a surname, he has risen, from a pandour and swineherd, to be a prince. This would rather have been an honour to him if even as a prince he would not have remained a pandour. Obrenovics is a borrowed name. It is the name of his mother's first husband, and as Milos had been in the service of the latter's brother, an Obrenovics, he adopted his name.

"His Prime Minister, Raj —— Zv——, is an old pandour. He is one of those who conspired against the last Prince, with the blessing of the priest Ranisics; and he has been three times condemned to death.

"H——, the Finance Minister, is a Bosnian peasant. He accompanied Milos in his exile to Vienna, and there acquired a slight knowledge of German.

"Ugr——, the Minister of Justice, is an ignorant, but honest man. He cannot write, but has been taught to sign his name.

"Mel——ko, at one time a valet in the service of Milos, is now his principal assistant and chief counsellor.

"One cannot trust to these men, or such as they.

"My mission therefore remained a secret to them, as Prince Michael also desired. Only the Prince's secretaries, Zukics and Lesjanin, and Garashanin, conferred with me; Magazinovjcs, a trusted friend of Garashanin, whom I used to meet at the Sardinian consulate, was also let into the secret.

"The Sardinian Consul engaged an hussar refugee from the Bácska as interpreter, and with his help, and that of another young Hungarian settled there, some 400 Hungarian coachmen, menservants, and journeyman mechanics, &c., were conscribed to take up arms, and declared themselves to be ready to come forward if called upon. But it was and will always be impossible to manage the affair seriously in Belgrade. Some out-of-the-way place, nevertheless, situated near the Danube, is required for that. But that there should be a good result, a Garashanin is needed.

"I maintain my connection with the Sardinian Consul and

Garashanin, in order that we may not lose the thread of events there.

"Moldo-Wallachia, even apart from its vicinity to Transylvania, is of great importance to us: 30,000 Hungarian souls in Bucharest alone, and I do not know how many thousands in Galatz and Jassy, and the "Csángos"*—it is no small matter.

"But I can assure you that Klapka was very much mistaken when he thought that he had won over Couza and his government to our cause. They are the enemies of our country. They are more particularly your personal enemies. Faith and alliance are so many empty words with them; they are even worse—a mask! I cannot free myself from the suspicion that Daco-Roumanian intrigues were hidden under the first plan. They hate you so much, because, by your insisting so determinedly upon the sending of a French army to Hungary, you have upset their plans. Had that not happened they would themselves have occupied Transylvania.† The Emperor Napoleon, in his speech from the throne, also brought forward the Wallachian question, in order to be able to put all the more shortcomings to the debit of Austria, from which to manufacture a *casus belli*. And then, when the papers were full of the regeneration of the Roumanian nation, they in Bucharest surrounded the Hora Gloska affair with the nimbus of national glory! and Klapka believed that he would create a Hungary with the help of Roumania! Before he had had time to look round they would have shoved him out of the way, had not your 'either a French army or we shall not move' prevented them.

"Possibly in these intrigues Couza was only more of an instrument in the hands of others than an instigator. Possibly, but not certainly. But it is a fact that Couza, if he could rely upon anybody, could do so only on the 'Jeune Roumanie' party, which was formed in 1847, is led by a secret society, and is presided over by J. Ghika, the late Governor of Samos. The Hungarian Daco-

* Hungarian settlers in Moldavia. (Translator's note.)
† This view was not without ground, as will be seen from the second volume of my "Memories."

Roumanians, who were rejected by the former government, are now in office.

"Besides, I think that, though Couza may hold the firman in his hand, and may grandly style himself "Nous Jean Alexandre, 1ᵉʳ prince regnant," his days are numbered; he cannot support himself; he has nothing to stand upon, has no root, and is powerless moreover, only protected by the wings of the French imperial eagle. But how long will this protection last?"

After this, Ludvigh also speaks about Turkish affairs. On account of the changes that have since taken place, it will be sufficient to give the following extract from this part of his letter :—

"The Bosnian Mussulmans are nothing less than the old lords of the land. Though they belong to the same nationality as the Servians, still they are afraid of them, and of their own peasants too, lest they should be deprived of their property as the Servian Turks were. But they are also afraid of the tanzimat, and therefore wish to be emancipated from the immediate rule of the Porte, and to remain in a mere tributary relation, having a government of their own, like the Danubian Principalities. .

"(Signed)   LUDVIGH."

CHAPTER VI.

JOURNEY TO ITALY.

I LEFT England on the 16th of June. The *Times* in its second edition of the same day published an alleged proclamation of General Klapka, addressed to the Hungarian regiments of the Austrian army. That proclamation was never issued. Klapka did not even sign it. It was a mere draft, which by the indiscretion of some busybody had found its way into a Turin paper, which mistook an undecided step for an accomplished fact. The *Times* copied it. Such being the case, there is no necessity to reproduce it here. But the reproduction of the leading article which accompanied the publication may be of some interest, as a record of the manner in which my departure from England was looked upon at that time. The *Times* wrote as follows:—

"It is announced that M. Kossuth has left England with a French passport, given him by superior orders, and that he will be employed at once in acting on the Hungarian regiments in the Austrian service, and, if possible, producing a revolt in Hungary itself. At the same time we receive a proclamation from General Klapka, published at the French head-quarters. The meaning of these proceedings is not doubtful. The Austrian Empire is to be attacked beyond the limits of Italy. The war is to be carried into the other hereditary dominions of Francis Joseph, not, indeed, by a French army—at least for the present—but by a revolutionary propaganda, supported by the whole strength of the French, and perhaps the Russian, Court. It would be useless to affect unconcern at this new development of Franco-Russian policy. The consequences may be of the very greatest importance. In the present state of Germany on the one side, and the Danubian populations on the other, a second revolutionary outbreak in Hungary may light up a war from the Baltic to the Black Sea.

" With the abstract merits of the cause which M. Kossuth advocates we have happily nothing to do. That the position of both the Magyar and Slavic races is at present most uneasy, and that hatred of Germans will impel the former, and sympathy with Russia may seduce a part of the latter, to waver in their loyalty to the Imperial house is not impossible. Austria has hitherto succeeded in maintaining her authority, and in the Hungarian war she was able to play off the one race against the other. What may be the condition of Hungary at the present hour we have no means of determining. Diametrically opposite opinions reach us from the same spot, and it is evident that even in Vienna they are uncertain whether the animosities of 1849 are in full practical working, whether the undoubted encouragement of the Czar has revived the national feeling, or whether, on the other hand, the common danger of the empire has recalled the Hungarians to at least a temporary loyalty. It would seem that, while there is a favourable spirit among the people, the superior classes keep aloof from the government, much after the fashion of Lombardy. The most reasonable supposition seems to be, that if left alone the Hungarians would reconcile themselves to the Imperial crown, and gradually forget the traditions for which they fought under Bem and Goergey. But they may not be proof against the temptation held out by two powerful despots who threaten to crush the whole fabric of Austrian domination. When they find the Italian Peninsula throwing·off the yoke, and when, by the most open and ostentatious means, the French Emperor invites them to renew the rebellion of 1849, it is possible that the stimulant will be too powerful for the moderate party to counteract. No one can tell what another month may bring forth, and it may prove that the promise of ' localising ' the war, so often reiterated in April, at a time when the Austrians were in force on Piedmontese territory, may be disregarded in July, when they are struggling to maintain themselves at the limits of their own Italian kingdom.

" Up to the present time this has been a purely Italian question, and neither England nor Germany had any right to object to the expulsion of the Austrians from a country which hates their rule and gives no strength to their empire. Putting aside, indeed, every consideration but that of the balance of power, the severance of Italy from the Austrian crown would not be in itself an evil. If Austria is necessary to the strength of Central Europe, if it forms a barrier to the ambition of Paris and St. Petersburg, if from the necessity of its position it is the ally of England, it will be able more effectually to perform these services to the world when it has been released from the duty of keeping down by force five millions of Italians. English statesmen, whose so-called sympathy with Austria means only that they see the advantage of having a strong power in the geographical position which Austria occupies, would care little if Francis Joseph gave up his Italian possessions to-morrow. Indeed, the efforts of all sensible ministers have been directed for years to bestowing practical independence on Lombardy and Venice under some system which should save the pride of Vienna. But when we find an aggressive power taking it in hand to redress by war the wrongs of populations not its own, a dangerous principle is being established in Europe. No potentate can pretend to confine the limits of war which has once broken out; no general engaged in a deadly struggle can afford to disregard any means of success. The discontent of Hungary with Austrian rule is too great a temptation for a commander on the banks of the Mincio to resist. Moreover, the 'understanding with Russia' has a direct tendency to encourage such a diversion. So it happens that within a fortnight after the first victory on Lombard ground Louis Napoleon is employing Hungarian refugees to revolutionise a distant province of his enemy.

" The effect on the English people of this new move will, of course, be small. *This country has determined on a strict neutrality, and a government would no more be allowed to go to war to keep the Austrians in Hungary than to keep them in Italy;* but several considerations arise from it which are not unworthy of notice. In the first place, the direct call to insurrection in the central and eastern provinces of the empire must have its effect on the Germans, who, as it is, are sufficiently excited. What influence the change of ministry in England and the menace of Russia may have on the Prussian Regent remains to be seen; they may induce him prudently to preserve the peace, or they may rouse him to gratify his subjects and the minor states by an active participation in the war. Within the last few days the Prussian army has been mobilised; everything, it is said, is ready for the transport of troops through Saxony and Bavaria, and, however much the world may count on the slowness and irresolution of Germans, it cannot be denied that the present aspect of things is threatening. Hitherto, however, Prussia has wanted a pretext for entering into the lists. The war has not spread to the Germanic Confederation, and the French Emperor has made the most earnest and repeated protestations that his views are limited to Italy, and that Germany has nothing to fear for her interests or honour. Moreover, the port of Trieste has not even been blockaded, and the whole commercial marine of Austria may lie safely in its harbour under the protection of the German Bund. But if Kossuth and Klapka be seriously commissioned to kindle the flame of revolt in a remote province of Austria, the Germans may have that *casus belli* which the more hotheaded among them desire. It is beyond a doubt that the preservation of general peace will be made much more difficult by such an extension of Louis Napoleon's programme.

"What the French Emperor proposes to himself must for a time remain a secret. Most probably his views for the present are confined to weakening the Austrian generals by promoting disaffection among the Hungarian regiments. But we may be sure that two such men as Kossuth and Klapka will not confine themselves to working for Italian independence. Their object is not to weaken the garrisons of Verona or Mantua, but to raise a revolt in Hungary, now nearly denuded of Austrian troops. The French Emperor must be aware of this, and it is certainly strange to see a sovereign who holds his throne as the champion of order in league with revolutionists and republicans against the model despotism of the Continent. Should he persist in the scheme which the proclamation of Klapka and M. Kossuth's departure from England indicates, it will be a sign that he is ready to wade into the deepest waters of European commotion."

I.

Letters written by Kossuth to his Wife, during his journey in Italy (among them an account of his meeting with the Emperor Napoleon at Valleggio).

1.

" *Paris, June* 16*th,* 1859.

" MY DEAREST ANGEL,

" It is not yet eight p.m., and I have not only arrived, but am already able to take pen in hand and write.

" The sea was calm, and I was not ill. In Boulogne my valet (who is a capital fellow), arriving with the horses before me, cleverly managed to inform the authorities that I was coming this morning; and it appears that they must have had instructions, for the custom and passport officials received me, uncovered, with the greatest politeness. They did not even allow my luggage (in which even arms were packed) to be taken to the custom-house. My name was a free pass everywhere. The Inspector of Police himself took my passport to be stamped, and, while I was dining, the sub-prefect sent to make an apology for the fact that, in undergoing the formality of having my passport *visé,* I was put to the trouble of passing through the room where that was being done, instead of simply having the barrier removed to let me step into the carriage without any further formality. On the railway they put me into a separate compartment, and begged me to take no notice of the rule against smoking. On my arrival at Paris I was not even stopped with my luggage. In one word, up to the present I have met with nought but complaisance and kindness.

" My friends at Genoa attach great importance to some sort of public reception being given to me on my arrival. I shudder at the very thought of it. You know how they have tormented me with public receptions on two Continents;—I have had enough of them. But perhaps my friends are right. In such agitated times the "voice of the people" may somewhat clear the atmosphere in which we live of that mist with which "high diplomatists" would like to surround us, that they may make use of us in the dark unperceived. I do not discuss the question, but make up my mind to undergo the ordeal. It will be soon over. I shall therefore send a telegram to Genoa this evening to know whether the arrangements made for my reception permit that I should arrive otherwise than by sea; if they do, I should like to go to Switzerland to see the country, where in three weeks I hope to press you to my heart with all the warmth of my languishing soul, and to be your guide among those wonders of nature, the sublimity of which will act like balm upon your distracted mind, my dear suffering angel!

"My eyes can even now see nothing but the grief and sorrow which overwhelmed you in the moment of parting, life of my life! Tears fill my eyes when I think of it. But console yourself, dear angel—console yourself by anticipating the joy of our meeting again; console yourself with the thought that, amid so much extraordinary adversity, some nameless Power has watched over us not in vain. We can say of ourselves what the poet wrote of our country, 'We have expiated the past and the future.' It is impossible that there should not be in store for us what alone our souls long for—a rest in the evening of our lives. Free from care, only living for each other, and seeing our lives rewarded by the love and assured prospects of our good children, we may smilingly look back upon the storms through which we have had to pass in order to reach the safe port.

"May this thought give strength to your soul, dear angel, that the strength of your soul may invigorate your body to be able to withstand the storms which are yet in store for us. You see, knowing the sincerity of your angelic love, I wish to be selfish enough to remind you that I stand in need of your strength, that, joining hands with you, I may be able to bear the weight of cares that rest upon my shoulders. If I knew that your heart is grieved, and noticed suffering in your face, I feel it at this instant that I could not tolerate the burden of cares. But, after all, there is something in the idea that perhaps we may be destined, when beholding a prosperous nation, to say to each other, 'This is our work.'"

2.

"*Marseilles, June* 20*th*, 1859.
(EXTRACTS FROM THREE LETTERS.)

"The reply of our friends in Genoa to the telegram I sent to them from Paris reached me at Lyons. They insist upon my going by sea, so as to give them an opportunity of making some display, which they think will be advantageous to our cause. I therefore came here with the intention of taking the boat for Genoa to-morrow (Tuesday). But, of course, their display can only take place in case the ship arrives in the daytime. This, however, is utterly impossible. Since the beginning of this month the boats start no longer at noon, as formerly, but in the morning, and therefore arrive at Genoa the following morning at five o'clock, when there is scarcely a soul in the streets. The end of the matter, therefore, is that I expose myself, to no purpose, to the inconveniences of a twenty-two hours' voyage; I who, as you know, am continually ill while on the sea. The very smell of the sea which comes through my window from the well-filled harbour already disgusts me. I ought to lie down, but my room looks as if myriads of bugs were waiting to feed upon me through the night. Well, perhaps, they will not devour me altogether. All this is but a trifling inconvenience, spiced with a little vexation, which one must get through somehow; but it is a calamity that the news which reaches me about the progress of our cause is not reassuring, especially as it appears that an inauspicious wind commences to blow from the Russian side. I shall see, but I shall certainly not bate any of my conditions.

"Otherwise, my journey to-day would have been interesting. From beautiful Lyons we travelled along the valley of the lovely Rhone, encompassed by a picturesque chain of mountains; on every peak the ruins of a castle, the mouldering monument of a time when mail-clad knights lorded it over the people of the valley from their strongholds, built like the nests of eagles, high up in the mountains, before that great leveller of human life, gunpowder, had brought them down to the level of other mortals.

"In the distance, on our right, the Pyrenees were sometimes visible, to the left the Alps; and the steam-horse, which nothing astonishes, carries us in one short day through distinct climates. In the morning I only saw the green, undeveloped ears of corn, at noon already harvest-work; after apples, pears, and such fruit, came the grapes; after the grapes, the mulberry-tree, stripped of its foliage, which the worm that was brought us from China makes into silk; till, at last, the olive is visible, first isolated and afterwards in groups on the rocky terraces, and the sultry and enervating atmosphere reminds us that we have arrived in southern regions. The sky is as intensely blue to-day as it was when the Provençal troubadours took their inspiration from it. But everything else has changed except the mercenary souls of men. Train after train carried the vivacious Frenchmen to die—not for their own country, but because they were ordered to. Train after train brought the Austrian prisoners of war, who fought at command, without knowing for what, and are now prisoners, far away from their country, without knowing why?

"I myself spoke to some soldiers of a transport. They were Czechs, but their faces brightened up all the same on hearing my name.

"I have sent my assistant to pay a visit to the camp of the prisoners of war. To-day the prisoners from the regiment 'Wilhelm' are in camp here; they will go on to-morrow. He found *seven* Hungarians amongst them, and heard from them that the Hungarians are all mixed up in the German and Slavonic regiments. That is how the Hungarians disappear. They told me that in Genoa all who wore bakkancs and tight trousers had to step forward from the ranks of the prisoners, and that they, too, repeatedly declared that they were Hungarians, but as they wore wide trousers they were marched off.

"In France I had no trouble whatever with those obstacles to the free intercourse of the human family, called custom-house officers, and I hope I shall have still less in Italy, as Villamarina, the Sardinian ambassador in Paris, has specially 'recommended me to their good graces,' and in the note he gave me in addition to my passport, has asked the custom-house and frontier officials 'd'avoir des égards particuliers' towards M. Kossuth, who, with his suite, was travelling to the dominions of the King.

"But I shall have plenty of anxiety in Italy in our own circle, and with the domestic troubles of our band of refugees. How those discordant elements will be able to work harmoniously together, I do not know. When once the authority of power is in my hands, I shall be able to remove what is bad and stimulate the influence of what is good, but under present circumstances it is certainly a painful position that is in prospect for me. On the one hand, enraged impetuosity of goodwill in which the vanity of the dear 'I' always gets the upper hand; on the other hand, goodwill with impotence; then, again, animosity, intrigues, petty ambitions, discord, and I amongst all these with no other power than that supplied by my personal moral influence. Well, no wonder if I too lose patience.

"However, you may rest assured that I shall never become a ball in anybody's hands."

3.

" *Genoa, June 23rd,* 1859.

" I cannot write much, I can only give you facts.

" I suffered much, very much on the sea. As I have informed you, we arrived here very early, and a reception was out of the question. Of course, the Hungarians came on board, and as the landing took some time, a few hundred people assembled on the shore and shouted 'Evviva.' People here and in Turin speak of a serenade. I do not know, but I think there will scarcely be time for anything of the kind, even if the intention exists. What strikes one as peculiar in this Genoa is, that the people are not enthusiastic for the war—not in the least.

"After landing, I had scarcely reached my handsome, cleanly

lodgings, free from all disagreeable insects, when I received a telegram from Turin, sent by Cavour, congratulating me on my arrival, and expressing his desire to speak with me as soon as possible.

" I therefore go to Turin to-day.

" Thence to-morrow to Piacenza to see the Prince.

" Thence, again, the day after, to the Emperor at Brescia.

" Not one has spoken with the Emperor of our Hungarian countrymen since they arrived here. I shall not make much ceremony, as I wish to know in a few days how we really stand in the whole matter.

" The question of the legion (as we must employ this term, but only in the French and Italian languages; in Hungarian it is called ' Hungarian Army in Italy') does not look so well as I could wish, yet is not so bad as I had suspected. The banner will be Hungarian, the uniform Hungarian (if there is to be a uniform, for the poverty is great); the oath says, that they swear obedience and allegiance to the Hungarian National Government, as soon as this begins its operations for the liberation of our country; and while *they are on Italian soil* they swear allegiance to the King of Piedmont. The words '*while on Italian soil*' are the chief obstacle, because they imply that, if desired, they must fight. It is dreadful to contemplate that Hungarians should have to fight against Hungarians in an alien country and for an alien cause. On the other hand it cannot be denied that it would be a delicate point for us to wish that an armed force, independent of the King of Piedmont, should exist in his land. Suppose the Polish legion had refused to swear allegiance to us in 1848 : should we have suffered it ? I know that our position now must be essentially different, for our compatriots only wish to fight for our country, and for nothing else. It will not be easy to satisfy all these different pretensions, but I console myself with the thought that everything depends upon the chief question, and if I can solve that satisfactorily these secondary difficulties will disappear of themselves; and if this chief question does not come to a satisfactory issue, everything else will be rendered problematical, and the men can easily make their choice; they either enter Piedmontese service or they again become French prisoners, and are replaced in their former position. However, I shall endeavour to procure their exemption from taking the oath.

"The men already form two battalions; their number exceeds one thousand. The battalions are weak, consisting of four companies. We could increase the number of the men, but I certainly shall not do much towards this increase until the chief question is clearly settled.

"The proclamation of Klapka which was published by the *Times* was a draft only, and has not been issued with Klapka's knowledge; he had not even signed it. By some indiscretion it came to the knowledge of some newspaper editor, who published as a fact that which was merely a project. It will be stated in the papers that the publication was made without authority. But the awkward part of the matter is that simply to revoke it would be a greater misfortune than its publication. Of course, its success is *nil*. It could have no success. Strange that these men cannot understand that a man wastes his influence by taking a step in public which can have no success!

"I shall not issue a proclamation unless I can say, 'Come, I'll lead you home.'

"Who do you imagine was the first man who shook hands with me when I landed? Regaldi, the improvisatore, who, by his passionate declamations, made the children in Kutahia roar with laughter.*

---

* Regaldi is a well-known Italian poet, who specially enjoys great reputation as an improvisatore. He was travelling in the East when I lived with my family in Kutahia. He was my guest for a few days. One morning I begged him to improvise something to amuse us with his poetical genius in our prosaic solitude. He was kind enough to do so. My wife and three children seated themselves close to each other on the Turkish divan " harrend der Dinge die da kommen sollen." After a few minutes' *recueillement*, Regaldi, with all the southern heat of poetical enthusiasm, commenced to declaim powerfully. My children, still very young, coloured to the tips of their ears, fixed their eyes upon him, and pressing their lips together with a twitching of the muscles of the face, listened for a time. Of course, they did not understand the

"The Governor of Genoa came '*pour présenter ses hommages*,' as he was pleased to express himself.

"Genoa, as much as I have yet seen of it, deserves its historical name :—' Genova la superba :' but it bears the stamp of *past* grandeur.

"Under my window the Aqua Sola, a park-like promenade, with its shady trees and ever-murmuring cascade, is agreeable, but the climate is trying for a foreigner. It is necessary to be very careful about diet. Many of our countrymen suffer from intermittent fever and dysentery; we have a large sick-list.

"If we remain in Italy we must transfer our quarters to some other place, for it appears to me that as the war progresses Genoa will become a useless and inconvenient place for us.

"I spent a whole day yesterday in receiving the reports of the Committee, and making myself acquainted with everything. I did not retire to rest until two o'clock in the morning. More sleep would have been beneficial to me, but to get up and write to you before starting for Turin is much pleasanter.

"I shall endeavour to write to you every day, but it is possible that I shall not always be able to do so in time for post; pray, therefore, make allowances if sometimes you receive two day's letters by the same mail.

"To-day is Corpus Christi; the narrow, dark streets (that peculiarity of hot climates), formed by houses six storeys high, are covered over for the occasion with canvas along the route which the procession will take, as a protection against the sun. The many varied forms of the priests and monks are a strange sight to me; it is a long time since I have seen this species of the human race in such numbers.

"I am looking forward to much work with little hope; but whatever may happen, we shall in any case have a peep at Switzerland and North Italy together.

language, but the raving intonation and the excited gesticulation so impressed them that suddenly all the three broke out into loud laughter, which it was impossible to check.

There was an end to the improvisation.—KOSSUTH.

"Pulszky can now ascertain at the Ministry what is the latest move of Prussia or Russia (?). The key to our situation lies there."

The following reports will explain the last paragraph of the preceding letter :—

"PULSZKY TO THE GOVERNOR.
"*London, June* 24*th*, 1859.

" 1. I have been to Monckton Milnes.* I told him that I had hoped to congratulate him as Under Secretary of State for Foreign Affairs. He replied that as Lord John had chosen to sit in the Lower House, the Under Secretary had to be a member of the Upper House. ' Lord John,' he continued, 'is quite at sea ; he does not know what is to be done; but in any case he tries to bring about peace, and expects much of the Prussian propositions, and the conditions of Eszterházy.' I told him that the Prussian propositions, whatever they might be, would at all events not be acceptable, and that Eszterházy had no conditions at all—that he comes to feel his way. (This has since proved perfectly true. The Prussian proposal is ridiculous. The ' restitution ' of Lombardy to Austria, the cancelling of the special treaties with the minor Italian states; and a congress. In a word, the old basis of Lord Cowley, which was not accepted before the war. As regards Eszterházy, he has in fact no proposal to make.) Milnes further mentioned that Bavaria intends to ' defend ' Hungary, and to send garrisons there. With this he very likely wished to frighten me. I denied it categorically, as I had learnt from Persigny that the report had no foundation, and that German neutrality would in that case be as much violated as if the Bavarians sent their troops to Italy.

" From all this I perceive that here they wish to procure peace at any price, and are afraid of the Hungarian diversion. They have no idea of a wider and bolder policy, and would like to patch up the *status quo* anyhow.

* Member for Pontefract; since raised to the peerage as Lord Houghton.

"Milnes said that he would soon come to see me, and that we shall continue our talk on this subject.

"2. The son-in-law of Horner,* on receiving the news of the Prussian mobilisation, wished at once to go to Berlin. He received a letter from the minister not to hurry himself, and not to be in anxiety about his two sons who had to join the ranks, but to go on comfortably to Paris, as he had originally intended, and to work there in the library; *there was no question of any conflict.*

"(Signed)   FRANCIS PULSZKY."

"TO THE GOVERNOR.

"*London, June 27th,* 1859.

"1. The Prussian proposals have not been made at Austria's request. Francis Joseph so confidently anticipated victory, which he did not gain after all, that he protested against peace being already talked about. What will now happen after he has been so shamefully beaten? Not only are we ourselves unable to supply an answer to this question, but very likely the Prussians themselves cannot do so yet, for their former proposal, which was much like that of Lord Cowley, and would have been based on the treaty of 1815, would now be ridiculous.

"2. I hold to-day the first conference to decide what is to be done in the press and by public meetings. Professor Newman will take the chair. It is now difficult here to bring the peop'e together, but I hope we shall systematise our efforts.

"3. I deem it wise for the present to propagate in the press, as well as in private circles, the following view:—The last battle has shown that Austria has no power of resistance. If peace were now

---

* The Horners are a universally respected and much esteemed English family, great friends of Hungary, who were in very intimate connection with the Pulszkys. One of the sons-in-law of old Mr. Horner was a German—a professor in Berlin, and was in such a position that the news received through him about the intentions of the Prussian ministry might be looked upon as perfectly trustworthy. Another son-in-law of Mr. Horner was the immortal geologist, Sir Charles Lyell. My friendly connection with this excellent family is one of my pleasant remembrances.—KOSSUTH.

concluded the Russians would soon find a pretext for war, and for occupying Hungary. If, therefore, Europe does not wish to witness the extension of Russia, an opportunity must be given to us of becoming independent.

" (Signed)   FRANCIS PULSZKY."

" SZARVADY TO IRANYI FOR COMMUNICATION TO KOSSUTH.
" Conduct of Prussia—Guarantees which she demands from France.
" *Paris, July* 1st, 1859.

" From the reports I receive here I suspect that people are beginning to get tired, and I am afraid that in order to pacify Prussia they will promise forthwith not to disturb Hungary.

" I have received the following information about the situation :—

" Count Walewski probably received a note from the Cabinet of Berlin through Pourtalés, in which a peaceful construction is put upon the mobilisation of the army. According to this note the army that has been mobilised only consists of 'Landwehr,' and the mobilisation therefore has no greater importance than the precautions taken by other states. Its object is solely to set at rest the minds of the second-rate powers of the German Confederation, and to strengthen the position of Prussia in a future congress. At the same time it is intended to give security to the German states in case revolution should break out in Hungary or Galicia. In the meantime the Prussian Government have decided not to defend Austria's position in Italy.

" It is alleged that the Cabinet of Berlin have submitted a programme to Russia and England, which defines the sphere of action of Prussia either alone or in company with other powers. From France they would require the following preliminary guarantees :—1. That the solution of the Italian question should be submitted to a congress. 2. That the territory of France should not be increased. 3. That no throne should be created for any member of the Napoleonic dynasty.

" If the fulfilment of this programme required war, they would, it is alleged, be ready for it.

"It has been rumoured that Leopold, King of the Belgians, was not ignorant of the concoction of this programme.

"(Signed)   SZARVADY."

(CONTINUATION OF KOSSUTH'S LETTERS TO HIS WIFE.)

4.

"*Turin, Thursday Evening, June 23rd,* 1859.

"To-morrow morning at ten o'clock I shall call on Cavour, and it is possible that I shall go afterwards by rail to Stradella on my way to see the Prince at Piacenza, which is indeed a long way off, and I therefore do not know whether I shall be able to write to you. So I write to-day, supposing that you are not tired of my gossip.

"Our difficulties with the Powers are no doubt great; the Austrians give up one position after another, and it is possible they will think that they can manage without us, which would be a calamity to our country, but would clear up matters as far as we are concerned. I have settled with myself what the great responsibilities resting upon me demand of me. I shall not draw back from my conditions, I shall not allow of our being led by the nose, or let them reap all the benefits they can from us, and afterwards discard us. If yes, yes; if no, no. Yes or no. And I am not afraid of gaining access to them. I go straight there, and when once I am there, the granting of an audience can only be a question of hours, not days. The other thing I wish to tell you is, that you cannot imagine how easily the differences in our own ranks disappear through the influence of my presence. I have no more apprehensions on that score.

"Now I shall give you a report.

"The Governor of Genoa and the Commander of Genoa have anticipated my visit; they both came to me before I could call on them.

"At five o'clock I started by rail for Turin. At the intermediate stations the sympathy of the people often manifested itself by loud cheering. At Alessandria we stopped for ten minutes, and I received a regular ovation. It so happened that at the station we just met 140 men of our own little force, who were on their way to Acqui as a new addition to Ihász's force. I had them ranged in a line, and passing along their ranks I spoke a few kind words to them. You cannot imagine the heartiness of the cheers of the poor fellows. Even after the train had started we heard above the shrill whistle of the engine the unceasing 'Éljens.' Of course enthusiasm is infectious; people collected, civilians and soldiers, priests and women, pressed to my carriage and shouted 'Evviva!' with beaming and often with tearful eyes. A Zouave, a true specimen of those intrepid fellows, with a hack in his nose that was just beginning to heal, pressed towards me; I shook hands with him, and he went away with a jubilant countenance, saying, 'Il m'a serré la main! ah! comme je suis content!' At Asti even the old general and commandant of the place, covered with decorations and his head bared, joined in the 'Evvivas.' Many wanted to kiss my hands. I could scarcely escape from them, and fancy! at Alessandria I delivered a little Italian speech. Where did I learn Italian? I do not know. But I heard them say to one another, 'How nicely he speaks Italian!' Marvellous, like my whole life!

"On my arrival here I found a letter from Cavour. He will receive me at ten to-morrow morning.

"This is a beautiful country! I cannot tell you how magnificent the Alps look from the distance. In one place, while admiring the gigantic Monte Viso towering up high into the sky to the left, the setting sun encircled a peak like a wreath of flames; its rays afforded such a beautiful sight, as no artist but nature can produce. And the country which is surrounded by these giants of mountains is so cheerful and lively, so young and pleasant!

"Oh, you must see this country, see it while leaning on my arm, that through each other we may doubly enjoy the magnificent impressions of nature."

"*Turin, June* 24*th*, 1859.

"This morning I was with Cavour for an hour and a half; he begged for another interview to-morrow morning at nine. I must, therefore, remain here to-day, and as the post to Paris goes only once a day (at 9 p.m.), I can add a postscript to the letter I wrote yesterday evening.

"I told Cavour on what basis I placed the offer of Hungary's co-operation, what encouragement I had received from the Emperor, what task I assumed with regard to England, with what success I carried it out, and that now I was here to say: 'I have governed a country amidst great difficulties; my life has been a great practical school. Let us, therefore, put aside all sentimentality. Do not let us talk about sympathy; that is but an empty word in politics. By interest, by interest alone and by nothing else, can you be influenced to lend me a hand for accomplishing the independence of Hungary, on conditions; from which, acting upon my conscience, I shall not withdraw, and without the fulfilment of which I shall not allow my country to be turned into a field of slaughter.' The Count agrees with me that the Italian question cannot be definitely settled without Hungary's being made independent; he agrees with me that the independence of Italy, from friend and foe, can only be secured by the alliance with an independent Hungary; I therefore do not doubt that the will exists to accomplish what the Emperor led me to hope for. 'But, it is possible,' I said, 'that there are political obstacles by which you find yourselves forced not to insist upon a final solution, but to be content with a partial solution, leaving the future to take care of itself. I know therefore that if your interests require it, and you deem it possible to accomplish what your interests require, you will realise the hopes the Emperor has held out to me; if your interests do not require it, you will not realise these hopes; I do not delude myself with the belief that I can persuade you to realise them. I implore you, do not appeal to sympathies, but simply say, as a practical man of the world to a practical statesman, Let us clear the matter up: tell me plainly and decidedly, can we, or can we not, rely upon the prospects which were opened to us in Paris being realised? If you tell me, "We should like to, but we cannot," well and good. Possibly a bitter tear may fall from the eye of a patriot. I will resign myself to the inevitable—to the prospect that I shall die an exile, but taking with me as a consolation the conviction that only I myself shall be compromised, not my country, whose future will remain unhurt. If you say, " We shall do it," we shall concert the ways, means, and time for its execution; or if you say, " We shall do it, but you must wait till such and such time," I shall wait, on condition that meanwhile you should not wish to draw us into some engagements of secondary importance, which would be of a delicate nature to us. For instance, the Emperor invited me, when I had finished the agitation in England, to come here, and to form a committee under my presidency, and, amongst other things, to address a proclamation to the Hungarian army. I answered, " Yes, when the time comes." " And when will the time be?" " When we can hope that the proclamation will have a success." " When can that be?" " When we can say, Come, we lead you home, to fight for the liberty of our country, in alliance with the powerful Emperor of the French." This conversation reveals the relations subsisting between us. Does the Emperor wish that the proclamation should be issued now?' ' No,' was his answer, ' not yet; towards the end of May.' ' Well,' now I ask, ' how do we stand? What are our prospects? Can we reveal the project to the world? If not, then I shall not sign the proclamation, for I do not know a greater mistake than to take a step which I know cannot be successful. Yes, but others who cannot well understand the situation were partly persuaded to issue a proclamation. What was the success? *Nil.* The error is therefore clear, but my compatriots have commenced organisation among the prisoners of war; the time for taking the oath will soon come. Those poor fellows know nothing of "identity of interests." We talk to them in vain about Italy. They only understand " Fight for our country," and if they be called upon to swear, the dreadful possibility will present itself to their minds that in a foreign land they should be engaging themselves to raise a fratricidal hand, Hungarian against Hungarian, and so they will not swear. Consider, your Excellency, how serious would be the consequence of this! But, if I can tell them, " I guarantee you that we are going home, and that you will only fight here if the enemy stands in our way; the oath is necessary to enable you to start for home;" then they will take the oath, and gladly, too. But in order to enable me to give them this assurance and guarantee, I must possess them myself, for, if I am not myself sure of them, it would be deceitful to raise their hopes. You see, therefore, that even this question of secondary importance depends on the solution of the chief question. I am justified, certainly, in wishing that we should not be kept in uncertainty. All the more because, to keep the nation in a state of excitement by holding out to them dubious hopes, would be a very dangerous game, that might lead to most deplorable consequences.'

"This was the substance of my statement. The minister gradually became visibly impressed, and finally acknowledged that he considered what I had said perfectly just and reasonable, and promised that he would support it by his influence with the Emperor, and requested me to put down my views on paper, to which I replied that I thought it better to proceed direct to the Emperor, without loss of time, after having spoken with the Prince. He agreed with me that this would be the more correct proceeding, and offered to send his confidential agent (Mr. N——), whom he had employed in this matter up to the present, to assist me, and to support me in his (Cavour's) name, at the two head-quarters. At the same time he begged me to pay him another visit on the following morning at nine, that he might properly instruct Mr. N——. I replied that I accepted his invitation with the more pleasure, as I had to arrange with him the question as to the legion.

"In this matter I had made up my mind even as to the smallest detail.

"I shall also have to arrange the financial question. As Pietri is not in Genoa, there are scarcely more than a few thousand miserable francs in the cash-box. Things cannot go on in this way: I shall see to it.

"Whichever way our affairs go—even if nothing comes of them —your dear old man clings to the much-cherished hope, and clings to it with a beating heart, that you, dear angel, and our children will come here as soon as possible,—if our cause is taken up, in order that we may bear together cares and troubles (you see, dear angel of my heart, how selfish is your dear, wicked old man; I ought to give you joy, but my poor, tossed head appeals to your faithful love to share cares and troubles); if, however, our cause falls to the ground, you must come to see the Alps, Switzerland, and Italy. I rejoice at the thought as a child rejoices over its innocent pleasures. As often as I read your letters—those true interpreters of your feelings (and I read them often)—my heart beats, and tears come into my eyes—but I am not ashamed of these tears, because they wet the eyelashes of a man who can face the devil without his pulse beating the faster, if the holy feeling of duty appeals to him in the cause of country and liberty—but, amidst the tears, a smile passes over my face when I think that I shall see you soon in these glorious places, and that you will lean on my arm and say, 'How wonderfully beautiful is eternal nature to him who can comprehend its beauty and can feel!' Therefore, you will come, will you not? even if you only pass through these countries like the bird of passage that comes and goes, without having a country.

"I cannot write any more now. Now and again a sympathising Italian forces his way into my room, and takes up my time. I drove out in the afternoon to have a look at the town and the country round about. The crowds barred my way, shouting 'Evviva!' A brave officer of Garibaldi's Alpine Chasseurs is just leaving my room; he walks on crutches, as he was wounded at Lemno. He served with us in the Monti Legion, and our medal of merit adorns his breast. He is as proud of it as he would be, I know not of what other medal. The modest silver wreath makes him a head taller; and though they have just extracted the bullet from his leg, he declares that he will not die contentedly if he cannot once more fight for Hungary in Hungary. The name of our country has a strange charm about it, and it is doubly strange that I, who have never courted glory, or great name, find in foreign countries so much of that which I did not seek. And why? Perhaps just because I do not seek them, and because, though I have no merit, even my enemies cannot throw doubt upon the fact that my character is modestly but unselfishly honest."

5.

"*Parma, Sunday, June* 26*th*, 1859.

" Yesterday, at two o'clock, I was still at Turin; to-day, at two, I am already at Parma. From Turin I went by rail to Alessandria and Stradella, in the direction of Piacenza. On my way I passed Tortona, Pontecurone, Voghera, Casteggio, Montebello, St. Giulietta, which were the scenes of the first battle fought in the present war, called the battle of Montebello.

"I do not know how it happened (perhaps through my telegraphing for a carriage and horses to take me from Alessandria to Stradella), but the people knew everywhere that I was coming by train, and crowds were waiting at the station, and everywhere the air resounded with the endless 'Evviva l'Ungheria! Evviva Kossuth!' and every one seemed to be happy who could shake hands with me, or kiss my hand, which I was not always able to prevent. I was especially interested by Casteggio, where the inhabitants themselves bravely arrested the Austrians, who were pressing forward towards Stradella, and where, in the course of the day, the Piedmontese cavalry made that brilliant attack, in which 200 out of 500 of the brave fellows were killed.

" My way, I can say, was a triumph, but afterwards an incident happened so inexplicable as to astonish even me, wearily accustomed as I am to such things.

"I must say first, that I reluctantly left Turin. I mentioned in my last letter that I had been to see Cavour. I stated what had been the theme of our conference, and that I had reason to be in every way satisfied with its result, also that we had arranged a second interview for nine o'clock yesterday morning to settle the details.

" In the evening, however (*i.e.*, of the day before yesterday), Valerio, the Deputy, came to me by Cavour's desire, and later on the Chief Secretary in the Ministry of Foreign Affairs (Minghetti) informed me by letter that Cavour had, at 5.30 p.m., received a telegram from the Imperial headquarters, in consequence of which he was obliged to start at 6.30 p.m., to go thither, and that it was therefore impossible that we could keep the second interview as arranged, but that I should receive a letter from the Ministry of Foreign Affairs to the governor of the province of Parma, instructing him to do all that I should wish, in order to enable me to arrive as soon as possible at the headquarters of Prince Napoleon; also that Cavour was sorry that, under existing circumstances, he could not possibly spare Mr. N——, whom he had promised to send with me, but whom he was now obliged to take with him.

"I was annoyed, for there remained many details to be settled, more especially with regard to the legion. 'However,' I thought, 'the chief question remains the chief question; everything depends upon that, and that cannot be settled at Turin, and as far as Count Cavour can have any influence upon it, I have already settled with him to my satisfaction.'

"I utilised my time in pacifying our battalions, or rather in exhorting them (by letter) to wait patiently, and in elaborating the conditions on which I was willing to organise a legion, and my recommendations with respect to the same. The next day I went to the Ministry for the letter to the governor of Parma (just when I was there the news of the victorious issue of the battle of Solferino arrived), and hearing that the Prince would be at Parma to-day, I started, and, travelling day and night, am here.

"The Prince has just sent to ask me to come and see him. I cannot write more. The post is going."

6.

"*Parma, June* 27*th*, 1859.

"Our affairs are taking a *serious* turn. I was yesterday for a very long time with the Prince. As always, he was full of good will, but by his unlucky secession, by which he is condemned to inactivity while gigantic battles are fought, he has not only been put into a false position towards his own nation, but has also lost the intimate knowledge of the situation. He would gladly go to headquarters, but the commander of an army corps cannot leave his force. I put the situation clearly as follows:

"I told him that the *sine quâ non* of my conditions was the despatch of a French army to Hungary, and a proclamation issued from the headquarters of such army; that I had been answered that there were two obstacles against it—England and the tactical unreadiness; that I was requested to remove the former, and was given to hope that the latter would be overcome in two or three months.

"'Since then nearly two months have elapsed. I have removed the former obstacle, and now ask—"Do you send an army or not?" I wish for a straightforward answer;—either that you will, in which case let us concert the time and ways and means; or that you will not, in which case perhaps my patriotic heart will break, but I shall resign myself to fate and return to England, a victim of the confidence I placed in the promises made to me. If we are told, "We shall send an army, but you must wait," we shall wait, but meanwhile we shall not consent to take steps which would compromise us without being helpful to our country. Such is my path, from which I shall not deviate. I beg for a clear answer.'

"In reply, political and tactical difficulties were mentioned; they had no soldiers; the struggle cost so many lives, that first they must accomplish the Italian affair; and they could not burden themselves with the other affair at the same time. Verona was a fearfully strong position, and what if they were beaten? No positive engagement could be entered into. But I should influence the Hungarian soldiers to come over and fight against Austria; and, if I did that, the Emperor would be under a moral obligation towards Hungary, and could not leave us.

"My answer was, 'I shall not do it. Neither do my duty towards my country and my conscience permit it, nor does my reason; for it would be madness to take a step which you know will not be successful. And the step could have no success unless I could say, "Come! with the assistance of the Emperor I will lead you home." If the struggle is sanguinary, if you are in want of men, if Verona is a hard nut to crack, and victory is doubtful, the operations in Hungary become the more necessary. To send 30,000 men into Hungary is a speculation which would bring the best return, for in two months it would give an auxiliary force of 150,000 to 200,000 men, would cut off the vital strength of Austria, and would solve the Italian question—which they can never, never do here.'

" *Enfin*—words, words, and again words. I want something different. I do not draw back from my conditions. Yes and yes, or no and no.

" I again go to the Prince to-day. He is to give me a letter to the Emperor. To-morrow I start for Brescia on my way to Cremona.

" He said, '*Ce serait fâcheux*,' if I returned. I think so myself. The prospects are small, very small.

" I continue the description of my journey, though in a serious mood.

" You know what a warm reception was accorded to me at every station as far as Stradella. Now comes the marvel.

" No railway runs beyond Stradella. I started at ten o'clock at night by carriage, and reached Piacenza at two o'clock in the morning. In the night at the post stations in the villages the intelligence as to who the traveller was died away. I arrived unknown at Piacenza; we could scarcely awake the gatekeeper of the fortress to let us pass in. We had to knock loudly, and he received us with a '*Che diavolo fate cosi tardi?*' I alighted at the St. Marco Hotel, where nobody knew me, and went to bed.

" Piacenza, as you know, is a border fortress of Parma, which the Austrians, after having garrisoned it by virtue of the Treaty of Vienna of 1815, therefore for forty-four years, left seventeen days ago, after having blown up many fortifications, and with wanton cruelty cut down the mulberry-trees standing along their route. Seventeen days ago the headquarters of three Austrian army corps were there; Culoz and Benedek stayed there too.

" I slept peacefully, and at eight o'clock sat down to breakfast still unrecognised. At this moment the waiter brought in the visitors' list. Nicholas Kiss entered my name; the waiter says, 'Grazie,' and goes. At the door he cast a look over the names, and looked back to us with eyes that can only be compared to the first eruptions of fire from a volcano. He ran like mad down the steps, and before five minutes—no, scarcely three minutes—had passed by, the 30,000 inhabitants knew it—they rushed into the streets as if the alarm-bell called them; they were coming from all directions, and stood underneath my window and shouted, ' Evviva ! ' as if they intended to bring down the firmament of heaven by their voices. The mayor and all the municipal officers came into my room to pay their respects to me, to offer their services, to beg my commands; the venerable Montanelli, a late Minister of Tuscany, who lost his left arm at Curtatone, where he fought as a volunteer in 1848, came accompanied by many officers of the civil guard, but he himself dressed like a private soldier; in a word, everybody came. Half an hour afterwards, when I was stepping into a carriage, everybody who could come near me kissed my hands and clothes. We moved along with great difficulty, and had scarcely reached the street when the people unharnessed the horses and themselves drew us through the town, while crowds streamed towards me from every street, thousands followed me, flowers were thrown from the windows, and the people honoured the poor homeless traveller with the perfect frenzy of young liberty's first intoxication. And why? Because they identify his name with that of liberty, the perception of which runs like a current of electricity through the nerves of humanity.

"And still how much servitude! How much oppression there is in this world! And for how long has it existed, and how long will it last!

"It was a scene such as you saw in Vienna in 1848. But here the five minutes were the 'marvel,' the clue to which I cannot find. Perhaps souls, too, have telegraphs which work more quickly than the electricity running along the wires.

" I arrived at Parma at two o'clock. The Prince having arrived the day before, the town was in gala attire, with its thousand banners and carpets and other hangings suspended from every window. When we turned into the hotel gate, one of two men who stood talking together said to the other (pointing to me), ' Cavour.' I shook my head by way of denial, upon which a beam of inspiration brightened his eye, and he shouted excitedly, ' Kossuth,

Kossuth! Evviva Kossuth!' By the time we reached the staircase a crowd numbering hundreds was around me, showing the same enthusiasm, even to kissing my hands and clothes, as at Piacenza, and by the time I came to my room thousands were moving up and down under my window. As soon as I showed myself at the window, yielding to the cries of 'Fori' and 'Evviva,' other thousands came forward, and this went on for hours and hours, until I drove to the Prince. Even to-day these scenes have not ceased—bouquets of flowers come down like so many rain-drops. Before my lodgings a guard of honour of the National Guard is posted. The governor of the province has placed a box at the theatre at my disposal. I did not go to see the performance lest I should appear to court popularity (which, as the Prince is here too, would have been bad policy), but though I was not present, they still cheered my poor name.

"In a word, if sympathy could save my poor country, it would be saved, but the people can only love; their fate, like ours, is in the hands of others. But whatever becomes of it, I shall not retract my conditions—either a French army to Hungary, or I go back into exile."

7.

"*Parma, Tuesday, June 28th*, 1859.

"I am still in Parma, and can only start to-morrow, the 29th. I shall go to Milan for the night, and on the 30th to headquarters. It is possible that I shall be detained there for two or three days, and possibly I shall not get back to Genoa before July 5th. In no case shall I be there before the 3rd."

"As regards our cause, the one thing which may be to your consolation is, that there is no longer, nor will there be, any more question of their wishing to persuade us to do something without a French army. When they saw my determination, they relinquished the idea, all the more readily since they are assured on all sides that without me certainly nothing can be done in the matter; and as I do not retract my condition, they have resigned themselves to the inevitable,—either that a French army must go to Hungary, or that Hungary will not budge.

"The question therefore is simply—Will they give us an army? for they know that if they do not, I shall not allow our nation to be brought into trouble, but shall throw up the whole negotiation without any ceremony.

"My impression is, that they will make a promise, but will keep the question as to the time of its redemption in suspense, as depending upon circumstances.

"If this is the result, we shall wait, and meanwhile our activity will be confined almost exclusively to the formation of an army, all the details of which I shall arrange on my present tour, so that the organisation shall rest upon a basis which will preserve the national character of our army, remove any doubt as to its destination, and any dissatisfaction, and make our work as far as possible independent of the retarding interference of red-tapism.

"I am daily with the Prince. Our prospects improve with every day. He will be with the Emperor in ten days, and, so he says, he will not again leave him.

"He attaches great importance to the organisation—says (that is another way of getting out of us as much as they can, and I quite well understand it) that if, by bringing over some ten thousand men from the Austrian ranks, I could introduce disorganisation into their army, such an obligation would rest upon the Emperor as to make it morally impossible that he could forsake Hungary without bringing shame and disgrace upon himself.

"I, of course, see that the proclamation is a necessity, as I said already in Paris, but I shall only issue it if I receive guarantees, and arrive at such an understanding that I can say, 'Come ! our object is to fight on Hungarian soil for Hungary's liberty; with the assistance of the Allied Powers, we have hopes of getting home.'

"As I intimated that I was going to the headquarters of the Emperor, the Prince offered to give me *sauf conduit* and a letter to the Emperor, but requested me to prepare a short draft of the proclamation, the issue of which I wished to be sanctioned by the Powers, and of the plan upon which I wished the organisation to proceed. He added that when he saw my answer on these points, he could tell me at once whether the Emperor would agree to them or not.

"I have accordingly prepared the report, and shall hand it in to-morrow.

"*En attendant*, the Prince tried to persuade me to-day not to go to headquarters until he had sent my proposals and his letter by an officer, and received an answer to them. But I did not give in. Fortunately Pietri has arrived to-day to confer with me. He understands our cause very well, and is a warm supporter of our interests. I told him what I wanted of the Emperor, and he said to the Prince in my presence that I was perfectly right, and might justly desire to comfort my conscience before I took any further steps. At this present moment, midnight, the matter stands thus: on handing in the project to-morrow, I receive the letter from the Prince, and also one from Pietri to one of his confidential agents. I start to-morrow. How the affair will look to-morrow, I do not know. Pietri promised to come after me; he assigned a good reason why he could not come at once with me.

"If I can I shall, to amuse you, copy the draft of the pro-. clamation,* and enclose the copy. Look at the date. If they allow that one to pass, they allow a good deal, but I scarcely believe they will.

"I have just received your kind letter of 23rd inst. The matter will end as you say. They will continue to protract it and postpone it; they will neither play the trump card, nor throw it away. But I always console myself that we are not compromising our country, and, as far as we are concerned, we shall be able to show that we did a sacred duty when we tried to do something in the interest of our country.

"P.S.—Pietri has this minute sent word that we shall go together; he received a letter from the Emperor, saying that he wishes to speak with me. Most of the minor obstacles, therefore, are overcome. Two days are gained by this message. This letter is to remain a secret, confined to our circle."

* See Paragraph III. of this chapter.

8.

"*Milan, Thursday Night, June* 30*th,* 1859.

"After having travelled eighty kilomètres by road (stepping into the carriage at 3 p.m.) I dined at midnight, and at two o'clock in the morning went to bed in the dirty room in which General Urban caroused for seventeen days. I rose at five to catch the train, and arrived at Milan only at eleven o'clock this evening, instead of at eleven in the morning; but either we had to wait several hours to let the train conveying wounded pass (there is only a single line of railway) or the railway clocks did not agree. At Buffalora the line and the magnificent bridge blown up by the Austrians are not yet re-opened to traffic; the diligence could not pass over the battle-field of Magenta, and we therefore went on foot (this is a wonderful place: since they succeeded in driving out the Austrians hence, they will drive them out from anywhere); *enfin,* on account of the many difficulties which were occasioned through the accumulation of traffic, I have only just arrived in this beautiful town, which I shall look at with you. I am very tired; I start again at four o'clock to-morrow morning, but still I cannot go to sleep without writing a few lines to set your mind at rest, to tell you that I feel quite well, and that there is nothing the matter with me, and to send to you, my dearest angel, and to our children a Good Night on the wings of my longing soul.

"Of our affair only this much: Pietri is with me; a telegram has arrived from the Emperor, couched in these words:—

"'*L'Empereur au Sénateur P.*—*Je vous recevrai avec plaisir avec votre ami là où je serai.*'

"What do you say to this? I hope to be with him to-morrow at Cavriana.

"The blessing of my love be with you."

9.

"*Valeggio, Imperial Headquarters, July* 2*nd,* 1859.

"That I write these lines from the headquarters speaks much for me; that the headquarters are at Valeggio, beyond the Mincio, speaks much as to the progress of the war.

"The Austrians, reinforced by two entirely new army corps (60,000 men), were over-confident, and instead of awaiting the French attack in their defensive position beyond the Mincio, they themselves attacked, but were supported in their forward movement by positions even stronger and more formidable than those of Magenta. I saw them both yesterday when I went over the battle-field of Solferino, where Death had such a rich harvest a few days ago. The French found 12,000 Austrians dead and 3,000 wounded after the battle. The latter are well cared for. The 7,000 prisoners are on their way to Genoa, in order that those who are willing to join our banner should be selected. The 12,000 dead were buried. I only saw their graves, strewn over this now trodden-down terrestrial paradise, and still covered with shakos, cartridge-boxes, and suchlike objects all riddled by bullets. There was a stench in the atmosphere arising from the dead bodies which a few days ago were living men, some of them with brave hearts and proud heads filled with ideas embracing whole continents; now they are decomposing matter, which in a few months will be turned up by the plough to grow wheat. . . .

" A melancholy sight! Impossible but that it should spur one on to work, so that, by some gigantic exertion, humanity may be placed in a state in which similar sights shall become impossible.

" But I have no time to meditate.

" The Austrians, having lost this great battle, in which 400,000 men fought on both sides, could no longer defend the Mincio, and have therefore given it up. Francis Joseph wept like a whipped child in the sight of the people at Novi, and then returned to Verona. When I started from Milan, the Emperor's headquarters were at Cavriana. When, after a railway journey of three and a half hours, I arrived at Brescia—notorious for the cruelties inflicted on its population by Haynau, in 1848—beyond which place there is no railway, the Emperor was said to be already at Novi. When I reached that place, he had already crossed the Mincio, and was at Valeggio. We went after him; it was a good thing that Pietri was with me. From high political considerations, I could not divulge my name to all the drivers who were taking artillery ammunition, provisions, wine, hay, officers' luggage, sutlers, reserve horses, straggling infantry, after the Imperial headquarters—it was the train belonging to an army corps of 200,000 men—and whose waggons in endless columns covered the narrow road for miles. But Pietri's words, '*Par ordre de l'Empereur*,' with the assistance of the camp |police interspersed here and there, made it possible for us to get on slowly, slowly, sometimes moving sideways like crabs, till at last an officer of the Engineers led us over a temporary bridge of planks, over which they allowed no carriages to pass, but only men and horses; and in this way we arrived at last, at ten o'clock, where—had there been no impediments—we should have arrived at six. Perhaps you saw a camp in 1849. Imagine a camp a thousand times larger compressed into the smallest possible space; imagine a quart of water in a pint glass, and you will have an idea of the conglomeration. So late in a camp in which even the Emperor rises with dawn, we should certainly not have obtained a spot to lay our poor heads upon, but as Pietri knew the *Grand Prévôt* (Colonel and Chief Commissioner of the Camp Police), the end of the matter was, that now we have beds even, and have had something to eat—part of a sausage, as thick as my arm, and strongly flavoured with garlic, which I could only digest with the assistance of camp air; but I have digested it, for it is now an hour past midnight, while I write, and I am quite comfortable, only sleepy as an owl, and my skin already smarts as I think that there will be plenty of fleas and bugs. But *par contre-coup* we have no water and no basin to wash off the dust, which covers me an inch thick.

"To-morrow (or rather this morning), at eight o'clock, I shall call upon the Emperor, and if he receives me at once, I shall start back in the course of the day—whither, and how far, the want of horses and obstacles alone can determine. But if the Emperor is pressing forward, and therefore cannot see me at once, it is possible that I shall finish this letter at Verona—for nothing is impossible to the French army. An Austrian colonel who was taken prisoner said to them, '*Je ne sais pas si le bon Dieu est avec vous; mais je sais que vous avez de diable avec vous, car vous vous battez comme des diables—il n'y a pas moyen de vous résister.'* And this is true."

10.

"*Milan, July 3rd,* 1859.

"I went to see the Emperor at eight o'clock in the morning. He not only received me at once, but kept me for a whole hour with him, and even the King of Sardinia was obliged to wait for about half an hour (he started early from Peschiera, which he is beleaguering). Pietri was present at the interview and said, when we came out, '*C'est étonnant, il vous a reçu avec des égards extraordinaires et vous a traité avec une considération affectueuse.*' And this is true. I cannot confide every secret detail to a letter, but from what I can write you will see, my dear soul and angel, that we certainly have not tried to mystify each other, but that we have spoken openly to each other and frankly stated, on both sides, how far we may rely on each other.

"First of all, I gave an account of the result of my mission to England. I did so only verbally, lest I should appear to be boasting; but Pietri interrupted: 'Yet the strangest part, Sire, is that M. Kossuth has in his pocket the letters of the English Cabinet Ministers, by which they engage that England will remain neutral, even if we go to Hungary.' 'Indeed!' said the Emperor, 'May I see them?' I handed him the letters. They seemed to interest him very much. He read them one after the other, smiling every now and again, and shook his head as if astonished.

"Then I spoke. 'Your Majesty can see,' I said, 'that I have not only faithfully carried out the task I had taken upon myself, but I have accomplished it with even greater success than I had promised, and I now feel compelled to ask, what are your designs with regard to Hungary?'

"*Emperor.* 'I have another obstacle—Prussia. I have already received a telegram from Lord John Russell, in which, in consequence of your journey hither (for European diplomacy attributes very, very great importance to your movements), he confirms, I may say officially, the assurance of England's neutrality, but expresses a belief that if I took up the cause of Hungary, I should provoke the Germans.'

"*Kossuth.* 'England's neutrality being assured, I do not consider this very probable. But supposing that the Germans were provoked, excuse me, Sire, if I ask whether Your Majesty is willing to accept a peace which will not solve the Italian question?'

"*Emperor.* 'Unless I am beaten, or a European "*médiation armée*" forces me, I shall not accept such a peace.'

"*Kossuth.* 'Neither of these alternatives will happen. Without England no European armed mediation is possible. An armed mediation is a conditional declaration of war; and England will not declare war—cannot do so; of that Your Majesty may be sure. I therefore say to Your Majesty, "Without us, this question cannot be solved. Recall to memory, Sire, the history of your own house. In the House of Austria there is some very lucky vitality. Your Majesty's great ancestor had often shattered it, humiliated it, prostrated it, but afterwards he made peace with it, and left it a power, and the House of Austria has risen again out of the dust (*s'est relevée*), and has become more dangerous to the Napoleonic dynasty than it was before."'

"*Emperor.* '*C'est vrai, parfaitement vrai.*'

"*Kossuth.* "*Eh bien, si vous ne l'écraserez pas, Sire, à présent*, when Your Majesty holds its fate in your hand, I say, "*elle se relevera plus dangereuse que jamais*," and not only will it be necessary to commence the Italian war again in a few years, and under less favourable circumstances than at present, but Austria will not rest until she has brought about a European coalition against Your Majesty. Ah! I have passed through Lombardy, and have seen the battle-fields of Magenta and Solferino. Whoever has lost such a country and such battles, revenge is inextinguishable in his bosom. It would be a great blunder not to deprive such a foe of the weapons with which he could inflict damage. But he can only be rendered harmless by making Hungary independent. Otherwise he will not only return to Italy, but will organise a European coalition against Your Majesty.'

"*Emperor.* 'Everything you say is well-founded,—is true. I

agree with every word you have uttered. I am convinced of all this.'

"*Kossuth.* 'If so, I ask Your Majesty whether you think, if you desire a substantial result, that it will be possible, by setting aside Hungary, to avoid war with Germany? I say it will not be possible. Let us suppose Your Majesty drives the Austrians out of Verona: if the principle of localisation is adhered to, Your Majesty cannot pursue them. The Austrians cross the Isonzo and laugh at you, because they are on German soil. To grant neutrality to a belligerent Power on its own territory is an absurdity for which I can find no adequate expression.'

"*Emperor* (interrupting). '*Ce n'est que trop vrai ; c'est absurde, absurde, on n'en pourrait jamais finir ; c'est absurde.*'

"*Kossuth.* 'Yes, "*on n'en pourrait jamais finir,*" and therefore, Sire, you will pursue the vanquished army beyond the Isonzo, on German territory, and that will be provocation. I therefore say that if Your Majesty does not send an army to Hungary you must violate German territory, and conflict will be certain: if, on the other hand, you go to Hungary, you completely annihilate Austria. Then, again, war with Germany is possible, but not at all certain, for Hungary is not in any sense German territory, and it is certain that if Your Majesty secures the alliance of a nation which puts in the field 200,000 combatants who fight like lions, Prussia will think thrice before unsheathing her sword, when on the Rhine the Duc de Malakoff moves against her with 160,000 men, and in her rear stand 30,000 to 40,000 Frenchmen, allied with 200,000 Hungarians.'

"*Emperor.* '*C'est pourtant vrai. Aussi, je vous dis franchement, loyalement :* I am decided, firmly decided, to make Hungary independent, unless something so unexpected intervenes that even you would be obliged to acknowledge that it is impossible. I see my interest. Without Hungary's independence I should not gain my object in Italy, and should expose the future to dangerous uncertainties. Therefore, consider it an accomplished fact. I wish to do it, *vous dis-je ;* let us talk about the how to do it, and the when. Are you still determined that you will not call your nation to arms without a French army being sent to Hungary?'

"*Kossuth.* 'I am more firmly determined than ever. I will tell you the reason why. *De deux choses une.* Either (for want of organisation) the movement would not be strong enough, and Austria would exterminate it before Your Majesty could send assistance, even supposing you intended to send it (and then a French army might come, but the Hungarians would not move for the next fifty years); or the movement would at once assume such force that Austria would be frightened, and would then leave Verona, leave Italy, make peace at any price, would send her whole army against us, and in case of need even call in Prussian assistance—and Prussia could safely go, for she would have to deal with us only, and not with Your Majesty as well. Great interests, Sire, are at stake—the life of a nation. The responsibility resting upon me is great. I must speak openly. In the case of the French flag's not being engaged on Hungarian soil, and Austria's offering such a peace with regard to Italy as Your Majesty desires, Your Majesty would accept it, and my poor country would be the victim.'

"*Emperor.* 'I respond to your loyal frankness with frankness. Yes, I would accept it. And you would do the same if you were in my place.'

"*Kossuth.* 'Possibly; but for this very reason I cannot expose my country to the chance of being victimised.'

"*Emperor.* 'Well, you act as becomes a good patriot. I accept the basis: I either send an army to Hungary, or I do not desire the Hungarians to rise. And I shall send an army unless it should be utterly beyond the limits of possibility. That I should be able to send an army, it is necessary that some operations should be concluded; only when I have fortunately accomplished one or two things, can I send an army. (I do not dare to trust these details to a letter.) If meanwhile Europe should oblige me (by armed mediation) to accept a peace which I deem acceptable, there will be no expedition to Hungary; in any other case there will be an expedition, and in the former case you have at least saved Hungary from being compromised. *En attendant,* try to form an army for yourselves; I give you money and every facility; it is for your interest that, if we go to Hungary, you should have an army of your own besides the French troops.'

"*Kossuth.* 'Doubtless; but *by the side of a French army—* that is a *sine quâ non*. As a man, I am satisfied with Your Majesty's word, but as a patriot I want to find guarantees in the French flag being engaged on Hungarian soil. If not, not.'

"*Emperor.* '*C'est entendu;* if not, not.'

"On taking leave, he most emphatically repeated this. We parted most cordially. '*Au revoir.*'

"I mentioned that the circular note of Gortchakoff, in which he too speaks of the localisation of the war, had created apprehensions in my mind as to whether the Russian policy had undergone a change or not. For if we had reason to be afraid of Russian intervention, this would much aggravate our position, you know, because of the Slavs.

"The Emperor completely reassured me on this point.

"I read the draft of the proclamation to him. When I came to the end where it says, 'Given at the French Imperial headquarters,' the Emperor smiled, and said, 'This would be a little too soon; it would be better to date it from some other place.'

"I believe so!

"Finally, we spoke also of the organisation of the army. He approved of my views. He also paid me a little compliment, by saying that I seemed to be an experienced army organiser. He places great importance upon my sending into his camp as soon as possible some battalions wearing the tight Hungarian trousers. I said that we could manage it in eight to ten days, if we had the necessary freedom in our movements. We shall have it. Pietri will come with me to Turin to remove the obstacles in the name of the Emperor. There will be no oath to the King of Sardinia. The Emperor said, '*Pour quoi faire? C'est de la folie que de le demander.*'

"In any case, come, my dearest angel. Come! hasten to my arms! If we go home, come because we go; if we do not go, come to be with me while I am here, and we shall return together or proceed. At all events we shall stay here for some weeks.

"I shall write to Pulszky the day after to-morrow. He is to prepare the contract as to a banknote-press, so that he can sign it as soon as I send money. I send some."

The rest of the details of my conversation with the Emperor at Valeggio are supplied by the second of the two reports sent to Hungary. It was sent off from Genoa on the fifth day after the conversation took place, and is given under Paragraph II. of this chapter.

11.

"*Turin, Monday, July 4th,* 1859.

"I arrived, after a long and often interrupted journey, amid heat of which I had no idea before. It is now 8.30 p.m. The wide and high windows of my room, which look on to the *piazza* before the royal palace, are open, and yet the heat is such that, as I hold the paper with my left hand, the perspiration *pours* down on my fingers. What must it be in the middle of the day!

"I am still as sound as a bell; I have just dined, and have eaten as much as a plough-boy. Yet, to set at rest my dear wife's anxiety, I take as much care of myself as a vain young lady. I wear flannel; I do not drink plain water—no foreigner must do so here; the Italian does not drink water at all; I eat little fruit—it is unwholesome for foreigners: and in consequence of these troublesome precautions, in spite of my tiresome journey of ten days, I have not even had a headache in this great heat.

" By telegraph I summoned hither the committee, the generals, and Ihász, so that, consulting with each other as to the organisation and other preparations, we can arrange to-morrow with the minister and delegate of the Emperor. To-morrow the number of our men will exceed 4,000; but do not be afraid,—even if it reached 50,000, *either with a French army, or without*—that is no longer an open question.

" I shall continue to-morrow my letter of yesterday; I cannot do so to-day, I have much work to do."

12.

"*Turin, Tuesday, July 5th,* 1859.

"I am so much occupied that it is quite impossible for me to redeem the promise I made to you, of giving you to-day an account of the other interesting details of my conversation with the Emperor.

"Yesterday we finally disposed of the details of the organisation of the army, besides a good many other things. To-day we have been to Count Cavour. I considered it necessary to give Cavour an account of my conference with the Emperor, in the presence of Pietri, so that I might be able to appeal to him as a witness that what I said was right, and that there might be no misunderstanding as to how I regarded the matter. Of course this report had its effect. Up to the present we were in want of a thousand things, and we met with a thousand difficulties in the organisation and equipment of the army. Now everything goes smoothly. What they cannot supply to us from their depôts we have made by contractors. We frame the contract, submit it for approval, and it is paid. I have made provision for the officers and men, in case we cannot reach home. We have no officers—we promote sergeant-majors, corporals,—in a word, every capable man, to the rank of sublieutenant; but there are not enough,—we are obliged to send for officers to England, America, and Turkey. The Government has also defrayed travelling expenses.

"One statement the Minister made was very significant: ' Now I put aside the diplomatist, and shall speak as an Italian patriot. If Hungary is not liberated we shall not gain much by the war, and at best can only look forward to a very dangerous future. *Eh bien!* European diplomacy is very much inclined to interfere in our cause, and to force upon us some half-satisfactory peace good for nothing. I wish to see this prevented, and your organisation is one means of accomplishing this. A Hungarian force of respectable strength, with the Hungarian flag, in Hungarian uniform, its organisation under Hungarian leaders, with the proclamation to be issued by you, will compromise us, and that is just what I should like. It is my desire that we should be compromised. If we are, there can be no patched-up peace, and through your independence that of Italy will be secured. On the whole, I quite understand Mr. K.'s policy. He looks for guarantees, and thinks that the engagement of the French and Piedmontese flags on Hungarian soil would supply these guarantees; and I say he is perfectly right.'

"Is not this an important statement?

"It is possible, certainly, that something may come of our affair, and my conscience tells me that I have done no little service to my country in so bringing it about, that if our cause is taken up it will be on a basis which reduces the danger and sufferings to a minimum, while it promises the greatest possible success, and excludes the possibility of my nation's being victimised.

"If our cause is not taken up, our country at least will not be compromised, nor shall we be; for every sane man must admit that it would have been a culpable neglect of our duty, not to attempt to make use of the present complications for the good of our country."

The rest of the letter refers to family and domestic affairs.

II.

Two Reports sent to Hungary.

1.

"31, *Salita dei Capucini, Genoa,*
"*June* 22*nd,* 1859.

"DEAR COMPATRIOT,

"Our colleague Ladislaus Teleki has communicated to us the contents of the letter which you were kind enough to address to him. The undersigned committee, duly appreciating your valued report, take this opportunity of sending the following reply:—

"The war carried on by the Governments of France and Piedmont against Austria promises to furnish an opportunity for reasserting the lost independence and liberty of the Hungarian nation.

"After preliminary consultations extending over several months, the Emperor of the French invited Mr. Kossuth to Paris at the beginning of last May, to confer with him personally about the participation of Hungary in the war. In agreement with Teleki and Klapka, Kossuth signified his readiness to co-operate in the said object on the following conditions:—

"1. That the insurrection of Hungary should not be used simply to make a diversion, but should serve completely and finally to accomplish the liberation of the nation.

"2. That the insurrection should be preceded, or rather promoted, by the advance of a French army of respectable proportions into Hungary.

"The Emperor of the French accepted these two *indispensable* conditions, and expressed the hope that in two or three months circumstances would enable him to despatch an army, ammunition, and the arms necessary for the equipment of the nation. In this case he would address a proclamation to the Hungarian nation, stating that, as the nation declared herself to be independent in 1849, he sent an auxiliary force into the country again to put in force this declaration. Our independence, when he had identified himself with it by this proclamation, would be thus assured beforehand.

"In return for this assistance, the Emperor does not ask anything except that, having acquired independence, we should establish not a Republic, but a Constitutional Monarchy. He would not further interfere in the settlement of our internal affairs.

"Taking into consideration their duty towards their country, and existing circumstances,—Kossuth as well as Klapka and Teleki, and the other Hungarian refugees—has accepted the offer and conditions referred to above, and the undersigned, conforming to the wish of the allied governments, have constituted themselves into a committee, under the name of the Hungarian National Committee, entrusted with the preparation and temporary conduct of the work of liberating the nation. Teleki and Klapka came last month to Genoa, with the intention, amongst other things, of forming an army of the fugitive, captured, and deserted Hungarians. Kossuth, however, at the wish of the Emperor, returned to London, to endeavour to secure the neutrality of the English Government.

"The organisation of an army, with Hungarian colours and under Hungarian officers, is progressing satisfactorily; and the second battalion is already in formation. Kossuth performed his task in England with astonishing success.

"The principal members of the new Cabinet have engaged themselves not to swerve from a policy of neutrality, even in case Napoleon should transfer the seat of war to Hungary. The sympathy for our country, to which the British nation gave expression at the public meetings organised by Kossuth, affords a guarantee that the Government will redeem their pledge.

"Having thus accomplished his most important mission, Kossuth, too, with the consent and passport of the French and Piedmontese Governments, arrived this day at Genoa to confer with his colleagues as to the further steps to be taken; and afterwards with the Piedmontese Government and the Emperor Napoleon. He will start to-morrow for Turin, and thence for headquarters. We had wished to defer our reply until such time had elapsed as would have enabled us to report the result of this fresh, and we hope decisive, meeting; but, fearing lest you should return home before receiving our letter, we lose no time in informing you of the present state of affairs, reserving it to ourselves to report to you their further progress later on, possibly in a few days.

"Premising thus much, we shall now proceed to investigate the questions to which you expect an answer and instructions.

"While, on the one hand, we do not doubt that at the proper moment the whole nation will rise like *one* man to reclaim the rights of which it has been deprived, on the other hand we must confess that not only every premature outbreak, but every such act as could call the enemy's attention to the approaching danger would be dangerous. The hope of liberation must be propagated among those who are faithful, and our countrymen true to the cause of their country must be reminded to keep themselves in readiness for taking up arms, but only when, and on condition that, a French army shall march into Hungarian territory. Until then, no organisation of any sort must be effected. However, we have agreed that even before then a few trustworthy men of sound judgment should be chosen in every district to remain in connection with you, and through you, with this Committee. For this purpose we do not hesitate to forward to you the enclosed letters of appointment. At this great distance we cannot pretend to be able to designate those gentlemen who would be most suitable for an office connected with so heavy a responsibility. We therefore leave it to your judgment to choose those persons, and to fill in their names in the spaces left blank for that purpose in the letters of appointments. Up to the present, nobody else has been entrusted with the centralisation of the arrangements at home. If you will take upon yourself to carry out the directions of the Committee, you will have our patriotic gratitude. The instructions enclosed herewith give further proof of the confidence we repose in you. But we have to inform you that our emissary met Mr. P. H. amongst others, last month. He informed that gentleman of what had occurred up to that time, and handed him 1,500 francs to defray the travelling expenses of the person employed to bring us the desired reports.

"The negotiations with the French and Piedmontese Governments referred to above will have shown you that we expect help thence and not from the East. Let this be a guide as to the receiving of proposals which have been, or may be, made from another quarter.

"We are rather short of money still, but we will send as much as possible soon. We hope that endeavours will also be made at home to raise funds towards our object.

"As regards the communication to be kept up with us, it would be best if you were to send your reports to us by special messengers; but in case this could not be managed often enough, we shall expect to receive your reports through, and shall address our answers to, Mr. Place, French Consul at Jassy, and Mr. Astengo, Sardinian Consul at Belgrade.

"Being aware of the object, you will know to what points to give your attention in your reports. Merely for the sake of example mention the following: the armed Austrian force stationed in the country, their numbers, nationality, garrison places, state of the fortresses, &c. It is very desirable that of the persons who are sent out here, one or another should be acquainted with the present administrative, judicial, and taxation systems, so as to let us know which laws will eventually have to be changed at once, and which temporarily left in force.

"We cannot yet give an opinion as to whether it will be necessary to send Honved officers, or not. But the district commissioners should schedule the names, addresses, ranks, and corps of the officers whom we could employ if the need arise. You will be kind enough to forward those schedules to us.

"There is one more subject of very high importance to which we must direct your attention, *i.e.*, our relation to the foreign nationalities. Try to ascertain the feelings and aspirations of the Wallachians and Saxons, Servians, and Croatians.* On this point please address yourself to the most influential representatives of the respective nationalities. While assuring them that on the basis of the territorial integrity of Hungary, and the laws of 1848, we are ready to grant them everything which one brother can offer another, please invite them to communicate their wishes to us—if they have any such—by sending to confer with us, if possible, a man chosen from their midst. Although we consider the laws of 1848 as our basis, it is by no means our intention to preserve them without alterations; on the contrary, we wish to extend and develop the principles laid down therein in such a manner as will completely reassure every interest, national as well as religious, under the protection of the Hungarian constitution. Take as a guide the enclosed draft of a constitution which the undersigned President has devised, and which, in its fundamental principles, has the approval of us all.

"And now we bid you 'Good-bye.' We confide to you a

---

* "Mr. John Ludvigh, late Deputy and Government Commissioner, is instructed to negotiate with the Croatians from Belgrade. If Croatia and Slavonia should not be willing to preserve the status of *ante* 1848, we are ready to grant them independence on certain conditions."

difficult but glorious work. May the mighty God of wisdom and justice direct your steps.

   " (Signed) Louis Kossuth, *President*.
   " (Signed) George Klapka.
   " (Signed) Ladislaus Teleki.

" The draft of the constitution referred to in the letter is much too bulky to be forwarded; and we shall therefore on this occasion only explain its fundamental principle, and that part referring to the question of nationality.

" Nationality, like religion, is an interest of society. The state, as such, has as little to do with the one as with the other. The constitution having secured the right of association, citizens have a right to defend and propagate their national interests as much as any others, and to unite and form associations according to communities, counties, and over the whole country; as the Protestants, out of regard for their religious interests, have associated according to communities, counties, and districts, and the members of the Augsburg creed also over the whole country. But like the religious associations, the national unions cannot claim territorial jurisdiction in civil matters, but will have to confine themselves to the cultivation of the interests of their nationality. In this respect they will have entire liberty—they will be allowed to choose superiors, to whom they may give any title they please; just as the religious congregations can choose superiors—calling them patriarchs, metropolitans, cardinals, bishops, superintendents, wardens, curators, or anything else. They may hold meetings and carry resolutions within the limits of the constitution and the law, and the state cannot require anything except that these meetings should be public. This principle will be applied to the Magyar as much as to the other nationalities; none will have the smallest privilege, and the Government, as such, will not prefer any one before any or all of the others. As far as the Government, the House of Representatives, the county, and the community want an official language, the principle enunciated above will be so applied, that the majority will everywhere decide in which tongue the public business should be carried on, while they do not violate the right of the minority. For instance, the assembly of the delegates of a county decide that in the ensuing year the public business is to be carried on in the Roumanian, Slavonic, Servian, German, or Hungarian language. Notwithstanding this, the persons speaking a different tongue will be allowed not only to petition, to carry on their lawsuits in their own tongue, but also to use it in the assembly of delegates. The Government, however, when sending their communications to a county which has adopted another language than the Hungarian as its official tongue, must attach to any document *written in the official Hungarian language* a translation in the tongue adopted by such county. The county will have to act on the same rule in its intercourse with the towns and villages lying within its jurisdiction. On the other hand, the county, if its official language is not the Hungarian, will have to attach a translation to its reports to the Government. All the laws will be translated into, and published in, the languages currently spoken in the country."

2.

" *My second meeting with the Emperor Napoleon after the battle of Solferino.* *

" *Valeggio, July 3rd*, 1859.

" Our compatriots have been informed by our letter of June 22nd of what happened prior to my journey to the Imperial headquarters; and about my first meeting with the Emperor in Paris at the beginning of May a still more exhaustive report has been sent home by a special emissary.

" To understand what we are now going to report, it will be necessary to recollect that with the consent of my colleagues I have stipulated as a fundamental condition of the participation of Hungary in the war, that the Emperor should send an army to Hungary, and

---

* Much that has already been said above in a letter is now repeated. But as this report also contains interesting details which are not mentioned in the letter, I did not think it right to omit it here.

thus give us a chance of developing and organising our national force, by throwing the honour of the French flag in the scale on Hungarian soil, and also assure us that no peace will be concluded at our sacrifice, or without the independence of our country being re-established. It must also be borne in mind that Napoleon thought he detected the chief obstacle to sending an army in the policy of England, because he was afraid that if he by his proclamation initiated the Hungarian revolution, England would be inclined to give material assistance to the German Confederation by extending its help to Austria. After I had conferred with Count Cavour in Turin and with Prince Napoleon in Parma, I arrived at headquarters at Valeggio on July 3rd in company with M. Pietri, a French Senator, whom the Emperor had informed beforehand by telegraph that he would see me with pleasure. And really he received me so cordially that Senator Pietri, who was present at our interview, could not refrain from remarking, '*Il vous a reçu avec des égards particuliers et vous a traité avec une considération affectueuse.*'

"I told the Emperor of the success of my activity in England, and convinced him by proofs that if he sends an army to Hungary and calls upon our nation to fight for its independence, he can not only rely upon the neutrality of the English Government, but he would by taking such a step positively secure the sympathy of the English people. The chief obstacle to which he had pointed being thus removed, I asked him whether he felt inclined to fulfil what he had promised me, and whether he was prepared to send an army to Hungary.

"The Emperor answered that there was yet another difficulty— Prussia, which was taking up a threatening position, and undoubtedly drew with herself every force of the German Confederation.

"I expressed my fears that the difficulty was to be found not so much in Prussia as in the change of Russia's policy; because I could not think that Prussia, if unable to depend upon any assistance from England, would dare to threaten France unless she were sure that she had nothing to fear from Russia. The Emperor requested me to give him the reasons which induced me to believe that Russian policy had undergone a change. Of several facts pointing to the same conclusion I laid the greatest stress upon the circumstance, that while the Emperor upon the occasion of our first meeting decidedly assured me that Russia did not oppose the liberation of one country, and would in no conceivable case assist Austria against us, I had since seen the Russian Government, by Prince Gortchakoff's well-known circular note, declare itself in favour of the localisation of the war, and the preservation of the so-called balance of power in Europe; that I knew that the latter signified the preservation of a powerful Austria, while the former made the extension of the war to Hungary impossible on such a basis as I consider it a duty to my country to lay down :—that I, however impatiently I may wait for the moment in which we can again resume the struggle for independence, still pray the Emperor with all my heart rather to relinquish the idea of drawing Hungary into the war than to draw upon us Russian intervention, because with two such opposite influences I did not dare anticipate the union of the people of my country, but was rather afraid of a rupture; and that I would prefer to die in exile than to lend a hand towards compromising, by fratricidal internal struggles, the union and the future of my country.

"The Emperor assured me in emphatic language that nothing had intervened from the Russian Government to make him fear that Russia would assume a hostile attitude either against the independence of Hungary or against France; but he acknowledged this much—that Russia did not quite like national struggles, because she was afraid that if, rising in Italy, this banner were carried through Hungary, it might also act as a stimulus to the Polish nation. '"*J'accepte le fait, mais je n'aime pas le mot,*' were the words of the Czar," said the Emperor; but he added that he did not fear hostile policy, and promised to obtain further assurances in this matter, since I had called his attention to it.

"The obstacles still in the way being thus confined to the German Confederation, I asked the Emperor whether he was inclined to conclude a peace which would leave the Italian question unsolved, and would not redeem the pledge he had given before

Europe, that Italy, from the Alps to the Adriatic, would be emancipated from Austrian rule.

"The Emperor answered that, unless he were beaten, he would not accept such a peace.

"Upon this statement I begged the Emperor to recollect that there is a fatal hardihood in the House of Austria, of which the House of Napoleon had had very bitter experience in the past:— that it had more than once been thrown to the ground by the Great Emperor; but as it is impossible to put this treacherous race under obligation by kindness, and its power was left to it, it rose, after every overthrow, more dangerous than before. I had passed through Lombardy, and examined the battle-fields of Magenta and Solferino, and I said I could affirm with deep conviction that he who had lost such a province and such battles would never forgive. There was no mistake more dangerous in politics than to offend somebody mortally, and to leave power in his hands for revenge. 'If, now when Your Majesty holds the fate of the House of Austria in your hand,' I said, 'you do not annihilate its power by making Hungary independent, not only will the blood of so many brave heroes have been shed in vain; not only will the Italian war, in a short time, but under less favourable conditions, have to be recommenced; but I also venture to assure you that the House of Austria will not rest until it leads an armed European coalition against the Bonaparte dynasty.'

"The Emperor exclaimed with emotion, 'True, true; every word true! I am deeply convinced of it.'

"I continued: 'If Your Majesty is convinced of this, why should you now be afraid of Prussia, when England's neutrality is assured, and Your Majesty trusts to the friendly neutrality of Russia? I reason thus: There has always been a great talk about the principle of localisation; but taken in theory, I consider it an absurdity, unheard of in history. In practice, however, I deem it utterly useless, unless Your Majesty is inclined to make a second Peace of Campoformio.'

"'I am not prepared for that,' interrupted the Emperor.

"'Let us suppose that the brave troops of Your Majesty drive the Austrians out of Verona. If the Austrians are allowed to retreat beyond the Tagliamento, and there to stand safely and say, " Your Majesty does not dare to pursue us, because we are on the territory of the German Confederation "—I do not understand why Your Majesty carries on war which can neither come to an end nor ever attain a result. There is no greater absurdity than to confirm to a belligerent power the advantages of neutrality on its own territory.'

" The Emperor said : ' *C'est vrai, c'est parfaitement absurde! Aussi je ne m'y soumettrai pas.*'

" ' If so,' I continued, ' Your Majesty's choice can only lie between two alternatives : either to pursue the vanquished Austrian troops on the territory of the German Confederation, or in Hungary and through Hungary to put an end to the war. In the former case Prussia, if she really does wish to interfere, will undoubtedly be provoked; in the second case, she may also intervene, but her interference is not certain, for Hungary is not German territory, and I really think that Prussia will think twice if she finds herself between two armies—on one side the Duc de Malakoff with 160,000 Frenchmen on the Rhine, and on the other side, advancing from Hungary, a French army and 200,000 Hungarian troops, which number may safely be depended upon.'

" To this the Emperor answered : ' Your remarks are well founded. I am convinced of the identity of our interests, and I therefore, give you my word that I wish Hungary to be independent, and am firmly determined to extend a helping hand during this war to the Hungarian nation to fight out its independence. This is a fact ; let us therefore speak no more about it, but let us confer as to the time, ways, and means. Do you still cling to the conviction that unless a French army is sent there the Hungarian nation should not rise ? '

" I answered, ' This conviction is stronger than ever, and if Your Majesty will permit me, I shall state the reasons why. One of two things would happen : our insurrection would be such that it would be suppressed by the Austrians before it could gain strength by organisation (and in this case I am sure that if Your Majesty in the course of the war should see the necessity of sending a French army to Hungary, the Hungarians, having suffered by the useless attempt, would with difficulty listen to Your Majesty's appeal), or it would be such as to seriously frighten Austria at once. I scarcely believe this, for strength lies in organisation, and we should have all the less time to accomplish this, because the Hungarian possesses a straightforward character; he cannot conspire. Yet if it should happen, nothing is more certain than that Austria would leave Italy, would offer peace at any price to Your Majesty, would throw her whole force upon us; and, if necessary, Prussia too would come to her help. And why should she not? She would only have to grapple with us, not also with Your Majesty. Excuse my frankness, Sire, in consideration of the importance of the matter. In such a case, not being yet engaged in Hungary, and being offered everything you wished with regard to Italy, Your Majesty would undoubtedly accept the peace, and my poor nation would be the victim.'

"Thereupon the Emperor stated that, wishing to requite my frankness by frankness, he would say that in such a case he *should* accept peace. 'You would do the same in my place,' he said. To which I rejoined that just because I considered it natural that he should accept peace under those conditions, I did not wish to sacrifice my country in order to facilitate the peace in Italy.

"The Emperor, appreciating these remarks, assured me that he had decided to send an army to Hungary, provided that, until such time as the course of the military operations permitted his intention being carried out, he should not be obliged by a European armed mediation to make peace. To which I again replied, that as in the case of a refusal of the conditions of an armed mediation, declaration of war became inevitable, nothing was to be feared from this obstacle either from England or Russia.

" In consequence of these assurances, I took the liberty of asking a question as to the time for which we had to prepare our nation to expect the expedition. The Emperor's reply referred partly to the completing of the organisation of his army on the Rhine, partly to the filling up of the gaps caused in the Italian ranks by the sanguinary encounters; to which I replied that the expedition of 30,000 to 40,000 men to Hungary was, even if done to gain strength, a good speculation, because in two months it would secure an allied army of 150,000 to 200,000 enthusiastic Hungarians. On the other hand, the Emperor's answer turned upon the accomplishment of a certain military operation, which I cannot enter upon here.* Suffice it to say that the question turned upon a port which would facilitate the embarkation of the troops destined for service in Hungary.

"After this the Emperor reminded me that it was to our interest to proceed with the formation of the Hungarian army, composed of the prisoners of war and deserters, with the greatest possible energy, and he desired me to use the utmost despatch in the organisation, so that we should as soon as possible be able to send some battalions, equipped in the Hungarian manner and with the Hungarian flag, to join his army, that it might be ascertained what influence the appearance of the Hungarian flag would exercise upon the Austrian army. I pointed out the obstacles which had hitherto prevented our organisation proceeding quickly, whereupon the Emperor ordered Senator Pietri to accompany me to Turin and to inform the Government there that it was his (the Emperor's) wish that our wants should be in every way satisfied, and that he recommended that our procedure should be altogether facilitated, so that our army might be formed, as soon as possible, entirely on a Hungarian basis, and be exempt from the oath of allegiance to the King of Piedmont.

"Matters standing as they did, I believed the time had arrived for addressing a proclamation to the Hungarians serving in the Austrian army. While our affairs did not rest on a sufficiently firm basis, no proclamation had been issued either in the name of the Hungarian National Committee or in that of any other proper authority, at least with my consent. I read to the Emperor the draft of the proclamation, which was so worded as to identify the Emperor as much as

* The capture of Venice, as without it (there being no port on the Adriatic shore at the Emperor's disposal) the troops destined for Hungary would have to embark at Genoa or Leghorn, which, on account of the distance, would be accompanied by endless difficulties. (Note added in September, 1859.)

possible with our cause. He made some comments, but agreed that the war must be extended to Hungary, because the independence of Italy could not be secured without the independence of Hungary; that our Hungarian flag should wave on Italian soil under the protection of the allied powers; that our army here should form the nucleus of the national forces to be developed at home, when our flag should wave by the side of the victorious French eagle; and that soon we might expect to be able to call upon our comrades to follow us home to reassert the independence and liberty of our country, with the assistance of the allied powers.

"Such was our interview; and when parting and wishing success to the arms of the Emperor, these were my last words, 'Lest there should be any misunderstanding between us, permit me, Sire, to repeat that I go hence with the conviction that, unless Your Majesty is meanwhile compelled to conclude peace, you will, after the capture of Venice, send an army to Hungary, call our nation to arms, and engage the French flag in the struggle for our independence, and that, without this being done, you will not endeavour to arouse the Hungarian nation into insurrection.' Shaking my hand heartily, the Emperor distinctly confirmed this statement.

"From the Imperial headquarters I went to Turin, and narrated to Count Cavour, the Prime Minister, what had taken place at my interview with the Emperor, not only in the presence of my colleagues Klapka and Teleki, but also in that of Senator Pietri. I requested the senator, as he had been present at the above interview, to say whether I had understood the Emperor aright. He answered without hesitation that I had, and even added that I had said rather less than more of what happened.

"The report made a perceptible impression upon Count Cavour. He not only agreed one after the other with our wishes with respect to the quick organisation, on a Hungarian basis, of the Hungarian army, but, as he put it, he even divested himself of the diplomatist for a moment, and as a patriot said : 'You want a guarantee that your nation will not be made use of for alien objects, and believe you find it—as we have heard now stated for the first time—

in the waving of the French and Piedmontese flags on Hungarian soil; and you are right.' He also stated that he feared European diplomacy would interfere in the affairs of Italy, and that, therefore, he wished to promote the organisation of a Hungarian army in every way possible, as this would compromise the allies in the eyes of European diplomacy, and he wished to be compromised.

" (Signed)   LOUIS KOSSUTH,
"President of the Hungarian National Committee.
" *Genoa, July 8th,* 1859."

III.

The proclamation previously referred to ran as follows :—

" In the name of our nation, greeting to you, brave Hungarians! the hope of our dear country's liberation !

" You remember the gigantic struggle which we carried on ten years ago for country and liberty against the perfidious House of Austria, when it ungratefully dared to raise above our country the axe of oppression and national perdition.

" The nation rose up in arms like one man.

" The combatants of the Hungarian Infantry Regiments tore away the yellow and black braid, that symbol of servitude, and, joining the Hungarian tricolour, made the name of ' Magyar Honvéd' known all over the world.

" The Hungarian Hussar, sword in hand, broke a way through hostile provinces to his native land, that he might have a share in the glory of saving our country.

" We stood alone in the gigantic struggle, forsaken by the whole world ; but love of our fatherland and our inherited bravery led us to victory.

" You held aloft the banner of law and liberty, and the God of

Justice, through your brave arms, dragged into the dust the symbol of despotism,—the Austrian yellow and black banner.

"We were victorious ! and as the deserved reward of our victory the nation unanimously declared that Hungary should no longer have a king of the Austrian dynasty, which was declared to have lost its claims to the throne for ever, because it had torn, with perjured hands, the compact existing between itself and our nation.

"The Hungarian soldier was legally relieved of his oath of allegiance to the House of Austria, and fidelity to it was declared to be treason.

"You know what followed : the Austrians implored foreign assistance against us, and with it and by treachery have put the yoke upon our country.

"And under this yoke our country has become a vale of misery. Our best men have perished by the hands of the executioner. Our constitution has been annulled ; our laws have been trampled under foot; our ancient liberty, which we had extended to the whole people without distinction of tongue, race, and creed, has been replaced by universal servitude; our country has been struck off the list of living nations. By overburdening imposts every morsel of food is taken from the mouths of your fathers and brothers. You, heroes, are by force dragged into foreign lands to shed your blood for the oppression of kindred nations; misery, distress, servitude spread over our country; the Hungarian, a slave in his own country, is the subject of German whim and German tyranny.

"Our Croatian, Servian, Wallachian, and Slavonian compatriots, who were deluded by promises ten years ago, but are now undeceived, were rewarded with the same lot and suffering which were imposed upon our race out of revenge. The House of Austria always repays fidelity by fraud and ingratitude. Such crime calls for retaliation—the poor oppressed country calls for liberation.

"Now is the time for retaliation ! now is the opportunity for liberation !

"The powerful Emperor of the French and the chivalrous King of Piedmont are the chosen instruments of Providence by which the righteous God punishes the crimes of the House of Austria, and wipes away the tears of suffering shed by these oppressed nationalities.

"But Heaven makes no gift of liberty—'Help yourself and God will help you,' is the law of Providence.

"The struggle commences on Italian soil, but it must extend to Hungarian ground. Our cause is identical; our oppressor is one and the same; our liberty is inseparable. The liberty of one cannot be secured without that of the other. And he who is the enemy of our country's oppressor is the natural friend of our country.

"The tricolour of Hungary was banished from the earth for ten years; but now, thank God, we are at liberty to unfurl it on Italian soil.

"And we have unfurled it on this friendly soil, under the protection of the allied powers.

"We have unfurled it with the object of collecting round it the faithful and brave sons of Hungary, to form them, under a Hungarian flag, Hungarian organisation, Hungarian leaders, into a Hungarian army, forming a nucleus round which the whole force of our nation may collect, and then in the course of the war our national flag will wave on the sacred soil of our country by the side of the French eagle, so accustomed to victory.

"We call you under this banner, heroes! comrades! We call you in the name of our suffering country, in the name of our liberty and independence! We call you in the name of glory and love of your native country! We call you in the name of that sacred country where your cradle stood, with the earth of which the ashes of your forefathers have mixed, and beyond which there is no room for the Hungarian in the whole wide globe.

"You will see this flag, the flag of the independence of Hungary, in the ranks of the troops of the allied powers on the battle-field.

"It is impossible that you should raise a sacrilegious hand against it.

"Your place is on this side, not on the other, where a despotic force retains you.

"You do not owe allegiance to Francis Joseph! He is not King of Hungary. According to our laws the Hungarian only owes allegiance to a King who is legally crowned. The power of Francis Joseph, acquired by alien brute force, has not been confirmed either by coronation or by election. He is a usurper who has been solemnly condemned by the universal will of the nation.

"You owe obedience to the nation, because you owe allegiance to your country.

"As often as you wield your bayonet and strike with your sword for the defence of the oppressor of our country, you wound the heart of your dear country.

"A deserter is he who forsakes the flag of his country: the flag of our country is in our midst. To follow this is a sacred duty; to forsake it is to desert.

"Come hither, then, ye heroes! where your country and glory call you, and where the blessing of the nation awaits you. Hasten to join the ranks of your comrades which we have already formed. Hasten to assist us to overcome the difficulties in our way, so that, if God wills as we will, we may soon be able to say to you: 'Follow us home, ye heroes! to reassert the independence and liberty of our country, fighting on its sacred soil, assisted by the victorious arms of the allied powers!

"Long live the allied powers, the liberators of Italy, the friends of the Hungarian nation!

"Long live the independence of Hungary! Long live liberty! Long live our native country!

"Given at the Imperial French Headquarters,* at . . . . July . . 1859."

Many data have come into my hands on the strength of which I can unhesitatingly assert, that if we had appeared in the country with a French army, the whole

* I read a French translation of this proclamation to the Emperor, and when I had come as far as "given at the Imperial French Headquarters" the Emperor smiled and said: "It will be better after all if you write Turin or Genoa."—KOSSUTH

nation, without distinction of race, tongue, or creed, would have risen like one man. The history of Hungary cannot show another instance of such universal concurrence of opinion as existed at this time in the country.

I do not think it necessary to prove this by detailed facts. To what purpose would proof be?

But I believe that the subjoined report from Pulszky will be read with interest, as showing how the situation at home was looked upon by such notabilities as I have certainly never classed among the most resolute champions of the independence of Hungary.

Whether those notabilities judged the situation at home aright, I leave to the decision of those of my readers who knew all the circumstances of the time, and can recollect them.

"PULSZKY TO KOSSUTH.

"*London, August* 19*th*, 1859.

"Just after I had closed my yesterday's letter, one of the present notabilities of Hungary, M———r L———y, came and gave me the following picture of the country :—

"The peasant, in spite of the taxes, has been doing well along the Theiss and in the Alföld.* He is in a better position than before: he only knows one name, that of Kossuth, curses the Germans, waits for liberation, and is ready for sacrifice. The lower nobility are ruined; they have become like peasants. The owners of 200 acres of land are almost as poor as farm labourers; they cannot give their children an education. The landowners of the middle class are more economical than before; . . . there are fewer spendthrifts amongst them. The great landowners, except those who live in

* Alföld – low lands. Name of the great Hungarian plain between the Danube and the Theiss. (Translator's Note.)

Vienna, have become good Hungarians. Among all these, there lives but the one idea—that of nationality. They do not want democracy: even the lower nobility are afraid of you, as certain persons have made them believe that you are a socialist, and endeavour to bring about a division of property. In this respect your last speeches have had a good effect: they were translated from the *Times*, and circulate through the country in manuscript. They have also read your former speeches, but liked them less, because they regretted that you abused the Emperor of the French, and placed yourself on a bad footing with one of the possible factors in the liberation of our country. Your new alliance has made you more popular with this class. When the news of the occupation of Lussin arrived, everybody, from the boy of fifteen to the man of sixty, was ready to take up arms and join the French army. But they expected, and still expect more from the Russians. Russian agents continually travel about in the country, and they are listened to. A Catholic bishop said that, if he could by this means rid the country of the Germans, he would go over to the Greek Church with his whole flock. The municipal spirit in the towns is still strong: their mayors are Czechs; the properties of the towns are mortgaged; and hatred of Austria is at its height there. The daughters of the middle class in Pesth speak Hungarian; an Austrian officer cannot get a partner for a dance at a ball; and the old men complain that their sons forget to talk German at school—though they are taught the sciences in German—because the *esprit de corps* of the youths has banished the German tongue from their conversation. But there is one bad generation—those who in 1848 were fifteen or sixteen years old. These are timid, subservient; their patriotism shows itself solely in their speaking Hungarian; in other respects they are cowards. The present generation of young men and school-boys, on the other hand, is better than ever. The old opposition has spent itself, is cowed with fear, and lacks courage. The old conservatives are better; they are ready for anything. New talents have not arisen, perhaps because they have no opportunity to distinguish themselves.

"The agricultural societies are now the only institutions the existence of which is tolerated by Austria. Their number is now increased so that there is one in every province, and these are the germs of the national government; they represent the provinces.

"Apponyi and Samuel Josika, at the commencement of the war, pointed out to Francis Joseph that the country was ripe for insurrection, and that insurrection would break out if he did not grant concessions. Francis Joseph thanked them for having called his attention to the subject, and said that for once there could be no question of concessions as, if granted, they would justify the complaints of the Sardinian Government before the world. L———y continued that, hearing of this, he and his friends informed Apponyi that *they would not be satisfied with anything short of the entire fulfilment of the principle of personal union*,* and that he was still convinced that the time for concessions had gone, that every Hungarian believed that there would shortly be a new French or Russian war, and that either of these powers would grant more than Austria; that, however, they rather expected the Russians than the French. The conflict about the languages had ceased. The Croatians and Servians were friends of the Hungarian, because they knew that only through Hungary could they save themselves from the Germans.

"L———y also gave me much news about different personages which may prove useful to us, but which I cannot entrust to a letter.

"(Signed)   PULSZKY."

* And since? "Quantum (*not* mutatus, *but*) mutati ab illis!!"—KOSSUTH.

CHAPTER VII.

THE ARMISTICE.

I.

The Catastrophe of the Armistice—End to our Hopes.

OUR affairs were in the position described. Full of hope, Klapka remained at Turin to press forward the execution of the contracts which we had entered into for the equipment of the army. With a similar object, and in order to keep up good spirits and preserve discipline in the ranks of our army, I went to Genoa on July 6th. And lo! on July 8th the papers brought the intelligence that an *armistice had been concluded.*

This news struck us like a thunderbolt, but the matter seemed so utterly incredible that as a drowning man catches at a straw, we found our last glimmer of hope in the fact that the papers simply mentioned an armistice, without giving particulars as to its nature.*

---

* They could not have given particulars. On July 6th, the Emperor Napoleon in strictest secrecy wrote a letter to the Austrian Emperor at Verona, offering through General Fleury an armistice as a preliminary towards peace. Nobody knew of this. The Austrian Emperor answered on July 7th. He accepted the offer, and left it to the Emperor Napoleon to decide upon a place and time for their meeting. On July 8th, the armistice was concluded by Marshal Vaillant on behalf of France, Baron Hess on behalf of Austria, and Count Morozzo della Rocca on behalf of Sardinia. The two Emperors met at Villafranca on July 9th. They conferred together in the house of Guadini Morelli without any witnesses being present. Prince Napoleon took the conditions of peace to Verona on July 11th. Francis

We tried to quiet ourselves. "It is not a prelude to peace," we said, "but a mere armistice suspending hostilities for a few days only, as is sometimes the case in warfare." But we had to ascertain how we stood. Uncertainty threatened to make our position untenable. Therefore, without losing any time, I addressed the following letter to Senator Pietri:—

"KOSSUTH TO PIETRI.
"*Genoa, July 8th,* 1859.

"It is only a few days since, in the presence of your Excellency, I was fortunate enough to receive such reassuring promises from His Majesty the Emperor, as not only to justify me and my colleagues in entertaining the hope that in the course of the present war the work of re-establishing the independence of Hungary would be taken in hand, but, at the express desire of the Emperor and the Government of Turin, to induce us as rapidly as possible to hasten the organisation of the Hungarian army.

"Already the fifth battalion is in course of formation. Their spirits are very high, and we have used every exertion to strengthen this feeling. Being in need of officers, we have, with the sanction of the Government of Turin, withdrawn our exiled compatriots from the several situations they held; we have sent appeals to England, Turkey, and America, calling upon them to join our ranks; and at home we have done what was necessary to prepare the nation for insurrection.

"And, amidst these circumstances, the news that an armistice has been concluded has struck us like a thunderbolt from a clear sky.

Joseph raised difficulties on some points, whereat Prince Napoleon threatened him with revolution in Italy and *Hungary*. The principal conditions of peace were signed the same day by the Emperor of Austria in Verona at 8 p.m., and by the Emperor Napoleon at Valeggio at 10 p.m. And King Victor Emmanuel exclaimed, "*Povera Italia!*"

"I would gladly seek reassurance as to its meaning in my own thoughts, without troubling your Excellency with a request for instructions, but I cannot conceal the fact that I and my colleagues are at a loss to understand the position which we shall have to assume in consequence of an armistice having been agreed to. If this armistice is a preliminary to peace, there will be an end to the activity which we were invited to display, and we stand seriously compromised. But we are prevented from believing that the armistice has such a meaning by the consideration that it can only be the preliminary to such a peace as would not satisfy the ends the Emperor has in view, would disappoint public opinion in Italy, all over Europe, and even in France itself; it would leave unsolved, not only the final settlement (which pre-supposes the independence of Hungary), but also the temporary solution of the Italian question; instead of securing peace to Europe, it would give rise to discontent and disturbances, would make it unavoidable that the war should be resumed in a short time, but under less favourable circumstances, and would even sow the germs of a future European coalition against France.

"These considerations lead us to hope that the armistice does not possess the meaning of peace preliminaries. In this case, however, we are still less able to reassure ourselves as to our position, for we fear that this armistice will render it very difficult to carry out the projects of the Emperor with regard to Hungary. I am convinced that this armistice will only serve the interest of Austria.

"From a tactical point of view, there is scarcely anything more dangerous than to stop an army which through great victories feels itself invincible, and to give time to an adversary to recover from demoralisation.

"Since the battle of Solferino the moral power of the Austrian army has been so much broken that it can scarcely accept another open battle; on the other hand, the provinces in Hungary commence to refuse recruiting, and generally the feelings of the people are so excited that, as we know from trustworthy sources, the military commanders pressingly urge for reinforcements, but are answered from Vienna that it is utterly impossible for the Austrian Government to send a single soldier to Hungary, and that conflicts with the populace are to be avoided at any price.

"In a word, the existence of the House of Austria as a first-rate power depends upon the Emperor's sufferance.

"In consequence of the armistice, all these circumstances will change in favour of Austria. The self-confidence of her demoralised army will be raised by the simple fact of an armistice having been concluded; the drafting in of fresh troops will re-establish it, by creating doubt as to the future; she may put a stop to that disintegrating process which has set in by the raising of the Hungarian flag in Italy; the armistice will shake the Hungarian nation in its determination; and if, while on one side the prospect of being forsaken will weaken the enthusiastic fervour, Austria, on the other side, grants some concessions, as it is to be expected she will do, it may be feared that the co-operation of Hungary will be irretrievably jeopardised.

"However, the Emperor has no doubt taken into consideration these consequences of the armistice, and, therefore, especially while confined to our present position, I cannot conceal from your Excellency that we have been brought into a most dreadful position by the conclusion of this armistice.

"What will become of our poor country, which has rejoiced at the news of our movements here—movements brought about by the sanction of His Majesty the Emperor; which has waited for our word of command; and, on hearing of the unexpected news, will despond of any better future, unless we can reassure it without loss of time.

"How shall we stand before our brave comrades who, trusting to our word, have enlisted under our flag?

"How shall we be able to deter them from taking desperate steps when they see their hopes thus baffled and themselves victimised? It was only yesterday that by the hope of our prospects I encouraged them to resolution, discipline, order, and patriotic self-sacrifice; and to-day, if they ask what they can expect, to what they can trust, we cannot answer them.

"It is but natural that these unfortunate men should ask what fate awaits them.

"And we ourselves, how shall we stand before these compatriots of ours, before our country and the world?

"There is no need for me to depict to your Excellency the dreadful position we are in. You will no doubt agree with me that our situation has, through the armistice, become untenable. For this reason I beg your Excellency, and I do so also in the name of my colleagues, to intercede with the Emperor that our position may be made clear.

"What can we expect? What are we to do? Shall we issue the proclamation submitted to the Emperor? Shall we go on with our armaments? Shall we extend them? And if not, what shall we do with those 4,000 soldiers who have collected round our banner?

"Interests of such immense importance are here at stake that it is impossible I should not urgently implore your Excellency to be kind enough to ascertain His Majesty's decisions with regard to us, and to communicate them to us.

"Accept, etc.
"(Signed) KOSSUTH."

Senator Pietri, in reply to this letter, informed me verbally that he only knew as much as he could learn from the papers. He did not understand, could not comprehend the matter, and believed it was impossible, so unexpected and so awful was it. He telegraphed to the Emperor and sent my letter by a courier. *"C'est impossible! impossible!"* There must be something behind the matter which we did not understand. He said that we should not lose hope, but wait. Meanwhile, we should go on with our work as if nothing had happened.

We went on amidst dreadful mental agony. In a few days Pietri came rushing to me with agitated mien and said, "*Malheur! malheur à nous! C'est fini. Tout est perdu! Lisez ceci!*"

He handed me an autograph letter addressed to him by the Emperor. I wept like a child, and could scarcely read it. The contents of the letter were to the following effect: "We have well considered the matter on all sides with the Prince and the King, and, however reluctantly, have come to the conclusion that we must make peace. This time we cannot go farther. There is now an end to the war. Tell M. Kossuth that I am extremely sorry that the liberation of his country must now be left alone. I cannot do otherwise. It is an impossibility. But I beg him not to lose heart, but to trust to me and the future. Meanwhile he may be assured of my friendly feelings towards him, and I beg him to dispose of me with regard to his own person and his children."

When I came to this point of the letter I could not control myself sufficiently to prevent my revolted feelings from venting themselves in a bitter exclamation. "Yes! yes!" I said, "such are those crowned heads! Such is their idea of the creature that is called 'man.' To the wind with the fatherland! A bag full of money to the man, and he will console himself! Senator, pray tell your master that His Majesty the Emperor of the French is not rich enough to offer alms to Louis Kossuth, and Louis Kossuth is not mean enough to accept them. He has turned me out of my position. Well, my sons will gain our living by their work. *Je vous salue.*"

All was over! There was nothing left to be done except to look after the honourable dissolution of our army, and the personal safety of those poor brave Hungarian fellows who had enlisted in it. Klapka saw the matter in the same light at Turin, whence he wrote the following letter to me at Genoa :—

"KLAPKA TO THE NATIONAL HUNGARIAN COMMITTEE IN GENOA.
" *Turin, July* 13*th*, 1859.

"I have just left Count Cavour. He has sent in his resignation. He is out of his mind in consequence of the indescribably miserable behaviour. It was Prince Napoleon more especially who insisted upon peace, who complained of everybody, of the Italians, of the Hungarians, and took upon himself to formulate* the peace preliminaries at the Austrian headquarters. Here everybody is downcast. Cavour has promised that he will provide for the legion. It is absolutely necessary that both the members of the Committee should at once come here to settle this matter, for in these quarters there is henceforth nothing for us to do. They used us to frighten Francis Joseph, to induce him to cede Lombardy as soon as possible. Since the meeting of the Emperors, Napoleon has not even received Cavour. That is how matters stand; I await your arrival. We have only one or two days left, therefore hurry yourselves.

" (Signed) KLAPKA."

We (Pietri, Teleki, and myself) therefore started for Turin, to settle this matter.

The settlement, during the negotiation of which many difficulties and unpleasantnesses arose, is treated of in another place.

* Rather to gain acceptance for them. He took the points prepared with him from Valeggio.

II.

Two Interesting Episodes—Security of Tuscany against Foreign Interference—Important Statement by Cavour.

In Turin two episodes occurred which I think worthy of note. Both are interesting. The second, furthermore, is an important historical incident.

I. We watched from our hotel window, which opened upon the *piazza* in front of the Royal Palace, as the Emperor and the King drove up in an open carriage. There were but few people in the square. Not a single "Evviva" was to be heard. Few people even raised their hats. *Sic transit gloria mundi!*

Late in the evening the brave (mutilated) Montanelli and Celestino Bianchi (afterwards confidential Under-Secretary of State to the Minister Ricasoli) came to me, and in the name of the Revolutionary Government of Tuscany requested that as we no longer stood in need of our legion we should give it to them—on loan! I laughed in their faces. "Gentlemen," I said, "we are not the masters of the legion, nor are we captains of *condottieri*, and our legionaries are neither slaves nor mercenaries. They are free men who were led by love of their country to join the Hungarian flag; but only that flag. If there is a man amongst us who is willing to accept your proposal, that is a matter to be arranged between himself and you; but we do not offer the insult to our countrymen of negotiating about their lives. Let us drop the subject; but I, as a friend of Italy, ask you, fortunate men, Why do you trouble yourselves about legions? Against whom do you wish to lead your legions, unless against the few dozen flunkeys in the Pitti Palace? for the Grand Duke of Tuscany does not stand at the head of an army. You are lucky men. You require a *plebiscite*, a ballot-box, but not an army. And then, excuse me, you do not calculate rightly. To take foreign mercenaries into your pay might provoke foreign intervention. Beware of this provocation. If you do not offer it, your affairs will go perfectly smoothly."

Bianchi. "But it is just because we are afraid of intervention that we are on the look-out for an army, and your legion is an organised force."

Kossuth. "Do not fear intervention. If you took a foreign legion into Tuscany there might be an intervention, because your movement would not possess the distinction of being of a purely Tuscan character. Perhaps it would assume larger proportions, and possibly there might be a powerful personage who would say, ' *Ça ne me va pas, je ne me laisserai pas déborder par la révolution*.' But if you strictly confine yourselves to the concerns of Tuscany, *after what has happened*, you need not be afraid of intervention. There will be none."

Montanelli. " Do you assure us of it ?"

Kossuth. "My dear, brave friend, with *my* assurances you certainly could not achieve much ; but I will tell you something." I took him to my window. " Do you see the light in that window on the second floor of the Royal Palace? It burns in the study of the King, and shows that His Majesty is still up. Go thither; tell the door-keeper to say to the King that *Tuscany* wishes to speak with him. True it is past midnight; but be not afraid, Piedmont will receive Tuscany even after midnight. Say to His Majesty, 'Sire, Kossuth tells Tuscany that there will be no intervention; is it true or not?' You will hear what he answers."

Montanelli rushed away. It was bright moonlight. I watched him from the window running across the square towards the Royal Palace, violently gesticulating with his one arm. He returned triumphantly in half-an-hour, and embraced me. "There will be no intervention! no intervention! the King has given me his word of honour."

"*Ecco!* Let me congratulate you! Lucky men!"

II. I went to Cavour's in company with Pietri, to discuss the arrangements for effecting an honourable dissolution of the legion. When we had entered, and had taken seats, Pietri commenced the conversation by saying, "It is rumoured, Your Excellency, that you have resigned. I hope this is not true."

Cavour. "It is true. I have resigned."

Pietri. "Oh! that is to be deplored, much to be deplored. The Emperor will be very sorry to hear it."

Cavour. "What do you say? In politics men often dispose of time and means, sometimes sacrifice even necessary principles; but there is one thing a human being never barters with; that one thing is honour. Your Emperor has disgraced me; yes, sir, *disgraced* me; *il m'a déshonoré*. My Lord and my God! He gave me his word, took an oath, that he would not stop until Austria had been finally driven out of Italy; in return, he stipulated that Savoy and Nice should be ceded to him. I persuaded my King to accept the bargain, to submit himself to this sacrifice for the sake of Italy.

My good and honest King, trusting to my word, agreed.
And now, your Emperor takes his reward, and deserts
us shamefully half-way. We are to be content with
Lombardy, and, to improve the bargain still, he wishes
to fetter my King with confederation with Austria
and the other Italian princes, under the presidency of
the Pope. I stand dishonoured before my King.
Dreadful! dreadful!"

Kossuth. " Dreadful, indeed! The Court of Vienna
itself has already—in 1848—offered unconditional surrender of the line of the Mincio (Lombardy). I know
this because I was then Minister, and had to do with
the question. And the provisional government of Lombardy was sufficiently Italian, sufficiently patriotic, not
to accept this offer without Venice being included.
And now you receive that same territory as a reward
for so much bloodshed. And you do not even receive
it gratuitously as the Lombardians might have done.
You must give in return Nice and Savoy. And then
that idea of a confederation! I picture to myself
the King of Piedmont as seventh in that grotesque
company over which the Pope presides, with Austria at
his right, and by her side the four Austrian satellites.
If Victor Emmanuel accepts that position, he lowers himself to the rank of a *prince médiatisé.*"

Cavour. " That is true—perfectly true. But I tell
you, and I say it before this gentleman, and to say it
before him is tantamount to telling it to his Emperor:
*Cette paix ne se fera pas: ce traité ne s'executera pas. Je
prendrai par une main Solaro della Margarita, par l'autre
Mazzini s'il le faut! je me ferai conspirateur!"* (striking
his chest) *" revolutionnaire! mais ce traité ne s'executera*

*pas. Non! mille fois non! Jamais, jamais!"** . . . .
(After a short pause, during which Pietri sat with downcast eyes, without speaking a word): "*Eh bien!* The Emperor of the French goes. Let him go! But I and you, M. Kossuth, we continue on our own way. Shall we not? We two shall accomplish what the Emperor of the French did not dare to finish. And, *pardieu*, we shall not stop half way!" (*Nous ne nous arrêterons pas à mi-chemin.*")

Kossuth. "Depend upon me, Your Excellency!"

This important statement of Cavour was the prologue to what passed between us in September, 1860.

But, dear Hungary, fate persecutes thee!

Cavour died in the spring of 1861.

---

* "This peace shall not come to pass! this treaty shall not be executed. I will take Solaro della Margarita" (the leader of the Clerical-Conservative party) "by the one hand and Mazzini by the other. If necessary I will become a conspirator! a revolutionist! but this treaty shall not be executed. No! a thousand times no! Never, never!"

CHAPTER VIII.

Contribution to the History of the Dissolution of the Hungarian Army in Italy.

IN the perplexity into which we were thrown by the first intelligence of the armistice of Villafranca, we caught at the hope, as a drowning man catches at a straw, that perhaps, after all, the armistice might not possess the character of a peace preliminary.

But this last ray of hope soon disappeared, and there was nothing left to us but to think of the honourable dissolution of the Hungarian army.

In the agreement of Villafranca only this much was stipulated: "A complete and plenary amnesty shall be assured by both of the belligerent powers, within their territory, to all persons compromised by late events." *

As we had undertaken the formation of an army not as our own venture, but at the instigation of the friendly powers, we could not be satisfied with this general stipulation of the amnesty, and considered that we could justly demand greater securities for those men of the Hungarian army who might decide upon returning home; that those, however, who did not go back to Hungary should be provided for, and individually receive an indemnification.

What we could obtain at once, and what we received encouraging promises about, will appear from the sub-

* "Traités publiques de la Maison de Savoye," Vol. VIII., page 660.

joined farewell address of the Hungarian National Committee to the army.

"THE HUNGARIAN NATIONAL COMMITTEE TO COLONELS AND COMMANDERS OF BRIGADE, DANIEL IHÁSZ AND NICHOLAS KISS.

"*Turin, July* 16*th*, 1859.

"We have already acquainted you that we have been officially informed by the Emperor of the French and the Piedmontese Government that, in the main conditions of the peace which has so unexpectedly put an end to our hopes, a general amnesty is stipulated for those who wish to return home.

"Being most solicitous about the fate of our brave countrymen, we deemed it incumbent upon us to urge that at the final ratification of the peace it should also be clearly stipulated that those who by virtue of this amnesty decide to return home, should not again be forced by the Emperor of Austria to do military service.

"It is a consolation to us that we are able to inform you that, yielding to our intercession, the Emperor of the French has promised to insert this condition in the peace.

"The allied powers have also promised to provide the necessary means of transport for those who wish to return home. Meanwhile the brigades will be preserved in their present state, under observance of the usual discipline; the officers, non-commissioned officers, and men will continue to participate in the same provisions as hitherto.

"The foregoing conditions are to be communicated to the men by general order, the officers to be informed besides that we have solicited and obtained from the allied powers permission to give them some indemnification as far as the money at our disposal will permit. The cashier of the committee has received the necessary instructions regarding this.

"Please to inform those gentlemen who were here promoted from non-commissioned officers to be officers, that it is for the interest of those who wish to return home not to adhere to their rank as officers in the lists of names which are to be prepared, as their rank would be taken as a sign of having entered active service against Austria, and they would either not be allowed to return as officers or expose themselves to persecution. Besides, their rank as officers could only have value at home in case the struggle for independence were resumed afresh; whenever this much wished-for day may arrive, it is a matter of course that their claim to the rank to which they have now been promoted will remain intact.

" We have further hope of procuring for the non-commissioned officers and the privates, on their departure, fifteen days' additional pay.

" General Klapka will remain here for some time yet, to complete his duties as commander of the army. Our corporate position as Committee, however, will for the present cease so far as the brave army is concerned.

" We dissolve this Committee with sorrow, but not without hope; bent by the sight of our ruined hopes, but not broken. We return to the path of joyless exile—ready to endure and suffer if necessary; determined to act whenever it is possible. No adversity will ever shake our sense of duty towards our country, and to this sense of duty there is added a conviction which, in spite of the unfortunate end, is confirmed by the present relations, namely, that the independence of our country is an inevitable condition of bringing Europe into a settled state, and one without which the Italian, or any other important European question, cannot be solved. It is, therefore, a religious belief with us that a free and independent future is in store for our country, if only our people individually and collectively remain true to themselves.

" We return into exile with the consciousness, the basis of which will not remain hidden from our nation and history, that we should have sinned against our duty as good citizens, had we neglected to try, when invited to co-operate at a time when a tremendous onslaught against the oppressor of our country was in preparation, whether we could not turn the prospects offered into an opportunity for accomplishing the liberation of our country.

" Fate decided otherwise; but we are consoled by the consciousness, which we are prepared to prove, that we placed our activity on a basis and obtained securities which, had the war not so soon and unexpectedly come to an end, would have placed the reassertion of our country's independence within the grasp of the manly determination of our nation, and which have, now that peace is concluded, at least saved our suffering country from a great misfortune.

"This is also a consolation, because the future of our country has remained unprejudiced, and without our precaution it might have been jeopardised.

"And now nothing remains but to say 'Good bye' to our comrades, and we do so with great emotion.

"For their faithful co-operation, we thank all those who have lent us a helping hand in the difficult task of accomplishing our sacred duty towards our country.

"We thank our brave comrades for the instinctive readiness with which, following the sacred impulse of their hearts, and full of love for their country, they joined our ranks.

"This readiness is an expression of the uncorrupted spirit of the nation, which only wants an opportunity to break the foreign yoke a foreign force has placed upon our necks.

"The opportunity may be delayed, but it will arrive, and with it the joyous day of the liberation of our country.

"We return thanks for the manly dignity and uprightness which have not only preserved the Hungarian name stainless in a foreign country, but have produced amongst the people here, and also in the judgment of the Powers, faith, trust, respect, and sympathy for the Hungarians. Let those who return to the country of our birth faithfully and unremittingly nourish in their bosoms the sacred flame of patriotism, and, as they carry with them our esteem and fraternal love, so we part from them in the belief that when Providence shall deem that our nation has suffered sufficiently, and shall cause the dawn of liberation to rise on the sad horizon of our country, the scattered members of the Hungarian army formed in Italy will rise again and distinguish themselves in the defence of their country and their liberty.

"Carry our greetings to our beloved country, and God speed you on your journey.

"A better future to our suffering country!
"The Hungarian National Committee.
" (Signed)   Kossuth, *President*.
" (Signed)   Ladislaus Teleki.
" (Signed)   General Klapka."

However, the fate of those members of our army who wished to return home depended upon the agreement of the powers negotiating the peace. And even to make a beginning in this agreement was no easy matter. France and Austria had decided that they would at once send plenipotentiaries to Zurich to change the preliminary stipulations of Villafranca into a treaty of peace. Hoping to have the matter settled speedily, they concluded the armistice till August 16th only.

The French Government, through their Ambassador, Prince La Tour d'Auvergne, invited the Cabinet of Turin, as early as July 19th, also to send a plenipotentiary to Zurich, but the Government of Turin first wished to know on which points it was intended to extend the negotiations. For King Victor Emmanuel had signed the preliminaries of Villafranca with the proviso that he should assume the responsibility only on those points which had reference to himself. He did this because the agreement of Villafranca also stipulated that the Princes of Tuscany and Modena should have their possessions restored to them, and that the two Emperors would promote the formation of an Italian Confederation ("*favorisent la création d'une confédération italienne*") of which Austria would also be a member by virtue of the possession of Venice. The Government of Turin by no means wished to give their consent to the restitution of the dethroned princes, or to limit the liberty of action of the people of Central Italy; and of the contemplated confederation, they (in Turin) were decided opponents, for they were very rightly convinced that if the project were carried out, the House of Savoy and Piedmont would not only be deprived of their rightful influence on Italian affairs, but would in reality become the vassals of the Emperor of Austria. In consequence of these difficulties the conferences of Zurich were delayed from the beginning. The plenipotentiary of Sardinia, Louis Desambrois, before going to Zurich paid a flying visit to Paris to gain information about the intentions of the Emperor. On August 3rd he was still in Paris, and when at last the conference was opened at Zurich, so many difficulties arose from the beginning that the first term of the armistice (August 16th) came and the negotiations had not yet led to any tangible result. They were spun out for four whole months, and only terminated on November 10th.

Uncertainty creates impatience. Uneasiness commenced to take possession of the ranks of our poor army, which felt as if confined to a *siralomház.** Serious excesses occurred, and the impatience had already at the beginning of August become so great as to increase more and more the number of those who wished to return home without any guarantee. The position of General Klapka, who, as Commander-in-Chief, had remained in Italy to superintend the dissolution of the forces, became daily more difficult. He himself took

* A room where, in days gone by, persons condemned to death were publicly exhibited prior to their execution. (Translator's Note.)

steps, and he requested me to do the same, to urge the Government in Paris to accelerate the solution of the question.

I prepared the following memorandum to be presented to the Emperor:—

"Memorial.

" A few days after we had, on the occasion of my last reception by the Emperor, agreed upon the conditions which were to serve as a basis for the organisation of the Hungarian army in Italy, we were surprised by the news of the Peace of Villafranca just at the very moment when we had taken in hand the execution of the task cast upon us.

" Therefore no time was allowed to complete our task.

" The consequence was that in the hope of being dismissed, the Hungarian forces remained without discipline, and, as they had no arms, unfit for service too; so that the difficulties of their disorganised state were further increased by the idleness enforced upon the men.

" We had no means in our hands of counteracting the drawbacks of this situation, except the moral influence which we could bring to bear upon the troops.

" Nevertheless, such was the spirit of the men that in spite of their dearest hopes being frustrated, this moral influence, combined with the promises the Emperor had made, were sufficient to prevent the want of discipline being perceived in deplorable consequences, all the while that the members of the army were supported in their resignation by the prospect of being able to return to their country, if not sooner, at least at the end of the first term of the armistice (August 16th), protected by the guarantees which they were allowed to hope for in consequence of the encouragements we gave with the sanction of His Majesty the Emperor.

" Meanwhile the armistice has been prolonged for two months, the peace conferences of Zurich are delayed, and the uncertainty arising from these circumstances having shaken to its very foundation the faith of the unfortunate men, not only create uneasiness among the ranks, but also gives room to agitation, which having already increased from voiceless discontent to loud complaints, may lead to attempts at the overthrow of order which we could not possibly suppress if the present uncertainty were to prevail any longer, and if the redemption of the given promises were deferred any further.

"In this state of affairs we, the members of the Hungarian National Committee constituted by desire of the Emperor, could no longer take the responsibility of preserving order in the ranks of the Hungarian army in Italy, because it would be the less possible for us to perform the duties connected with this responsibility, as the exchange of the Austrian prisoners of war has already been effected completely. Therefore we should not know what to say to those who, responding to the powerful words uttered by the Emperor, have gathered round the standard of national independence, and who felt so fortunate at being able to sacrifice their lives for the noble object which appeared to them to be identical with the cause of their own country.

"And there is another consideration still, and it belongs to a higher class of ideas.

"Though the turn of events is against us, even in the depth of grief to which we have been brought by the annihilation of our hopes, we will not and cannot part with the consoling belief that the benevolent feelings entertained by the Emperor towards our unhappy country have not changed.

"Animated by this belief, we fervently wish that, in return for these benevolent feelings, our nation may preserve that grateful trust in the Emperor which we were so fortunate as to perceive diffused among all classes of our nation on their hearing the news of those truly international relations which, at the beginning of the Italian war, were established under the auspices of His Majesty the Emperor, and which certainly will not be without importance in regard to those European difficulties with which the future is laden.

"But our wish in this respect could not be realised if the postponement of the guarantees given to the Hungarian army in Italy were to be accompanied by some lamentable excess, or if the return of the men without the promised stipulations were such a source of trouble and difficulties as to give them cause to regret having preferred service in the Hungarian army to the position of prisoners of war.

"We have heard with feelings of sincere gratitude that His Majesty the Emperor has deigned to give instructions not only with respect to the amnesty, but also that the members of our army should be exempted from Austrian military service, and sent home to their families free of expense to themselves.

"But considering the incalculable misfortunes with which we are threatened in case of further delaying the settlement of the questions to be solved prior to the final dissolution of the Hungarian army, we are obliged to petition His Majesty the Emperor to furnish his Zurich plenipotentiaries with the necessary instructions that the affair of the Hungarian army in Italy—though unimportant when compared with the other topics of the Conference, but most important to us, and also very urgent—should no longer be kept in suspense, but independently of the other conditions of the peace, and in conformity with the directions of the Emperor, should as soon as possible be decided in such a manner that, besides the amnesty stipulated in the agreement of Villafranca, the final dismissal (*congé définitif*) from military service and the free journey home should also be assured.

"May God grant that the realisation of the promised guarantees may not arrive too late.

"(Signed)   KOSSUTH.
"President of the Hungarian National Committee.
"*Vevey, August 20th,* 1859."

I wished this memorial to reach its destination through Pietri, as the Emperor had designated *him* the mediator between us. But as I also wished that it should be handed to the Emperor without delay, in case Pietri were absent, I sent the memorial to Paris by Colonel Emerich Szabó, the informant of the Committee on military matters, with instructions to address himself to Prince Napoleon in the absence of Pietri, who, at the request of General Klapka, had already used his influence with the Emperor in the interests of our men.

I subjoin a copy of my letter to Pietri :—

"KOSSUTH TO SENATOR PIETRI.
" *Vevey, August* 20*th*, 1859.

"The first term of the armistice expired on August 15th without the guarantees in favour of the Hungarian army in Italy having been definitely settled, and the dismissal of the men on their basis being rendered possible. In consequence of this, doubt, uneasiness, and impatience have taken possession of our ranks to such an extent that our position with regard to the army, which has been painful ever since the fatal day of Villafranca, has now, in the truest sense of the word, become wholly untenable.

" If in consequence of the protraction of the Conferences of Zurich the uncertainty were further prolonged, we fear we should not be able to avert disorders and *émeutes* in connection therewith.

" It is sufficient that we leave the situation in Italy with so much grief. We should wish at least to leave it without public scandal; we should wish to leave it without ourselves doing, or allowing our men to do the least thing which would be out of accord with the respectful consideration which we owe to the Emperor, and of which we should wish to give proof with the greatest discretion.

" In this state of affairs, patriotic duty and honour and humanity alike force me to appeal once more to the goodwill, or rather the pity, of the Emperor.

" As the two letters which we sent to you through my colleague, Ladislaus Teleki, have remained unanswered, we are afraid that some irregularities may have occurred in the postal arrangements. Considering the urgency of the present matter, I deemed it wise to send the bearer of these lines, Colonel Emerich Szabó, to Paris with instructions to hand to your Excellency a memorial of mine, and with the request that you will kindly submit it to the Emperor, and with your accustomed benevolence recommend it to his consideration.

"Colonel Szabó is further instructed to make to you, or (should he receive his commands) to the Emperor himself, a detailed report about the state of the Hungarian army in Italy.

"Permit me, your Excellency, to ask for your sympathetic interest in this matter, which is not less serious than urgent.

"I leave the Continent heart-broken. My journey will take me to Paris on or about September 2nd. I should very much like to shake your hand cordially and say 'good-bye' to you, and thank you for the sympathy you have shown to my unfortunate country, and for all the kindness you were good enough to bestow on me personally.

"I remain, etc.,
"(Signed) KOSSUTH."

As Senator Pietri was absent from Paris, Colonel Szabó, in accordance with his instructions, requested Prince Napoleon to forward my memorial to the Emperor. The Prince readily complied with his request, and at once sent my memorial, accompanied by a letter of recommendation of his own, by special courier to the Emperor at Biarritz.

From the report of Colonel Szabó (August 23rd) as to what the Prince said to him on this occasion, I think it worth while to quote the remark of the Prince that he did not like to hear that I was about to return to England, and that he was desirous of dissuading me from doing so. He said that Englishmen were egotistic; for years they had been agitating for the independence and liberty of Italy, and now that there was a prospect of realising their wishes, England was the greatest obstacle to the execution of the Emperor's intentions. He thought it would be better that I should remain in France, and cultivate my connection with the Emperor, which had made a good impression upon him; for as no question had been solved, the present state of affairs could not be permanent.

The Emperor's reply to my memorial was communicated to Colonel Szabó, by a letter of which I subjoin a copy:—

"*Paris, Sept. 3rd,* 1859.

"His Imperial Highness Prince Napoleon has been informed by the Emperor that Monsieur Bourqueney has a written promise from Count Rechberg, the Austrian Minister, that the soldiers of the Hungarian legion formed in Italy will be sent back to their homes (*seront renvoyés dans leurs foyers*). I am instructed by the Prince to request you to communicate this to M. Kossuth, in reply to his memorial.

"Believe me, etc.,
"(Signed)   Em. Hubaine.
"Private Secretary to the Prince.

"*To* Colonel Szabó."

The Austrian Government had then promised so much,—that our soldiers should be sent back to their homes.

I could not possibly rest satisfied with this ambiguous expression. Liberally constructed, it might have comprised final dismissal from military service, but it might also have meant temporary leave, and even less than this; and certainly we could not flatter ourselves with the illusion that the Austrian Government would put a favourable interpretation upon it.

General Klapka, who being on the spot could personally follow with attention the disposition of our men, shared my view, and in his letter of September 6th he asked me to apply to Prince Napoleon, and through him to the Emperor, that the ambiguous expression which had given rise to so much apprehension should be interpreted in a more reassuring sense, and the interpretation telegraphed to the General, as the discontent had taken such possession of the ranks that the dissolution could no longer be deferred without the danger of scandal and disorders.

This letter from General Klapka reached me in Paris as I was on my way back to England. I at once went to Prince Napoleon. He found that our apprehensions were well founded; he promised to intercede on our behalf, and as the Emperor was still at Biarritz, he (the Prince) requested me to prepare a note which he would forward with the greatest despatch to the Emperor, at the same time strongly supporting it.

Without loss of time I prepared a note the same day (September 8th). In it I stated that the expression "*seront renvoyés dans leurs foyers*" was much too ambiguous to assure to those of our soldiers who intended to go home complete exemption from further military service; that it was even so indefinite as to leave room for fear that, if the explanation rested with the discretion of the Austrian Government, it would be so construed in its execution as to make even the amnesty illusory. I therefore begged the Emperor to telegraph to his Plenipotentiary at Zurich, Monsieur Bourqueney, to obtain from Austria at once such an explanation as would afford security that by the expression "*renvoyés dans leurs foyers*," not a temporary leave of absence was understood, but final dismissal and exemption from further service. I also insisted in my note that the practical accomplishment of the dismissal made the appointment of special *ad hoc* Commissioners necessary, so that every soldier should receive a document which would prove the amnesty and the man's exemption from further military service. The dismissals after the capitulation of Komárom in 1849 were carried out in this way. It was therefore necessary that Monsieur Bourqueney should receive instructions to induce the Austrian Government to appoint a Commissioner and send him to Alessandria.

Prince Napoleon again manifested the sympathy for the Hungarians of which he had constantly given proofs. He sent my note the same day (September 8th) to the Emperor to Biarritz, supporting it warmly himself.

But for my note to go to Biarritz, for instructions to be sent thence to Zurich, for the negotiations there to be completed, and for the Austrian Plenipotentiary to receive a decision from Vienna—for this again to be communicated to the Emperor at Biarritz, and by him sent to Turin, naturally, took some days, and only by the use of the telegraph was it possible that the matter was after all settled within eight days.

Meanwhile the impatience of our troops manifested itself in such scenes as to render it impossible to keep the fast-dissolving army any longer together. General Klapka was therefore obliged, on the basis of the agreement come to with General Lamarmora, the Sardinian Minister of War, to take in hand the dissolution of the army and the transport of those who wished to return home before the result of the steps I had taken in Paris became known.

Fortunately, before the transport in smaller troops had been completed, the following message arrived at Turin, by telegraph, from the Emperor Napoleon (September 16th):—

"EMPEREUR AU ROI DE SARDAIGNE (TURIN).

" Le Comte de Rechberg a promis par écrit que les Hongrois de la Légion étrangère (hongroise) seront amnistiés et dégagés de tout service militaire. *Biarritz,* le 16 Sept."

This telegram was communicated to General Klapka while he was occupied with the transport of the men, and he was able to give those returning home as much consolation as can be derived from a written promise of the Austrian Government.

We took the necessary steps to inform ourselves whether the word given had been adhered to—whether the given promise had been redeemed.

The word was not adhered to, and the promise was not redeemed. " Es ist eine alte Geschichte, doch bleibt sie immer neu," says Heine. Of this faithlessness of Austria to her word I shall speak in the second volume of my " Memories."

The army which we took to be the vanguard of Hungarian liberty, was therefore dissolved.

Of the men, more than 4,000 in number who had gathered round the Hungarian standard, and who had mostly been recruited from prisoners of war, only ninety-five chose to remain in exile. The others were overpowered by home-sickness. If they could not return as champions of liberty, they returned home to endure and suffer. Under the command of a Hungarian captain, and accompanied by a Piedmontese officer, they were transported in troops of from 600 to 800 at a time, to Desenzano on the Austrian frontier, where they were handed over to the Austrian commander of the fortress of Peschiera, and all collected again at Verona, where they were classified according to their counties, and sent on to Hungary, "*dans leurs foyers*," as it has been said. But only said. Many of them never again set eyes upon their homesteads.

The Piedmontese Government took every care that our soldiers should be well provided with everything, and leave Italian soil with pleasant recollections. The transport by rail as far as the frontier was done gratuitously. Each man received fifteen days' pay, a military cloak, linen, and rations of bread and meat for the way. Each man who started for home received a letter of discharge, signed on behalf of the Sardinian Minister of War by General Pettiti, in which it was stated that the bearer thereof was one of those Hungarian soldiers who were amnestied by the agreement of Villafranca, and to whom the representatives of the parties who negotiated peace at Zurich had assured a free return to their homesteads.

A free passage had been secured to those who wished to go to the Danubian Principalities or to America. twenty-seven men went to the former place and twenty-four to the latter.

To the officers—to those who returned home as well

as to those who remained abroad—a gratuity equal to three months' pay was voted by the Piedmontese Government; and Senator Pietri, by command of the Emperor Napoleon, contributed 100,000 francs, which we distributed among the officers according to their rank. Of the non-commissioned officers and privates who decided to remain abroad, each private received 100, each corporal 120, and each sergeant-major 150 francs from the sum left of the cash which was transferred to the brigades.

Of the forty-three officers who had been employed in the dissolved Hungarian army twelve returned home, eleven went back to their former places of exile, and four (amongst whom my true friend and faithful sharer of my exile, Colonel Ihász) were admitted as officers on half pay (*in aspettativa*) into the Piedmontese service; sixteen officers and thirty-two non-commissioned officers and privates entered the service of Modena.

The last troop left Alessandria by rail on September 18th, 1859, for the Austrian frontier.

Of the Hungarian army in Italy nothing but the memory is left.

Consummatum erat.

I have mentioned that several of the members of our dissolved army enlisted in the service of Modena.

Lest anybody should by "Modena" understand that Duke of Modena who would have liked to colonise the Croatians from the Military Frontier along the French frontier, it will not be without interest to explain shortly what Modena it was in whose service my brave countrymen enlisted.

When the war between Austria and Sardinia had

broken out (April 29th) the inhabitants of the provinces of Massa and Carrara demolished the symbols of the Duke of Modena's rule, and proclaimed the King of Sardinia Dictator. The Government of Turin declared war against the Duke of Modena, assigning as a reason that, in spite of protests, and to the detriment of Sardinia, he had obstinately adhered to his treaty with Austria, which was opposed to European treaties, and that, besides, he had in his possessions accorded perfect liberty to Austria in her preparations for her attack on Piedmont.* The Duke of Modena asked for help from Vienna. Count Rechberg (who was the successor of Count Buol-Schauenstein in the control of foreign affairs in Austria, answered that the Emperor was exceedingly sorry that, being engaged with a powerful adversary, he could not spare a single battalion, and when the Minister Plenipotentiary of the Duke at Vienna, Count Volo, exclaimed in terror, that in that case his master and Prince would be obliged to leave his country, Count Rechberg said that he himself did not see that he (the Duke) had any alternative left; but he consoled Count Volo with the fact that Austria would take the Duke back to his throne.

The Duchess of Parma received a like consolation.

The Duke of Modena (Francis V.) left his country on June 11th. He took 3,000 Modenese soldiers with him, emptied all the cash-boxes of the public service of their contents (he found 2,690,000 Italian lire in them), and took with him all the silver objects and ornaments belonging to the crown, even the coins from the collections

* Note of Count Cavour to Forni, Minister of Modena (May 7th, 1859).

in the museums, and the valuable codices and manuscripts from the libraries. He also had eighty political offenders put into irons, and carried them with him to Mantua.

The reigning Duchess of Parma, on the other hand, endeavoured to save her possessions for her son by proclaiming that she .wished to be friendly with everybody, and the enemy of nobody (May 12th, 1859), and at the same time asked the English Government to help her to observe neutrality. In England, at that time, the Tories were still in power, and they on this occasion also gave proof of how much they were attached to Austria in spite of their pretended neutrality. Lord Malmesbury, the Secretary of State for Foreign Affairs, bitterly reproached the Government of Turin for having occupied a part of the Duchy of Parma. In reply, Count Cavour requested Lord Malmesbury to study the map of the seat of war a little, and to remember that Austria had made her preparations for the invasion of Piedmont, to a great extent, in Parma, so that Sardinia, as soon as she was attacked by Austria, found herself practically at war with Modena and Parma, as they had permitted their being made integral parts of the Austrian military system in Italy; that besides, the Duchess was a little too late in talking of neutrality, after she had sought by flight to escape from the fury of her late subjects.

Parma and Modena came into the possession of Victor Emanuel. To Modena Charles Farini was sent, a patriot of unmatched energy, one of those towering figures of history which stand like milestones on the road to Italian unity.

One of the points of the peace preliminaries of

Villafranca was that Duke Francis V. should be reinstated in the possession of Modena.

On July 15th Farini telegraphed to the ministers at Turin: "Do not leave me without instructions. Recollect that if by virtue of some treaties of which I have no cognisance, the Duke should make an attempt, I shall consider him an enemy of the country and the King, and treat him accordingly. I shall not allow myself to be driven away by any one, even if it costs me my life."*

But the danger was the most threatening in Modena, because the Duke was encamped with 5,000 men on the banks of the Po.

Let the reader remember those words of Cavour which, after the thunderbolt of Villafranca, he addressed to Pietri, and through him to the Emperor Napoleon: "*I shall become a conspirator, a revolutionist, but I shall not allow this treaty to be carried out.*" And he did as he had said; at once, even before he quitted office.

The agreement of Villafranca was signed. Officially he had to bow before it. Cavour *the Cabinet Minister* instructed Farini to leave Modena; but Cavour *the patriot-revolutionist* in his private palace had at dawn †

* Luigi Frapolli: "Cenni intorno a Luigi Carlo Farini," 1864.

† At dawn! That was Cavour's time of receiving people. When, in September, 1860, I was with Ladislaus Teleki and Klapka in Turin, in order to sign that compact which will be treated of in the second volume of my "Memories," one evening our conference with Cavour lasted till midnight. "It is late," he said; "we shall continue to-morrow." "At what time?" I asked. "At five in the morning. It will not be too late?" "Late! No, certainly not," I answered smilingly. He did not even smile, for he thought five o'clock so very late. And indeed, when we came to him at five in the morning, we could see, judging from the amount of candle he had burnt, that he had been already for some two hours at work.—KOSSUTH.

the next morning called to him the Republican Louis Frapolli, and received him with this question: "Do you want to co-operate for the salvation of Italy?" "Yes," was the answer. "Well, go at once to Modena, and place yourself at the disposal of Farini, if you still find him there. If, however, obeying the order which we were obliged to send to him, Farini has left, take the defence in hand yourself, turn every pale into a weapon, and should the Duke attempt to break into the Duchy, drive his army into the Po—those unworthy Italians who disown their country."

A few hours afterwards Malmusi, the President of the Assembly of Modena, called upon him and asked for arms. Cavour kissed him on the right cheek and on the left. "You are plucky men," he said. "I am no longer Minister of War, but let us try a little stratagem." He wrote a few lines, and said to Malmusi, "Go with this paper to the arsenal, and if they give you any arms on the strength of it, be off with them to Modena." They did give him arms, and he took them with him.

Farini received the order recalling him, and replied to it by wire as follows: "*The royal commissioner obeys, but the citizen immediately becomes a soldier with the people.*"*

He did more. Without soldiers, one day's march from the enemy, surrounded by a downcast people, he introduced himself on the balcony of the ancient palace of the Prince to the inhabitants of Modena as Dictator. He called out to them, "March on with the star of Italy! Italy has not signed the preliminaries of Villafranca!"

Cavour wrote on July 17th: "*The Minister is dead; your friend applauds your decision.*"

* Telegram of Farini from Modena, July 16th, 1859.

Dictator Farini appointed Frapolli Minister of War. Thus was formed the Modenese army in which my Hungarian compatriots enlisted.

And I? With a bleeding heart I returned to England, after having sought consolation for some weeks with my wife and sons in the Alps of Savoy and Switzerland.

On the arrival of the news of the catastrophe of Villafranca, the most extraordinary rumours were spread in England. It was said that I was taken prisoner, surrendered to Austria, and that they had done to me heaven knows what! Pulszky, on July 25th, informed me that letters from my friends in all parts of England and Scotland had reached him, all showing a sympathetic uneasiness. Gilpin was besieged in Parliament by men who wished to learn what he knew about me, whether I was in safety, &c. They frightened my poor wife so much that she became nervously ill, and in that condition started on her journey. I stopped her by telegraph at Aix-les-Bains, where we met.

When the bubbles of all the nonsensical rumours had disappeared, curiosity supervened. I received whole bundles of invitations to meetings; addresses expressing sympathy with me were put into circulation to give me an opportunity of making great "revelations," and of divulging my opinion on the events in Italy in voluminous answers. And it was just the very thing I did not intend to do. I considered discretion to be not only a conventional but also a patriotic duty, and just because I wished to avoid indiscreet interrogation, I neither went to meetings again nor delivered lectures, though I was sensible of the loss of the accustomed source of income.

But while I had decided, on account of the reason referred to above, not again to speak in public, I considered that I owed so much to my most intimate English and Scotch friends as to inform them with what feelings I returned from the Continent.

This debt I discharged in the following letter:—

"*London, September 24th,* 1859.

"The fatal day of Villafranca prostrated my hopes at a moment when we had the deliverance of my country within sight, nay, almost within the reach of our hands, like a ripe fruit ready to be plucked, and here I am again, a poor exile, as I was four months ago, only older by ten years from the bitter pangs of disappointment.

"I say designedly 'disappointment,' and not deceit; of deceit I cannot complain. I took good care to guard myself and my country against even the possibility of deceit. But I feel my heart nearly broken by disappointment, unwarranted by circumstances, unaccounted, and unaccountable.

"Without that thunderbolt from a clear sky—the Villafranca arrangement—this moment at which I write Hungary would have already filled a page in her history than which none equal stands on record. Because the whole nation was united, ready, and resolved as scarcely ever before. All the feelings which sometimes bring division into a national household—difference of religion, language, race, and distinction of classes, had melted into the one great common resolution to get rid of the banditti rule of the House of Austria as soon as the war would take its logical expansion.

"The positive knowledge of this fact only adds to the bitter pangs of my disappointment. To be thus stopped at the very moment when we were stretching out our hands to pluck the ripe fruit of liberty is distressing beyond description.

"Well, it is as it is, and must be borne. It shall be borne without despondency, though not without grief.

"I feel tranquil in my conscience that I have done the duty of an honest man and of a good citizen by not neglecting to try whether or not events might be turned on a solid basis to the profit of my native land.

"And some consolation I have besides. I had occasion to get reassured on the point that no diplomatic tricks, nothing that the craft of despots may devise will divert my nation from its unalterable determination to take advantage of every reasonable opportunity for reasserting its independence.

"I have been confirmed in the confidence that, with the bulk of my nation, this determination will as little be broken by terrorism as it can be shaken by any such concessions as the Hapsburgs may devise in the hour of their need. I have learnt that Hungary knows how to endure, how to wait, but will not abdicate her rightful claim to an independent national existence. I know that the nation is as well disciplined as it is determined.

"I have been strengthened, together with my nation, in the conviction that no great European question can receive its adequate and definitive solution without our co-operation, nor can Europe be brought to a settled condition without the rights and the legitimate claims of Hungary being taken into due account.

"From this conviction we derive a firm trust in our future. We believe in our future freedom; therefore we shall be free. The corresponding resolution has with the whole nation become a religious creed.

"To have learnt all this is some consolation. And I have one more.

"You will of course understand that it would be inconsiderate on my part to enter on the particulars of what has passed between us and the powers opposed to Austria. Regards to the interests of my country raise in my case the propriety of discreet reserve to the height of a patriotic duty. Therefore I shall only say this much, that I have the satisfaction to know that by not allowing myself to be influenced by promises, that by insisting on the guarantees of irretractable facts preliminary to my giving the signal for rising, I have preserved my country from great misfortunes for aims which were not our own, and have preserved its future uncompromised and intact. This, at least, is a bright speck on the dreary horizon of present disappointed hopes.

"I was particularly careful to warn my fellow-countrymen in exile not to be led away by impatience to throwing up positions which they may have gained by industry, before events took a turn which will warrant my calling on them. I even warned, in public papers, my countrymen in America to wait and not to stir. Thanks to this precaution, no harm has accrued to any one of them on my account.

"But the prisoners of war from the Hungarian regiments flocked spontaneously to our banner. We had already five battalions (upwards of 4,000 men) organised (alas! in three more weeks we might have had twenty-five thousand of them). When the war was brought to an untimely end, I considered it a duty to safeguard the condition of the gallant band. It appeared desirable that the great bulk of them should return home rather than be scattered in misery over the face of the earth, provided we could secure to them a safe return.

"We therefore insisted on a double stipulation on their behalf: that of entire amnesty, and that of exemption from further Austrian military service. We succeeded in both regards. France insisted in a peremptory manner, and Austria had to yield. Both points are guaranteed as far as stipulations can guarantee. Remains to be seen how Austria (false Austria) will execute them.

"On this point I want to be kept in knowledge. According to instructions received, it may be that some of our home-gone braves will write to me under your address. Excuse the liberty I have taken; and should any such letters come to your hands, do me the favour to forward them to me. There will be nothing in them of a compromising character. We are no conspirators, nor do we want to be conspirators. Our national cause has outgrown such swaddling clothes. Where the whole nation is one in purpose and determination, conspiracies are as useless as they would be unwise.

"I am like the birds of the air. I had given up my house here, and have yet none; in fact, have no spot on earth to rest my weary head upon. Therefore till further notice please—occasion rising—send letters to the care of . . .

"The little explanation I herewith furnish you, I considered to be due from me to the kind interest my English and Scottish friends have honoured me with. I feel forbidden from saying more. But once again I wish to have it clearly understood that a woeful disappointment has befallen me, but of deceit I cannot complain.

"Come what may it shall find me both ready and determined. The blessings of success rest with Him above,—with frail mortals the sense of duty and the honest striving inspired thereby.

"Allow me to trust that your friendly feelings towards me and mine have undergone no change by late events, and believe me

"Yours ever truly,
" (Signed)   Kossuth."

Though this letter was not intended for publication, it found its way into the newspapers, and supplied occasion for such observations respecting my person as could only increase the feeling of gratitude which I owe, and shall owe until my death, to the people of Great Britain.

IMPORTANT WORKS.

I.

The Life and Words of Christ. By CUNNINGHAM GEIKIE, D. D. New cheap edition. From the same stereotype plates as the two-volume illustrated edition. 8vo. Cloth. Price, $1.50.

This edition of Geikie's Life of Christ is the only cheap edition that contains the copious notes of the author, the marginal references, and an index.

"A work of the highest rank, breathing the spirit of true faith in Christ."—*Dr. Delitzsch, the Commentator.*

"A most valuable addition to sacred literature."—*A. N. Littlejohn, D. D., Bishop of Long Island.*

II.

Mind in the Lower Animals, in Health and Disease. By W. LAUDER LINDSAY, M. D., F. R. S. E., etc. In two volumes, 8vo, cloth. Price, $4.00.

"I have studied the subject of mind in other animals, as compared with that of man, for a series of years, simply as a *physician-naturalist.* . . . Regarding the whole subject of mind in animals from a medical and natural-history point of view, I have studied it from first to last without any preconceived ideas, with no theory to defend, support, or illustrate. . . . All that I attempt is to outline the subject of mind in the lower animals, to illustrate their possession of the higher mental faculties as they occur in man."—*Extract from Introduction.*

III.

Memoirs of Madame de Remusat. Complete in one vol., with an Index, 12mo, 740 pages, cloth, price, $2.00. In three vols., octavo, paper covers, price, $1.50; or, 50 cents each.

"'Madame de Rémusat's Memoirs' will remain as the most finished picture of the Napoleonic Court in its outward glory and its inner pettiness."—*London Athenæum.*

"Notwithstanding the enormous library of works relating to Napoleon, we know of none which cover precisely the ground of these Memoirs. Madame de Rémusat was not only lady-in-waiting to Josephine during the eventful years 1802-1808, but was her intimate friend and trusted confidant. Thus we get a view of the daily life of Bonaparte and his wife and the terms on which they lived not elsewhere to be found."—*New York Mail.*

IV.

Memoirs of Napoleon, his Court and Family. By the Duchess D'ABRANTES (Madame Junot). New edition. In two vols., 12mo. Cloth. Price, $3.00.

The interest in the first Napoleon and his Court, which has recently been so stimulated by the "Memoirs of Madame de Rémusat," has induced the publishers to reissue the famous "Memoirs of the Duchess d'Abrantes." These memoirs, which hitherto have appeared in costly 8vo volumes, are now published at a much lower price, to correspond with the De Rémusat 12mo volume. The work at the present juncture will be read with attention, especially as it presents a much more favorable portrait of the great Corsican than that limned by Madame de Rémusat.

V.

The Life of David Glasgow Farragut, First Admiral of the United States Navy, embodying his Journal and Letters. By his Son, LOYALL FARRAGUT. With Portraits, Maps, and Illustrations. 8vo. Cloth. Price, $4.00.

"The book is a stirring one, of course; the story of Farragut's life is a tale of adventure of the most ravishing sort, so that, aside from the value of this work as an authentic biography of the greatest of American naval commanders, the book is one of surpassing interest, considered merely as a narrative of difficult and dangerous enterprises and heroic achievements."—*New York Evening Post.*

For sale by all booksellers; or any volume sent by mail, post-paid, on receipt of price.

D. APPLETON & CO., Publishers, 1, 3, & 5 Bond Street, New York.

Historical and Biographical Works.

The Life of the Prince Consort.
By THEODORE MARTIN. With Portraits. Complete in 5 volumes. 12mo. Cloth, $2.00 each volume.

The English Reformation:
How it came about, and why we should uphold it. By CUNNINGHAM GEIKIE, D. D., author of "The Life and Words of Christ." With a Preface by the author for the American edition. 1 vol., 12mo. Cloth. Price, $2.00.

A History of England in the Eighteenth Century.
By WILLIAM E. H. LECKY. 2 vols., 8vo. Cloth, $5.00.

Prehistoric Times,
As illustrated by Ancient Remains and the Manners and Customs of Modern Savages. Illustrated. By Sir JOHN LUBBOCK, Bart., author of "Origin of Civilization, and the Primitive Condition of Man." Entirely new edition. 8vo. Cloth. Price, $5.00.

The French Revolutionary Epoch.
Being a History of France from the Beginning of the First French Revolution to the End of the Second Empire. By HENRI VAN LAUN, author of "History of French Literature," etc. 2 vols., 12mo. Cloth, $3.50.

The Historical Poetry of the Ancient Hebrews.
Translated and critically examined by MICHAEL HEILPRIN. Vol. 1. Crown 8vo. Cloth. Price, $2.00.

History of New York
During the Revolutionary War, and of the Leading Events in the other Colonies at that Period. By THOMAS JONES, Justice of the Supreme Court of the Province. Edited by EDWARD FLOYD DE LANCEY. With Notes, Contemporary Documents, Maps, and Portraits. In two vols., 8vo, 748 pp., 713 pp. Cloth, gilt top, price, $15.00. Printed for the New York Historical Society, in "The John D. Jones Fund Series of Histories and Memoirs."

The Last Years of Daniel Webster.
A Monograph. By GEORGE TICKNOR CURTIS. 8vo. Paper, 50 cents.

For sale by all booksellers. Any work mailed, post-paid, to any address in the United States, on receipt of price.

D. APPLETON & CO., Publishers,
1, 3, & 5 BOND STREET, NEW YORK.

www.ingramcontent.com/pod-product-compliance
Lightning Source LLC
Chambersburg PA
CBHW051854300426
44117CB00006B/387